BETWEEN SCHOOL AND WORK:
NEW PERSPECTIVES ON TRANSFER AND BOUNDARY-CROSSING

ADVANCES IN LEARNING AND INSTRUCTION SERIES

Series Editors:
S. Strauss, E. De Corte, R. Wegerif, K. Littleton

Further details: http://www.socscinet.com/education

Published

VAN SOMEREN, REIMANN, BOSHUIZEN & DE JONG
Learning with Multiple Representations

DILLENBOURG
Collaborative Learning: Cognitive and Computational Approaches

BLISS, SÄLJÖ & LIGHT
Learning Sites: Social and Technological Resources for Learning

BROMME & STAHL
Writing Hypertext and Learning: Conceptual and Empirical Approaches

KAYSER & VOSNIADOU
Modelling Changes in Understanding

SCHNOTZ, VOSNIADOU & CARRETERO
New Perspectives on Conceptual Change

SMITH
Reasoning by Mathematical Induction in Children's Arithmetic

KOZULIN & RAND
Experience of Mediated Learning

ROUET, LEVONEN & BIARDEAU
Multimedia Learning: Cognitive and Instructional Issues

GARRISON & ARCHER
A Transactional Perspective on Teaching and Learning

COWIE & AALSVOORT
Social Interaction in Learning and Instruction

VOLET & JÄRVELÄ
Motivation in Learning Contexts

Forthcoming Titles

DE CORTE, VERSCHAFFEL, ENTWISTLE & VAN MERRIËNBOER
Powerful Learning Environments: Unravelling Basic Components and Dimensions

Related journals — sample copies available online from:
http://www.elsevier.com

Learning and Instruction
International Journal of Educational Research
Computers and Education
The Internet and Higher Education
Early Childhood Research Quarterly
Journal of Early Childhood Teacher Education
Learning and Individual Differences

BETWEEN SCHOOL AND WORK:

NEW PERSPECTIVES ON TRANSFER AND BOUNDARY-CROSSING

EDITED BY

TERTTU TUOMI-GRÖHN
Helsinki University, Finland

YRJÖ ENGESTRÖM
University of California, San Diego, USA and Helsinki University, Finland

⊛ Earli

Published in Association with the European Association for Learning
and Instruction

2003

Pergamon
An Imprint of Elsevier Science

Amsterdam – Boston – London – New York – Oxford – Paris
San Diego – San Francisco – Singapore – Sydney – Tokyo

ELSEVIER SCIENCE Ltd
The Boulevard, Langford Lane
Kidlington, Oxford OX5 1GB, UK

First edition 2003

Library of Congress Cataloging in Publication Data
A catalog record from the Library of Congress has been applied for.

British Library Cataloguing in Publication Data
A catalogue record from the British Library has been applied for.

ISBN: 0-08-044296-X

∞ The paper used in this publication meets the requirements of ANSI/NISO Z39.48-1992 (Permanence of Paper).
Printed in The Netherlands.

Contents

Contributors

Frank Achtenhagen   Institute of Economics and Business Education and Management Training, Georg-August-University, Germany

Petra Angervall   Department of Education, Göteborg University, Sweden

King Beach   Transitions Research Group, Michigan State University, USA

Lara Dessagne   Groupe de Recherche sur les Communications, Laboratoire de Psychologie de l'Interaction, University of Nancy 2, France

Yrjö Engeström   Center for Activity Theory and Developmental Work Research, Helsinki University, Finland

Bärbel Fürstenau   Department of Business Management and Economics, Dresden University of Technology, Germany

Gary Granville   National College of Art and Design, Ireland

David Guile   School of Lifelong Education and International Development, University of London, United Kingdom

Anton Havnes   Oslo University College, Norway

Leif Chr. Lahn   Institute of Educational Research, University of Oslo, Norway

Pirjo Lambert   School of Vocational Teacher Education, Helsinki Business Polytechnic, Finland

Sten R. Ludvigsen   InterMedia, University of Oslo, Norway

Mary Reilly   Education Department, National University of Ireland, Maynooth, Ireland

Annalisa Sannino   Department of Education, University of Salerno, Italy

Roger Säljö   Department of Education, Göteborg University, Sweden

Christa Teurlings   IVA Tilburg, Institute for Social Policy Research and
                          Consultancy, Department of Education and Culture, The
                          Netherlands

Per-Olof Thång   Department of Education, Göteborg University, Sweden

Alain Trognon   Groupe de Recherche sur les Communications, Laboratoire
                          de Psychologie de l'Interaction, University of Nancy 2,
                          France

Terttu Tuomi-Gröhn   Center for Activity Theory and Developmental Work
                          Research, Helsinki University, Finland

Johan van der Sanden   Teacher Training Department of Science and Technology,
                          Eindhoven University of Technology, The Netherlands

Susanne Weber   Institute of Economics and Business Education and
                          Management Training, Georg-August-University, Germany

Michael Young   Institute of Education, University of London, United
                          Kingdom

Chapter 1

From Transfer to Boundary-crossing Between School and Work as a Tool for Developing Vocational Education: An Introduction

Terttu Tuomi-Gröhn, Yrjö Engeström and Michael Young

Many strong claims have been made for the importance of transfer in education. Transfer of learning makes survival possible by allowing people to adapt to new situations. Schools are not able to teach students everything they will need to know for the rest of their lives; they must equip students with the ability to transfer — to use what they have learned to solve new problems successfully or to learn quickly in new situations.

This book is a result of the work of Working Group 2 of Cost Action A 11 "Flexibility, Transferability, Mobility as Targets of Vocational Education and Training". Our task was to concentrate on the issue of transfer in vocational education and training. This includes transfer from the school to the worksite and from worksites back to school. There was also a need to find new conceptual tools for the promotion of transformative learning to facilitate effective coping with changed situations, and to influence working conditions and behavior in different contexts. This book is a result of our work.

The debate on transfer started in the beginning of the last century (Judd 1908; Thorndike 1924; Thorndike & Woodworth 1901); in the last fifteen years this debate has become intensified (Analoui 1993; Cormier & Hagman 1987; Detterman 1993; Detterman & Sternberg 1993; McKeough, Lupart & Marini 1995; Singley & Anderson 1989). However, this transfer discussion was mainly concentrated on the transfer of knowledge from one task to another in school or in laboratory settings. This perspective on transfer problems has only limited relevance from the viewpoint of learning at workplaces and the transfer of knowledge between school and workplaces.

However, the new situated approach to learning (Lave 1988) did focus on the learning in workplaces. According to this approach learning occurs most effectively when it is an incidental by-product of genuine participation in meaningful activities, such as work. Although some representatives of the situated approach (e.g. Lave 1988) have argued that transfer of knowledge may not exist at all since knowledge cannot be decontextualized. Most theorists recognize that transfer of learning can be socially mediated and that guided forms of learning have potential for enhancing the likelihood of transfer across tasks and contexts taking place (Volet 1999: 626). Recent situated cognition research (Greeno 1997, 1998; Greeno, Moore & Smith 1993) has emphasized the critical importance of the affordances that learning contexts and activities provide for participants. The issue is not to determine the influence of a prior task to an unchanging subsequent task, but to understand the continuity of activity and learning from one changing everyday situation to another. The situated approach to learning gives hints as to how to approach the transfer of learning in workplaces, but cannot address transfer between school and work.

The topicality of the transfer issue is illustrated by the recent lively debate between the proponents of constructivist and situated approaches to learning (see Anderson, Reder & Simon (1996, 1997) and Greeno (1997) in *Educational Researcher*). The discussion was continued in the 1999 issue of the *International Journal of Educational Research* (de Corte 1999) (see also Beach 1999; Brandsford & Schwartz 1999; Packer 2001). Wake & Williams (2002) summarize the discussion by arguing that while cognitivists view the situated cognition theorists as unscientific, and the implications for schooling drawn from their work as dangerous. The situated cognition theorists view the research base of classical psychology as invalid and culturally decontextualized, and its implications for schooling are seen as narrow at best, and inequitable at worst.

The debate concerns the relevance and justification of schooling. If there is minimal transfer of school knowledge to the activities outside school, how can we justify the massive expenditure of money and time spent on formal school systems? The debate is aptly crystallised in the titles of articles like *Transfer on Trial* (Detterman & Sternberg 1993) and *The Transfer Dilemma* (Carraher & Schliemann 2002).

Achieving significant transfer of learning has proved to be a difficult task. Gruber, Law, Mandl & Renkl (1996) and Mayer & Wittrock (1996), among others, have presented excellent analyses of the lack of transfer in learning. Transfer has proven to be difficult even within school context. Laboratory studies have shown that learning how to solve problems often does not help students to solve other problems that look different but can be solved in the same way (Gick & Holyoak 1980, 1983; Hayes & Simon 1977; Reed, Ernst & Banerji 1974; Simon & Reed 1976). Classroom studies also indicate that in spite of the claims that thinking skills programs improve intellectual ability, they often fail to reveal convincing evidence that such programs result in general transfer of learning to new kinds of problems (Nickerson, Perkins & Smith 1985; Segal, Chipman & Glaser 1985). Field studies also reveal that problem solvers commonly fail to apply school-taught mathematics procedures to solve mathematics problems they encounter out of school (Lave 1988; Lave & Wenger 1991; Nunes, Schliemann & Carraher 1993).

However, some reports have indicated success in the transfer of skills to new tasks. Judd's (1908) and Katona's (1940) early reports indicated that the understanding the central principles of a task was transferred to other similar tasks. Palinscar & Brown (1984), similarly Catrambone & Holyoak (1989) showed that the transferability of knowledge can be dramatically increased by manipulating contexts and contents of problems to be worked on. There are also examples of more recent research demonstrating forms of successful transfer (Brown 1994; Singley & Anderson 1989). All these studies have, however, remained limited to the school or to the laboratory. They did not address the question of crossing the boundary between school and working life.

In a changing world there are new demands for expertise. Dominant approaches to cognition share a narrow and "vertical" view of expertise in which some have more knowledge than others. Characteristically they distinguish between "stages" or "levels" of knowledge and skill. Such a vertical image assumes a uniform, singular model of what counts as an "expert" in a given field. In recent research, an argument for a broader, multi-dimensional view of expertise has been put forward (Engeström, Engeström & Kärkkäinen 1995). While the vertical dimension remains important, a horizontal dimension is rapidly becoming increasingly relevant for the understanding and acquisition of expertise. In this research, experts are viewed as operating in, and move between, multiple parallel activity contexts. These multiple contexts demand and afford different, complementary but also conflicting cognitive tools, rules, and patterns of social interaction. Criteria of expert knowledge and skill are different in the various contexts. Experts face the challenge of negotiating and combining ingredients from different contexts to achieve hybrid solutions. The vertical master-novice relationship, and with it in some cases the professional monopoly on expertise, is problematized as demands for more dialogical problem solving increase.

Central features of this newly emerging landscape of expertise may be designated as polycontextuality and boundary-crossing. Polycontextuality means that experts are engaged not only in multiple simultaneous tasks and task-specific participation frameworks within one and the same activity and are also increasingly involved in multiple communities of practice.

A number of novel approaches to transfer, pay attention to this horizontal dimension of expertise and learning, and to boundary-crossing between communities of practice. These approaches are the sociocultural approach which conceptualizes transfer as consequential transitions between different organizations (Beach 1999) and the approaches based on the activity theory and expansive learning (Davydov 1990; Engeström 1987).

Beach (1999, this volume) introduces the concept of consequential transitions to reconceptualize transfer. Beach is concerned with the process of generalization. However, the generalization he is interested in is not located within the developing individual, nor can it be reduced to changing social activities. Rather, it is located in the changing relationship between individuals and sets of social activities. For Beach, generalization is located at the interface of persons and activities, embodied in systems of artifacts, and symbolic objects that are created with human intent. As its core the concept of transition involves consequential change in the relation between the individual and one or more social activities across time. All forms of transition involve the construction of knowledge and skills understood as transformation rather than as the mere application or use of something that has been acquired elsewhere.

This approach, based on the activity theory and expansive learning (Davidov 1990; Engeström 1987, 2001) moves the scope of learning from the individual to relations between activity systems. From the point of view of activity theory, previous accounts of transfer are inadequate in that the unit of analysis, the learner, is still depicted as the individual, confined in his/her relatively enclosed 'domain of situations'. An activity-theoretical view of learning (Engeström 1987; Leont'ev 1977) redefines the unit of analysis of cognition and learning as a collective activity system. Significant learning processes are achieved by collective activities. In this view, meaningful transfer of learning takes place through interaction between collective activity systems. For example, the school and the workplace may engage in collaborative interaction in which both activity systems learn something from each other. What is transferred is not packages of knowledge and skills that remain intact; instead, the very process of such transfer involves active interpreting, modifying and reconstructing the skills and knowledge to be transferred. In this way the scope of learning is radically broadened. In relation to the interface between school and work it is assumed that the two activity systems can together find and create mutually relevant projects in which both benefit from collaboration. Most formal programs of vocational education already have built-in sequences of internship and work practice. These periods, often extended and definitely remodeled, are the natural starting point and site for the new kind of collaboration between school and work. This process is multi-directional and multi-faceted, involving transitions between activity systems like school and workplace; on account of its dynamic nature, this process is called *developmental transfer.*

Boundary-crossing as a Tool for Promoting Learning and Transfer

Boundary-crossing is a broad and little studied category of cognitive processes. Classic studies of innovation and creative thinking emphasize the potential embedded in transporting ideas, concepts and instruments from seemingly unrelated domains into the domain of focal inquiry. Yet, such processes seem to be rare and quite demanding. Crossing boundaries involves encountering difference, entering into territory in which we are unfamiliar and, to some significant extent therefore, unqualified. In the face of such obstacles, boundary-crossing seems to require significant cognitive retooling.

Konkola, Lambert, Tuomi-Gröhn & Ludvigsen (manuscript) suggest some of the conceptual tools that help us to understand how the process of boundary-crossing takes place.

Wenger (1998) introduces the concept of a *broker* and how brokers are able to make new connections across communities of practice, facilitate coordination and open new possibilities for new meanings. From the perspective of boundary-crossing brokers have an important role because they can introduce new elements into a practice from other communities of practice. The role of a broker is above all a form of intervention. It assumes that teachers and students collaborate voluntarily, introducing elements of themselves into what they do. In addition, teachers and students must act like translators by way of conveying the demands of various parties in an appropriate language. Vocational education students are in a unique position to act as mediators, bringing the new instruments and insights from their work experience (internship) into the school and from the school to the workplace.

Konkola (2001) has introduced the concept of a *boundary zone* as a sphere which resembles a "no-man's land", free from prearranged routines or rigid patterns. It is also a place where each activity system reflects its own structure, attitudes, beliefs, norms and roles. This means that elements from both sides are always present in the boundary zone. Gutiérrez, Rymes & Larson (1995) have used the concept of the third space in a similar vein when describing the learning and development that takes place as ideas and needs from different cultures meet, collide and form new meanings. Because it is a hybrid, polycontextual, multi-voiced and multi-scripted context, the boundary zone is considered as a place where it is possible to extend the object of each activity system and to create a shared object between them. In that way, the activity itself is reorganized, resulting in new opportunities for learning.

Wenger (1998) discusses boundary encounters, such as meetings, conversations, and visits, which are single or discrete events that provide connections. Although Wenger's concept is useful for designing different forms of boundary encounters, it is not, however, enough to explain the dynamics of learning and change in these encounters. It is necessary to examine the boundary encounter as a discursive space and a hybrid learning context. Using activity theory as a framework, Lambert (this volume) has presented the idea of a *boundary-crossing place* as a model for promoting developmental transfer in teacher education. She describes the Learning Studio as a place for student teachers to present their developmental projects in the context of multi-voiced discussions, in which all the parties involved in the developmental work could participate. This boundary-crossing place offered an opportunity to reconstruct the knowledge and skills produced in teacher education in a hybrid learning context.

The idea of boundary-crossing puts great emphasis on the new intellectual and practical tools that boundary-crossers or brokers (Wenger 1998) bring into processes of change. One example is the boundary object discussed by Star (1989), and Star & Griesemer (1989). This concept is useful in analyzing objects that inhabit several intersecting social worlds and satisfy the informational requirements of each of them. Boundary objects are, according to Star (1989) "both plastic enough to adapt to local needs and constraints of the several parties employing them, yet robust enough to maintain a common identity across sites". Like "a blackboard", a boundary object sits in the middle of a group of actors with divergent viewpoints (Star 1989: 46). Bowker & Star (1999) present different kinds of classifications as objects of cooperation between different social worlds, as boundary objects. They see boundary objects as developing straightforwardly from the problems that emerge in the collisions of different classifications. Thus, boundary objects are something that emerge over time from the interaction between different communities.

The concept of a boundary object is useful in denoting a tool used to join activities together (Bowker & Star 1999). People who have different approaches to what they do can coordinate their activities around an object, which gives some common meaning across the settings where the activities take place. At the collective level, this object seems to be weakly structured, but for an individual actor it might be strongly structured. Tensions in regard to the meaning of the boundary object are part of what actors have to take into account in their attempts to coordinate their differing interests.

Structure of this Book

The many failures make it clear that transfer of learning, especially between school and work is not easy to achieve. However, successful experiments demonstrate that transfer of learning to new situations or tasks is not impossible; furthermore, some form of transition to working life does occur for most people. This very multiplicity and partial incompatibility of findings and interpretations points to the need to deepen our theoretical understanding of transfer and of educational arrangements used to facilitate it. In this book, we will present an overview of different theoretical approaches to transfer, including recent attempts at reconceptualization. Our emphasis is on a view of learning as boundary-crossing between organizations. We do not view this process as merely the transfer of intact knowledge and skills from task to task or from the school to the workplace. Increasingly there is evidence that in the process of transfer the knowledge and contexts are changed.

The book is divided in three parts: (I) Boundary-crossing as a theoretical basis for research on transfer; (II) Learning and transfer in vocational education; and (III) Learning in workplaces. The book ends with an epilogue which comments on the previous chapters and the book as a whole.

Part I: Boundary-crossing as a Theoretical Basis for Research on Transfer

In Chapter 2, Tuomi-Gröhn and Engeström provide a historical overview of approaches to transfer. The chapter includes a discussion on the important new approaches such as those based on sociocultural and activity theories which have been missing in most of previous overviews.

In Chapter 3, Beach criticizes the way previous approaches to transfer conceptualize the generalization of individuals' knowledge across contexts as "transferring" something from one place to another. He proposes an alternative approach to understanding generalization as a developmental process within which learners and social organizations exist in a mutually constitutive relation to another over time. Changes in their relations can occur through a change in the individual, the activity, or both. Transition, then, is the concept the author uses to understand how knowledge is generalized across social space and time. A transition is consequential when it is consciously reflected on, struggled with, and shifts the individuals sense of self or social position. Thus, consequential transitions link identity with knowledge propagation. Beach describes four primary types of consequential transitions: lateral, collateral, encompassing and mediational.

Chapter 4 by Guile and Young, provides links between different approaches to transfer. In particular they discuss the relationship between the situated knowledge acquired in workplaces and the codified knowledge that constitutes the school curriculum. They also discuss the implications for vocational education of different approaches to the distinction between horizontal and vertical development. The authors try to link activity theory approaches to learning to a sociological approach to knowledge and discuss how they can be used to providing a basis for a "vocational curriculum for future". They claim that recent changes in the organization of work are making demands for new kinds of skill and knowledge on those leaving school and therefore, call for a new approach to the curriculum. The idea of "authentic learning" is questioned. Authors address a number of fundamental issues: (1) The reconceptualization of transfer as transition by separating its "horizontal" and "vertical" elements; (2) the importance of recognizing that contexts serve two functions — providing meaning and helping give coherence to learning; and (3) The need to distinguish between tacit, situated and codified knowledge as a basis for reconceptualizing the vocational curriculum. They argue that in order to foster transfer it will be necessary to give greater attention to supporting students in relating their "situated" knowledge of workplaces to the "codified" knowledge that they acquire through the curriculum.

Part II: Learning and Transfer in Vocational Education

Chapter 5 by Fuerstenau, describes "exploration tasks" as tools for transfer and boundary-crossing between vocational school and working life in businesses. The tasks are based on the action-control theory, systems-oriented business administration and elaboration theory. The design of the learning environment is described and its results are compared to the jig-saw puzzle model of instruction, where genuine boundary-crossing and contact with the working life are missing. The results give hints that genuine boundary-crossing provides a basis for disregarding irrelevant or wrong relationships between concepts and thus improves the knowledge networks of students.

In Chapter 6, van der Sanden and Teurlings are concerned with the role that the theories of learning held by individuals play in competence development. They assume that scientific learning theories have their individual and non-scientific counterparts. The authors review a number of empirical studies on work-related learning processes during practice periods in different vocational educational settings from the viewpoint of individual learning theories. The chapter goes on to describe how to design a competence-oriented learning environment that fosters learning and boundary-crossing competencies as the ability to learn constructively and to progressively recontextualize knowledge and skills. An experimental study with regard to word processing competencies is described.

In Chapter 7 Achtenhagen criticizes the whole discussion of transfer and its problems, and argues that it neglects the curricular dimension of the corresponding teaching and learning processes and does not sufficiently distinguish the learning objectives as they are given for initial vocational education. Achtenhagen emphasizes that all different approaches to solve transfer problem, need to be enriched by the development of curricular structures which support learning by reformulating the role of teachers, curricula, teaching, learning methods and media. He demonstrates how an evaluative-constructive curriculum approach, based on the concept of "learn-acting" can contribute to a solution of the transfer problem. According to the criteria of action orientation and learn-acting the complex teaching-learning environment and virtual enterprise are developed. The virtual enterprise provides a training guide for the official apprenticeship for industrial office workers.

In Chapter 8, Weber deals in her chapter with boundary-crossing in the context of intercultural learning. She begins with a critical analysis of traditional intercultural training programs and their theoretical frameworks and introduces a new intercultural encountering model. This model is based on Ting-Toomey's approach called "mindful identity negotiation". Weber, however, expands the theoretical basis of the model to include not only individual learning but also social or collective learning and bases her reflections on Engeström's idea of expansive learning. She argues that when studying social interaction the unit of analysis has to go beyond story telling, cross-cultural descriptions and adaptation measures; the process itself has to be embedded into social, cultural and historical contexts. The author introduces an innovative theoretical model for intercultural learning that seeks to overcome the shortcomings of previous models.

In Chapter 9, Granville and Reilly focus on the boundaries between school and work, between different school subjects and between different forms of teaching and learning. A new Leaving Certificate (LCVP) was created in Ireland to help young people to cross the boundary between secondary education and work life. Drawing on Beach's conception of consequential transitions the authors describe different transitions from the viewpoint of students. The boundaries between school learning and work-based learning were successfully crossed on many cases through the LCVP modules. Within the school setting of LCVP, however, the boundaries between school subjects remained uncrossed except in very rare circumstances. The students studied displayed little success in respect of cross-curricular boundary-crossing. A new type of teaching and learning was, however, created: it was work-related and activity-based and operated in the zone where school meets work. It was manifested in collaborative teaching and learning experiences, in changed student-teacher relationships and in situated learning of a kind hitherto unacknowledged in formal education programs in Irish schools.

In Chapter 10, Tuomi-Gröhn describes and evaluates one attempt to produce developmental transfer. The concepts of developmental transfer and zone of proximal development (as introduced by Vygotsky) were applied in the additional training program for nurses in Finland. The aims of the internship were based on these premises. They were: (1) to create a collaborative team during the internship, involving people from the school and the workplace; (2) to create fruitful interrelationships between the theoretical knowledge in the school and the everyday experiences of the practitioners; (3) to create networks and boundary-crossing outside the team; and (4) to find new knowledge and as a result to develop advanced collaborative practices at the boundaries between the two activity systems of school and work. Three different cases are analyzed with very different results from the viewpoint of developmental transfer. The reasons for success or failure are discussed.

The research reported in Chapter 11 by Lambert, is based on activity theory and aims to create and analyze a new model for promoting developmental transfer in vocational teacher education. This model is called the "learning studio"; it is an intervention that aims to promote innovative learning in vocational institutions where student teachers were working as teachers. In the learning studio, student teachers present their developmental projects to teachers and practitioners in health care and social welfare.

The learning studio is an example of a boundary encounter between a teacher education institute, vocational schools and workplaces. The chapter focuses on analyzing how the boundary objects were developed as tools for constructing an object for different partners: students, teachers and practitioners. It shows how the boundary object was an important element in producing innovative learning. In this chapter a new tool for boundary-crossing between different activity systems, the Learning Studio, is developed. The Learning Studio is presented as an innovative tool for promoting transfer not only at an individual but also on the collective level in different participating organizations.

Part III: Learning in Workplaces

Chapter 12 by Angervall & Thång, describes how the employees in the Swedish engineering industry are willing to collaborate in different learning projects within a program of continuing education. The results indicated, that the learning opportunities offered to blue collar workers that are independent of their work activities were not experienced very positively. The authors discuss the gender issue and why it is that women take more advantage of educational opportunities than men. They question why it is difficult to motivate men into participating in learning activities that are not directly related to work activities. The chapter considers whether, if formal learning activities such as learning centers that are not directly related to work are necessary at all, or whether the learning centers referred to in the study might be serving a different purpose than that which they were aiming at. This chapter illustrates the importance of relating learning activities to work in continuing education. The disconnection of learning and work activities does not motivate new learning.

Chapter 13 by Sannino, Trognon and Dessagne, attempts to define the kind of learning demands in various occupational contexts in order to improve the transition from educational institutions to the working world. The objective of the chapter is to analyze processes of training leading to the acquisition of professional skills and identities within the framework of alternance-based vocational training. The original, situated interactions of tutor-apprentice couples are recorded and analyzed as natural exchanges at a moment when the transmission of training and the reappropriation of skills are taking place The methodology takes the mechanisms of the transmission of expertise and the adaptation of the trainee into account, as well as the elaboration of mutual skills in conversation. Thus, it has similarities with the situated apprenticeship approach advocated by Lave. The results indicate that these paired interactions are more complex and more capable of improving the learning of the apprentices than the classical interactions of the individual at work. The authors illustrate how discursive and manual activities are intimately intertwined in the learning process.

Chapter 14 by Ludvigsen, Havnes and Lahn, question the notion of knowledge as stored in the heads of individuals and transported from school into working life. Instead, a situated view of learning is presented which focuses on the links between different, situations or contexts. The unit of analysis expands from the individual to the contexts of interaction and communication. In the chapter, the work of sales engineers and the context of their learning process are analyzed. The intention is to conceptualize the complexities of learning among engineers as a process that is rooted in social practices, where agents move in and between activity systems. Horizontal movements are analyzed by using the concepts of boundary-crossing, boundary object and poly-contextuality. The chapter illustrates the division of labor that must exist between formal educational institutions (providing general knowledge) and other activity systems where people are going to operate. The use of general knowledge has to be negotiated in various practices through a learning process in which the learner moves from the general to the specific.

In the epilogue, Säljö takes a critical stance to the use of the concept of transfer. He points out that the meaning of this term is completely dependent on the theory in which it is based. Scholars drawing on different epistemological backgrounds use the term with different meanings since, different theoretical perspectives have radically different units of analysis in the study of learning. Säljö concludes, (based on Smedslund), that the concepts of learning and transfer cannot be distinguished. The problem of predicting transfer is the problem of what will be learned, thus, the concept of transfer may at best serve as a general reminder of, problems of seeing connections and parallels between situations and practices. To learn is to appropriate powerful intellectual and physical tools, and to realize how they can be put to productive use in a range of continuously changing practices. The more powerful the tools, the more of boundary-crossing has to be part of the learning process.

The author comments on the different chapters in the book by drawing attention to two issues that are addressed by the authors. The first concerns the alleged gap between learning in formal institutions and other activity systems. The second point he makes reinforces the significance of studying learning as a problem of the relationship between collectives and individuals, and the need to attend to the dynamics at both levels.

Comparison of the Empirical Studies of this Book

Table 1 summarizes and compares the different studies presented in Parts II and III of this book. The comparison is based on the following characteristics: unit of analysis used, what kinds of tools are created to foster learning and transfer, and how learning and transfer are conceptualized in each study.

Unit of analysis ranges from individual cognition in studies based on the constructivist approaches to individuals learning in different school and work settings in studies based on a sociocultural approach. Studies based on activity theory use two or more collaborating activity systems that are embedded in a social, cultural and historical process as their unit of analysis.

Tools for promoting transfer and boundary-crossing between school and work include the creation of diversified tasks and working methods: explorative tasks, or the "mindful identity negotiation" approach. Also new curricular developments are created : Examples are vocational link modules included in the upper secondary education and curriculum embedded mastery learning. The third group of tools include different kinds of collaboration between different partners: for example, the transmission of expertise

Table 1: Comparison of the empirical studies presented in this book.

Approach: Cognitive/ constructivist	Unit of analysis	Tool for learning and transfer	Intended kind of learning and transfer
Fuerstenau	Individual cognition	Explorative tasks to analyze real firms	Conceptual structure
Van der Sanden & Teurlings	Individual cognition	Cognitive apprenticeship learning environment	Ability to learn constructively and to progressively reconceptualize knowledge and skills
Achtenhagen	Individual cognition	Curriculum embedded mastery learning	
Situated/ sociocultural			
Weber	Individual learning process embedded into social, cultural and historical process	Mindful identity negotiation approach	
Granville & Reilly	Individual in different contexts, school and work	Vocational subjects and vocational link modules included in the upper secondary education	Equipping students with skills of consequential transitions between school and working life
Sannino & Trognon	Paired interactions in everyday work settings	Transmission of expertise and elaboration of mutual skill in conversations between tutor-apprentice couples	Acquisition of professional skills and identity

Table 1: Continued.

Approach: Activity theory	Unit of analysis	Tool for learning and transfer	Intended kind of learning and transfer
Ludvigsen et al.	Two activity systems embedded in a social, cultural and historical process	(Boundary object)	Horizontal or collateral transfer of knowledge
Tuomi-Gröhn	Two activity systems embedded in a social, cultural and historical process	Creation of collaborative zone of proximal development	New advanced practices in both activity systems
Lambert	Three activity systems embedded in a social, cultural and historical process	Learning studio as the boundary crossing place	Innovative learning in vocational institutions

between tutor-apprentice couples, collaboration between school and workplaces and between vocational teacher education, vocational school and work organizations.

Intended kinds of learning and transfer range from transition of conceptual structures, the acquisition of professional competence and identity, equipping students with skills of consequential transitions between school and working life, and the creation of new advanced practices in different activity systems.

Based on this table, it is easy to agree with the argument by Säljö in the epilogue that the meaning of the term transfer is completely dependent on the theory in which it is based. Scholars drawing on different epistemological backgrounds use the term with different meanings since different theoretical perspectives have radically different units of analysis in the study of learning. However, the diversity of studies reported in this book indicate the different kinds of possibilities in fostering learning and transfer.

References

Analoui, F. (1993). *Training and Transfer of Learning*. Newcastle upon Tyne: Athenaeum Press.

Anderson, J. R., Reder, L. M., & Simon, H. A. (1996). Situated learning and education. *Educational Researcher, 25* (4), 5–11.

Anderson, J. R., Reder, L. M., & Simon, H. A. (1997). Situative versus cognitive perspectives: Form versus substance. *Educational Researcher, 26* (1), 18–21.

Beach, K. (1999). Consequential transitions: A sociocultural expedition beyond transfer in education. *Review of Research in Education, 28*, 46–69.

Bowker, G., & Star, S. L. (1999). *Sorting things out. Classification and its consequences.* Cambridge, MA and London, U.K.: MIT Press.

Brandsford, J. D., & Schwarz, D. L. (1999). Rethinking transfer: A simple proposal with multiple implications. In: A. Iran-Nejad, & P. D. Pearson (Eds), *Review of research in education* (Vol. 24, pp. 61–100). Washington, D.C.: American Educational Research Association.

Brown, A. L. (1994). The advancement of learning. *Educational Researcher, 23* (8), 4–12.

Carraher, D., & Scliemann, A. D. (2002). Transfer dilemma. *The Journal of Learning Sciences, 11* (1), 1–24.

Catrambone, R., & Holyoak, K. J. (1989). Overcoming contextual limitations on problem solving transfer. *Journal of Experimental Psychology: Learning, Memory and Cognition, 14* (6), 1147–1156.

Cormier, S. M., & Hagman, J. D. (Eds) (1987). *Transfer of learning.* New York: Academic Press.

De Corte, E. (1999). On the road to transfer: an introduction. *International Journal of Educational Research, 31*, 555–559.

Davydov, V. V. (1990). Types of generalization in instruction: Logical and psychological problems in the structuring of school curricula. *Soviet Studies in Mathematics Education, 2.* Reston, VA: National Council of Teachers of Mathematics.

Detterman, D. K. (1993). The case for the prosecution: Transfer as an epiphenomenon. In: D. K. Detterman, & R. J. Sternberg (Eds), *Transfer on trial: Intelligence, cognition and instruction.* Norwood: Ablex.

Detterman, D. K., & Sternberg, R. J. (Eds) (1993). *Transfer on trial: Intelligence, cognition and instruction.* Norwood: Ablex.

Engeström, Y. (1987). *Learning by expanding: An activity-theoretical approach to developmental research.* Helsinki: Orienta-Konsultit.

Enheström, Y., Engeström, R., & Kärkkäinen, M. (1995). Polycontextuality and boundary crossing in expert cognition: Learning and problem solving in complex work activities. *Learning and Instruction, 5*, 319–336.

Gick, M. L., & Holyoak, K. J. (1980). Analogical problem solving. *Cognitive Psychology, 12*, 306–355.

Gick, M. L., & Holyoak, K. J. (1983). Schema induction and analogical transfer. *Cognitive Psychology, 15*, 1–38.

Greeno, J. G. (1997). Response: On claims that answer wrong questions. *Educational Researcher, 26*, 1, 5–17.

Greeno, J. (1998). The situativity of knowing, learning, and research. *American Psychologist, 53* (1), 5–26.

Greeno, J. G., Smith, D. R., & Moore, J. L. (1993). Transfer of situated learning. In: D. K. Detterman & R. J. Sternberg (Eds), *Transfer on trial: Intelligence, cognition and instruction.* Norwood: Ablex.

Gruber, H., Law, L., Mandl, H., & Renkl, A. (1996). Situated learning and transfer. In: P. Reimann & H. Spada (Eds), *Learning in humans and machines: Towards an interdisciplinary learning science.* Oxford: Pergamon.

Gutierrez, K., Rymes, B., & Larson, J. (1995). Script, counterscript, and underlife in the classroom: James Brown vs. Brown v. Board of Education. *Harvard Educational Review, 65* (3), 445–471.

Hatano, G., & Greeno, J. G. (1999). Commentary: alternative perspectives on transfer and transfer studies. *International Journal of Educational Research, 31*, 645–654.

Hayes, J. R., & Simon, H. A. (1977). Psychological differences among problem isomorphs. In: N. J. Castellan, P. B. Pisoni, & G. R. Rotts (Eds), *Cognitive theory* (Vol. 2). Hillsdale: Lawrence Erlbaum.

Judd, C. H. (1908). The relation of special training and general intelligence. *Educational Review,* *36*, 28–42.

Katona, G. (1940). *Organizing and memorizing.* New York: Colombia University Press.

Konkola, R. (2001). Harjoittelun kehittämisprosessi ammattikorkeakoulussa ja rajavyöhyketoiminta uudenlaisena toimintamallina. [Developmental process of internship at polytechinc and boundary-zone activity as a new model for activity]. In: T. Tuomi-Gröhn, & Y. Engeström (Eds), *Koulun ja työn rajavyöhykkeellä – uusia työssäoppimisen mahdollisuuksia* [At the boundary-zone between school and work — new possibilities of work-based learning] (pp. 148–186). Helsinki: University Press.

Konkola, R., Lambert. P., Tuomi-Gröhn, T., & Ludvigsen, S. *Developmental tools for promoting learning and transfer between school and work* (Manuscript).

Lave, J. (1988). *Cognition in practice: Mind, mathematics and culture in everyday life.* Cambridge: Cambridge University Press.

Lave, J., & Wenger, E. (1991). *Situated learning: Legitimate peripheral participation.* Cambridge: Cambridge University Press.

Leont'ev, A. N. (1977). *Activity, consciousness, and personality.* Englewood Cliffs: Prentice-Hall.

Mayer, R. E., & Wittrock, M. C. (1996). Problem-solving transfer. In: D. C. Berliner & R. C. Calfee (Eds), *Handbook of Educational Psychology.* New York: Simon & Schuster.

McKeough, A., Lupart, J., & Marini, A. (1995). *Teaching for transfer. Fostering generalization in learning.* Hillsdale: Lawrence Erlbaum.

Nickerson, R. S., Perkins, D. N., & Smith, E. F. (1985). *The teaching of thinking.* Hillsdale: Lawrence Erlbaum.

Nunes, T., Schliemann, A., & Carraher, T. (1993). *Street mathematics and school mathematics.* Cambridge: Cambridge University Press.

Packer, M. (2001). The problem of transfer, and the sociocultural critique of schooling. *The Journal of Learning Sciences, 10*(4), 493–514.

Palinscar, A. M., & Brown, A. L. (1984). Reciprocal teaching of comprehension fostering and comprehension monitoring activities. *Cognition and Instruction, 1,* 117–175.

Reed, S. K., Ernst, G. W., & Banerji, R. (1974). The role of analogy in transfer between similar problem states. *Cognitive Psychology, 6,* 436–450.

Segal, J. W., Chipman, S. F., & Glaser, R. (Eds) (1985). *Thinking and learning skills.* Hillsdale: Lawrence Erlbaum.

Simon, H. A., & Reed, S. K. (1976). Modeling strategy shifts in a problem solving task. *Cognitive Psychology, 8,* 86–97.

Singley, M. K., & Anderson, J. R. (1989). *The transfer of cognitive skill.* Cambridge: Harvard University Press.

Star, S. L. (1989). The structure of ill-structured solutions: Boundary objects and heterogenious distributed problem solving. In: L. Gasser & M. N. Huhns (Eds), *Readings in distributed artificial intelligence* (Vol. 3). Menlo Park, CA: Morgan Kaufmann.

Star, L. S., & Griesemer, J. R. (1999). Institutional ecology, "translations" and boundary objects: Amateurs and professional in Berkeley's museum of vertebrate zoology 1907–39. *Social Studies of Science, 9,* 387–420.

Thorndike, E. L. (1924). Mental discipline in high school studies. *Journal of Educational Psychology, 15,* 1–22, 83–98.

Thorndike, E. L., & Woodworth, R. S. (1901). The influence of improvement in one mental function upon the efficiency of other functions. *Psychological Review, 8,* 247–261.

Wake, G., & Williams, J. (2002). Using college mathematics in understanding workplace practice. *Learning, Teaching and Assessment.* The University of Manchester.

Wenger, E. (1998). *Communities of practice. learning, meaning and identity.* Cambridge: Cambridge University Press.

Volet, S. (1999). Learning across cultures: appropriateness of knowledge transfer. *International Journal of Educational Research, 31,* 625–643.

Part I

Boundary-crossing as a Theoretical Basis for Research on Transfer

Chapter 2

Conceptualizing Transfer: From Standard Notions to Developmental Perspectives

Terttu Tuomi-Gröhn and Yrjö Engeström

The tension between cognitive/constructivist and situated notions of transfer (see Tuomi-Gröhn, Engeström & Young, this volume) may be seen as the current backdrop of the discussion we will present in this contribution. While we are strongly in favor of moving beyond the cognitive notions, we are not inclined to accept the situated approach as such, at least not without critical examination. Instead, we will sketch a new developmental perspective on transfer that attempts to go beyond the opposition between the cognitive notions and their situated challenges. To accomplish this without too many shortcuts, we will now discuss a series of conceptualizations of transfer. This series begins with two classical notions of transfer: identical elements by Thorndike (1924) and general principles by Judd (1908). We then move to more current cognitive views (e.g. Gick & Holyak 1980; Reed 1993; Sternberg 1990). They are followed by theories of situated learning (Greeno, Smith & Moore 1993; Lave 1988; Wenger 1998). Very recent sociocultural views are represented by Beach (1999). Finally, transfer views of cultural-historical activity theory are presented, drawing on the work of Davydov (1990) and expanding this legacy in the formulation of our own ideas of expansive learning and developmental transfer.

Classical Theories of Transfer

Thorndike and Identical Elements

Early psychological ideas of transfer were based on the notion that intellectual performance depends on certain mental faculties such as memory, attention, and judgment. According to this view, training of basic mental functions was thought to have general effects that would transfer to new situations (Wolf 1973: 207). Exercise on mental tasks strengthens abilities of memory, reasoning, concentration and the like in

Between School and Work: New Perspectives on Transfer and Boundary-crossing
Copyright © 2003 by Elsevier Science Ltd.
All rights of reproduction in any form reserved.
ISBN: 0-08-044296-X

ways that will generate to the full range of other activities that call on these abilities. An important educational application of this general transfer view was the doctrine of formal discipline — the idea that certain school subjects such as Latin and geometry improved students minds by making their thinking more logical and disciplined (Mayer & Wittrock 1996: 49).

Thorndike and his colleagues proposed the specific transfer view as an alternative to the doctrine of formal discipline. In a series of classic studies, Thorndike (1924) disproved the doctrine of formal discipline by showing that, on tests of intellectual development or reasoning, students who studied Latin and geometry performed no better than students who studied other subjects. Thorndike argued that transfer would occur when the specific content of one subject was needed to learn another subject. For Thorndike, transfer rested on the availability of "identical elements" between the original learning and transfer situations, that is, connections that could be reinstated in the new setting (Mayer & Wittrock 1996: 49–50; Shulman & Quinlan 1996: 405).

> The mind is . . . a machine for making particular reactions to particular situations. It works in great detail, adapting itself to the special data of which it has experience . . . Improvement in any single mental function need not improve the ability in functions commonly called by the same name. It may injure it. Improvement in any single mental function rarely brings about equal improvement in any other function, no matter how similar, for the working of every mental function-group is conditioned by the nature of the data in each particular case (Thorndike & Woodworth 1901: 249–250).

An educational implication of the focus on identical elements was that the curriculum should be analyzed into specific behaviors and taught in sequence so that lower level basic skills were taught before the higher level skills that included them. Drill and practice of specific skills became the hallmark of educational arrangements based on this view of transfer (Mayer & Wittrock 1996: 50). It is easy to see a continuity from these ideas to more modern doctrines of specific behavioral objectives of instruction (e.g. Mager 1967).

Judd and General Principles

Thorndike's view was questioned by Judd (1939), who proposed that transfer does not depend on identical elements but on grasping the general principles or generalizations of the subject matter. Judd thus, maintained, that broad transfer occurs when the same general strategy or principle that was previously learned in a task A is also required in learning or performing task B.

A famous experiment was run by Judd & Scholckow (Judd 1908). They had children practice throwing darts at an underwater target. One group of subjects received an explanation of the principle of refraction of light, which causes the apparent location of the target to be deceptive. The other group only practiced, receiving no conceptual instruction. Both groups did equally well on the practice task, which involved a target 12 inches under water, but the group with conceptual information did much better when asked to transfer to a situation where the target was now under only four inches of water.

For Judd, education was an enterprise of the "higher mental processes" and a broad conception of transfer was essential to such a view.

> The psychology which concludes that transfer is uncommon or of slight degree is the psychology of animal consciousness, the psychology of particular experiences. The psychology of higher mental processes teaches that the end and goal of all education is the development of systems of ideas which can be carried over from the situations in which they were acquired to other situations. Systems of general ideas illuminate and clarify human experiences by raising them to the level of abstract, generalized, conceptual understanding (Judd 1936: 201).

Judd rejected Thorndike's atomistic reductionism in his commitment to an educational psychology of higher mental processes. The essence of Judd's argument was that transfer occurred because of *what* was transferred, namely principles, and *how* instruction of principles was undertaken, namely, intentionally, self-consciously, and reflectively. Transfer does not occur effortlessly and mindlessly, as a reflex. The contrast between learning as reflection, and learning as reflex, identifies the fundamental difference between Thorndike and Judd. For Judd, teachers must actively and purposively teach for transfer, and students must thoughtfully learn for transfer, if the feat is to be accomplished (Shulman & Quinlan 1996: 405).

Building in part on Judd's (1908) work on transfer, Gestalt psychologists provided substantial empirical evidence for transfer of a general principle from one situation to another (Katona 1940; Wertheimer 1945). Bower & Hilgard (1981: 323) summarize this view as follows:

> A pattern of dynamic relationship discovered or understood in one situation may be applicable to another. There is something in common between the earlier learning and situation in which transfer is found, but what exists is not identical piecemeal elements but common patterns, configurations, or relationships. One of the advantages of learning by understanding rather than by rote is that understanding is transposable to wider ranges of situations, and less often leads to erroneous applications of old learning.

Judd's approach may be seen as a predecessor of later views, most notably those formulated by Jerome Bruner (1969, 1972), that emphasize the understanding of deep structures and general principles in different curricular subjects as the foundation of transfer. While they offer a much more optimistic view of human cognitive potentials than the notion of identical elements, a key problem in these views is that they seem to uphold the institutional and epistemological separation of school from life.

Cognitive Views of Transfer

Theories of Cognitive Schemas and Metacognitive Monitoring

A number of cognitive psychologists and cognitive scientists see the concept of schema as the theoretical basis for understanding transfer. Schema theories are focused, on the one hand, on how information is represented and organized in memory, and on the other hand, on processing aspects: how these structures are developed, updated, and used (Danserau 1995: 99). Thorndyke (1984: 167) defines a schema as a cluster of knowledge that provides a skeleton structure for a concept that can be instantiated or filled out by the detailed properties of a particular instance. Schemas are formed by induction from numerous previous experiences with various exemplars of a general concept. Thorndyke lists five characteristics of schema models that are generally shared by theorists who propose these models. The characteristics are abstraction, instantiation, prediction, induction, and hierarchical organization. According to Reed (1993: 46), algebra word problems fit rather nicely into a schema interpretation. Students typically categorize problems and use equations associated with problem categories as a basis for solving problems.

A version of the symbolic schema idea is used by Reed (1993) for problems presenting numerical values of quantities that are solved using formulas. Formulas are abstract representations that can be used to specify arithmetic operations that result in the needed answer. Reed discusses transfer of solution methods that include the use of the same formula for a transfer problem that was used in solving problems, presented in initial learning. In most versions of the symbolic schema theory model of solving word problems in arithmetic, use of a solution method depends on recognizing a pattern of relations among the quantities that are described in the problem. In problems involving the use of a formula, it is supposed that the mental representation in a learning situation would include a symbolic schema that represents the pattern of quantitative information in the initial learning problems, along with a representation of the formula that can be used to solve problems, and a representation of the quantitative properties and relations. Transfer will occur if the pattern of quantities in the transfer problem is recognized to fit the same schema that was used in initial learning. Transfer, therefore, requires the ability to interpret the learned symbolic schema in the transfer situation (Greeno *et al.* 1993: 143).

Cognitive views of transfer commonly emphasize the role of metacognition, that is, awareness of the cognitive processes that one uses in "monitoring and consequent regulation and orchestration of those processes" (Flavell 1976: 232, see also Morris 1990). In the metacognitive transfer view, successful transfer occurs when the problem solver is able to recognize the requirements of the new problem, select previously learned specific and general skills that apply to the new problem. The problem solver is seen as an active participant in the problem-solving process, as one who must manage the way the prior knowledge is used to solve a new problem (Mayer & Wittrock 1996: 50). Sternberg (1990: 269) characterizes this view of transfer as follows:

> Recognizing the existence of a problem, deciding upon the nature of the problem confronting them, selecting a set of lower order processes to

solve the problem, selecting a strategy into which to combine these components, selecting a mental representation upon which the components and strategy can act, allocating one's mental resources, monitoring one's problem solving as it is happening, and evaluating one's problem solving after it is done.

Gick & Holyoak (1983: 39–40) draw a distinction between perceived similarity of the training and transfer situations, based on salient common features of their representations, and objective structural similarity, based on the actual components determining appropriate responses. Transfer is affected by both types of similarity. Perceived similarity determines whether transfer will be attempted, whereas objective structural similarity determines whether transfer will be positive or negative.

Many studies based on cognitive views do not involve intentional learning of a transfer task. Instead, transfer is reflected in the performance of transfer task on the basis of knowledge acquired by performing an initial task. The basic assumption is that transfer results when the original encoding of Task A can be applied to guide the performance of transfer task B (Gick & Holyoak 1983: 12).

Several cognitively oriented educational psychologists, for example Ausubel, Novak & Hanesian (1978), advocate the use of explicit structural schemas — or advance organizers — by instructors during the presentation of new information to enhance its organization and to illustrate its relationships to other areas of the knowledge domain. While this may indeed facilitate better performance in text-based school tasks, it remains unclear just what relevance such in-school improvement may have for the transfer of school knowledge to life situations and activities outside school.

Dispositional Theory of Transfer

Within a broadly conceived range of cognitive views of transfer, Bereiter's dispositional view deserves a separate discussion. Bereiter (1995: 22–23, see also Bereiter 1997) distinguishes between two kinds of transfer in teaching and learning. The first, *transfer of principles*, has to do with students' recognition of new cases where the principles acquired can be applied. The second kind, *transfer of disposition*, focuses on whether the students in fact do apply the principle acquired in a real situation.

Bereiter argues that only the second kind of transfer poses problems of teaching for transfer. Research on teaching for conceptual change provides good reasons to believe that transfer of principles depends preeminently on how thoroughly and deeply the principles are understood. Bereiter argues that when it comes to transfer of principles, the teacher is better off forgetting about transfer and concentrating on teaching for understanding. It is a different problem, however, with transfer of dispositions. Drawing on cases of moral education and scientific thinking, Bereiter (1995: 23) claims that no matter how well a principle, such as respect for human life or scientific thinking, is understood, it is uncertain whether respect for human life will function in situations of crisis or mass emotion, or whether students will actually think scientifically when there is no teacher to guide them. Whatever is learned in the classroom tends to vanish outside the classroom, and this is the real problem of transfer.

The dispositional view is based on reinterpreting what are usually thought of as mental abilities or cognitive skills and treating them instead as dispositions (Bereiter 1995: 21). For instance, critical thinking has been reinterpreted in this way — treating it as a virtue, similar to honesty and kindness, rather than as a mental skill similar to deductive reasoning and problem-solving. The dispositional view on transfer, based on a combination of personal characteristics, is different from other views on transfer because transfer is not usually thought of as an ability but rather as an event, and the potential for transfer is not usually thought of as residing in the learner but rather in whatever has been learned. A consequence of the dispositional view is that transfer is no longer thought of as skill training or strategy instruction, but as something more like character education.

But can schools be expected to teach transferable dispositions? The transfer of dispositions depends on their incorporation into the student's character. To understand the transfer of dispositions, Bereiter conceptualizes it as *transfer of situations* rather than transfer *across* situations (Bereiter 1995: 29–30). Learning to participate in thoughtful, critical discourse in a classroom may not imbue children with the reflective disposition to think that way in general, but it may dispose them to seek out companions and situations for that same kind of discourse. The result sought after is a disposition to seek out and to create situations similar to those in which reflective discourse was experienced initially. This is different from the idea that having got children to act reflectively in certain situations of classroom discourse, we imagine that they now have a little reflective module planted in their heads and we vainly hope that it will be activated in other situations (Bereiter 1995: 31).

For Bereiter, what typically fails to transfer from one situation to another is learned intelligent behavior. If education were seriously to aim at transfer of dispositions and to invest in the possibilities of transfer of situations, it would not be sufficient for teachers to create situations that are more or less characterized by desirable kinds of thinking and cooperative efforts. Teachers would need to work toward enabling students to create those situations for themselves, with different participants, and with different constraints. Then there might be reason to expect that intelligent behavior acquired in school situations would reappear as people recreate similar situations later (Bereiter 1995: 33).

Bereiter's view is refreshing in that it shifts our attention to everyday situations outside school and emphasizes the creation of situations rather than merely the 'correct' reaction to given problems and tasks. At the same time, Bereiter puts the dispositions firmly inside individuals, thus upholding the Cartesian bias of the dominant cognitive views. The possible cultural, communal and socially distributed nature of dispositions — powerfully explored by Moscovici and others (Farr & Moscovici 1984) under the rubric of social representations, by D'Andrade & Strauss (1992) under the rubric of cultural motives, and by Holland *et al.* (1998) under the rubric of cultural identities — is all but ignored by Bereiter.

Situated Views of Transfer

Jean Lave (1988: 43) criticizes cognitively oriented transfer research as in the following terms:

> Its central characteristics include separation of cognition from social world, the separation of form and content implied in the practice of investigating isomorphic problem-solving, and a strictly cognitive explanation for continuity in activity across situations. All these *dissociate* cognition from its contexts, and help to account for the absence of theorizing about experiments as social situations and cognition as socially situated activity.

Cognitive experiments are based on the idea that transfer should take place between two versions of the same story or problem. The cognitive view represents the static quality of transfer in experimental practice: it is treated as a process of taking a given item and applying it somewhere else (Lave 1988: 37).

The important notion in a situated view of transfer is that what is transferred is not knowledge from task to task but patterns of participatory processes across situations (Greeno 1997: 12; for a more comprehensive presentation of different views of transfer in situated learning theories, see Gruber, Law, Mandl & Renkl 1996).

James Greeno (1996) proposes a situated view of transfer. He draws on Gibson's (1986) notion of affordances to explain the mechanisms underlying situated cognition: "We call the support for particular activities created by relevant properties of things and materials in the situation affordances. For a practice learned in one situation to transfer to another situation, the second situation has to afford that practice and the agent has to perceive the affordance. If a learned practice is to transfer, it has to be learned in a form that is invariant across changes in the situation or that can be transformed as needed, and transfer depends on an ability to perceive the affordances for the practice that are present in a changed situation" (Greeno, Smith & Moore 1993: 102).

To a great extent, the affordances that enable our activities are properties of artifacts that have been designed so that those activities can be supported. The functions of these properties as affordances are shaped by social practices. People learn these practices, including the utilities of affordances, mainly by participating in them along with other people. The range of situations that provide affordances for an activity constitutes an important aspect of the socially constructed meanings of the properties of those situations, so that the potential for transfer between situations is shaped by social practices in which people learn the activities (Greeno, Smith & Moore 1993: 102).

The issue of perceiving affordances is crucial in Greeno's theory of situativity. It depends significantly on Gibson's pivotal concept of direct perception, which implies that environmental stimuli are simply picked up instead of being conceived with the mediated symbolic representations; for instance, a chair is perceived as "sit-on-able" and a path is perceived as "walk-on-able" (Greeno, Smith & Moore 1993: 104).

Hatano & Greeno (1999) propose to use the term *productivity*, rather than transfer, to refer to the generality of learning, and they claim that we should pay more attention both to practices of productive learning and to the activities involved in using the results of prior learning in novel situations, as well as to how we can help these processes.

For Greeno, symbolic cognitive representations can play an important role in transfer, but they are considered as instrumental parts of the activities that occur in the initial learning and in transfer situations, rather than being fundamental and ubiquitous. Greeno believes, transfer that depends primarily on symbolic cognitive representations that are learned in one situation and applied in another is not the only kind of transfer. Indeed, Greeno believes that transfer mediated in that way by abstract, symbolic representations is probably atypical. The Greeno's focus is on activities or practices rather than on representations. Transfer, in this view, is enabled by structural invariance in the interactions of agents in situations. These interactions can be described as action schemata, referring to the organizing principle of the activity rather than to symbolic cognitive representations. In Greeno's view, the structure that enables transfer is in the interactive activity of the person in the situation. The structures are general, and transfer occurs because of general properties and relations of the person's interactions with features of a situation. A physical or cognitive symbolic representation may play a role in that activity, but symbolic representations are not necessary conditions for transfer (Greeno, Smith & Moore 1993: 146).

In order to result in transfer, instruction should influence the activity so that it includes attention to affordances that are invariant across changes in the situation and that will support successful interactions in situations that have been transformed. With his epistemological assumption that learning involves construction of knowledge rather than its passive acquisition, Greeno (1996) suggests that learning environments should include collaborative settings where teachers act as partners, coaches as well as models, and where students can work together as well as engage in exploration of ideas.

Greeno's view of instruction is a version of the apprenticeship approach that focuses on turning peripheral novices into central experts, and therefore, targets the characteristics of established expert practice as what should be learned (Lave & Wenger 1991). Instead of transfer, the basic metaphor for learning is participation. In a community of practice, learning takes place without much teaching, as an incidental by-product of productive activity and often with tremendous efficiency, due to the strong motivational basis (it is for real, not just for school) and the richly supportive environment (everybody in a community of practice functions as a teacher).

Greeno's view of transfer is promising in that it switches the locus of learning from an isolated Cartesian individual to a novice participating in a community of practice. In so doing, it also expands the structures of knowledge to include not just mental and symbolic representations but also physical artifacts and recurring patterns of social practice. However, learning is still ultimately depicted as an individual achievement, albeit as that of an individual situated in a communal setting. Furthermore, the learning trajectory of the individual is curiously unidirectional, moving in a rather traditional fashion from the periphery of not-knowing to the center of knowing. The theory depicts communities of practice as stable formations; it does not address outward movement, radical innovation, and change in communities of practice.

Sociocultural Reconceptualization

Drawing on a number of socio-culturally oriented theories, King Beach (1999, also this volume) has recently suggested a bold reconceptualization of transfer. For Beach, most current notions of transfer presuppose that tasks or situations across which transfer occurs are unchanging. Hence the process of *creating tasks* is excluded from being considered as part of the transfer process. A similar logic excludes emerging historical relations between institutional situations such as the family and the school from being part of transfer across them. This is problematic, given that these same notions of transfer acknowledge that relations between tasks and situations partially determine whether, and how, transfer occurs. The effect is an over-emphasis on the role of the individual learner, excluding from the transfer process humans involved in the construction of tasks or collectively and historically linking situations.

Beach argues that learners and social organizations exist in a recursive and mutually constitutive relation to one another across time. Consequently, our experiences of continuity and transformation across time and social situations are neither a function of the individual nor the situation, but rather of their relation.

Beach introduces the concept of *consequential transitions* to reconceptualize transfer. This concept is closely related to Bronfenbrenner's (1979) earlier concept of ecological transitions.

> An ecological transition occurs whenever a person's position in the ecological environment is altered as the result of a change in role, setting, or both. . . . every ecological transition is both a consequence and an instigator of developmental processes (Bronfenbrenner 1979: 26–27).

But Beach expands the argument to construct a whole alternative view of transfer-related phenomena. The first assumption underlying the construct of consequential transitions is that generalization, or the continuity and transformation of knowledge, skill and identity across various forms of social organization, involves multiple interrelated processes rather than a single general procedure. The second assumption is that generalization is never distanced or decontextualized in its relation to various forms of social organization. The decontextualization of mediational means (Wertsch 1985), or the formation of symbols and concepts at ever increasing distances from particular contexts and referents (Hatano & Inagaki 1992), does not provide an adequate basis for explaining and facilitating generalization.

The generalization Beach is interested in, is not located within the developing individual, nor can it be reduced to changing social activities. Rather, it is located in the changing relationship between persons and activities. Numerous studies demonstrate the centrality of symbols, technologies, texts, or systems of artifacts in constructing continuities and transformations across social situations. Thus generalization is located at the interface of persons and activities, embodied in systems of artifacts, symbolic objects that are created with human intent.

The interrelated processes and systems of artifacts weave together changing persons and social organizations such that the person experiences becoming someone or something new. Thus the experiences of continuity and transformation are important to, reflected on, and struggled with by individuals *participating in multiple social activities*. In so far as many of these experiences are life-transforming, they have a developmental nature and they bear witness to some notion of progress.

Studying history or making a transition from student to professional involves transformation; the construction of new knowledge, identities, ways of knowing, and new positions of oneself in the world. They are consequential for the individual and are developmental in nature, located in the changing relation between individual and social activities.

Given that it is generalization across broader domains of human experience with which education is ultimately concerned, analyses of local attempts at facilitation across tasks and problems need to be understood within an interpretative framework that encompasses relations between larger social practices and institutions (see also Lemke 1997). Relations between larger forms of social organization may also be a fruitful starting point for understanding local attempts at facilitating generalization across tasks and problems.

As its core, the concept of transition involves consequential change in the relation between the individual and one or more social activities across time. All forms of transition involve the construction of knowledge and skills, understood as transformation rather than as mere application or use of something that has been acquired elsewhere. Consequential transitions often involve changes in identity as well as knowledge and skill.

Beach identifies four primary types of consequential transition: *lateral, collateral, encompassing, and mediational*. Lateral and collateral transitions involve persons moving between preexisting social activities. Encompassing and mediational transitions are made by persons moving within the boundaries of a single activity, or into the creation of a new activity.

Beach's framework depicts transfer above all as movement across the boundaries of activity contexts. It is not only knowledge that moves — the entire human being moves, and in so doing reconstructs his or her relation to the context. Transitions can be multi-directional and reciprocal. However, the locus of learning is still firmly in the individual. Also, while Beach points out that multiple processes are involved in consequential transitions, he does not really elaborate the specific nature of these processes.

Activity-theoretical Views

Davydov and Theoretical Generalization

In cultural-historical activity theory (Chaiklin, Hedegaard & Jensen 1999; Engeström, Miettinen & Punamäki 1999; Leont'ev 1978), the unit of analysis is a historically evolving, collective, artifact-mediated *activity system*. Activity is oriented at a culturally significant object which also forms the motive of the activity. Activity must be distinguished from action. Actions are produced by individuals and groups as they pursue a collective activity. Actions are oriented at goals and relatively short in duration.

They are performed with the help of operations, automatic routines oriented at the given tools and circumstances of the action.

Most learning consists of learning actions embedded in activities whose object and motive is not learning as such. Thus, learning in school typically happens in relatively discrete learning actions embedded in what might be characterized as schoolgoing activity (Engeström 1987; Miettinen 1999).

On the basis of an extensive critique of dominant forms of school instruction, V. V. Davydov (1988, 1990) introduced the concept of learning activity as a new type of learning. For Davydov, the object and motive of learning activity is the formation of a theoretical relationship to reality — or theoretical thinking for short. The core of theoretical thinking consists of *substantive, theoretical generalizations*. Theoretical generalization requires that the learners first analyze and identify a primary general relationship in the system to be mastered, at the same time making the discovery that this relationship is operative in innumerable other particular manifestations of the domain. Identifying and isolating such an initial abstraction — a kernel or a *germ cell* — leads to the modeling and examination of this general relationship. Learning activity proceeds step by step to establish links between the primary abstraction and its diverse particular developmental forms and manifestations. In other words, learning activity proceeds by *ascending from the abstract to the concrete*.

> *Content-related generalization discloses the essence* of things as the guiding principle of their development, as that which determines their development. To make such a generalization means to discover a principle, a necessary *connection* of the individual phenomena within a certain whole, the law of the formation of that whole. Disclosure of the general nature of some real relationship occurs ... in the process of *analyzing* those of its features that allow it to be the genetic base of a developed system (Davydov 1990: 295).

Over the course of some thirty years of experimental research on instructional programs based on the principle of ascending from the abstract to the concrete, Davydov and his colleagues have produced an impressive amount of evidence for their theoretical claims (e.g. Davydov 1988; Lompscher 1999). Davydov identifies a sequence of six learning actions constitutive of theoretical generalization:

(1) transforming the conditions of the task in order to reveal the universal relationship of the object under study;
(2) modeling the identified relationship in an item-specific, graphic, or literal form;
(3) transforming the model of the relationship in order to study its properties in their 'pure guise';
(4) constructing a system of particular tasks that are resolved by a general mode;
(5) monitoring the performance of the preceding actions;
(6) evaluating the assimilation of the general mode that results from resolving the given learning task (Davydov 1988, Part II: 30).

While this sequence is general, the contents of each action in it are specific to the system under investigation. When fully developed, such an interconnected system of epistemic actions becomes a theoretical concept. The formation of a theoretical concept leads to an 'on-the-spot' ability to grasp and solve a particular problem as an instance of a general relationship. Imagination is a crucial vehicle for such a very quick insight into the nature of a problem.

As a theory of transfer, Davydov's framework requires a deep epistemological and logical paradigm shift, from formal logic and empiricism to dialectics and the study of developing systems. The method of ascending from the abstract to the concrete offers a possibility to overcome the empiricism and verbalism predominant in educational institutions. It identifies specific processes — learning actions — behind the achievement of transfer. But it also opens up a number of questions: What if there are multiple alternative and competing 'germ cell' abstractions in a domain? What is the role of dialogue and debate in the formation of theoretical generalizations?

Above all, Davydov's work suffers from the fact that its applications were practically confined within schools and classrooms. Davydov never studied transitions between school and work. Thus, the locus of learning also remained individual. Transformations in collective activity systems and institutions (e.g. schools and workplaces) were not integrated into his theoretical framework. Paradoxically, in spite of the theoretical intent, collective activity systems did not become units of empirical analysis and experimentation during the Soviet regime.

Expansive Learning and Developmental Transfer

In our own work over the past fifteen years, we have used and developed activity theory to analyze and design learning processes in which new types of transfer may be achieved (Engeström 1987, 1991; Engeström, Hakkarainen & Hedegaard 1984). We find Davydov's concepts of learning activity and ascending from the abstract to the concrete a useful foundation, yet also restrictive in their exclusively school-based focus within Davydov's work. Our work centers around the concepts of expansive learning and developmental transfer, situated at and around the boundaries between multiple activity systems, typically schools and workplaces.

We take Leont'ev's (1978) idea of collective activity system as unit of analysis seriously. This means that learning is distributed in an object-oriented activity system, mediated by instruments, rules and division of labor (Figure 1). The learning of the activity system and the learning of an individual are intertwined, and the individual's learning is understandable only if we understand the learning of the activity system. This does not mean that the subject position and agency are handed over to a mysterious collective entity. Different individuals and groups involved in an activity system take and leave the subject position as they produce specific goal-oriented actions. Thus, the detailed configuration of the activity system changes in each action.

Expansive learning is initiated when some individuals involved in a collective activity take the action of questioning the existing practice. This can lead to an escalating process of debate and collaborative analysis of contradictions in the current state of

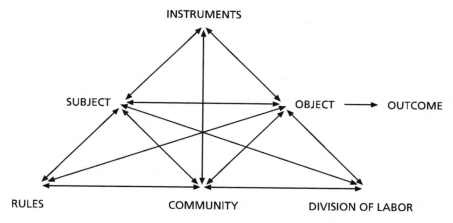

Figure 1: General structure of an activity system (Engeström 1987: 78).

affairs, which may lead to a projective modeling of a developmentally new form of the activity, in which the contradictions are resolved. The model is a germ cell or initial abstraction of the next developmental form of the activity system. The model and its implications are examined, and it is implemented step by step in practice. This leads to consolidation and proliferation of the new practice, and to reflective evaluation of the process. In our intervention studies, we have documented and analyzed numerous cases of such expansive learning cycles in work organizations (e.g. Engeström 1991, 1994, 1999a). Expansion happens substantively, by constructing a more encompassing object and motive for the activity, and socially, by recruiting a growing number of participants in the transformation effort.

It is relatively easy to see the affinity between Davydov's six learning actions and the actions we have found in expansive learning cycles. The two sets of actions are summarized in Table 1.

There are three main differences between the two models of learning. First, Davydov's model begins with transforming the conditions of the given task in order to find out the general relationship within it. This corresponds to the second action —

Table 1: Davydov's learning actions and expansive learning actions.

Davydov's learning Actions	Actions of expansive learning
– transforming the conditions	– questioning
– modeling	– analysis (historical and actual-empirical)
– transforming the model	– modeling
– constructing a system of tasks	– examining the model
– monitoring	– implementing
– evaluating	– consolidating and proliferating
	– evaluating

analysis — in our model of expansive learning. The difference is that we do not take the learning task as a given. In work settings, interesting problem-solving and learning processes are typically not triggered by an instructor giving a task to be learned. To the contrary, these processes are commonly triggered when some practitioners reject the given wisdom and begin to question it. We cannot emphasize enough the importance of such actions of questioning in processes of expansive learning (see Engeström 1999b; Pihlaja 1999).

The second difference between the two models is in the meaning of modeling. For Davydov, modeling means that students discover a general relationship in the task and model it graphically, symbolically, or by other means. The expected model is known ahead of time by the instructor, and the model has primarily explanatory and diagnostic functions in the further course of learning. In our framework, modeling has an explicitly dual character. On the one hand, the practitioners model the past and present contradictions in their activity system in order to understand where the causes of trouble lie and on which aspects of the activity they shall focus their change efforts. On the other hand, the practitioners model also a future vision of their activity, in which they depict expansive solutions to the contradictions. This latter model has primarily the functions of projection and design — something that is not highlighted in Davydov's framework.

The third difference is in the ascending to the concrete. In Davydov's framework, the critical action for the occurrence of transfer is constructing a system of particular tasks to be resolved by means of the general relationship found. In our framework, two actions are critical for transfer, namely implementation of the new model in practice and consolidation/proliferation of the new practice. In other words, we are interested in: (a) the transfer of new models into practice (implementation); and (b) in the transfer of local innovations and new forms of practice into other activity systems and organizations (proliferation). In both cases, the original models and new practices will themselves be transformed and renegotiated as they are transferred.

From the point of view of educational institutions, such as vocational colleges, the idea of expansive learning translates into *turning the school into a collective change agent* that works in partnerships with local community organizations and workplaces. The school offers its expertise to work organizations going through transformations. This means that the school needs to prepare its teachers and students not just to do their assigned routine jobs but to work also as boundary-crossers between the school and the work organization, bringing new intellectual and practical tools and insights into the change process.

From the student's point of view, one's future workplace will inevitably be caught in developmental turmoil. Thus, the best way to learn is to become engaged in real life processes of change already when one is in school. Relative novices and outsiders can be tremendously valuable in change efforts because they see things from a fresh angle, they have time to reflect and take initiatives, and they are not caught in the routines and turf battles of the workplace. During their internships and work practice periods, students in collaboration with their teachers can work as change agents in various transformation and redesign projects of local work organizations. The collective capabilities and resources of the schools are brought into these change efforts. Teacher and students act as mediators between educational institutions and workplaces.

Most formal programs of vocational education already have built-in sequences of internship and work practice. These periods, often extended and definitely remodeled, are the natural starting point and site for the new role for schools as change agents. In these change projects, a collaborative team consisting of practitioners, students and their teachers will have to develop — pull together, elucidate and negotiate — knowledge and skills (cognitive tools) that meet the challenges of the project. This is done by constructing and combining heterogeneous networks and 'knots' of expertise (on knotworking, see Engeström, Engeström & Vähäaho 1999). This we see as the practical essence of developmental transfer. Chapters by Lambert (this volume) and Tuomi-Gröhn (this volume) provide some initial examples and findings from projects of developmental transfer in vocational education.

In such projects of expansive learning and developmental transfer, three parties learn in collaboration and dialogue: the school, the student, and the workplace. They are all engaged in constructing their partially interdependent zones of proximal development (Engeström 1987, 1994).

Conclusions

Every conceptualization of transfer reflects its own time and the concept of learning related to it. Transfer conceptualizations can be divided roughly into three groups according to the basis of transfer which are task, individual and context, or actually interaction between individual and context. Different conceptualizations of transfer are summarized in the following table along with indications as to the basis and mode of transfer in each group.

The first group of the notions of transfer is based on the transition of knowledge used in one task to solve another task. According to Thorndike this is the case when two tasks have identical elements, and according to Judd when the same principles can be used in solving different tasks. According to the views based on the cognitive approaches, a problem solver has to identify in the new task symbolic schema that are similar to those used in the previous task and to benefit from them when solving the new task. All these conceptualizations and research on transfer were made in school settings involving a transition of knowledge from one task to another.

Bereiter emphasizes the importance of the individual instead of the task. According to him transfer is most of all an individual disposition where an individual tries to create or seek such situations in which he can use the principles learned in school. Novel in this conceptualization is that transfer also includes situations outside school. What is learned in schools should be used in situations outside school. In addition, situations where learned principles are used are not characterized as static but an individual is able to develop and change them. The basis of transfer is the creation of situations needed in applying learned principles in practice. According to transfer conceptualizations based on tasks, so-called transfer tasks are given and the changes that take place in them are not taken into account in transfer research.

Most recent are the conceptualizations of transfer that are based on context. These views started from the situated notions where the basis of transfer is not in the transition

Table 2: Different conceptualizations of transfer.

Author	Basis of transfer	Mode of transfer
Task		
Thorndike	Identical elements	Specific transfer
Judd	General strategies	Broad transfer
Cognitive view (e.g. Sternberg)	Schemas	Specific and broad transfer
Individual		
Bereiter	Dispositions, intelligent behavior	Transfer of situations
Context		
Situated view (e.g. Greeno)	Individual actions in static situations	Transfer of social participation
Socio-cultural view (e.g. Beach)	Individual actions in different changing social organizations	Individual developmental transfer
Activity theory (e.g. Engeström, Davydov)	Collective activity in different social organizations	Collective developmental transfer

of knowledge but in patterns of participatory processes as a part of the social and material context. The basis of transfer research is everyday participation in social processes. In addition transfer includes not only mental, symbolic representations in the form of cognitive views but also physical artefacts and social interaction. However, transfer is still far unidirectional, moving in a rather traditional fashion from the periphery of not-knowing to the center of knowing. Communities of practice are still depicted as stable formations, they do not address change and innovations.

The conceptualization of transfer based on socio-cultural views takes into account the changing social situations and individual's multidirectional movement from one organization to another, from home to school or from workplace to school and back. Based on activity theory, this conceptualization expands the basis of transfer from the actions of individuals to the collective organizations. It is not a matter of individual moves between school and workplace but of the efforts of school and workplace to create together new practices. Novel is also that new knowledge and practices are consciously created, instead of focusing on the transition of knowledge from one organization or community of practice to another. In developmental transfer, new practices expand also to the other collaborating activity systems, not only to the original ones.

Different conceptualizations of transfer do not exclude each other. Vocational education needs learning based on situated approaches when young novices should adopt the practices of the more experienced ones. This kind of transfer increases vertical expertise and deepens the knowledge and practices in the basic professional area per se. In addition to this, learning and transfer based on socio-cultural views are needed when an individual moves between school and workplace. It is important to strengthen the knowledge and skills which can be beneficial when one moves from one community of practice to another when solving new tasks. Surprising boundary-crossings can be very useful in creating new expertise. In this case it is a matter of horizontal expertise. But the modern word needs also developmental transfer where the basis expands from individual to the collective organization, activity system. Teams and groups cooperate to find solutions to problems with no previous answers. Multi-voiced solutions, involving different kinds of expertise are more efficient than "uni-voiced" problem-solving. To this extent, transfer is about changing communities rather than individuals.

References

Ausubel, D. P., Novak, J. D., & Hanesian, H. (1978). *Educational psychology: A cognitive view.* New York: Holt.

Beach, K. (1999). Consequential transitions: A sociocultural expedition beyond transfer in education. *Review of Research in Education, 28,* 46–69.

Bereiter, C. (1995). A Dispositional view of transfer. In: A. McKeough, J. Lupart, & A. Marini (Eds), *Teaching for transfer: Fostering generalization in learning.* Hillsdale: Lawrence Erlbaum.

Bereiter, C. (1997). Situated cognition and how to overcome it. In: D. Kirschner, & J. A. Whitson (Eds), *Situated cognition: Social semiotic and psychological perspectives.* Hillsdale: Lawrence Erlbaum.

Bower, G. H., & Hilgard, E. R. (1981). *Theories of learning* (5th ed.) Englewood Cliffs: Prentice-Hall.

Bronfenbrenner, U. (1979). *The ecology of human development: Experiments by nature and design.* Cambridge: Harvard University Press.

Bruner, J. (1969). *The process of education.* Cambridge: Harvard University Press.

Bruner, J. (1972). *Beyond the information given.* London: Allen & Unwin.

Chaiklin, S., Hedegaard, M., & Jensen, U. J. (Eds) (1999). *Activity theory and social practice.* Aarhus: Aarhus University Press.

D'Andrade, R. G., & Strauss, C. (Eds) (1992). *Human motives and cultural models.* Cambridge: Cambridge University Press.

Danserau, D. F. (1995). Derived structural schemas and the transfer of knowledge. In: S. M. Cormier, & J. D. Hagman (Eds), *Transfer of learning.* New York: Academic Press.

Davydov, V. V. (1988). Problems of developmental teaching. Parts I–III. *Soviet Education, XXX,* 8–10 (whole issues).

Davydov, V. V. (1990). *Types of generalization in instruction*. Reston:. National Council of Teachers of Mathematics.

Engeström, Y. (1987). *Learning by expanding: An activity-theoretical approach to developmental research*. Helsinki: Orienta-Konsultit.

Engeström, Y. (1991). Developmental work research: Reconstructing expertise through expansive learning. In: M. I. Nurminen, & G. R. S. Weir (Eds), *Human jobs and computer interfaces*. Amsterdam: Elsevier.

Engeström, Y. (1994). The working health center project: Materializing zones of proximal development in a network of organizational learning. In: T. Kauppinen, & M. Lahtonen (Eds), *Action research in Finland*. Helsinki: Ministry of Labour.

Engeström, Y. (1999a). Expansive visibilization of work: An activity-theoretical perspective. *Computer Supported Cooperative Work*, 8, 63–93.

Engeström, Y. (1999b). Innovative learning in work teams: Analyzing cycles of knowledge creation in practice. In: Y. Engeström, R. Miettinen, & R-L. Punamäki (Eds), *Perspectives on activity theory*. Cambridge: Cambridge University Press.

Engeström, Y., Engeström, R., & Vähäaho, T. (1999). When the center does not hold: The importance of knotworking. In: S. Chaiklin, M. Hedegaard, & U. J. Jensen (Eds), *Activity theory and social practice*. Aarhus: Aarhus University Press.

Engeström, Y., Hakkarainen. P., & Hedegaard, M. (1984). On the methodological basis of research in teaching and learning. In: M. Hedegaard, P. Hakkarainen, & Y. Engeström (Eds), *Learning and teaching on a scientific basis*. Aarhus: Aarhus Universitet, Psykologisk Institut.

Engeström, Y., Miettinen R., & Punamäki, R-L. (Eds) (1999). *Perspectives activity theory*. Cambridge: Cambridge University Press.

Farr, R. M., & Moscovici, S. (Eds) (1984). *Social representations*. Cambridge: Cambridge University Press.

Flavell, J. (1976). Metacognitive aspects of problem solving. In: L. B. Resnick (Ed.), *The nature of intelligence*. Hillsdale: Lawrence Erlbaum.

Gibson, J. J. (1986). *The ecological approach to visual perception*. Hillsdale: Lawrence Erlbaum.

Gick, M. L., & Holyoak, K. J. (1980). Analogical problem solving. *Cognitive Psychology, 12*, 306–355.

Gick, M. L., & Holyoak, K. J. (1983). Schema induction and analogical transfer. *Cognitive Psychology, 15*, 1–38.

Greeno, J. G. (1983). Forms of understanding in mathematical problem solving. In: S. G. Paris, G. M. Olson, & H. W. Stevenson (Eds), *Learning and motivation in the classroom*. Hillsdale: Lawrence Erlbaum.

Greeno, J. G. (1997). Response: On claims that answer wrong questions. *Educational Researcher, 26*, 1, 5–17.

Greeno, J. G., Smith, D. R., & Moore, J. L. (1993). Transfer of situated learning. In: D. K. Detterman, & R. J. Sternberg (Eds), *Transfer on trial: Intelligence, cognition and instruction*. Norwood: Ablex.

Gruber, H., Law, L., Mandl, H., & Renkl, A. (1996). Situated learning and transfer. In: P. Reimann, & H. Spada (Eds), *Learning in humans and machines: Towards an interdisciplinary learning science*. Oxford: Pergamon.

Hatano, G., & Greeno, J. G. (1999). Commentary: Alternative perspectives on transfer and transfer studies. *International Journal of Educational Research, 31*, 645–654.

Hatano, G., & Inagaki, K. (1992). Desituating cognition through the construction of conceptual change. In: P. Light, & G. Butterworth (Eds), *Context and cognition: Ways of learning and knowing*. Hillsdale: Lawrence Erlbaum.

Holland, D. *et al.* (1998). *Identity and agency in cultural worlds.* Cambridge: Harvard University Press.

Judd, C. H. (1908). The relation of special training and general intelligence. *Educational Review, 36*, 28–42.

Judd, C. H. (1936). *Education as cultivation of higher mental processes.* New York: Macmillan.

Judd, C. H. (1939). *Educational psychology.* New York: Houghton Mifflin.

Katona, G. (1940). *Organizing and memorizing.* New York: Colombia University Press.

Lave, J. (1988). *Cognition in practice: Mind, mathematics and culture in everyday life.* Cambridge: Cambridge University Press.

Lave, J., & Wenger, E. (1991). *Situated learning: Legitimate peripheral participation.* Cambridge: Cambridge University Press.

Lemke, J. (1997). Cognition, context, and learning: A social semiotic perspective. In: D. Kirschner, & J. A. Whitson (Eds), *Situated cognition: Social semiotic and psychological perspectives.* Hillsdale: Lawrence Erlbaum.

Leont'ev, A. N. (1978). *Activity, consciousness, and personality.* Englewood Cliffs: Prentice-Hall.

Lompscher, J. (1999). Activity formation as an alternative strategy of instruction. In: Y. Engeström, R. Miettinen, & R-L. Punamäki (Eds), *Perspectives on activity theory.* Cambridge: Cambridge University Press.

Mager, R. (1967). *Developing vocational education.* Belmont: Fearon-Pitman.

Mayer, R. E., & Wittrock, M. C. (1996). Problem-solving transfer. In: D. C. Berliner, & R. C. Calfee (Eds), *Handbook of educational psychology.* New York: Simon & Schuster.

Miettinen, R. (1999). Transcending traditional school learning: Teachers' work and networks of learning. In: Y. Engeström, R. Miettinen, & R-L. Punamäki (Eds), *Perspectives on activity theory.* Cambridge: Cambridge University Press.

Morris, P. F. (1990). Metacognition. In: M. W. Eysenck (Ed.), *The Blackwell dictionary of cognitive psychology.* Oxford: Basil Blackwell.

Pihlaja, J. (1999). *Innovation as collaborative learning: An activity-theoretical analysis of expansive learning in a Post Office.* Paper presented at the conference 'Researching Work and Learning', Leeds, September 10–12 1999.

Reed, S. K. (1993). A schema-based theory of transfer. In: D. K. Detterman & R. J. Sternberg (Eds), *Transfer on trial: Intelligence, cognition and instruction.* Norwood: Ablex.

Schulman, L. S., & Quinlan, K. M. (1996). The comparative psychology of social subjects. In: D. C. Berliner, & R. C. Calfee (Eds), *Handbook of educational psychology.* New York: Simon & Schuster.

Simon, H. A., & Reed, S. K. (1976). Modeling strategy shifts in a problem solving task. *Cognitive Psychology, 8*, 86–97.

Sternberg, R. J. (1990). *Metamorphs of mind: Conceptions of the nature of intelligence.* Cambridge: Cambridge University Press.

Thorndike, E. L. (1924). Mental discipline in high school studies. *Journal of Educational Psychology, 15*, 1–22, 83–98.

Thorndike, E. L., & Woodworth, R. S. (1901). The influence of improvement in one mental function upon the efficiency of other functions. *Psychological Review, 8*, 247–261.

Thorndyke, P. W. (1984). Applications of schema theory in cognitive research. In: J. R. Anderson, & S. M. Kosslyn (Eds), *Tutorials in learning and memory.* San Francisco: Freeman.

Wenger, E. (1998). *Communities of practice. Learning, meaning and identity.* Cambridge: Cambridge University Press.

Wertheimer, M. (1945/1959). *Productive thinking.* New York: Harper & Row.

Wertsch, J. V. (1985). *Vygotsky and the social formation of mind.* Cambridge: Cambridge University Press.
Wolf, T. H. (1973). *Alfred Binet.* Chicago: University of Chicago Press.

Chapter 3

Consequential Transitions: A Developmental View of Knowledge Propagation Through Social Organizations

King Beach

This chapter begins with an ancient puzzle. How can human intellectual progress occur simultaneously with experiences of personal and epistemological continuity across time? This has been pondered in various arenas since the dawn of recorded history. Both Plato's philosophical dialogue in the *Meno* dating from 380 B.C. (1961) and Dignaga's 5th century A.D. Buddhist discourse on the dependent origination of concepts (Thurman 1984) take on a form of the puzzle: the origins of knowledge and identity, and their generalization across time, events, and generations. Generalization necessarily involves both constancy with change, which is how developmental psychology has frequently characterized the puzzle (Brim & Kagan 1980). Educational psychology's rather more restricted version is found in the works of Watson, Thorndike, and Judd, where it is conceptualized as transfer.

Learning from one task later applied to learning a new task — understood as transfer — invokes the metaphor of transporting of something from one place to another. The metaphor continues to be influential in educational psychology today (Anderson, Reder & Simon 1996, 1997; Bransford & Schwartz 1999; Detterman & Sternberg 1993; Mayer & Whittrock 1996; Pressley 1995). The historical robustness of the metaphor is due in part to its association with schooling. As Hanks points out in his introductions to Lave and Wenger's *Legitimate Peripheral Participation* (1991), our schools are designed with the assumption that knowledge and skills are portable to new events and activities, and to students' futures beyond their confines. Transfer has face validity as an appropriate metaphor for studying portable epistemologies. The metaphor shares functionalist assumptions with the behaviorist and cognitive traditions of educational psychology and much of American education (cf. Packer, in press). It also has been reified into its own phenomenon from its origins as a theoretical construct and metaphor. For all these reasons transfer continues to be the principle means by which educational psychology thinks about the generalization (constancy and change) of individuals' knowledge across contexts. It also explains why the concept endures in the face of repeated critiques of its shortcomings. Several of the more salient shortcomings are:

- transfer is logically no different than "just plain learning", or alternatively, it defines a narrow and isolated aspect of learning;
- transfer splits its agency between mental representations and external environment without adequate means for understanding their relation; and
- the formation of transfer environments are not assumed to not be an actual part of the transfer process, but rather are seen as differentially supporting or interfering with it.

Perhaps the strongest criticism is based on commonsense, which suggests that generalization from old tasks and events to new ones must happen for us on a daily and even moment-to-moment basis. Yet when we go to study generalization as transfer, it is difficult to find, and appears even more difficult to intentionally facilitate.

The purpose of this chapter is not to add to the existing critiques of transfer, of which there have been many (LCHC 1986; Rogoff & Gardner 1984; Pea 1987; Lave 1988; Guberman & Greenfield 1991; Detterman 1993; Gruber, Law, Mandl & Renkl 1996; Greeno 1997; Kirshner & Whitson 1997; Cox 1997; Lobato 1996; Cobb & Bowers 2000) including my own (Beach 1999). Rather, the chapter proposes a viable alternative for understanding how knowledge generalizes across social context. Though the construct of transfer is problematical, issues that underlie the phenomenon of generalization continue to be of importance to the organization of schools, families, communities, and workplaces as people move among and between them.

Broadening the Phenomenon: Generalization as Knowledge Propagation

Cultural-historical and activity theories provide the grounds for reconceptualizing generalization as a developmental concept in which learners and social organizations exist in a mutually constitutive relation to one another over time. However, we first need to expand the phenomenon of generalization that we are concerned with beyond the constraints imposed by the transfer construct. The process of placing boundaries on phenomena is never fully independent of the processes by which we create constructs to study them. Yet as we can see from the history of transfer research, the danger of loosing analytic power by confounding our conceptual tools with the phenomenon we are trying to understand is quite real. I will therefore, first characterize the general set of phenomena we are seeking to understand. The characterization includes but goes beyond what has been studied as transfer. Then, I will propose a concept — consequential transition — that can be used to study the broader phenomena.

Generalization, or the continuity and transformation of knowledge across various forms of social organization involves multiple interrelated processes rather than a single general procedure A similar point is made by Cox (1997) in his developmental-historical analysis of transfer, suggesting that even early Gestalt notions questioned the existence of a general procedure for transfer. Second, knowledge generalization is never separate or decontextualized from social organization, through it may become distanced from particular social organizations over time. Arguing from the position of dialectical materialism, Davydov (1990) states that curriculums and teaching should support generalization that moves toward increasing integration of the diverse aspects of a concept, and reveals the interconnected nature of its different aspects. Abstract or decontextualized representations that reveal common properties in a class of things or phenomena are impoverished descriptions of reality (Falmagne 1995), and of generalization.

Third, generalization involves changes in both individuals and social organizations, and therefore, their changing relations to each other are central to understanding generalization. Social organizations are not simply the backdrop to, or support for, generalization. Fourth, the starting point for understanding generalization among people as they move within and between organizations and activities that are historically related to one another. This stands in contrast to transfer research which takes the task as the starting point for understanding generalization — making the assumption that what is understood at the level of the task is later applicable to knowledge generalization between large scale social institutions such as school and work. We argue the reverse, that generalization is best understood as a set of processes that relate changing social organizations and individuals, and that this will in turn help us better understand generalization between tasks embedded in, and constituted by, this larger set of relations.

Finally, generalization consists of the construction of associations among social organizations. These associations can be continuities, or constancies, which is how generalization has typically been thought of under transfer. But associations can also be constituted as distinctions and contradictions. As all of these forms of associations — even continuities — are active constructions rather than transportations of knowledge, we will refer to this view of generalization as *propagation* to distinguish our phenomena of interest from that considered more narrowly under transfer.

Knowledge propagation at the interface of persons and activities cannot happen without systems of artifacts; symbolic objects that are created with human intent (cf. Cole 1996). Whitson's (1997) Peircean analysis of a case of inappropriate transfer, Walkerdine's description of students' mathematical mastery (1988), Lemke's (1997) interconnected ecosocial systems, Evan's (1999) re-analysis of Noss & Hoyles (1996) study of 'banking maths', and my studies of adults becoming bartenders (1993) and Nepali students becoming shopkeepers (Beach 1995a, 1995b) all emphasize the centrality of symbols, technologies, and texts, or systems of artifacts, in propagating knowledge across social situations.

Knowledge propagation with systems of artifacts weave together changing individuals and social organizations in such a way that the person experiences becoming someone or something new, similar to Dewey's (1916) notion of development as "becoming". Thus these experiences of knowledge propagation are important to, reflected on, and struggled with by individuals participating in multiple social activities: playing, studying, working, parenting, loving, and so on. In so far as these experiences are life-transforming, they have a developmental nature to them along with some notion of *telos* or progress. The developmental constitution of the phenomenon has also been noted by Saxe (1989, 1991).

Experiences such as learning algebra after years of studying arithmetic, becoming a machinist, founding a community organization, teaching your first-born to walk, an elementary school class writing a letter to a local newspaper, collaborating with NASA scientists on a classroom project via the Internet, making the transition from student to teacher, and negotiating your identity as an Asian-American between your home and the school are all potential examples of the sort of generalization we are concerned with. Each of these experiences involve propagation; the construction of new knowledge, identities, ways of knowing, and new positionings of oneself in the world. They are consequential for the individual and are developmental in nature, located in the changing relations between individuals and social activities. Knowledge propagation clearly extends well beyond transfer's view of what generalization is, but includes the educational terrain that transfer had reduced, metaphorically, to the carrying and application of knowledge across tasks.

The Concept of Consequential Transition

We define transition as a developmental change in the relation between an individual and one or more social activities. Changes in their relation can occur through a change in the individual, the activity, or both. Transition, then, is the concept we use to understand how knowledge is generalized, or propagated, across social space and time. A transition is *consequential* when it is consciously reflected on, struggled with, and shifts the individual's sense of self or social position. Thus, consequential transitions link identity with knowledge propagation. A college student becoming a teacher, a worker trying to adapt to a management-reorganized job, a middle school student doing well in math for the first time in his life, and high school students taking part-time work in fast food restaurants are all potential examples of transitions that are consequential both for the individual and for the particular social organization. Etienne Wenger's outstanding volume on communities of practice and the negotiation of their boundaries speaks to a similar set of phenomenon and concerns (Wenger 1998), but emphasizes the practices themselves as a unit of reflection and analysis.

We have distinguished four primary types of consequential transition: *lateral, collateral, encompassing, and mediational.* Lateral and collateral transitions involve persons moving between preexisting social activities. Encompassing and mediational transitions have persons moving within the boundaries of a single activity, or into the creation of a new activity. This typology is necessarily simplistic, and in fact one form of transition can segue into another. The typology does, however, expresses the different principal forms of relational change between individuals and social activities while sharing a core set of characteristics that define each as a form of consequential transition.

- Transitions involve the propagation of knowledge across social space and time through the construction of associations embodied in artifacts, and constituted by continuities, discontinuities, and contradictions. Knowledge is constructed and reconstructed during transitions.

- Transitions that are consequential involve a change in identity: a sense of self, social position, or a feeling of becoming someone new with knowledge propagation. Individuals and institutions are therefore often highly conscious of consequential transitions, and have particular, sometimes publicly debated agendas for how and why they should or should not take place. Transitions therefore involve notions of progress for the individual and are best understood as developmental in nature.

- Consequential transitions are not changes in the individual or in the social activity, per se, but rather are changes in their relationship. There are always multiple ways in which that recursive relationship can change.

Lateral Transitions

Lateral transitions occur when an individual moves between two historically-related activities in a single direction. Examples would include moving from school to work, such as a student becoming an airline pilot and moving from one sub-discipline to another, such as a student taking a first course in algebra after many years of arithmetic. Participation in one activity precedes and is replaced by participation in another activity during lateral transition. Lateral transition most closely resembles classic transfer in its unidirectionality. Lateral transitions generally involve some notion of progress embedded in the particular sequence of activities, and thus, in the individual's movement between the activities. Often the activity one is in lateral transition to is considered a developmental advance beyond the previous activity, which is seen as preparation for the new activity. For example, high school students saw themselves as becoming shopkeepers during their apprenticeships to shopkeepers, not as students who happened to be learning about shopkeeping (Beach 1995b). The unidirectional notion of progress associated with lateral transitions was closely tied to explanations of how and why the students transformed their mathematical reasoning in the process of becoming shopkeepers.

Lave & Wenger's (1991) account of as Alcoholics Anonymous group contains the distinction between lateral transitions, which are linear and are generally seen as irreversible, and collateral transitions which are non-linear and highly negotiated. Becoming an alcoholic involves a massive and irreversible transformation in knowledge and identity in the eyes of A. A. members. However, becoming a non-drinking alcoholic generally involves much back-and-forth collateral participation in the community of drinkers as well as non-drinkers, even though becoming a non-drinking alcoholic is what constitutes progress. It is to a far more complex form of transition that we now turn.

Collateral Transitions

Collateral transitions involve individuals' relatively simultaneous participation in two or more historically-related activities. The notion of collaterality was first developed in the dissertation work of Reineke (1995) in which he examined children's homework as it moved between school and home. Examples of collateral transitions are daily movement between home and school, participating in part-time work after school, and moving between language arts and science classes during the school week. Collateral transitions occur more frequently in life than do lateral forms, but are more difficult to understand because of their multi-directionality. Back and forth movement between activities may or may not have an explicit notion of developmental progress tied to the movement itself. As we can see from the following example, development during collateral transitions can run in opposition to societal notions of progress as often as it runs with them.

During our study of Nepali students becoming shopkeepers, we also followed adult shopkeepers attending adult education classes (Beach 1995a, 1995b). Schools did not exist in their village when the shopkeepers were of school age, hence the evening adult education class was their first participation in schooling. The shopkeepers collaterally participated in both school and work, but did not see themselves as becoming students. Instead they attended literacy and numeracy classes to gain skills in arithmetic and written literacy that would be of use to them as shopkeepers. They were not becoming better students so much as better shopkeepers. This runs contrary to the Nepali societal notion that participation in school constitutes a form of developmental progress in and of itself.

Collateral transition did not fit with extant American notions of developmental progress in our study of high school students learning to work part-time in a fast food restaurant (Beach & Vyas 1998). Students learned nothing beyond what they already knew about math, science, and language from school. Furthermore, the skills they acquired in making sandwiches were seen as cognitively low-level and low in social status by the fast food corporation. It is not surprising that this particular collateral transition between school and work does not fit our existing conceptions of development progress. Yet our findings do suggest that high school students develop during this collateral transition. Students struggle with and develop the ability to learn in a production activity devoid of a supportive agenda for their learning, unlike schooling.

As a final illustration of collateral transition, Bowers (1996) examined third-grade students learning arithmetic during a nine-week teaching experiment in which the students constructed new ways of symbolizing the process of combining and separating quantities (see also Cobb & Bowers 2000). These students also participated in daily mathematics lessons with their regular classroom teacher who taught standard paper-and-pencil algorithms for combining and separating quantities. Bowers found that two-thirds of the students became able to use the new ways of symbolizing the process to develop numerical meanings for the column algorithm in their regular math class. However, the remaining students simply switched between instrumental uses of standard computational algorithms in their regular classroom, and their constructed means of symbolizing the combination and separation of quantities in their experimental class. Thus, collateral transition consisted of the transformation of knowledge for some, and mathematical code-switching for others. Other examples of collateral transition can be found in studies of teachers and students drawing community-based knowledge and wisdom into their classroom literacy practices (Moll 1992), parents and teachers co-

constructing math homework with their children/students (Reineke 1995), and the relation of social class and parental involvement at home to elementary students participation in school (Lareau 1989).

More than any other form of transition, collateral transition raises questions about extant societal notions of developmental progress. These notions generally value knowledge proportional to the degree to which it is seen as higher in a hierarchy of distance from its origins in particular social activities. Collateral transitions make an exclusive concentration on this vertical dimension of developmental progress problematical.

Encompassing Transitions

Encompassing transitions occur within the boundaries of a single social activity that is itself changing. In the broadest sense, all social activities are changing, even if only through collective efforts to maintain the constancy of activity through rituals, routines, revivals, and rules. One form of encompassing transition is captured in Lave and Wenger's conception of legitimate peripheral participation. The activity is stable relative to the changing individual becoming a full participant in that activity. "By this we mean to draw attention to the point that learners inevitably participate in communities of practitioners and that the mastery of knowledge and skill requires newcomers to move toward full participation in the sociocultural practices of a community" (Lave & Wenger 1991: 29). A second form of encompassing transition occurs when activities undergo rapid change relative to the lives of its participants. Examples are, experienced teachers responding to new education reform initiatives or conventional machinists learning to run newly introduced computer controlled machines.

Like lateral transitions, encompassing transitions generally involve a clear notion of progress, though it is associated with the direction taken by the changing activity rather than the direction of individuals moving between activities. Unlike either lateral or collateral transitions, encompassing transitions take place within a single activity with boundaries that change, albeit at different rates with different consequences relative to the individual. It should be noted that this sense of boundary is not absolute or hermitic. Rather an activity boundary is one that can be crossed developmentally (Engeström, Engeström & Kärkkäinen 1995; Gutierrez, Rymes & Larson 1995) and through the use of boundary objects sufficiently flexible to be adapted across multiple activities (Star 1989, 1996).

Individuals participating in encompassing transitions often experience the process as adapting to existing or changing circumstances in order to continue participation within the boundaries of the activity. Encompassing transitions can result in generational reversals in expertise and instructional roles. Younger generations of participants often assist older generations in acquiring necessary knowledge, and are seen as more expert. This generational reversal in roles in the face of rapid societal change was first noted by Margaret Mead in her classic ethnography, *Coming of Age in Samoa*. Many of us experience it today when we request assistance from our students, daughters, or sons in learning a particular piece of computer software.

Our research on machining activity changing with the introduction of computerized machines illustrates encompassing transition (Hungwe 1999; Hungwe & Beach 1995). Machining parts traditionally involved machinists using lathes, milling, and grinding machines that were controlled using mechanical linkages, dials, levers, and gauges. The recent introduction of computer numerical control (CNC) machines into American manufacturing also introduced symbol-based computer programs that mediate the relation between the machinist and part creation. Traditional machinists learn CNC machining by transforming prior machining knowledge into the representations and organizational structures of the program code, and by adapting to the asynchronous nature of their actions that control the machines through the program. Many of the upcoming generation of machinists have not had years of mechanical machining experience prior to learning on CNC machines. Thus, the nature of becoming a machinist, their status within the machining community, and their identity as craftsmen differs from the previous generation of machinists with whom they work.

Becoming a machinist at different periods in the technological transformation of machining activity illustrates the heterochronous relation of changing persons and a changing activity that is characteristic of encompassing transition. Heterochronicity has also been studied as a key feature in the genesis of after-school computer clubs (Nicolopoulou & Cole 1994) and in the development of a school-based court of law (Wilcox & Beach 1996).

Mediational Transitions

Mediational transitions occur within educational activities that project or simulate involvement in a yet-to-be-fully-experienced activity. Examples of this form of transition are particularly prevalent in vocational and adult education (Beach 1993), but can also be seen in activities as diverse as a school play store (Walkerdine 1988), instruction in writing (Palinscar & Brown 1984), learning the concept of area (Sayeki, Ueno & Nagasaka 1991) and community- and work-based apprenticeships (Lave & Wenger 1991). Mediational transitions exist along a continuum from classroom-based activities that have "as if" or simulated relations to the world beyond the school, to partial or peripheral participation in the activities themselves. No matter where they are on the continuum, however, they always maintain a "third object" or mediating status with regard to where the participants are currently, and where they are going developmentally, roughly equivalent to Vygotsky's concept of a zone of proximal development (Vygotsky 1978). Thus mediating transitions always embody a particular notion of developmental progress for its participating individuals.

An example of mediating transition is provided in an earlier study of mine that examines how adults participating in a private vocational school learn to become bartenders (Beach 1993). The bartending class occupied a middle position between where its students were — highly literate part-time actors, restaurant managers, graduate students — and where they were going: part- or full-time work as a bartender or supervising bartenders. Drink recipes were initially memorized using written materials, but the pressure to achieve speed as well as accuracy in drink mixing meant that students were assisted in shifting away from the use of written materials toward memonic materials more closely associated with the mixing of the drinks themselves. The vocational school activity existed as a bridge between two other systems of activity and embodied a developmental agenda for its students who chose to participate in it.

These four forms of transition — lateral, collateral, encompassing, and mediational, as diverse as they may seem, share a common set of features that justify engaging them as a whole. Each involves the propagation of knowledge and engages identities rather than the application or use of something that has been acquired elsewhere. Each involves one or more notion of progress for the learner and are best understood as a developmental process. Finally, each form of consequential transition consists of changing relations between persons and social activities represented in signs, symbols, texts, and technologies, or more generally, in systems of artifacts. This not only acknowledges the recursive relation between persons and activities, but makes it the explicit object of study.

Studying Consequential Transitions

Studying consequential transitions requires new methodology. By methodology I do not mean the particular nuts-and-bolts methods or tools of analysis, of which we already have many at our disposal. Rather, drawing on Valsiner's broader notion of methodology (Valsiner 1989; Kindermann & Valsiner 1989), I use the term to refer to new ways of constructing data, thinking about designs/methods, and asking appropriate questions that relate the construct of consequential transition to knowledge propagation: the broad set of generalization phenomena we are concerned with. I will take up four key aspects of a methodology for studying consequential transitions, and will illustrate what such a methodology "buys" us with findings from several of our research group's studies.

Developmental Coupling as a Unit of Analysis

The concept of coupling comes from the work of Varela, Thompson, and Rosch in their book, *The Embodied Mind* (1991; also see Maturana 1975; Varela 1981). In it they draw on post-Darwinian evolutionary biology and connectionist theory to describe co-evolution as a changing relationship between a species and its environment, a structural coupling of the two systems over time — not as a property of the species, the environment, or an interaction between separable systems. We think of the concept of developmental coupling in a similar manner.

A developmental coupling encompasses aspects of both changing individuals and changing social activity. The coupling itself is the primary unit of study and concern rather than the individual or the activity, *per se*. The coupling assumes that individuals move across space, time, and changing social activities, rather than being hermetically situated within an unchanging context. If a context does appear unchanging, it is because much collective effort is being put into maintaining it in place. Similarly, if an individual appears constant, effort is usually being put into maintaining that constancy.

The coupling itself transforms or develops. Its directionality and causal relations are not efficient, or antecedent/consequent, but rather are correlational or relational in nature. Finally, developmental coupling necessarily involves artifacts: objects that embody human intention and agency in some form, and that extend beyond a particular individual participating in a particular social organization at a particular time.

The mathematical concept of area is a nice illustrative analogy to the developmental coupling as a unit of analysis. Area has the properties of both length and width and does not exist without both properties. Changing the length or the width will change the area, but changes in both may, or may not, change the area. Length and width can theoretically be studied independent of one another, just as a mathematical point can be studied as the lack of both length and width. However, only the relationship of length to width over time with change tells us anything about area. Similarly, the propagation of knowledge can only be understood as the developmental coupling of changing persons and changing social activities.

Our first illustration of developmental coupling as a unit of analysis will be from the previously mentioned study of arithmetic reasoning during transitions between school and work in rural Nepal (Beach 1995a, 1995b). It involves instances of both lateral and collateral transition. The second will be from a study of machinists making an encompassing transition from mechanical to computerized technology within a large American automobile manufacture (Hungwe & Beach 1995; Hungwe 1999).

The initial purpose of the study was to understand how adolescents' and adults' arithmetic reasoning changed during transitions between school and work in a Nepali village. At the time of the study, two major societal changes in relations between of school and work were underway in rural Nepal. One change involved increasing numbers of high school graduates and dropouts becoming merchants in local shops. As a high school education became less valuable in obtaining work outside of agriculture, shopkeeping became an option for those who did not want to continue with their family in subsistence agriculture. The other change consisted of increasing numbers of shopkeepers attending adult education classes. Adults had previously not attended school because schooling was outlawed in the Kingdom when they had been of school age. The shopkeepers saw the classes as providing them with written forms of literacy and arithmetic that would be of benefit in their shops. These societal-level changes were simulated voluntarily at a local level by apprenticing graduating high school students to local shopkeepers, and by enrolling shopkeepers in adult education classes. Changes in arithmetic reasoning were then tracked over a period of several months as the students participated in shopkeeping, and as the shopkeepers participated in schooling.

The students constructed new forms of arithmetic reasoning in their lateral transition to shopkeeping. They moved away from using written column algorithms and toward decomposition and interation calculation strategies that included monetary and measurement structures and created a previously unseen system of written notation to support these strategies. This transformation in arithmetic reasoning did not have its origins in schooling or shopkeeping activity, but rather in the transition process between two activities. Power and status played a role in this transition, and in the arithmetic reasoning of the students. Prior to the introduction of schooling in the village, arithmetic originating outside of school had the status of *hisaab*, or mathematics. With the introduction of schooling, *hisaab* gradually became those calculations associated with column algorithms and paper and pencil notation, relegating other forms of arithmetic to *andaji*, or estimation. The students were clearly reluctant to move away from some form of written notation, having spent a decade studying *hisaab* in school. At the same time, they clearly saw themselves as becoming someone new, a shopkeeper, and found that using column algorithms was often unwieldy in the context of converting prices across different systems of measurement and totaling customer purchases. Over half of the students participating in the study in fact went on to become shopkeepers.

The transition for shopkeepers attending adult education classes was collateral. Shopkeepers attending the classes were doing so because they wished to expand the nature and complexity of the goods they could sell. They consequently used the adult education classes to supplement their already existing repertoire of arithmetic strategies with written column algorithms. Shopkeepers were not on a linear trajectory to becoming students, but rather were enhancing their economic viability as shopkeepers. A clear illustration of this in the shopkeepers' arithmetic reasoning was their lack of use and rapid forgetting of the arithmetic operations signs upon completing the class. The reason for this was that operations signs are not needed for column algorithms when the practices within the activity make explicit what needs to be done with the numbers.

Lateral and collateral transitions, and the particular couplings that developed between the individuals and the activities appeared quite different, at least within the domain of mathematical reasoning. They differed despite the fact that both were transitions between school and work, and both shopkeepers and students became able to deploy a variety of written and non-written strategies and artifacts. Therefore, neither the nature of the particular activities nor the participants' different backgrounds offer adequate explanations of these consequential transitions. Nor can an interaction between persons and activities, because, it would require the two to be analytically separable though they always co-occur in life, thereby, creating a "black box" right where the recursive relation between persons and society is played out.

Though developmental coupling is a viable concept for understanding changing local relations between persons and activities, it remains a partial explanation of consequential transition. A more macro level of explanation exists in conjunction with the local, and involves two additional methodological concepts: leading activity and heterochronicity. These will be described later after first illustrating developmental coupling during an encompassing transition.

The second illustration comes from a compendium of studies in which we follow machinists during a major encompassing transition from mechanical to computerized machining in American industry. It is a re visitation of work that was begun almost a decade ago with Laura Martin and Sylvia Scribner (Martin & Beach 1992; Martin & Scribner 1992).

Over the past thirty years, American machining has undergone a tremendous change in response to economic pressures from abroad. One of the major changes has been from the making of parts with mechanically-controlled machines to the use of program or computer-controlled machines to cut metal, ceramics, and plastic parts. Machinists with experience on mechanically controlled machines that range from a couple of years to several decades, find themselves in transition because the activity in which they participate is itself transforming. We set out to study the process for transition from mechanical to computer numerical controlled machining among these machinists.

In his dissertation, Kedmon Hungwe (1999), described a developmental coupling consisting of three components: artifact, object, and machinist's role. A change in any one or two of the three components constitutes transformation, the creation of a new relation between machinist and the activity of machining. Rather than define each component, I will describe each as it changes during the encompassing transition from mechanical to computerized machining.

The creation and use of artifacts shifts from primary to secondary artifacts during the course of the transition. Primary artifacts bear a direct material relation to the cutting operation of the machine and to the parts being made. They consist of levers, dials, and gauges as well as the smells, sights, and sounds of tools cutting metal. They are deployed in real-time with the operation of the machine. The shift to secondary artifacts in the form of written program codes means that the system of artifacts used to control the machine no longer directly draws on the structure of the machine and the cutting process for its organization. See Wartofsky (1979) for a detailed exegesis of his concept of primary and secondary as well as tertiary artifacts: social objects that embody human intent. Programing does not operate in machine-time, but rather occurs prior to the operation of the machine, often in an office removed from the shop floor. Traditional machinists learning computerized machining struggled with apparent but not always actual similarities, and differences in the organization of the two systems of artifacts.

What constitutes an "object" shifts from the actual parts produced by the machinist to the computer program which can be used to produce thousands of parts. With minor adjustments a program can direct a machine to produce a new part that is a modification of an old one; avoiding the lengthy set-up required on mechanical machines for each change in a part. Thus, the program controlling the machine is in the long-term often more valuable to the company than the parts. Machinists doing programing are often concerned with the elegance and efficiency of the program as an object in its own right. While this seems quite natural for younger machinists who have learned machining largely on computerized machines, the shift in objects is difficult for highly skilled tool and die makers who may have spent twenty years on mechanical machines prior to learning computerized machining.

The third component, that of the machinist's role, is directly tied to the machinist's identity as a highly skilled craftsman. The expansion of the activity to include computerized machining split the machinist's job into operator and programmer. Machine operation consisted in setting up the machine and monitoring it during its operation. Control of the machining processes rested in the hands of the programmer. Neither operators nor programers had total responsibility for crafting the part and experienced a resulting loss of identity as a craftsman. This was sufficiently profound for some more experienced machinists that they left computerized machining and returned to work with mechanical machines on the shop floor, despite a decrement in status, though not in pay. In contrast, younger machinists who had trained on computer-driven machines saw computerized machining as a way of increasing their status and making themselves more marketable within and beyond the company.

The consequential transition from mechanical to computerized machining was of the encompassing form. Developmental changes in the relation between machinists and machining activity took place within the confines of the activity that was itself changing. Instances of continuity in knowledge and identity were rare, as were pure instances of discontinuity. Most of what we found in the transition were transformations in the relation between artifacts, objects, and role: a developmental coupling that embodied aspects of identity and economics in addition to knowledge.

Leading Activities and Heterochronicity

Consequential transitions cannot adequately be understood only at the level of local developmental couplings between persons and activities. Activities exist in relation not only to individuals, but also to broader institutional, societal, and cultural forces. An activity is

> ... the non-additive, molar unit of life for the material, corporeal subject. In a narrower sense, it is the unit of life that is mediated by mental reflection. The real function of this unit is to orient the subject in the world of objects. In other words, activity is not a reaction or aggregate of reactions, but a system with its own structure, its own internal transformations, and its own development (Leont'ev 1981: 46).

Activities such as machining, bartending, or schooling are developmental entities in their own right. Relations between various types of activity are not neutral or simply additive for individuals participating in them, however. As Leont'ev describes it, human life

> ... is not built up mechanically ... from separate types of activity. Some types of activity are leading ones at a given stage and are of greater significance for the individual's subsequent development, and other types are less important. Some play the main role in development and others a subsidiary one (1981: 95).

For example, playing, followed by schooling, working, and retirement is a sequence of leading activity categories characteristic of most European and North American societies. Each leading activity serves as preparation for the next. In some subsistence agricultural societies the sequence of leading activities may only be play followed by work that is highly integrated with family and community. This should not be interpreted as meaning that a given society defines a developmental sequence of activity categories which in turn fully dictate individual development. Rather, whether or not an activity is "leading" and therefore, dominant in influence compared to other activities the person may be participating in is co-determined by the sequence of activity categories characteristic of a society *and* the period in an individual's history at which he or she participates in the activity (Beach 1995a). Changes in persons, activities and societies are heterochroneous with respect to each other. This means that the general rate of change for individuals is less than that for activities, which in turn is less than that for societies. That being said, the most revealing cases of consequential transition are instances in which activities and societies change within the time span of the individuals participating in them. Heterochrony (see Hutchins 1995, for an elaboration of the concept within distributed technological systems), or the timing of relations between persons, activities, and more macro social processes often determines the nature of the consequential transition and the developmental coupling.

I will return to the Nepal study to illustrate how the concepts of leading activity and heterochronicity are useful for understanding consequential transitions. Two generations of villagers with radically different relations to the transition between school and work lived in the village at the time of our study. The younger generation had spent an extensive period of time in school before apprenticing to shopkeepers, but had not done shopkeeping work prior to this time. The older generation had not had the opportunity to attend schools when they were of school age, and had spent a minimum of four years working as shopkeepers before attending adult education classes. These two generations of villagers differed in their temporal relation to schooling and shopkeeping, and to broader changes in Nepali society. Heterochronicity between the villagers' lives, the activities, and the society figures prominently in our understanding what actually happens during transitions between schooling and shopkeeping.

Students apprenticed to shopkeepers were making a lateral transition from one leading activity to another, following a school-to-work sequence characteristic of generations to come in Nepali society. However, the two activities are defined by motives that bear little relation to one another, at least in rural Nepal. The motives are learning for a credential, with learning up front as the object of the activity, and becoming a shopkeeper, with selling goods for profit up front as the object. These unrelated motives allow schooling and school forms of arithmetic with it to achieve a status disconnected from and above that of arithmetic embedded in village work activities. We have evidence that the difference in status partially explains students' reluctance to drop the more visible portion of arithmetic originating in school while learning to become shopkeepers.

However, shopkeepers enrolled in the adult education class were participating in a collateral transition between a leading activity and a non-leading activity, following a work-to-school sequence characteristic of only a couple of previous generations in Nepali society. The motive for the shopkeepers' participation in the adult education class was to acquire additional knowledge which could benefit them in the running and expansion of their shops. This was reflected in their developing a flexible repertoire of arithmetic artifacts, organizations, and operations through the adult education class, in contrast to the students becoming shopkeepers.

School and work are clearly categories of leading activities in rural Nepali society. However, the period in the development of an individual, or of a generation of individuals, at which they participate in an activity has as much to do with whether it is leading or not as the societal sequence of activities. It is in this way that activities mediate between large-scale societal change and the local coupling of individuals with activities. A similar heterochronic relation can be found in the machining study.

Individuals who participated in mechanical machining prior to the introduction of computerized machining to the activity exhibited a different developmental coupling in learning of computer-controlled machines than did those who became machinists after computerized machining had become widespread in American industry.

A Horizontal Notion of Development

If we are to take seriously the notion that consequential transitions are developmental phenomena, then we must address what constitutes *telos* or progress in consequential transition. Most grand notions of human development characterize progress as movement through some form of vertical hierarchy, toward greater levels of abstraction, and away from the tangibilities of our world. While genetic epistemology displays this most clearly, Vygotsky's cultural-historical theory is not an exception to this: a point that has also been made by Engeström (1996) and by Van Oers (1998). Notions of progress are important to study and critique. They often serve as a focus for practical action, and thus, should be taken seriously by any developmental theory. This is rather different, however, from a theory promoting a particular notion of progress. Theories possessing a singular notion of developmental progress run the risk of having its notion wander away from being an analytic tool to become a prescription for action, a yardstick for progress, or a call for reform. This is particularly true in the education arena. If we accept the premise that a society expresses its agendas for individual progress through its institutions and their activities, embedding that notion of progress in a theory of learning and development will, at best, reduce the analytic tension between the theory and the phenomenon, and thus any analytic power. At worst, it will create a measuring stick for developmental progress derived from those who hold dominant and controlling interests in that society, and will silence, coerce, and stigmatize other. Thus the concept of consequential transitions needs to include notions of developmental progress without an *a priori* privileging of one notion over the other.

Contrasting views of what constitutes developmental progress during consequential transition clearly emerge in our study of high school students becoming part-time assistants in a fast food restaurant (Beach & Vyas 1998). It is a collateral transition between two long-associated activities: the high school and the fast food restaurant. The fast food restaurant industry is a major employer of high school-age youth in the United States. Paradoxically, becoming a fast food restaurant team member also runs against extant notions of what counts as individual progress in American society. Because fast food restaurants are the largest single employer of high school students in the United States, they provide many students with their first work experience outside the home. Thus, many students who participate in school activity with learning as it defining object first encounter the need to learn in a work activity at the fast food restaurant, where production rather than learning is the object of the activity.

The United States has seen a notable increase in attention paid to issues of school-to-work transition in recent years. A report published in 1988 by the W. T. Grant Foundation titled, "The Forgotten Half: Non-College Youth in America" pointed out that slightly over 50% of America's youth do not attend four year colleges (W. T. Grant

1988). By indicating that a majority of American youth do not fit our society's dominant model of intellectual and economic progress, the report initiated a series of heavily funded school-to-work programs designed to facilitate, sanction, and formalize an alternative pathway to personal and economic success: one that does not involve obtaining a four year college degree.

Fast food work is considered in the school-to-work movement only as an example of what school-to-work should not be: preparation for low knowledge, low skill, low wage employment. A highly influential report issued by the U.S. Department of Labor in 1991 (U.S. Department of Labor 1991) titled "What Work Requires of Schools" describes the economic future of American society as being in "high skill, high tech, high wage, knowledge-intensive" jobs (p. 22). This rhetoric has been widely adopted by American industry and education policy makers. Note that this has embedded in it a metaphorical marking of individual progress as proceeding upward through a hierarchy of knowledge and skill. The final section of the report is devoted to outlining a series of generic work-related skills and abilities that all students should acquire in school; independent of whether they will attend college, and independent of the particular job they may eventually acquire. This conceptualization of skills and abilities is based upon assumptions of individual epistemological progress toward greater levels of abstraction and decontextualization.

The notion of human progress dominant in American society and, as we have noted, in major developmental theories, is upward through a hierarchy of knowledge and skills, and away from the specifics of human activities. We question the fruitfulness of such a singular notion of developmental progress. The collateral transition that students in our study make is between schooling, heavily invested in the dominant notion of progress, and participation in fast food restaurants, which runs counter to that notion. This provides the opportunity to examine how we might characterize couplings between individuals and activities, and relations between activities and society, as developmental though they may run counter to a dominant notion of progress.

The corporate-designed training for fast food assistants consists of videotapes that are specific to each restaurant work station and a written mastery test to be completed at the end of each video. Successful completion of a test for a particular work station should be followed by training at the actual station with a more experienced member of staff. The corporation's view of knowledge and skill is consistent with the place occupied by fast food work within the intellectual hierarchy of American jobs. In other words, it is near the bottom. Each of the training videos breaks a station-job down into a series of behavioral elements and repeats the sequence three times for the viewer. This view of knowledge separates it developmentally from that which is acquired in school because it does not advance students' understanding of a particular subject matter such as math, science or language arts. Thus, the corporate view of knowledge is both consistent with the societal hierarchy of jobs, and places a developmental boundary between it and schooling. However, we are not suggesting that becoming a staff member has nothing to do with one's participation in school. In fact, the structure of learning activity in school has everything to do with what needs to be learned in a production activity such as fast food work.

The official training curriculum has little to do with what actually takes place in becoming a fast food staff member. Because of high turnover rates among employees, most new employees were hired to immediately fill vacant positions in the store and never saw a training video. While some had a period of introduction to the work that was marked as training, most started out by operating a particular station where they were needed to maintain the collective production of the assistants. The activity is highly time-driven and places pressure on the member of staff to perform his or her job rapidly and accurately. Speed becomes more important than accuracy at times when the shortage of one particular product holds up the production of other members of the staff. This places the students in the position of needing to learn how to learn while maintaining production, something that runs counter to their participation in schooling. The students developed new means for learning while maintaining production, and were assisted in this by the more experienced members of staff who may or may not have been designated as the students' trainers. Learning to learn in a production activity was not easily and smoothly achieved by the high school students. Rather, the students struggled with creating opportunities to learn in the midst of production.

There are multiple reasons for viewing the collateral transition of youth between school and fast food work as having nothing to do with development or progress. Certainly this is true in the vertical sense of development. Nothing new was learned about school subjects, nor were there many opportunities to use knowledge of math, science, or written literacy on the job. The corporate view is consistent with this. Knowing how many pickles and how much mustard to place on a burger is local declarative knowledge that must reside at the bottom of any hierarchy of developmental progress. Furthermore, knowledge gained at the restaurant are not seen as sufficiently abstract and conceptual to generalize to other more societally valued activities.

We propose an alternative conception of developmental progress that is horizontal. First ventured by Engeström (1996), horizontal development as we define it is closely tied to the concepts of consequential transition, developmental coupling, leading activity, and heterochronicity. It consists of transformation or the creation of a new relation between individuals and social activities; not continuities or discontinuities, though these may be experienced by the participants at some points in the transition. Thus, horizontal development is never removed or distanced from social activities. The appearance of distancing, decontextualization, or vertical development is a special case of horizontal development — one that generally involves new layers of symbolic mediation that give the appearance of generality because their referents are assumed to be unchanging while new layers of mediation are added. As we can see from our studies of machinists, however, referents shift along with the addition of new layers of symbolization. A program rather than a part becomes the referent for the machinist-programmer's actions.

Though vertical-appearing versions of horizontal development are generally tied to dominant societal notions of human progress, this does not mean that such notions should simply be deconstructed and ignored. What, then, does it mean to "find" development in, how high school students learn to learn in becoming fast food assistants? First, it means that if our society's dominant notion of progress were embedded in our theoretical framework it would have precluded the possibility of seeing collateral transitions as a form of horizontal development. Second, the fact that horizontal development does occur is consistent with a very local notion of progress bounded within fast food staff activity, but is related to other notions of developmental progress and activities, even if in opposition to them. Finally, it would be disingenuous to suggest that by showing that students are struggling to figure out how to learn in a production activity, and that there is a developmental coupling, we are suggesting that there is more of value to becoming fast food staff than society acknowledges, or that it is satisfying work that prepares students for future work, or that it allows workers to survive economically. It does, however, allow us to pose new questions about how horizontal development can take on the appearance of vertical progress during consequential transitions. It also allows us to move our beliefs about human progress out from behind psychological theorizing into the realm of education and society where they can be studied, critiqued, and when deemed appropriate, altered.

Some Challenges for the Future

Understanding knowledge propagation, the broad form of generalization that we are concerned with — and its facilitation in practice, presents us with a number of productive challenges when conceptualized as consequential transition. One challenge is explaining how continuity is produced across social time and context. Continuity is often taken to be indicative of strength, endurance, stability, and consistency of character in the individual. Change is conversely seen as difficult, stressful, and challenging. This difference has not been lost on an educational psychology that proposes multiple processes and complex explanations for epistemological change, but uses a simplifying assumption that individuals carry and apply knowledge when it comes to continuities across contexts and tasks. That individuals and organizations often put much effort and strategy into maintaining a stable sense of identity, a scientific concept, or a ritual across time and context argues against such a simplifying assumption. Consequential transition requires adequate descriptions and explanations of the interrelated processes that produce constancy as well as change when knowledge is propagated across contexts.

Another challenge is understanding how identity-making, or identity craftwork as Lave (1996) describes it is ontogenetically linked with the propagation of knowledge during consequential transitions. Not all changes in knowledge have direct and apparent consequences for one's sense of self and social position. Learning that two plus two equals four after having learned that one and one are two is not likely to have a direct consequence for one's identity. However, this is not simply a function of that knowledge, but also of the social circumstances of which it is a part. One can conceive of situations such as the one in which the "dumb" student in a class is the first to publicly get an otherwise trivial math problem correct at the blackboard. This may at least perturb the student's sense of self as well as his or her social position within the class. Consequential transition also makes us consider that identity craftwork drives knowledge propagation as much as it is shaped and perturbed by it. Gover's (2001) recent analysis of consequential transitions in the autobiographies of three public intellectuals (social essayist Richard Rodriguez, journalist and educator Mike Rose, and former president of Harvard University, Jill Kerr-Conway) suggests that disruptions of sense of self and social position lead to the seeking out or creation of activities through which new forms of knowledge that connect the past with the future are possible.

Understanding knowledge propagation as the construction of complex associations, dialectical associations that include contradictions and distinctions as well as similarities is yet another challenge. We have just begun to examine the formation of such associations between electrical codes, certification examinations, and work practices in an electrical apprentice classroom (Beach 2001). National and state movements toward standardized code created the need for a trade class, a mediational transition, devoted to interpreting electrical codes both for use in local work practices and for the purpose of passing the state master electrician examination.

Thus far, our research program has focused on consequential transitions that are chronologically contiguous for the individuals. Yet knowledge propagation also occurs among events that are chronologically distal from the perspective of the individual. Learning how to add and subtract during your first several years of school and balancing your checkbook for the first time as a young adult are non-contiguous events in your life. Note, however, that the development and distribution of balance books for checking accounts by banks is predicated on heavy citizen participation in school. Though the activities of learning arithmetic in school and later balancing the checkbook are distance in linear chronological time for the individual, schooling and banks' continued issuance of balance books are historically contiguous. Analysis of historical contiguities among activities are necessary if we are to understand the full scope of knowledge propagation as consequential transition.

Education, whether it be in the school, the family, the community, or the workplace prepares people to adapt to existing society, thereby maintaining a degree of continuity in our collective knowledge, values, and beliefs across generations. It also must prepare individuals to participate in the transformation of society. It is this second concern to which consequential transition is directed, though it necessarily presupposes the existence and legitimacy of the first. It is a concern that echoes from the writings of both Dewey & Vygotsky (Dewey 1985; Prawat 1999; Vygotsky 1987). Consequential transition is the conscious reflective struggle to propagate knowledge linked with identity in ways that are consequential to the individual becoming someone or something new, and in ways that contribute to sociogenesis; the creation and metamorphosis of social activity and ultimately, society. Producing culture in addition to reproducing it. Education and economic policy aimed at achieving smooth and "seamless" transitions from one institutions to another, such as home to school or from school to work, emphasizes knowledge continuity and reproduction over transformation. Viewing these as consequential transitions forces us to think about how to take advantage of their productive developmental nature, rather than trying to smooth the process by making the school more like work, or the home more like school. At the same time, consequential transitions should not be so challenging and disruptive that groups of individuals opt out of making the transition altogether and become disadvantaged. This is perhaps the ultimate challenge laying ahead for our work.

References

Anderson, J. R., Reder, L. M., & Simon, H. A. (1996). Situated learning and education. *Educational Researcher, 25* (4), 5–11.

Anderson, J. R., Reder, L. M., & Simon, H. A. (1997). Rejoinder: situative versus cognitive perspectives: form versus substance. *Educational Researcher, 26* (1), 18–21.

Beach, K. D. (1993). Becoming a bartender: The role of external memory cues in a work-directed educational activity. *Journal of Applied Cognitive Psychology, 7* 191–204.

Beach, K. D. (1995a). Sociocultural change, activity and individual development: some methodological aspects. *Mind, Culture, and Activity, 2* (4), 277–284.

Beach, K. D. (1995b). Activity as a mediator of sociocultural change and individual development: the case of school-work transition in Nepal. *Mind, Culture, and Activity, 2* (4), 285–302.

Beach, K. D. (1999). Consequential transitions: a sociocultural expedition beyond transfer in education. *Review of Research in Education, 24,* 101–139.

Beach, K. D. (2001). *Generalization between the certification and work activities in an apprenticeship class: An illustration of a mediational consequential transition.* Invited presentation. Department of Psychology, Aarhus University, Denmark.

Beach, K. D., & Vyas, S. (1998). *Light pickles and heavy mustard: Horizontal development among students negotiating how to learn in a production activity.* Paper presented at the Third International Conference on Cultural Psychology and Activity Theory, Aarus, Denmark.

Bowers, J. (1996). *Conducting developmental research in a technology-enhanced classroom.* Unpublished Ph.D. dissertation, Vanderbilt University.

Bransford, J. D., & Schwartz, D. L. (1999). Rethinking transfer: A simple proposal with multiple implications. *Review of Research in Education, 24,* 62–92.

Brim, O. G., & Kagan, J. (1980). *Constancy and change in human development.* Cambridge: Harvard University Press.

Cobb, P., & Bowers, J. (2000). Cognitive and situated learning perspectives in theory and practice. *Educational Researcher, 2,* 4–15.

Cole, M. (1996). *Cultural psychology: A once and future discipline.* Cambridge: Harvard University Press.

Cox, B. D. (1997). The rediscovery of the active learner in adaptive contexts: A developmental-historical analysis of transfer of training. *Educational Psychologist, 32* (1), 41–55.

Davydov, V. V. (1990). *Types of generalization in instruction: Logical and psychological problems in the structuring of school curricula.* Soviet studies in mathematics education (Vol. 2). Reston, VA: National Council of Teachers of Mathematics.

Detterman, D. K. (1993). The case for the prosecution: Transfer as an epiphenomenon. In: D. K. Detterman, & R. J. Sternberg (Eds), *Transfer on trial: Intelligence, cognition, and instruction* (pp. 1–24). Norwood, NJ: Ablex.

Detterman, D. K., & Sternberg, R. J. (Eds) (1993). *Transfer on trial: Intelligence, cognition, and instruction* (pp. 1–24). Norwood, NJ: Ablex.

Dewey, J. (1916). *Democracy and education: An introduction to the philosophy of education.* NY: Macmillian.

Dewey, J. (1985). *Essays on education and politics* (Vol. 8). Carbondale, IL: Southern University Press.

Engeström, Y. (1996). Development as breaking away and opening up: A challenge to Vygotsky and Piaget. *Swiss Journal of Psychology, 55,* 126–132.

Engeström, Y., Engeström, R., & Kärkkäinen, M. (1995). Polycontextuality and boundary crossing in expert cognition: Learning and problem solving in complex work activities. *Learning and Instruction, 5,* 319–336.

Evans, J. (1999). Building bridges: reflections on the problem of transfer of learning in mathematics. To appear in *Educational studies in mathematics*.

Falmagne, R. J. (1995). The abstract and the concrete. In: L. Martin, K. Nelson, & E. Tobach (Eds), *Sociocultural psychology: Theory and practice of doing and knowing* (pp. 205–228). New York: Cambridge University Press.

Gover, M. (2001). *Identity is a verb*. Unpublished Ph.D. dissertation.

Greeno, J. G. (1997). Response: On claims that answer the wrong questions. *Educational Researcher, 26* (1), 5–17.

Gruber, H., Law, L., Mandl, H., & Renkl, A. (1996). Situated learning and transfer. In: P. Reimann, & H. Spada (Eds). *Learning in humans and machines: Towards an interdisciplinary learning science* (pp. 168–188). Oxford: Pergamon.

Guberman, S. R., & Greenfield, P. M. (1991). Learning and transfer in everyday cognition. *Cognitive Development, 6*, 233–260.

Gutierrez, K., Rymes, B., & Larson, K. (1995). Script, counterscript, and underlife in the classroom: James Brown versus Brown v. Board of Education. *Harvard Educational Review, 65*, 445–471.

Hungwe, K. (1999). *Becoming a machinist in a changing industry*. Unpublished Ph.D. Dissertation, Michigan State University.

Hungwe, K., & Beach, K. (1995). *Learning to become a machinist in a technologically changing industry*. Poster presented as part of an interactive poster session titled, "Learning and Development Through Work" at the Annual Meeting of the Educational Research Association, San Francisco, CA.

Hutchins, E. (1995). *Cognition in the wild*. Cambridge, MA: MIT Press.

Kindermann, T., & Valsiner, J. (1989). Research strategies in culture-inclusive developmental psychology. In: J. Valsiner (Ed.), *Child development in cultural context* (pp. 13–50). Lewiston, NY: Hogrefe and Huber Publishers.

Kirshner, D., & Whitson, J. A. (Eds) (1997). *Situated cognition: Social, semiotic, and psychological perspectives*. Mahwah, NJ: Erlbaum.

Laboratory for Comparative Human Cognition (1986). Culture and cognitive development. In: W. Kessen (Ed.). *Manual of child psychology: History, theory and methods* (pp. 295–356). New York: Wiley.

Lareau, A. (1989). *Home advantage*. NY: The Falmer Press.

Lave, J. (1988). *Cognition in practice*. NY: Cambridge.

Lave, J. (1996). Teaching, as learning, in practice. *Mind, Culture, and Activity, 3* (3), 149- 164.

Lave, J., & Wenger, E. (1991). *Situated learning: Legitimate peripheral participation*. NY: Cambridge University Press.

Lemke, J. (1997). Cognition, context, and learning: a social semiotic perspective. In: D. Kirshner, & J. A. Whitson (Eds), *Situated cognition: Social, semiotic, and psychological perspectives* (pp. 37–56). Mahwah, NJ: Erlbaum.

Leont'ev, A. N. (1981). The problem of activity in psychology. In: J. V. Wertsch (Ed.), *The concept of activity in Soviet psychology* (pp. 37–71). Armonk, NY: Sharpe.

Lobato, J. E. (1996). *Transfer reconcieved: How sameness is produced in mathematical activity*. Unpublished Ph.D. dissertation, University of California, Berkeley.

Martin, L. W., & Beach, K. D. (1992). *Technical and symbolic knowledge in CNC machining: A study of technical workers of different backgrounds*. Technical report. National Center for Research on Vocational Education, University of California, Berkeley.

Martin, L. W., & Scribner, S. (1992). Laboratory for cognitive studies of work: a case study of the intellectual implications of a new technology. *Teachers College Record, 92* (4), 582–602.

Maturana, H. (1975). The organization of the living: a theory of the living organization. *International Journal of Man-Machine Studies*, *7*, 313–332.

Mayer, R. E., & Whittrock, M. C. (1996). Problem-solving transfer. In: D. C. Berliner, & R. C. Calfee (Eds), *Handbook of Educational Psychology* (pp. 47–62). NY: Simon & Schuster Macmillian.

Moll, L. C. (1992). Funds of knowledge for teaching: using a qualitative approach to connect homes and schools. *Theory into Practice*, *31* (1), 132–141.

Nicolopoulou, A., & Cole, M. (1994). Generation and transmission of shared knowledge in the culture of collaborative learning: the fifth dimension, its play-world, and its institutional contexts. In: E. A. Forman, N. Minick, & C. A. Stone (Eds), *Contexts for Learning* (pp. 283–314). NY: Oxford.

Noss, R., & Hoyles, C. (1996). The visibility of meanings: modeling the mathematics of banking. *International Journal for Computers in Maths Learning*, *1* (1), 3–30.

Packer, M. (in press). *The problem of transfer, and the sociocultural critique of schooling.*

Palinscar, A. M., & Brown, A. L. (1984). Reciprocal teaching of comprehension-fostering and comprehension-monitoring activities. *Cognition and Instruction*, *1* (2), 117–175.

Pea, R. D. (1987). Socializing the knowledge transfer problem. *International Journal of Educational Research*, *11*, 639–664.

Plato. (1961). *Meno*. Cambridge, U.K.: Cambridge University Press.

Prawat, R. S. (1999). Social constructivism and the process-content distinction as viewed by Vygotsky and the pragmatists. *Mind, Culture, and Activity*, *6* (4), 255–273.

Pressley, M. (1995). A transactional strategies instruction Christmas carol. In: A. McKeough, J. Lupart, & A. Marini (Eds). *Teaching for transfer: fostering generalization in learning* (pp. 177–214). Mahwah, NJ: Erlbaum.

Reineke, J. W. (1995). *To home and back: The influence of students' conversations on their completion of school mathematics tasks*. Unpublished Ph.D. Dissertation, Michigan State University.

Rogoff, B., & Gardner, W. (1984). Adult guidance of cognitive development. In: B. Rogoff, & J. Lave (Eds), *Everyday cognition: Its development in social context* (pp. 95–116). Cambridge, MA: Harvard University Press.

Sayeki, Y., Ueno, N., & Nagasaka, T. (1991). Mediation as a generative mode for obtaining an area. *Learning and Instruction*, *1*, 229–242.

Saxe, G. B. (1989). Transfer of learning across cultural practices. *Cognition and Instruction*, *6* (4), 325–330.

Saxe, G. B. (1991). *Culture and cognitive development: Studies in mathematical understanding*. Hillsdale, NJ: LEA.

Star, S. L. (1989). *Regions of the mind: Brain research and the quest for scientific certainty*. Stanford, CA: Stanford University Press.

Star, S. L. (1996). Working together: Symbolic interactionism, activity theory, and information systems. In: Y. Engeström, & D. Middleton (Eds), *Cognition and communication at work* (pp. 296–318). New York: Cambridge University Press.

Thurman, R. A. F. (1984). *The central philosophy of Tibet*. Princeton, NJ: Princeton University Press.

U.S. Department of Labor (1991). *What work reguires of schools: A SCANS report for America 2000*. U.S. Department of Labor: The Secretary's Commission on Achieving Necessary Skills.

Valsiner, J. (1989). *Human development and culture*. Lexington, MA: Heath.

Van Oers, B. (1998). The fallacy of decontextualization. *Mind, Culture, and Activity*, *5* (2), 135–142.

Varela, F. J. (1981). Autonomy and autopoiesis. In: R. Gerhard, & H. Schwegler (Eds), *Self-organizing systems: An interdisciplinary approach* (pp. 14–23). New York: Verlag.

Varela, F. J., Thompson, E., & Rosch, E. (1991). *The embodied mind: Cognitive science and human experience.* Cambridge, MA: MIT Press.

Vygotsky, L. S. (1978). *Mind in society: The development of higher psychological processes.* Cambridge, MA: Harvard University Press.

Vygotsky, L. S. (1987). *The collected works of L. S. Vygotsky* (Vol. 1): *Problems of general psychology* (N. Minick, ed. and trans.). NY: Plenum.

Walkerdine, V. (1988). *The mastery of reason.* London: Routledge.

Wartofsky, M. W. (1979). *Models.* Boston: D. Reidel Publishing.

Wenger, E. (1998). *Communities of practice: Learning, meaning, and identity.* NY: Cambridge University Press.

Whitson, J. A. (1997). Cognition as a semiosic process: From situated mediation to critical reflective transcendence. In: D. Kirshner, & J. A. Whitson (Eds). *Situated cognition: Social, semiotic, and psychological perspectives* (pp. 97–150). Mahwah, NJ: Erlbaum.

Wilcox, C., & Beach, K. D. (1996). *Order in the court: The development of a play activity and its elementary school participants.* Paper presented at the Biannual Meeting of the International Society for the Study of Behavioral Development, Quebec City, Canada.

W. T. Grant Foundation (1988). *The forgotten half: Non-college youth in America.* Commission on Work, Family, and Citizenship.

Chapter 4

Transfer and Transition in Vocational Education: Some Theoretical Considerations

David Guile and Michael Young

Introduction

In this chapter we wish to explore some aspects of the issue of the transfer of knowledge and skill in vocational education and training. Transfer has been a problem intrinsic to general and vocational education in advanced industrial countries since the beginning of mass schooling and the growth of college-based programmes of vocational education. With the demise of old industries and the expansion of learning demands by new industries, most European governments are trying to find ways of tackling the problem and more generally of improving the quality of vocational education. In the reformed vocational courses, students are expected not only to acquire more broad-based skills and knowledge not previously associated with vocational education but to be able to apply what they learn in workplaces (Lasonen & Young 1998).

Two types of reform of vocational education can be distinguished, at least analytically. We can refer to them as *external* and *internal* (Young in Stenstrom & Lasonen 2000). External reforms refer to attempts to tackle the low status of vocational programmes and their tendency to only recruit lower achieving students who have been rejected for general or academic courses. External reforms involve changes in the relations between the VET system and the system of general education and are concerned with such issues as qualifications and funding (Green & Lucas 1999; Green, Wolf & Leney 1999). These *external* reforms are important in changing the wider context in which VET takes place; however, they do not concern us directly here. *Internal* reforms, on the other hand, involve attempts to change the pedagogy and curriculum of VET programmes; they aim to improve both the relevance of the knowledge and skills that students acquire on VET programmes and the effectiveness with which both are transferred to workplaces.

Examples of such *internal* reforms are:

- increasing the knowledge content of VET programmes;

- developing innovative modes of assessment that provide evidence that students can apply the knowledge they have acquired in the workplace;
- enhancing the opportunities for students to acquire *generic* skills and knowledge that are not tied to particular jobs or bodies of knowledge.

All these reforms aim to increase the likelihood that students on VET programmes will have the relevant knowledge and skills and be able to apply them in the workplace. However, despite their advantages, they take for granted the actual process of transfer of knowledge and skill from school to workplace. It is assumed that students learn how to transfer knowledge and learning from education to work and that their employability is improved. Furthermore, transfer is seen as a largely one-way mechanical process in which students acquire knowledge in vocational school and relatively unproblematically 'apply' it in the workplace.

Two fundamental issues are avoided by these assumptions. The first is that though the transfer of learning between schools and workplaces does take place, it is anything but a simple mechanical process. Following Beach (1999), Engeström (forthcoming) and Van Oers (1998, 1999), we shall argue that it is useful to see transfer in three ways. Transfer can be seen as: (a) a process of *consequential transition* which involves changes in both the identity of the individuals involved, and the contexts between which they are moving; (b) a form of *expanded learning* between different activity systems; and (c) the *recontextualisation* of activities between different contexts. The second issue is that VET curriculum reforms, at least in the U.K., concentrate on changing the knowledge and skill content of programmes, without considering the assumptions about knowledge that are involved. VET programmes, like the school curriculum generally, treat knowledge as a body of content to be acquired, and as we shall argue later in this chapter, as more like information. This idea of knowledge as a 'body of content' is closely linked to a view of learning as a process of transmission between programme and learner which either does, or as is the case of many VET programmes, does not take place. With such a *delivery* model, the continuing low performance of VET programmes[1] can only be explained in terms of the individual attributes of the student/ trainees such as poor motivation or lack of basic skills. On the other hand, educational researchers working in the *socio-cultural* tradition (Guile & Young 1998; Young 2000) have explicitly recognised the limitations of these assumptions about knowledge and learning. They have emphasised that the acquisition of knowledge and skills is fundamentally a social process involving participation by learners in new contexts and that knowledge cannot be seen as simply a body of content to be transmitted. Socio-cultural theory stresses that the knowledge to be acquired is not just what is codified in textbooks; it is also embedded in specific contexts. Researchers in the socio-cultural tradition also point out that like learning, knowledge is a property of groups and organisations as much as something possessed by individuals (Cook & Seely Brown 1999).

---

[1] Less than 30% achieve a qualification in the high profile VET programme for 16 year olds in the U.K. known as Modern Apprenticeship

Socio-cultural approaches to learning are understandably determined to free themselves from school-centric models and the idea that learning is always in some way a product of teaching (Lave 1993). However, Lave's preference for examples from non-industrial societies means that school-centric models are replaced by the idea of a learning curriculum in which the most important knowledge can somehow be picked up through experience of specific contexts. This idea of a learning curriculum plays down the significance both of the relationship between the pedagogic structuring of learning in the workplace and the formal learning that occurs through VET curricula. It also under-emphasises the need in modern economies, for future employees to acquire knowledge that is not experience-based, situated or limited to what is codified in particular workplaces (Young 2000).

In drawing on an activity theory approach to learning (Engeström 1987; Engestrom, forthcoming; Leontiev 1978) and linking it to some of our own work on the organisation of knowledge in curricula (Young 2000), we have two aims. The first is to attempt to reformulate the problem of transfer in vocational education in a way that contributes to the wider theoretical debates about learning (Tuomi-Gröhn & Engeström; Oenstenk, this volume). We argue that this reformulation can generate new insights about the pedagogic implications of supporting students to act as 'boundary-crossers' within and between education and work. Second, we will link our reformulation of transfer to epistemological issues concerning knowledge (Cook & Seely Brown 1999; Seely Brown & Duguid 2000) and the curriculum (Young 1998, 2000) and the development of more grounded reforms of vocational education.

The Idea of 'Authentic' Learning and School-to-Work Transitions

EU and national government policy documents concerned with combating disaffection and low achievement among 14–19 year old students frequently assert that workplaces can give an 'authenticity' to learning that is absent from most school classrooms. It follows that a work-related, and more generally a vocational curriculum is seen to offer an important source of motivation for those students who have become disaffected from mainstream schooling. The assumption of reforms designed to *vocationalise* the curriculum for 14–19 year olds is that both school attainment and school-to-work transitions can be enhanced by providing low achieving students with better access to workplaces (Stern & Wagner 1999) and by implication to work-related learning. Work related learning is seen as providing a 'context' that can make learning meaningful for these students; something that 'normal' classrooms systematically fail to do.

There are two questions about this approach to disaffection and low achievement which we will consider; both suggest that much more fundamental questions about learning need to be asked. First, in so far as the outcomes of general and vocational programmes are comparable, there is no conclusive evidence that slow learners achieve better on the latter. All it is possible to say is that they may drop out of work-related courses less quickly. Second, we have to ask why, if authenticity and 'real-life' contexts are so important as conditions for learning, do a growing number of students succeed in the presumably 'inauthentic' classrooms offering general or academic programmes with little conscious attention to 'real-life' contexts. Two answers to these questions can be suggested at this point. First, the assumption that low achievers, who invariably though not always come from lower social classes, are in some way more motivated by education that is closely linked to their future employability is a legacy of history and product of ideology; not necessarily based on research. In earlier phases of industrialisation, this section of each cohort of 14+ year olds would have left school with minimal formal skills and knowledge and have been comfortably absorbed into the ranks of the unskilled working class. It is a legacy of this history that shapes the assumptions of policy makers who believe that despite the disappearance of employment opportunities for young people, work related programmes can motivate them to learn. Second, the idea that workplaces can be primary opportunities for authentic learning because they provide 'real-life' contexts is based on a misleadingly simplistic understanding both of contexts and their role in supporting learning and the process of transition between school and work. It is the argument of this chapter that only if we clarify the concepts of *transition* and *context* will we have a more realistic basis for improving vocational education and developing the educational potential of workplaces.

The Problem of Knowledge in Vocational Curricula

Before focusing more explicitly on the link between contexts and learning, it is important to say a bit more about the implications of the socio-cultural approaches to learning initiated by the research of Lave & Wenger (1991) and others. First, as a result of this research, learning theory and research can no longer avoid addressing how people actually learn in everyday life. Second, learning has to be seen as an intimate part of people's lives as *social* beings; it can no longer be treated as a disembodied process that 'goes on in individual minds'. Third, Lave and Wenger show how learning is inescapably a process of interaction that includes peers as well as teachers, parents and others with formal educational responsibilities; it is not just a transmission process between the expert (teacher, parent or manager) and the learner. People learn, as Lave and Wenger put it, 'by participating in communities of practice'. This is an important and perceptive insight; however, it is not adequate on its own as a theory of learning on which to base a vocational curriculum. Learning in modern workplaces is a process of participation but it also involves the acquisition of knowledge which may or may not be available in the 'communities of practice' in which people find themselves. In other words learning in workplaces raises issues of knowledge, curriculum and pedagogy which cannot be addressed if learning is seen as only a process of 'participation' (Young 2000).

In the emerging knowledge economy many workplaces require young people who are qualified for specific jobs and can provide evidence of broader capabilities. This means that VET programmes need access to some form of workplace learning, but that this on its own is not enough. Apart from some types of low skill work, there are increasingly few workplaces in which the knowledge that can be acquired from them is an adequate basis for becoming a qualified worker.

Traditional approaches to the transfer of knowledge in vocational education have taken knowledge for granted in one of two ways. Either they assumed that it could be acquired through experience — the *craft apprenticeship* model — or that on-the-job learning could be unproblematically supplemented by off-the-job college-based programmes which concentrated on the transmission of technical knowledge — the *technician apprenticeship* model. Socio-cultural approaches to learning have a much more sophisticated concept of how and what knowledge is acquired in becoming a member of a workplace community. However, they also take knowledge for granted, treating it as unambiguously embedded in workplaces. However, modern workplaces are extremely diverse and even 'promiscuous'[2] in the learning and knowledge demands that they make.

The issue of 'knowledge' has been increasingly recognised in the organisational science literature, usually under the rubric of 'knowledge management'. However, as Cook & Seely Brown (1999) point out, because the priority in such research is *management* — in other words, achieving specific ends, the concept of knowledge easily degenerates into something more like information, which in contrast to knowledge, can be controlled, moved about and distributed at will. Knowledge, they argue is far less amenable to 'management' as it cannot be separated from who knows it and how they use it and therefore, from all the issues of power and identity that are features of any organisation. We suggest that there are parallels between this view of knowledge as 'information' that pervades the knowledge management literature and the view of knowledge 'as something to be transmitted' that underpins the traditional concepts of learning transfer referred to earlier. Cook & Seely Brown (*op. cit.*) make a valuable point in arguing that we need to think not of knowledge but of types of knowledge. They make useful distinctions between both tacit and explicit knowledge and between the knowledge possessed by individuals and that associated with groups and go on to point out that there been a tendency in industrial societies to neglect the tacit in favour of the explicit and the knowledge associated with groups in favour of that possessed by individuals. However, as with many researchers who adopt a broadly sociological or anthropological view of knowledge which stresses the interdependence of knowledge and the knower, their approach has its own limitations. By prioritising the different ways that knowledge can be organised, whether this refers to its embeddedness in particular contexts or its codification as 'bodies of knowledge', they tend to neglect questions of knowledge content (in other words the 'knowledge itself') that may at least in part transcend issues of social organisation. As a result they are led to avoid a number of issues that are crucial to the question of transfer in vocational education.

As Cook & Seely Brown (*op. cit.*) rightly point out it is important to see tacit and explicit knowledge as not necessarily reducible to one another other. Their example to illustrate this is that the *explicit* knowledge one has about bicycles makes little

---

[2] The promiscuity of some workplaces with regard to knowledge refers to the fact that the knowledge that underpins them bears no necessary relationship to the hierarchies in which knowledge is structured in school and college curricula. For example employees in an electronics factory might require a combination of relatively low level craft knowledge about materials and a knowledge of laser physics that would only be familiar to graduates in physics.

difference to whether one has acquired the *tacit* knowledge involved in being able to ride a bicycle. However the extent to which such so-called 'know-how' knowledge is tacit varies and in a sense the bicycle example is misleading. The knowledge involved in any activity is always a mixture of the tacit, the situated and the explicit, in variable proportions. Whereas, it maybe useful to know about gears if one is going to ride a bicycle, it is not necessary. On the other hand, one needs a considerable amount of explicit knowledge about jet planes if one is going to pilot one. This point is directly relevant to the problems facing vocational educators. As the intellectual demands of work increase the balance between explicit and tacit knowledge in vocational programmes has to change. At the same time the new balance creates problems in combining knowledge with different characteristics in the design of curricula.

The second clarification that is needed is to distinguish between tacit knowledge which cannot be made explicit and situated knowledge which is embedded in particular contexts. Unlike tacit knowledge, situated knowledge can be made explicit; it may, as Hutchin's (1993) studies of the process of navigation in aircraft and seacraft illustrate, be distributed throughout a team of workers and therefore be tied to specific contexts and relationships within those contexts. Whereas tacit knowledge is not, as Cook and Seely Brown point out, a hidden form of explicit knowledge waiting to be codified, situated knowledge can be made explicit or codified as in the case of recipes, textbooks and handbooks. This does not of course mean that codification provides a complete account of knowledge as all who have tried to follow instructions for equipment or in a cookery book will know.

The final clarification that we need to introduce that appears neglected by even the most reflective organisational knowledge theorists Cook and Seely Brown (1999); Seely Brown and Duguid (2000), is the distinction between different forms of codification. The form of codification depends on its purpose. The purpose of codification may be the discovery of new knowledge as in the case of research disciplines. In some cases researchers may be forced to recodify knowledge by going beyond existing disciplinary boundaries and constructing new knowledge categories. The purpose of codification may be for instruction (as in the case of handbooks) or education (as in the case of school subjects and textbooks). Educational purposes may be defined narrowly when they take on the features of instruction or broadly defined when they overlap with the priorities of research. Equally, the purpose of codification may be to protect the interests a community of specialists.[3]

To summarise, we suggest the need to make three distinctions between types of knowledge:

- *Tacit and situated knowledge*
  Whereas situated knowledge is that knowledge which is embedded in specific contexts but can be made explicit or codified, tacit knowledge refers to the knowledge associated with activities that cannot be codified.

---

[3] The classic example is Max Weber's description of the bookish knowledge of the Chinese mandarins.

- *Situated and codified knowledge*

  This distinction recognises the difference between knowledge which is embedded in specific contexts and can be acquired by participation in those contexts and knowledge that is codified in bodies of rules that apply in a range of contexts.
- *Corporate, disciplinary and pedagogic knowledge*

  These distinctions between forms of codified relate to the different purposes that it can have. *Corporate knowledge* refers to the knowledge an organisation codifies for its own needs; it is the explicit knowledge that people have to acquire if they are to be accepted as members of an organisation. *Disciplinary knowledge* is the form of codification traditionally associated with research and the production of new knowledge; it is largely located in universities and concerned with providing criteria for scholarship. *Pedagogic knowledge* is knowledge codified for instructional purposes — the paradigm form is the school subject.

These distinctions raise important questions for vocational educators. Historically, most vocational curricula have treated theory (codified knowledge) and practice (situated and tacit knowledge) separately. Responsibility for transmitting 'theory' has fallen on vocational schools or colleges, while workplaces have assumed responsibility for socialising apprentices into occupational cultures and inculcating work-related knowledge and skills. In most VET programmes the question of how students or trainees learn to use the theory in workplaces (in other words the relation between theory and practice) is taken for granted, though some researchers have identified how the work-based component of vocational or professional education can be used as an opportunity to develop tacit and situated knowledge (Eraut 1999). Our distinctions between tacit, situated and codified knowledge suggest that the relationships between types of knowledge and sites of learning is more complex. We can indicate briefly some of the implications of our analysis for students and teachers involved in VET programmes.

First, VET students will need to understand that though tacit knowledge is necessary in performing particular work place tasks, it is unlikely that by itself to be an adequate basis for a more broad based workplace capability. Second, students will need to recognise that they are unlikely to gain access to the full range of knowledge and expertise that resides in specific 'communities of practice', unless they acquire the 'situated' knowledge that allows them to learn from and within those workplace communities. Third, students and their teachers will have to understand that depending on whether the purposes of codification are organisational or disciplinary, the codification of knowledge will support quite different ways of working and learning. This awareness will assist students in completing their formal written assignments as well as in working with experts to mediate the relationship between different forms of codified knowledge that support social, scientific and technological innovation; likewise it will assist teachers who, with employers, have to design assignments and learning programmes. Finally, programmes designed to support students intending to work in knowledge-intensive workplaces will involve re-thinking the relationships between the knowledge acquired in school and that in workplaces. We discuss this issue in the next section.

The Idea of 'Horizontal Development' and Its Relevance for Vocational Education

Historically, vocational education curricula have mirrored dominant psychological ideas about learning and development (Piaget 1980; Vygotsky 1978) and in particular, that learning involves a hierarchical (or vertical) process of apprehending sets of concepts of ever greater abstraction. In this way the learner achieves a broader and more inclusive mastery over the environment and him or herself. Recent work in activity theory (Beach 1999; Engeström 1996; Van Oers 1998, 1999) has, however, introduced the idea that learning involves a horizontal as well as a vertical process. In this section of this chapter we will consider three different ways in which the horizontal/vertical distinction has been developed by drawing on the work of Engeström, Beach and Van Oers and their implications for VET research.

Movement Across Borders

Engestrom (1996) argues that one of the main challenges that people and groups face in modern societies is learning how to cross the social and cultural borders between different activity systems. He describes this 'boundary-crossing' as a form of *horizontal development* and is therefore, very different from the traditional *vertical* notion of mastering a skill or a hierarchical body of knowledge. Drawing on the concepts 'contradiction', 'zone' and 'mediation' that have a long tradition in activity theory (Leontiev 1978; Vygotsky 1978), Engeström identifies three main challenges facing boundary-crossers. First, they have to learn how to overcome the contradictions that manifest themselves in everyday life; for example, the conflict between positive, enjoyable and rewarding experiences and the negative, destructive and explosive events that help to shape the way a person's character and identity develops. Second, they have to be prepared to change the course of their lives by learning to work with other people in ways that will constrain action and shape their intellectual development. It follows for Engeström, who has a different emphasis to Vygotsky, that the 'zone of development' ought to be viewed as a collective process of transformation as well as an individual process. Third, people have to learn how to move from immaturity and incompetence towards maturity and competency. According to Engeström, this involves people in using conversation, cultural artifacts and social situations to mediate their understanding of the world and in conceptualising new relationships, new forms of knowledge and new work practices. From Engeström's perspective, facing these challenges involves people and groups working to create new objects, to new meanings, and new activity systems (Engeström, forthcoming).

New Relationships Between People and Social Activities

Beach also questions the assumption in developmental psychology that learning is primarily a process of *vertical* development. However, he draws on a slightly different range of concepts from activity theory such as 'leading activity' and 'heterochronicity' as well as the idea of 'developmental coupling' from evolutionary biology Maturana (1987).

Beach is interested in demonstrating how people's knowledge, skill and identity change over time as a result of the relationships they develop with social institutions and groups. He uses the concept of 'developmental coupling' to describe the close attachments that people form to the social activities in which they are involved; the concept of 'leading activity' refers to how people become identifed with certain activities which come to exert a dominant influence over them; he uses the concept of 'heterochronicity' to suggest that there is a temporal dimension to the process of development that means it is never fixed and immutable. Beach views development as a series of transitions between different activity contexts; the *horizontal* aspect of development refers to the way people actually encounter, and develop knowledge and skill both in workplaces and in classrooms and the way their identities change over time.

Recontextualising Knowledge

Van Oers also draws on activity theory to help him to formulate his concept of horizontal development, though he also appears to retain a role for the vertical development that is more explicit than in either Beach or Engeström. Van Oers argues that if people are to learn to 'free themselves' from the constraints that specific situations impose upon them, they must be able to envisage a 'theoretically constructed world'. He uses the concept of 'activity development' to illustrate how a 'theoretical world' can be constructed. Initially he argues that the object of any action (i.e. writing an essay) can become a motivating force for a new set of related actions and thus stimulate the invention of new strategies and the use of new 'tools' (i.e. books, computer programmes). Instead of seeing the development of abstract thought a question of the *decontextualisation* of actions and thoughts, Van Oers suggests it can be seen as a process of continuous progressive *recontextualisation*. According to Van Oers, this process of recontextualisation can occur in one of two ways. It can either occur as a *horizontal* form of development (when familiar activities are realised in a new context), or as a *vertical* form of development (when new activities are developed by drawing on insights derived from 'theoretically constructed worlds'(his example is mathematics).

The interpretations of the concept of horizontal development by Engeström, Beach and Van Oers, all throws new light on the questions of transition and the transfer of knowledge between school and work which are at the heart of vocational education programmes, whether they are predominantly school or work-based. Traditionally, school-to-work research has conceptualised transition as though it was merely a matter of 'launching' a student from one context (school) into another (work). The idea of horizontal development warns vocational educators against ignoring or playing down the significance of the contextual features of workplaces, since they are key determinants of both the learning that may occur and the knowledge that may be developed.

Transitions and Contexts

Beach's work (1999, Chapter 3) offer's an approach to understanding the problems that students on vocational courses face as 'boundary-crossers' within and between education and work that is complementary to that of Engeström. Instead of viewing transfer as a process of learning to re-produce pre-existing activities, he argues that greater account needs to be taken of how, in the process of transfer, identities and even the contexts themselves change. Beach argues that this implies reconceptualising transfer as a process of what he refers to as *consequential transition*.

Beach identifies four different types of consequential transition — lateral, collateral, encompassing, and mediational — although he acknowledges that there are certain affinities between the first and second pair. Lateral and collateral transitions involve people moving between sets of activities that are changing slowly compared to the changes that individuals are experiencing as they move between them. In contrast, encompassing and mediational transitions refer to situations when the rate of change of the contexts is relatively rapid when compared to the change that is required by the individuals involved in the transition.

According to Beach, each type of transition involves a form of horizontal development and has quite different implications for learners and organisations. In lateral and collateral transitions, learners have to come to terms with shifting between the particularities of different contexts. In one of his examples, high school students working in a fast food restaurant had to learn how to develop an attachment to the 'rules' of the restaurant and acquire the ability to produce and deliver hamburgers (Beach & Vyas 1998). In encompassing and mediational transitions, the leading activity in which people are expected to engage may cause reversals to occur in the normal conceptions of expertise and instructional roles. For example, in Hungwe & Beach's (1995) account of changes in the machine tool industry as a result of the introduction of CNC systems, employers and workers faced different but related challenges. Workers had to learn how to develop the new skills required by collaborating with one each other and trying out how to use the new technology since even the more experienced workers and managers did not understand the new system.

The concept of consequential transition is relevant to the reconceptualisation of the issue of transfer in vocational education in two senses. First, it can be used to question the idea of 'employability' (Taylor 1998) and the assumption that moving from school-to-work is relatively unproblematic provided the student has the appropriate skills and personal attributes. Such a view leads to prescriptions for 'employability skills' to be built into school/work curricula that take no account of the actual transitions involved nor the influence of contexts in the development of such skills. Second, it can be used to remind vocational educators that transition is not merely a matter of 'launching' a school student to learn in a workplace; workplaces are very different, and learning opportunities are not distributed equally across them. In 'knowledge-poor' workplaces (e.g. Fast Food restaurants), learning goes on and is expected, but it is not a high priority, relative to delivery; there are no separate activities which have learning as their primary goal. Knowledge of a kind has to be acquired in such workplaces but is knowledge essential to doing the job and closely tied to specific contexts; it has no value outside that context. It is of course not codified (or if it is as in the case of the training video in Beach's example, it is in a form that is largely disregarded). In contrast, in 'knowledge-rich' workplaces (such as hospitals) medical students are likely to have opportunities to participate in specialist communities of practice' (such as intensive care wards) and be encouraged to engage in activities that allow them to acquire broader forms of knowledge and skill.

Beach's analysis of transitions highlights the horizontal development involved in learning in workplaces. His study of school students in the Fast Food restaurants illustrates how they acquired certain knowledge and skills in order to survive. His analysis, however, has only limited value for vocational educators. By focusing on the idea that the primary determinants of learning are active engagement in a 'leading activity' (in his example, delivering hamburgers) and forming attachments (i.e. 'developmental coupling') with members of a workplace community, Beach's analysis cannot deal with the contribution that formal education might make in supporting work based learning. Furthermore, although he acknowledges that contexts are an important influence on learning, he tends to limit the role of contexts to helping people to personalise their experiences. As Van Oers shows it is possible that contexts have a more strategic role in learning than Beach allows for.

According to Van Oers, contexts have two functions in learning. First, they support the *particularisation of meanings* by constraining cognitive processes and eliminating some meanings as not relevant — we can refer to this as the *specification function* of contexts. Second contexts bring about coherence with the larger whole (they provide meaning in the sense of 'putting things in context') — we can refer to this as *the connective function* of contexts. Under pressure from governments to provide solutions to the problem of disaffected learners, vocational educators stress the *specification* function of contexts by assuming that for disaffected learners, workplaces are nearer to 'real-life' than classrooms. At the same time they neglect the broader *connective* function of contexts and the possible role of general education in vocational curricula that it implies.

Van Oers argues that traditional cognitive psychology and the newer constructivist approaches have both emphasised the importance of context. However, whereas the former sees context in terms of external cognitive structures, the latter locate it in social situations experienced by learners. At the same time, both retain the idea of the individual IN situations in which the two functions of contexts emerge. As a result it is easy for contexts to be separated from individuals and becoming more like circumstances acting on them from outside. However, how and why some circumstances become determining at different times and others do not remains unclear.

Activity theory offers a more dynamic approach both by seeing context as an activity involving both contextualising and recontextualising processes and by refusing to separate the individual from the context in the first place (Engeström 1996). Van Oers discussion of context opens up a very different perspective on the question of 'authentic learning' to that traditionally associated with vocational educators (Lewis 1998) who often cite Dewey as providing the rationale for introducing real-world problems to promote learning. Furthermore, various concepts such as 'cognitive apprenticeship' (Brown, Collins & Duguid 1989) and 'problem-based learning' (Boud & Felitti 1998) have been employed to encapsulate the idea of using problems that professionals experience in day-to-day practice to enhance the quality of learning in formal educational contexts (i.e. school, college, university).

For activity theory, it is not working on a problem by itself that causes people to become motivated to learn. It is the nature of the activity system in which both the problems and the interpretations of the learner are embedded that makes the difference as to whether people are able to personalise and generalise from their experience of addressing a 'problem'. As Van Oers has suggested (1999), the key determinants of learning are similar and irrespective of whether learners are working in a classroom (Cobb & Bowers 1999) or in a workplace (Brown & Duguid 2000), First, learners need to be supported to participate in an activity system that encourages collaboration, discussion and some form of 'risk taking'. Second, learners need to have opportunities to share and be inspired by a common motive for undertaking a specific learning task. However, while activity theory stresses how activities are needed that enable students to re-locate what they already know as a step to acquiring new knowledge, it has little to say about the form or content of this knowledge.

Knowledge and Context in Vocational Education: Perspectives from Activity Theory

At the beginning of this chapter we introduced two aspects of the issue of transfer in vocational education, the problem of knowledge in the vocational curriculum in the emerging global economy and the issue as to whether workplaces can provide contexts for 'authentic' learning, especially for low achieving students. In this section of the chapter we draw on our earlier discussion and suggest how the approaches to activity theory of Engeström (see Chapter 2) and Van Oers (1999) offer a way of tackling these problems.

Both Engeström (1978), Tuomi-Gröhn & Engeström (this volume) and Van Oers stress the importance of Davydov's work and refer to his idea of a 'germ cell' as an abstract structuring tool which is designed to guide student activities in a variety of situations to enable them to acquire knowledge. Davydov's theoretical model constrains the kinds of activities that are open to students and is another way of formulating what earlier we referred to as *the specification function* of contexts. As Tuomi-Gröhn and Engeström put it, Davydov's model identifies specific processes and learning actions that lie behind the achievement of transfer. The main weakness of his approach from the point of view of vocational education is that it is limited to classroom settings and cannot deal with the problem of learners moving from school to work.

Van Oers and Engeström develop activity theory in very different ways to Davydov. Both shift the balance from developing a theoretical model to encouraging activities and therefore can conceptualise learning across the contexts of school and work. Van Oers describes what he calls a 'post modern' approach which involves a shift from Davidoff's rather rigid epistemology to a more liberal view that emphasises to the need for meanings to be negotiated by peers and teachers and for learners to be able to 'articulate their interpretations of activity and actions'. However, these 'activities' are not bounded by a pre-given theoretical structure as in Davydov's approach but by the shared understandings of a community. In the case of vocational schools this community would need to include employers as well as students and teachers. However, there are dangers in adopting the 'post modern' approach referred to by Van Oers with its emphasis on individual variations of perspective in the negotiation of meaning. As in sociocultural approaches to learning, the wider question of knowledge tends to be subsumed into the knowledge shared by particular communities; it cannot therefore provide a basis for developing a vocational curriculum that can enables learners to move beyond the communities that they find themselves in.

In other words, the problem of knowledge remains for both Davydov and the 'post-modernist' interpreters of activity theory. The former underplays the extent to which his theoretical model is itself socially located. It sees no need, therefore, to allow space for a dialogue between teachers and learners in which its limitations as well as its strengths can be made explicit. In contrast, the 'post modern' approach tends to reduce knowledge to 'communities of knowers'.

Engeström develops activity theory as a result of his critique of Davydov in a rather different way with his concept of 'expanded learning'. Instead of stressing the theoretical model, he focuses upon the activity system itself. As a result, he and his colleagues' research (Tuomi-Gröhn; Lambert, this volume) has focused support individuals and groups in identifying the contradictions within and between activity systems as a way of beginning to question existing forms of practice. Engeström defines this process as *expanded learning*. From the point of view of vocational educators, expanded learning would involve students, teachers and employers agreeing to focus upon the organisational context of the workplace and the school as well as on organisational practices. Each could be seen as engaged in constructing 'partially independent zones of proximal development'.

Expanded learning begins with the learner questioning existing knowledge and, with the help of the teacher or instructor, modelling existing circumstances and future possible activities. Tuomi-Gröhn & Engeström (this volume) state that expanded learning is different from traditional approaches in three ways. First, it requires learners to select the specific problem that is the starting point of learning. Second, it encourages learners to 'model' the perceived contradictions they experience and determine the type of modification or innovation required to overcome them. Third, it provides opportunities for learners to test out, and consolidate, their proposed solutions and, hence, pave the way for implementing them through new forms of practice in different activity systems. They describe this cycle of questioning, modelling, implementing and reviewing any proposed innovation as a form of *developmental transfer*. In other words, expanded learning impacts on the activity system itself as well as on those individuals and groups who work within it.

The concept of expanded learning provides a useful framework for re-thinking the question of transfer in vocational education. First, Engeström stresses that the focus of learning should fall upon the *set of relationships* that constitute the activity system and not only specific elements of that system. It follows that VET research needs to focus on developing new types of *learning relationships* between schools and workplaces and between teachers, instructors and students. Second, it implies that issues about pedagogy and relations between organisations, curriculum and qualifications need to be addressed simultaneously and not treated as separate sets of issues. Third, the emphasis on identifying the contradictions that exist between and within activity systems raises issues for both schools and workplaces. In the case of the former, it suggests that students should be encouraged to identify mismatches between what they are expected to learn in the curriculum and what they find that they need to know as trainees or in employment. In the case of employers, the implications are that they should make explicit any possible mismatches between the knowledge possessed by their employees and the knowledge such employees may need to cope with new production demands.

In applying the idea of 'expanded learning' to the question of transitions in programmes of vocational education, Tuomi-Gröhn and Engeström suggest that schools should become 'change agents' in partnership with companies. By including consolidation and proliferation in his expanded learning cycle, Engeström certainly offers an innovative approach to boundary-crossing between school and work, though it does not address the knowledge question which we outlined earlier. It is not clear how learners are encouraged draw upon the forms of codified knowledge that may be necessary to deal with the contradictions that emerge in a particular workplace but that do not directly emerge out of practice or negotiations with employers. Although the 'expanded learning cycle' identifies the need to model new solutions, Engeström and his colleagues play down the extent to which students are encouraged to draw upon their curriculum knowledge as a resource. Without such encouragement, students on vocational programmes, especially if they have previously been unsuccessful in school, will be unlikely to appreciate the potential of codified subject knowledge in helping them to tackle workplace problems.

In schools and colleges, unlike in most workplaces, the knowledge that students are required to learn is codified in the curriculum as text books and in syllabuses. However, very little research has focused on the 'situated' knowledge that is required if the subject knowledge of the curriculum is to be acquired. Nor has much attention been given to the way that such knowledge may support or inhibit students in transferring learning between subjects or between school and work. Both the school knowledge associated with the official curriculum and the situated knowledge involved in classroom learning and in transferring that learning to workplaces tend to be taken for granted rather than made explicit.

The concepts of contradiction, mediation and zone of development and their role in expanded learning are important if schools and workplaces are to develop a shared understanding about their respective roles in helping students to develop their 'boundary-crossing' skills and in producing new curriculum concepts that connect school and work- based knowledge. However, Engeström's concept of expanded learning seems to rest upon the assumption that schools and workplaces share goals and therefore will collaborate in supporting the transfer of knowledge and skill across contexts. It is this assumption that is problematic in countries like the U.K. in which there is no social partnership tradition. On the other hand, the model might have direct application to the question of transfer between universities and industry where the mutual benefits of partnerships are more widely recognised. In ways that only rarely involves vocational schools,[4] universities frequently have links with companies through research contracts. The challenge for vocational educators is to try and establish links with employers as a basis for collaboration over vocational programmes that link school and workplace knowledge in new ways.

Transfer, Context and Knowledge

We have argued that it is useful to reformulate transfer as a process of 'transition' between activity systems. We have also argued that contexts have a dual function in the learning process and identified the potential of the expanded learning cycle in supporting students as 'boundary-crossers' between school and work. We now return to how this analysis might illuminate the relationship between 'codified' and 'situated' knowledge in vocational curricula. We propose that it is useful to reformulate the question in the following way. First, how can students interrogate the knowledge they acquire in workplaces from the perspective of the knowledge that is codified in the curriculum? And, second, how can students give meaning to the codified knowledge of the curriculum from their experience of the workplace. To tackle these questions we return to Van Oers' concept of 'activity development' and his idea of re-contextualisation (Van Oers 1998).

Van Oers, like Beach and Engeström, starts from the premise that the process by which people acquire concepts cannot be separated from the context in which they find themselves. It follows, he argues, that it is mistaken to believe that thinking abstractly can be understood as a process of decontextualisation. Such a view is premised on the false idea that there can be a kind of thinking that is not 'in context'. Van Oers goes on to suggest that in order to overcome the constraints on thinking that are imposed by specific contexts, people have to have access to new contexts in which they can develop alternative ideas and visions about their current situation. As we noted earlier, he employs the concept of 'activity development' to refers to the processes through which people 'free themselves' from the constraints that specific situations might impose upon them. He argues that the development of abstract thought provides a paradigmatic example of how to accomplish this objective. However, rather than seeing the development of abstract thought as a process in which people decontextualise their actions and thoughts, he views it as a process of continuous progressive *recontextualisation*.

He identifies two principles that underpin his argument that the process of recontextualisation is an iterative and interpretative activity. First, he argues that any activity that humans undertake can be realised in different 'forms of activity patterns'. In other words, although one can write with a pen or a computer, they each evoke different patterns of thought and action. Second, he argues that in any situation, the object of an action (i.e. writing an essay) can motivate someone to engage with more complex activities than they ever originally envisaged and, thus, stimulate innovation

---

[4] The nearest equivalent to vocational schools in the U.K. are Further Education Colleges most of which also offer general education programmes.

and creativity. Thus, Van Oers suggests that learning as a process of recontextualisation occurs when individuals and groups act upon the recognition that any situation provides, at least in principle, an opportunity for alternative courses of action. For Van Oers recontextualisation involves seeing an original activity from a new perspective rather than trying to extract it from its original context.

As we discussed earlier, Van Oers distinguishes between 'horizontal' and 'vertical' forms of recontextualisation. The former occurs when people carry out a known activity in new context. In vocational education an example would be when students on work placement undertake tasks that they have already carried out in a school workshop. Vertical recontextualisation occurs when individuals and groups use the problems that arise while undertaking a task as the basis for developing a new pattern of activity in a new context. An example is when a student nurse recognises that 'taking a patient's temperature' is not just a task on it own; knowledge of a patient's temperature can help a nurse to diagnose the state of his or her health. With appropriate pedagogic support and access to new knowledge, a nurse can develop her or his knowledge of diagnosis out of the activity of measurement.

According to Van Oers 'vertical recontextualisation' can lead people to develop new goals, new actions and new strategies in order to grasp the connection between different activities. This process may take two forms. First, new patterns of activity and new meanings may emerge from the original context which constitute a modification of the original activity rather than an alternative realisation of that activity. Second, it may not be possible to resolve the original problem unless there is contact with ideas that lie outside of the immediate situation. For example, in order for a nurse to see the connection between temperature and diagnosis, he or she would have to be able to conceptualise it in terms of a 'theoretically-constructed-world' that takes account of medical science as well as the state of health of any patient.

Envisaging 'theoretically-constructed-worlds' involves developing concepts that are not just about particular situations. Van Oers argues that the principle of 'activity development' is central to this process. Through activity development people can be motivated to recontextualise their experiences and with the support of an expert or teacher, try out concepts and ideas that have been developed and debated over a period of time in relation to many similar practical problems (Guile & Young 1999). As he notes, this recontextualisation involves learners in two processes. First, they have to come to terms with how the codified knowledge is constructed. Second, they have to acquire the capability to interpret new situations in workplaces in light of the concepts they have developed as well as to deal with counter interpretations. It is through engaging with both of these processes that students on vocational education programmes learn to relate the codified knowledge of the curriculum to their situated knowledge of workplaces.

Activity Theory and Vocational Education: Some Lessons for Future Research and Practice

In this chapter we have argued that in addressing the problems of 'transfer' between school and work that are faced by students, teachers and employers, vocational educators have much to gain from the insights of activity theory. At the same time, a focus on the boundary between school-based and learning requires activity theory to acknowledge its own tendency to neglect curriculum issues and more broadly the question of knowledge.

Vygotsky emphasised the importance of knowledge in the process of human learning and development with his distinction between scientific and everyday concepts. However despite Davidoff's 'germ cells' and the important role given to mediation in Engeström's theory of expansive learning, the question of knowledge and the role of scientific concepts seems to have got lost in recent developments in activity theory with their stress on activities, contexts and horizontal development. This trend is most evident in what Van Oers refers to as 'post modernist' interpretations where activity becomes synonomous with negotiation. However, the 'knowledge question' and the power relations that it embodies are crucial in decisions about the vocational curriculum. Such decisions may be concerned with the balance between general knowledge and vocational skills, what knowledge of production processes that students are given access to by employers or a more fundamental question as what counts as the knowledge needed by a technician or professional employee.

Earlier in this chapter we indicated that vocational educators have been inclined to adopt one of two positions with regard the question of knowledge. They have either treated the general (i.e. the 'codified') and vocational (i.e. the tacit and situated) elements of the vocational curriculum as the separate responsibilities of colleges and employers and leave students to make the connections between them, or they have affirmed the distinctive importance of the 'situated' (or experiential) knowledge that can be picked up in workplaces and underplayed the role of codified knowledge.

Activity theory provides new conceptual tools for addressing aspects of the process of learning in vocational education that have other wise been ignored, such as supporting boundary-crossing, However, there are issues that students on vocational courses face that activity theory has not up to now addressed. First, students have to acquire the knowledge relevant to particular occupations that has been 'codified' and demonstrate their mastery of it; they also have to learn to use it as a resource to help them to transform work practice and work organisation. Second, during their work placements, students need to be helped to identify issues that may lead them to question the design of their curriculum. In order to provide a theoretical framework for tackling these problems, activity theory has to go beyond its current concerns in two ways. First, it has to go beyond the very general notion of 'theoretically constructed worlds' to how such worlds are constructed (the processes of codification and recontextualisation). Second, it has to take its analysis of 'boundary-crossing' a step further. Boundary-crossing is not a generic process, even one incapsulated in terms of Beach's four types of transition. Whereas some boundaries (for example the boundary between home and an unskilled workplace like a Fast Food Restaurant) are between two contexts, both of which have embedded knowledge which can be acquired through experience. Others (for example the school and many technical workplaces) are between contexts in which the forms in which knowledge is embedded and codified are very different and pose quite specific problems for students and designers of vocational curricula.

Conclusions: Reconceptualising the Transition between School and Work in Vocational Education

We began with the problem of transfer in vocational education and how it has become more acute as a result of recent changes in the organisation of work. In particular, we have been concerned with how these changes are making demands for new kinds of skill and knowledge on those leaving school or college and the implications of these changes for the vocational curriculum. We commented critically on the idea of 'authentic' learning, and in particular on policies assuming that providing students with access to workplaces or 'real-world' problems will promote attainment and employability. In contrast, we argued that if students are to be prepared for the demands of working in the global economy, a number of more fundamental issues have to be addressed. First, it will be necessary to explore the implications of reconceptualising transfer in vocational education as transition and separating its 'horizontal' and 'vertical' elements. Second, instead of assuming a simple link between 'real-life' contexts and learning, it is important to recognise that contexts serve a dual function — providing meaning *and* helping give coherence to learning. Third, we stressed the importance of distinguishing between tacit, situated and codified knowledge as a basis for exploring their possible relationships in the vocational curriculum. This led us to argue that if students are to become 'boundary-crossers' between school and work in vocational education programmes, teachers will need to give greater attention supporting students in relating their 'situated' knowledge of workplaces to the codified' knowledge of the curriculum. We suggested that our understanding of this process might be developed by drawing on the concepts of 'activity development' and 'recontextualisation'. We see this chapter as a first step in linking activity theory approaches to learning to a sociological approach to knowledge and how they can be used to providing a basis for a VET 'curriculum of the future'.

References

Beach, K. (1999). Consequential transitions: A sociocultural expedition beyond transfer in education. *Review of Research in Education, 24*, 101–139.

Beach, K. D., & Vyas, S. (1998). *Light pickles and heavy mustard: Horizontal development among students negotiating how to learn in a production activity*. Paper presented at the Third International Conference on Cultural Psychology and Activity Theory, Aarus, Denmark.

Boud, D., & Feletti, G. I. (1998). *The challenge of problem-based learning*. London: Kogan Page.

Brown, J., Collins, S., & Duguid, P. (1989). Situated cognition and culture of learning. *Educational Researcher, 18*, 32–42.

Brown, S. J., & Duguid, P. (2000). *The social life of information*. Harvard, USA: HBP.

Cobb, P., & Bovers, J. (1999). Cognitive and situated learning perspectives in theory and practice. *Educational Researcher, 28* (2), 4–15.

Cook, S. D. N., & Seely Brown, J. (1999). Bridging epistemologies: the generative dance between organizational knowledge and organizational knowing. *Organization Science, 10* (4), 381–400.

Engeström, Y. (1996). Development as breaking away and opening up: a challenge to Vygotsky and Piaget. *Swiss Journal of Psychology, 55*, 126–132.

Engeström, Y. (forthcoming). *Expansive learning at work: Toward an activity-theoretical reconceptualization.* University of California, San Diego/Academy of Finland.

Green, A., & Lucas, N. (Eds) (1999). *FE and lifelong learning: Realigning the sector for the twenty-first century.* London: Institute of Education Bedford Way Papers.

Green, A., Wolf, A., & Leney, T. (1999). *Convergence and divergence in European education and training systems.* London: Institute of Education Bedford Way Papers.

Guile, D., & Young, M. (1998). Apprenticeship as a conceptual basis for a social theory of learning. *Journal of Vocational Education and Training, 50* (2).

Hungwe, K., & Beach, K. (1995). *Learning to become a machinist in a technologically changing industry.* Poster presented as part of an interactive poster session titled Learning and Development through Work at the Annual Meeting of the Educational Research Association, San Francisco, CA.

Hutchins, E. (1995). *Cognition in the wild.* Cambridge MA: MIT Press.

Lasonen, J., & Young, M. (1998). *Strategies for achieving parity of esteem in European upper secondary education.* Finland: University of Jyvaskyla.

Lave, J. (1996). Teaching, as learning, in practice. *Mind, culture and activity, 3* (3), 149–164.

Lave, J., & Wenger, E. (1991). *Situated learning: Legitimate peripheral participation.* New York: Cambridge University Press.

Leontiev, A. N. (1978). *Activity, consciousness, and personality.* Englewood Cliffs, NJ: Prentice-Hall.

Maturana, H. (1975). The organization of the living: a theory of the living organization. *International Journal of Man-Machine Studies, 7* (3), 313–332.

Piaget, J. (1980). *Experiments in contradiction.* Chicago: The University of Chicago Press.

Seely Brown, J., & Duguid, P. (2000). *The social life of information.* Boston, MA: Harvard Business School Press.

Stenstrom, M-L., & Lasonen, J. (2000). *Sharpening post 16 education strategies.* Finland: University of Jyvaskylä.

Stern, D., & Wagner, D. A. (1999). *International perspectives on school-to-work transitions.* Creskill, NJ: Hampton Press.

Taylor, A. (1998). Employability skills: from corporate wish list to government policy. *Journal of Curriculum Studies I, 30* (2), 143–64.

Van Oers, B. (1998). From context to contextualizing. *Learning and instruction, 8* (6), 473–488.

Van Oers, B. (1998). The fallacy of decontextualization. *Mind, culture and activity, 5* (2), 35–142.

Vygotsky, L. S. (1978). *Mind in society: The development of higher psychological processes.* Cambridge, MA: Harvard University Press.

Young, M. F. D. (1998). *The curriculum of the future.* Brighton: Falmer Press.

Young, M. (2000). Brining knowledge back in: Towards a curriculum for lifelong learning. In: A. Hodgson (Ed.), *Policies and practices in lifelong learning.* London: Kogan Page.

Part II

Learning and Transfer in Vocational Education

Chapter 5

Exploration of an Industrial Enterprise as a Method of Boundary-crossing in Vocational Education

Bärbel Fürstenau

Goals, Demands and Problems of Apprenticeships in Vocational Education

One of the central goals of vocational education is to help students attain and develop competency in action so that they can meet current and future professional challenges and participate in defining their vocational lives.[1] For industrial clerks (in German: Industriekaufleute), this means preparing them to work with complex interdepartmental cases and procedures (Sekretariat der Ständigen Konferenz der Kultusminister der Länder in der Bundesrepublik Deutschland 1995). In addition, they should be able to cooperate across departments, jointly solve problems with customers and purchasers and constantly keep track of markets and competitors. These are different forms of boundary-crossing, and they require both vertical and horizontal expertise (Engeström, Engeström & Kärkkäinen 1995), e.g. domain-specific knowledge about products and business processes, the ability to acquire new knowledge independently, as well as to generate, communicate and exchange knowledge as needed in each situation. Currently, schools and firms are meeting this goal with only limited success. Students have difficulties understanding complex interrelationships and applying knowledge in new situations and to new tasks. Transfer occurs neither in the sense of identifying identical elements and general principles nor in the sense of developmental processes (Tuomi-Gröhn & Engeström, this volume).

Educational politicians and educational researchers name the following as some of the causes:

---

[1] This is a description of what we call "Handlungskompetenz" in Germany. In the international context, it may be more appropriate to use the term "skill" if skills include not only visible action or automatized actions but also a structured knowledge basis which enables higher-order and reflective thinking.

Between School and Work: New Perspectives on Transfer and Boundary-crossing
© 2003 Published by Elsevier Science Ltd.
ISBN: 0-08-044296-X

(1) In vocational schools, teacher-oriented instruction from the front of the classroom and instruction-oriented thinking dominate teaching-learning processes. This kind of instruction can be rather efficient for memorization of single knowledge facts. For self-regulated and active learning and knowledge application however this process is comparatively inefficient (Frey & Frey-Eiling 1993; Reetz 1984; for the international discussion Schank & Cleary 1995).

(2) Goals and contents to be taught, as outlined in the curricula and in textbooks, are often out of date and no longer relevant in practice or in theory. In addition, the apprenticeship of industrial clerks is organized according to functions (e.g. purchasing, sales, production), and these are treated separately, in isolation from one another (Sekretariat der Ständigen Konferenz der Kultusminister der Länder in der Bundesrepublik Deutschland 1995; Der Bundesminister für Wirtschaft 1978). Complex interrelations and the social dimensions of enterprises are often disregarded. Thus, students are inefficiently prepared to cope with modern work structures and organizations. Though this modernity lag was diagnosed in the 1970s, it has not been rectified up to now (Achtenhagen, Tramm, Preiss, Seeman-Weymar, John & Schunck 1992; Krumm 1973; Rebmann 1994; Reetz & Witt 1974).

(3) For the firms, difficulties arise because the apprentices are often given only routine tasks. In many cases, apprentices become acquainted only with parts of complex business processes and are not allowed to take on responsibility. The learning potential of workplaces is not exploited. The preparation for future work as an employee is deficient (Achtenhagen, Nijhof & Raffe 1995; Keck 1995; Noß 2000).

(4) Inefficient *cooperation* also causes apprentices to experience *school* and *workplaces* as different worlds (Feller 1995: 43). They have difficulty connecting their real-life experience with the abstract body of knowledge learned in school. Initiatives have been taken to improve communication and cooperation among the participants and institutions by setting up working and discussion groups, by initiating or improving internships for teachers and possibilities for educators to observe during instruction (Pätzold & Walden 1995, 1999). However, these attempts have not contributed effectively to the reduction of boundaries between learning in schools and in workplaces, according to the perceptions of the students.

From the perspective of situated learning (Brown, Collins & Duguid 1989; Lave & Wenger 1991; Wenger 1998) one could say that the fact that knowledge and skills are situated differently in schools and workplaces (and sometimes in the workplaces of employees and those of apprentices) is often ignored (Guile & Young, this volume). Consequently, too little effort is made to reconcile or bridge these differences. Another problem results from the need to redefine the division of (apprenticeship) labor between school and workplaces in response to the development of new information and communication technologies. Tasks that are performed by computers and can no longer be physically experienced by the apprentices have to be visualized or simulated in schools.

To solve these problems, education policy makers recommend relating apprentice-ships more closely to practice and workplace reality by flexibly matching goals and contents to regional or branch-specific needs (Deutscher Industrie- und Handelstag 1999; Sekretariat der Ständigen Konferenz der Kultusminister der Länder in der Bundesrepublik Deutschland 1998),[2] by relocating teaching-learning processes from special training departments back to the shop floor and by structuring curricula according to workplace assignments and business processes (Sekretariat der Ständigen Konferenz der Kultusminister der Länder in der Bundesrepublik Deutschland 1999: 14). Some educational researchers hold similar views. The idea of situated cognition (Brown *et al.* 1989), for example, is based on the premise that knowledge is situated in contexts. The goal of these endeavors is to do a better job of applying learning, from the point of view of both method and contents, to the contexts of knowledge and skills in which it is used in order to promote processes of acquisition and the application of knowledge.

The project described in this chapter begins with this task. The aim is to promote students' action competence and transfer by relating school-based and work-based learning, by linking learning to practice and real workplace situations, and by systematically facilitating boundary-crossing between schools and workplaces. For that purpose, two teaching-learning arrangements were developed and tested. One is a so-called exploration, which takes place both in the school and the workplace. The jigsaw, on the other hand, takes place exclusively in the classroom. The main thrust of the evaluation was to determine to what extent the exploration setting and the jigsaw setting help students develop a cognitive structure or a mental model of the "company as complex economic system". Knowledge structures, or knowledge conceptualization, is regarded as a central component of action competence and transfer. Since the exploration allows "peripheral participation" in vocational practice, whereas the jigsaw does not, the evaluation can also be understood as an effort to discover to what extent vocational and school contexts have different effects on the development of knowledge.

In the course of designing teaching-learning arrangements, both the teaching-learning processes and the content are subjects of discussion and decision making. With regard to the teaching-learning processes, it is important that students' learning be active and self-regulated. Furthermore, it is necessary to support students in combining the situated knowledge and more abstract knowledge learned in schools. Concerning subject matter, it is necessary to model current structures and the organizations of workplaces. In order to foster boundary-crossing through the selection of appropriate subject matter, it should be interesting and important for both school and workplaces and should have the potential to be applied and elaborated on (differently) in schools and workplaces.

In the following, theoretical considerations concerning the design of the teaching-learning processes and the subject matter are presented. The design of the teaching-learning arrangements is based mainly on action-control theory and the idea of boundary-crossing. Selection and modeling of the subject matter is based on systems-oriented business administration. The acquisition of action competence is a long-term process. In the course of designing a single teaching-learning arrangement, long-term sequence decisions must be taken into account. Here, elaboration theory is

---

[2] Though the recommendations of the mentioned groups differ in several aspects, they share the idea of intensifying practice orientation.

addressed. Starting from these theoretical considerations, the teaching-learning arrangements and the research design are introduced. Preliminary results are explained and discussed.

Theoretical Framework

Basic Ideas of Action-Control Theory

Teaching-learning processes have to be arranged efficiently because the context and manner of knowledge acquisition influences retention, integration, availability, and applicability of knowledge. Action-control theory (in German: Handlungstheorie or Handlungsregulationstheorie) provides hints for effective learning.[3] This conception is based on several different theories, among them Soviet activity theory from the materialist and Marxist research traditions (Galperin & Talysina 1972; Leontjew 1979; Rubinstein 1977), psychological action or action-control theory and psychology of work and engineering (Hacker 1978; Hacker & Skell 1993; Lompscher 1979; Volpert 1980), cognitive psychology (Miller, Galanter & Pribram 1973), and the work of Aebli (1980, 1981), which aims at integrating different psychological approaches.[4] In addition, it has some similarities with activity theory[5] and expansive learning due to their shared theoretical basis (Engeström 1987; Engeström & Miettinen 1999). In broad terms, these theories share a common ground in their understanding of the concept of action[6] (in German: Handlung) (Achtenhagen *et al.* 1992: 28–29; Preiß 1999; Tramm 1992).

Acting is a conscious, goal-oriented and cognitively controlled process. The attribute of goal-orientation or object-orientation discriminates between actions[7] and other forms of behavior.[8] In order to act, individuals must, at a minimum, be rational, reflective, constructive, self-regulated, and have the ability to participate in social processes (Hurrelmann 1983; Söltenfuß 1983). Action is the central process of interaction between

---

[3] Action-control theory is largely compatible with constructivistic learning conceptions based on the idea of situated learning (see overviews of Gerstenmaier & Mandl 1995; Reinmann-Rothmeier & Mandl 1994).

[4] Additional approaches stem from social-cognitive learning theory, socialization research, and symbolic interactionism (Tramm 1992: 59).

[5] "Activity theory has its threefold origins in classical German philosophy (from Kant to Hegel), in the writings of Marx and Engels, and in the Soviet Russian cultural-historical psychology of Vygotsky, Leont'ev, and Luria" (Engeström 1999a: 19–20). Since 1920 or 1930 activity theory has been developed in different disciplines and can now be regarded as a multidisciplinary theory (Engeström & Miettinen 1999; Engeström 1999a).

[6] The concepts "action" and "activity" are largely used as synonyms in the literature. The same is true for the concept "operation", which is closely connected to the term "action". Terminological differences result from different Eastern and Western research traditions (Klauser 1998: 46).

[7] Goal or object-orientation is a common ground between activity theory and action-control theory. However, compared to action-control theory, activity theory differentiates more clearly between actions and activities. Activities are oriented toward objects and driven by superior durable motives. An activity is composed of a set of actions. In contrast to activities, actions are goal-oriented and have a clear-cut beginning and end. Goals do not explain why an action emerges; often they are explicated retrospectively (Engeström 1999b: 380–381).

[8] The radical withdrawal of behaviorist assumptions is evident.

individual and environment. Both the individual and the environment change as a result of the action. Thus, actions play a decisive role in learning and developmental processes. The environment provides subject matter to be acquired or to be dealt with, and it also supplies challenges, hints, incentives and/or information which influence the respective interaction. However, environmental factors only become important to the degree to which they are perceived and processed internally. This process, again, depends on the existing knowledge base that guides people in perceiving and evaluating situations. Following the result of the evaluation, the individual plans the action (searches for, evaluates and decides on alternatives), carries out the action, and evaluates the outcome (Von Cranach, Kalbermatten, Indermühle & Gugler 1980: 83–99). The whole action process is moderated by emotion and motivation. In the course of the action process individuals experience problems, contradictions etc. which lead to critical reflection and expansion of knowledge and skills.[9] So far, action comprises processes of assimilation and accommodation in the sense of Piaget. In other words, action is at the same time an adaptive and constructive interaction of individual and environment. Acting suspends the duality between thinking and doing (Aebli 1980, 1981, 1989).

Action competence, then, is the ability to plan, carry out, control and generate actions on the basis of available declarative (subject matter, facts, objects) and procedural (cognitive operations and transformations) knowledge (Aebli 1980, 1981; Volpert 1979), the current state of emotion, motivation and environmental conditions. Action competence presupposes an adequate (e.g. structured, complete and sophisticated) internal representation of the situation, and the ability to plan and carry out actions (Tramm & Rebmann 1997: 14). While acting plays a central role in everyday life, we are mainly interested in learning as a specific kind of action in the context of instruction. Contrary to other goal-oriented actions (working or playing), learning is dominated by the goal of expanding and modifying knowledge, skills and attitudes (Tramm 1992: 102).

As stated above, not only the individual, but also the environment plays a decisive role in the process of acting or learning by providing hints, challenges, incentives etc.

---

[9] The notions that action is a process of interaction between individual and environment and that action is composed of phases are similar to activity theory and expansive learning (Engeström 1987). Expansive learning assumes that activity systems can be regarded as dynamic developing and learning entities. These processes can be conceptualized by the expansive cycle. The expansive cycle is sparked off by perceived contradictions and comprises the following steps: questioning, analyzing the situation, modeling the new solution, examining the new model, implementing the new model, reflection on the progress and consolidation of the new practice (Engeström 1999b: 383–385). The full dialectic of an expansive cycle covers both adaptation to environment and active intervention, in other words resolution and production of contradictions. In this respect, expansive learning is characterized by the interdependence of internalization and externalization. The point that developmental processes are caused by contradictions is compatible with Wygotski's (1964) notion of the zone of proximal development: perceiving and solving of contradictions is the key to enter the zone of proximal development. Differences between activity theory and action-control theory concern the fact that expansive learning is a process that takes longer than an individual action. Furthermore, in the context of schools, actions are initiated by teachers or trainers rather than determined by students. According to Wygotski (1964) the dialectic relationship between guided and self-regulated learning (in the sense that self-regulation needs guidance, at least at the beginning) must be acknowledged. Pure expansive learning can best be realized by running projects (Frey 1990) or by open learning.

In order to conceptualize environmental conditions and understand the situatedness of acting, it is useful to have a closer look at activity theory. Activity theory illuminates especially social and cultural aspects of acting and learning. The main idea of activity theory is that activity (in German: Tätigkeit) is always embedded in so-called activity systems and mediated by artifacts. Activity systems are groups or communities with partially shared objects, partially shared knowledge, and partially shared practice. The basis of activity systems is defined by a community, its rules and division of labor (Engeström 1999a: 29–32). Mediating artifacts are coined by culture and society, so that in the end, society mediates between subject and object. Mediating artifacts include ". . . *tools and signs, both external implements and internal representations such as mental models*" (Engeström 1999b: 381). The social and collaborative nature of activity becomes especially obvious through the characteristics of activity systems and artifacts.

Concerning the dual system of vocational education in Germany, both schools and workplaces or their sub-systems can be regarded as activity systems. The activity systems have different objects, they consist of different rules, communities and divisions of labor, so that learning is situated differently in each of the activity systems. However, with regard to apprenticeships, schools and workplaces share some objects and goals and thus have to collaborate in reaching them together. Especially for the students — who are apprentices at the same time and thus have to act in different systems — it is important to cognitively relate different experiences and to use and elaborate knowledge learned in one system in another system. As a consequence, it is necessary to construct effective relationships between the different activity systems. Possible ways to cross boundaries between activity systems will be shown in the following section.

Boundary-crossing — Interaction of Activity Systems

Activity systems need to interact in order to solve common problems or to coordinate perspectives (Star 1989; Wenger 1998). Thus, interaction and cooperation, or boundary-crossing, require common or complementary (at least partially shared) objects and/or goals. Different forms of boundary-crossing can be categorized either as "reification", "participation" or a combination of both (Wenger 1998: 103–123). *Reifications* are, for example, so-called *boundary objects*, such as repositories, ideal types or platonic objects, terrains with coincident boundaries or forms and labels (Star 1989: 48–51; Star & Griesemer 1989: 410–411). Engeström *et al.* (1995) extends this notion of a boundary object as an external representation to the effect that internalized cognitive artifacts, like shared mental models, can also be considered boundary objects. Boundary objects can be interpreted as mediating artifacts. They have to meet different requirements: "*Boundary objects are objects that are both plastic enough to adapt to local needs and constraints of several parties employing them, yet robust enough to maintain a common identity across sites*" (Star 1989: 46). Not every object is a boundary object. Objects are only boundary objects if perspectives need to be coordinated (Wenger 1998: 108). Boundary-crossing as *participation* can take the form of brokering. Brokering means that people use their common membership in various activity systems to coordinate perspectives, to transfer ideas or to introduce elements of one practice into another (Wenger 1998: 105). Boundary encounters, such as meetings, conversations and visits *combine reifications and participation* in the course of boundary-crossing. Another way to relate activity systems is *practice* itself. Contrary to boundary encounters, practice is not a single or discrete event, but involves related activities engaged in over a longer period of time (Wenger 1998: 113). Different forms of practice can be distinguished: peripheries, boundary practice and overlaps. Peripheries refer to activity systems that offer people casual access to their own practice by letting them observe or engage in their activities. Boundary practices establish boundary encounters on a regular basis and build an ongoing forum for mutual engagement. Overlaps result from a direct natural and sustained overlap between two practices.

Often it is not easy to cross boundaries. Crossing boundaries "*involves encountering difference, entering onto territory in which we are unfamiliar and, to some significant extent, therefore, unqualified*" (Suchman 1994: 25). Obstacles to boundary-crossing can be such phenomena as groupthink (Janis 1982) or fragmentation of viewpoints. The potential for boundary-crossing depends on several factors, such as the way boundary objects are used and whether they are communicated, discussed, and critically reflected by all involved parties (Engeström *et al.* 1995).

In the dual system of vocational education in Germany, it is necessary to cross boundaries between schools and workplaces and their respective activity systems because both schools and workplaces share responsbility for fulfilling a common educational commission, and thus obliged to correlate teaching-learning processes.[10] This correlation process requires teachers and trainers, as well as apprentices, to cross various boundaries either in the course of planning teaching-learning processes or in the course of learning itself: In planning the apprentices' learning processes, teachers and trainers have to define objects/tasks, etc. which are interesting and important for both activity systems and could therefore initiate boundary-crossing. One can assume that the planning process first and foremost requires boundary encounters. One goal of the encounter could be developing boundary objects (such as repositories or ideal types) that are later used for the learning process in school or in the workplace and can be adapted to the needs of the activity systems, for example in a more situated or a more abstract way. In the course of their apprenticeship, students are members of several activity systems (departments, working groups, groups, courses etc.). Thus, they have to cross different boundaries in order to cognitively combine different learning experiences and to form a holistic understanding of the subject matter. For the students, boundary-crossing occurs in all kinds of reification, participation or in combinations of both.

The following chapter describes one of the goals pursued by both the vocational school and the firm, namely that the students/apprentices understand how the enterprise functions. Experiences in school as well as in the firm should contribute to this understanding. In order to understand the functioning of the firm, it is necessary to cross boundaries. This process is supported when experiences in vocational school and in the

---

[10] The focus here is on the process of correlating instruction between the school and the firm. However, it should be mentioned that different activity systems are present in the school and in the firm, and that boundaries between these systems must be crossed.

firm can be related to a common reference, for example an academic model of a firm that can be interpreted as a boundary object. This common reference should conform to the interests of the school as well as to those of the firm. Currently, systems-oriented business administration (Ulrich 1968)[11] presents itself as the best approach for understanding modern labor structures and processes.

Systems-Oriented Business Administration or "The Company as a Complex Social System" as a Boundary Object for Vocational Education in Schools and Workplaces

Systems-oriented business administration is an application-oriented and pragmatic science. It provides usable knowledge for managers and employees. Human beings as decision makers play a decisive role in this theory. It uses general systems theory and cybernetics to describe, explain and predict economic processes (Ulrich 1985: 18). According to systems-oriented business administration, enterprises are characterized by the following features of a system: openness, dynamics, purpose-orientation, goal-orientation and complexity. As structured social formations they produce goods and services for customers (other institutions or individuals). Business processes of enterprises have material, social, communicative and financial dimensions (Ulrich 1984: 24). Enterprises consist of subsystems (departments, sections etc.) that receive input and produce output. Subsystems or individuals can define goals, decide on the organizational structure and the operative management.

Using systems-oriented business administration as a reference field for school-based and workplace learning has some advantages (Keck 1995: 91; Preiß 1999: 47): (1) Its normative orientation is compatible with major pedagogic principles and with a pedagogic view of human beings (Preiß 1999: 43–44); (2) In step with current apprenticeship goals, systems-oriented business administration enables an integrative understanding of the functions of different departments or subsystems. The general context is always transparent, even when single aspects are focused on. In addition, this approach clearly shows the relationship between basic processes on the one hand and steering and adaptation processes on the other hand, and the links between information, goods and finances; (3) Systems-oriented business administration is compatible with other views on the same subject matter, e.g. the factor theoretical approach or the decision theoretical approach; (4) The systems-oriented approach emphasizes formal characteristics of business processes, thus fulfilling the principle of exemplary learning. On the basis of structural insights into subject matter, transfer (as understood in classical and some cognitive views, Tuomi-Gröhn & Engeström, this volume) may be facilitated; (5) The systems-oriented approach emphasizes the opinions of both managers and employees and the significance of learning and development processes on the level of the whole enterprise, its subsystems or individuals. It is assumed that actions or activities of enterprises are goal-oriented and socially and culturally embedded so that

---

[11] Systems-oriented business administration can be interpreted as a secondary artifact (Engeström 1990: 188). In addition to systems-oriented business administration, there are a number of other approaches to the subject.

it is possible to interpret enterprises as activity systems. Thus, at least in some respects, activity theory and systems-oriented business administration are compatible; (6) By intensively studying systems-oriented business administration, students learn the boundary-crossing requirements of their future jobs: boundary-crossing between company and customers, between departments or working groups, between strategic and operational levels etc.; and (7) Finally, the subject matter is important for all involved activity systems and thus suitable as a boundary object.

Sequence Decisions

The development of action competence and transfer is a long-term process and cannot be achieved with the help of only one teaching-learning arrangement. Thus, when constructing individual teaching-learning arrangements, long-term ordering and structuring of goals and contents must be taken into consideration. A comparatively new approach, elaboration theory (Reigeluth 1999; Reigeluth & Stein 1983), offers guidance for scope and sequence decisions. Elaboration theory[12] aims both to extend and integrate existing theories, such as Bruner's notion of a *spiral curriculum*, Ausubel's *subsumptive sequencing* and Norman's notion of *web learning* (Reigeluth & Stein 1983: 337, 339). Elaboration theory utilizes seven major strategy components, of which the so-called "elaborative sequence"[13] is the one of main interest here. Elaborative sequencing differs according to types of contents, relations among topics and expertise aspired to. Reigeluth & Stein (1983: 343) define three types of contents: concepts, principles and procedures. Accordingly, the elaborative sequence can have a conceptual, a theoretical or a procedural organization. Conceptual and theoretical elaborative sequences lead to domain expertise, which is knowledge of and orientation within a body of subject matter. Procedural elaboration sequences, on the other hand, lead to task expertise (which one can compare to action competence), which is the ability to carry out a specific task (Reigeluth 1999: 434–445).

In principle, an elaborative sequence is a "simple to complex sequence" in which general ideas of a single type of content are epitomized rather than summarized. Epitomizing means teaching fundamental and representative ideas of a content at the application level with concrete examples and practice as well as with abstract generality (Reigeluth & Stein 1983: 343, 346). The type of content which is epitomized is the so-called organizing content. The other two types of content are only introduced when they are relevant to organizing content ideas. This is referred to as supporting content (Reigeluth & Stein 1983: 344). The epitomized content, or the epitome, is elaborated on several levels, so that it becomes more and more detailed and complex. A "simple to complex sequence" is hypothesized as resulting in stable cognitive structures, good long-term retention and transfer, high motivation due to meaningful contexts and

---

[12] Elaboration theory was developed in the context of instructional design, but is compatible with newer constructivist approaches (Preiß 1999: 129).

[13] The latest version of elaboration theory includes the so-called simplifying conditions method as a sequence to epitomize and elaborate procedures (Reigeluth 1999).

enabling learner control over the selecting and sequencing of content (Reigeluth & Stein 1983: 356).

Design of Teaching-Learning Arrangements

In order to promote effective learning by organized boundary-crossing, teaching-learning arrangements should be designed keeping the following landmarks in mind[14]:

- The starting point of the learning processes should be a representative epitome in the form of a complex problem situation (not single concepts or facts). A medium complexity factor seems to be appropriate to provoke contradictions which lead the learner into the zone of proximal development (Wygotski 1964). Situated experiences should be systematized in order to structure and abstract knowledge. Thus, students are enabled to combine action, operation and concept as described by Aebli (1989). In order to promote transfer, knowledge and skills should be practiced, repeated and used in new situations and tasks. Depending on students' prior knowledge and achievement level, new situations and tasks can be designed ranging from those very similar to the initial ones to those very different from these. In this way, knowledge and skills can be expanded systematically. The initial situation can serve as mental anchor and continual reference point for further teaching-learning processes. To guarantee effective goal-oriented actions and a sustainable outcome, students should regard the subject matter as significant and important.
- Problems or tasks should require holistic (cognitive, emotional and psychomotoric) and complete (planning, carrying out and controlling) actions. The students should be given a basic orientation to the whole action.
- Boundary-crossing usually does not function automatically, but must be organized or at least supported in the beginning by different means of reification and/or participation, e.g. by a subject matter which is relevant for all involved activity systems (such as understanding the functioning of an enterprise from the systems perspective), or by enabling social and communicative experiences with peer groups or experts.

The Teaching-Learning Arrangements Exploration and Jigsaw

Aims and Curricular Embedding

The starting point of the construction of both teaching-learning arrangements is the curriculum for training of industrial clerks/managers and the corresponding guidelines of the state of North Rhine-Westphalia. These guidelines are divided into subjects, which are composed of several learning areas. The teaching-learning arrangements operationalize the learning area, the "market as impetus for industrial production", as part of the subject "Business Administration for Industrial Enterprises".

---

[14] Each landmark has to be specified according to the goals involved, the learner, and the available research.

This learning area is meant for the initial phase of the apprenticeship aiming at the following competencies. The students should develop a holistic understanding of companies as complex economic systems involving organizational structures and processes. More precisely, the students should recognize how different departments (e.g. purchasing, production, manufacturing control, personnel, internal sales or accounting) of an enterprise work together and likewise how the departments work with external institutions or enterprises (e.g. customers, banks, suppliers, employees, owners or the state) in order to produce marketable goods. Students should be capable of explaining the flow of information, goods and finances within the enterprise and between the enterprise and other economic or societal institutions. And finally, the students should be knowledgeable about the products, the legal form and the goals of the enterprise (Der Kultusminister des Landes Nordrhein Westfalen 1997).[15] The goals of the teaching-learning arrangement — roughly outlined here — must be specified when the arrangement is designed. In the case described in this paper, order processing, one of the most important areas in the functioning of an enterprise, was chosen. Using this process, the interrelationship of the various departments within the firm, between the firm and its environment and between the differing kinds of flows can be demonstrated. In addition, the topic could be subjectively meaningful for the students' apprenticeship and for their future jobs because order processing will be an integral part of their work.

Characteristics of Exploration

Explorations, in general, should support students in understanding abstract economic concepts and cause/effect relationships by effectively harmonizing learning at different venues (school and workplaces). For that purpose, students should experience reality (e.g. an industrial enterprise) by social contact, by observation and/or by working. All three possibilities can be interpreted as participation as defined by Wenger (1998, see Chapter 2.2). Contents and aims of explorations have to be embedded in the curriculum. Explorations aim at equipping students with the competence to orient themselves in new situations and to acquire knowledge as a prerequisite to action competence. Explorations always require techniques of gathering and processing information. These techniques are at the same time the prerequisite to and result of the learning process.

The "Exploration of an Industrial Enterprise" was developed in cooperation by teachers of the private vocational school of the Bertelsmann Corporation, employees of Mohn Media Mohndruck Company (a profit center of the Bertelsmann Corporation) and the Institute of Economics and Business Education of the University of Goettingen. The "exploration" is subdivided into four main phases: Preparation, Introduction, Exploration and Systematization.

In the *Preparation Phase*, teachers of the vocational schools, company trainers involved in the project and the university research group discussed and worked out how

---

[15] This holistic access to an enterprise may be interpreted as an epitome which has a procedural order. But, at this point of the apprenticeship, students are not asked to process orders themselves. Other levels, then, elaborate on the epitome. Students should then have the chance to expand knowledge and skills. The exploration serves as a reference point for the learning processes in the school and in the enterprise.

the actual processing of an order functions, in what degree of detail the students should be instructed and how to divide labor between school and workplace. The group used written information about the product, department goals and department tasks etc. as aids. The outcome of this process was twofold: (1) a jointly developed order processing model with written explanations; and (2) working agreements between the participating persons and institutions. In terms of boundary-crossing, the preparation phase can be regarded as a boundary encounter. The outcomes (e.g. the order processing model and the job sharing agreements) can be seen as written reifications of shared mental models that can serve as boundary objects in the further course of the apprenticeship.

The *Introductory Phase* served to clarify the problem situation and the assignment to the students. An authentic case served as a starting and reference point in the learning processes of the apprentices. In the case presented here, a publishing company would like to have 300,000 copies of a magazine printed by a company (Mohn Media Mohndruck GmbH). The students were required to independently explore the course this order takes from the customer's inquiry to payment for the product. They worked in groups on this case. Most of the relevant information was to be gained by interviewing experts from all essential areas within the enterprise (production, sales, purchasing, personnel, accounting, manufacturing control) and by observing the production process.

The task during the main *Exploration Phase* was to prepare, conduct and evaluate interviews, and then to present the results to company experts, fellow students and teachers. The process of acquiring information was to be organized by the students themselves. For that purpose, they were prompted to develop guideline questions for each interview. To prepare the guideline questions and to carry out the interviews, the students were given several information leaflets. These made basic information available to the students in the form of real material about Mohn Media Mohndruck. In addition, the students were provided with basic information about how to conduct interviews. In order to reflect on their experiences, to gradually improve their own learning processes and to gradually conduct interviews more efficiently, the students kept a learning journal in which they took notes on each interview and evaluated its contents and atmosphere. In addition, students were supported in preparing the presentations by instructional lessons about presentation techniques. During the exploration phase, boundary-crossing had the form of boundary encounters. The main goal of this kind of practice was to research and understand the processing of an order. When company experts participate, the presentations can be regarded as boundary encounters. The contents of the presentation can be regarded as shared mental model of each group and the written or graphical material as its reifications.

In the *Systematization Phase*, students should learn the specific facts of order processing (e.g. the particulars of printing magazines compared to telephone books), on the one hand. Otherwise, they can neither perceive changed circumstances nor adapt their actions to them. On the other hand, using the concrete case as an example, they should learn important concepts and relationships on an abstract conceptual level and apply this knowledge to other examples. The conceptual systematization is done according to systems-oriented business administration (see Chapter 2.3). To support the process of the application of knowledge and to increase flexibility between concrete and abstract knowledge, simulated enterprises can be used in the classroom. The aim is to relate situated and more abstract knowledge in order to create a holistic learning process at several different places of learning. This can be regarded as a preparation for the brokering of knowledge. During the remainder of the apprenticeship, students are often required to broker knowledge they have acquired in the school and in the workplaces and use their multiple membership in both activity systems to coordinate perspectives for themselves and others. With the help of the initial knowledge structures and with all resources from the exploration (all written materials and charts etc.), brokering may be supported.

Characteristics of the Jigsaw Teaching Method

Jigsaw (Aronson, Blaney, Stephan, Sikes & Snapp 1978; Clarke 1994) is a teaching method in which students play the roles both of teachers and of students. The jigsaw is composed of several phases. In the first phase, after being introduced to the goals and subject, students work together in groups on a topic or part of a topic (that is to say: as a piece of a larger puzzle or task). In the case presented here, each group of students worked on the aims, tasks and relationships of a person or his or her department (e.g. sales, purchasing, accounting etc.). One group worked on all the external institutions (customers, suppliers etc.). In the next phase, the groups of the first phase reorganized themselves into new learning groups so that each new learning group was composed of different students, one from each former group. Each "expert" of a special department taught the new group his/her knowledge (e.g. his or her piece of the puzzle). In the end, all students should have the same level of knowledge about the processing of an order in by Mohn Media Mohndruck. The results were then presented to the class and discussed.

In contrast to the exploration group the jigsaw group exclusively worked in the classroom, using written materials about order processing. The material was created from a model about order processing, which teachers of the vocational school, company trainers and the university research group discussed and worked out in the course of preparing the teaching-learning arrangements. Thus, it could be guaranteed that the students in the jigsaw group received the same information as the students in the exploration group.

Evaluation

Treatment

The learning environment was evaluated using a quasi-experimental design with two experimental groups. While the students in the first experimental group conducted the exploration, the students in the second experimental group learned the same contents using written materials in the classroom in the "jigsaw" teaching-learning arrangement. Both groups had different boundary-crossing possibilities, but were otherwise largely comparable, in that they both did group work, they both had access to information leaflets, and they were both required to present their results.

Subjects

The first experimental group consisted of 21 high-school (Gymasium) graduates, aged 19.6 on average. The second experimental group consisted of 23 students, the majority of whom had graduated from a two-year advanced business trade school. As a result, most of the students in the control group had economic knowledge that they had learned systematically. Their average age was 18.9. The average age of the six interview partners was 40.6. On average, they had worked for 18 years at Mohn Media Mohndruck. Four of them were department heads, one was an assistant department head and one was an assistant.

Indicators and Instruments

Interconnected knowledge   In order to measure changes in the students' cognitive structures concerning the company as a complex economic system, the students of both experimental groups showed what they knew about the processing of an order in the form of a multi-relational network with named relations before beginning and after completing the exploratory or instructional phase.[16] Networking techniques were used for different purposes. One of the main areas of application is modeling and diagnosis of knowledge (e.g. Collins & Quillian 1969; Dörner 1976; Norman & Rumelhart 1978; Shavelson & Ruiz-Primo 1999; White & Gunstone 1999; for an overview, e.g. Opwis & Lüer 1996; Tergan 1986) and subjective theories (Scheele & Groeben 1984; Becker, Oldenbürger & Piehl 1987). In addition, networking techniques are used as tools in order to structure and coordinate problem-solving and decision-making processes (e.g. Axelrod 1976). Numerous variants of networking techniques exist (Jonassen, Beissner & Yacci 1993). Many approaches share the notion that knowledge can be reconstructed as propositions. Propositions are semantic units which consist of concept-relationship-concept structures. Concepts are terms of objects, in this case departments of the enterprise or external institutions (e.g. printing department, publishing company, processing department, internal sales). Relationships, in this case, specify transactions involving information, goods and finances (e.g. sends magazines, orders paper) which flow between the "concepts".[17] In addition to being able to describe these relationships verbally, students were asked to use the abbreviations "I" (flow of information), "G" (flow of goods) and "F" (flow of finances) to designate what kind of flow was described

---

[16] The initial knowledge structure can be interpreted as current achievement level.

[17] It should be noted that only the current state of the knowledge structures at any given point in time can be reconstructed on the basis of the students' verbal data.

by each relationship. Finally, they were asked to number the relationships to show the chronological order of the transactions in order processing.

Three examples below illustrate this analysis technique:

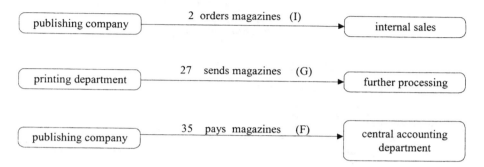

The students were given a glossary of terms containing concepts as components of the network to use as an aid.[18] However, the students were required to define the relationships without any help. If the students were given a glossary of terms containing relationships they probably would have been supported in guessing propositions after learning the concepts and relations. The relationships were categorized after the exploration on the basis of a content analysis procedure.

Motivation To measure the students' motivation for their teaching-learning arrangement, questionnaires were used after the exploration/instruction. The questionnaires contained several items concerning six variants of learning motivation (Prenzel, Kristen, Dengler, Ettle & Beer 1996: 109–110) that were to be rated on a scale ranging from 1 (exactly true) to 6 (not at all true). The six variants of learning motivation differ in the degree of self-determination and the degree to which the content is meaningful in the students opinion. The three variants "lack of motivation", "external motivation" and "introjected motivation" describe externally determined learning, as well as learning situations which are subjectively judged as insignificant. The degree of self determination increases from "lack of motivation" to "introjected motivation". The variants "identified motivation", "intrinsic motivation" and "interest" are descriptive of more self determined learning and subject matters that are judged as increasingly important and challenging. "Interest", for example, implies that students want to delve deeper into the subject matter beyond their learning situation (see Figure 1).

The six variants of learning motivation operationalize a theory of learning motivation which is oriented to pedagogics. Contrary to other theories of learning motivation, it aims to consider the perceived significance of the subject matter and the extent to which the students find it motivating. It is based on the theory of Deci and Ryan (1993) and the pedagogical theory of interest (Prenzel, Krapp & Schiefele 1986).

---

[18] These concepts are the result of an investigation which was conducted with a comparable group of students.

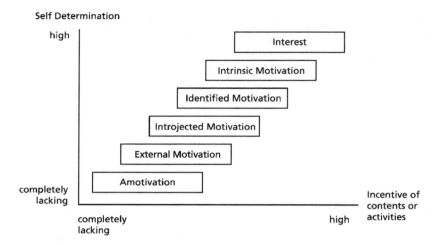

Figure 1: Six variants of learning motivation (Prenzel, Drechsel, Kliewe, Kramer & Röber 1998: 8).

Other Data

(1) Subsequent to the exploratory/instructional phase, students were asked to assess positive and negative aspects of their teaching-learning arrangement. To that end, they were asked to answer two open questions on a questionnaire. The answers were categorized with the help of a content analysis. (2) The other data collected included biographical data, learning success, quality and atmosphere of the interviews, the atmosphere within the group and the cooperation within the group itself, and lastly, the capability and readiness of the students to work in groups.

Results

Interconnected Knowledge

Knowledge networks can be assessed both quantitatively and qualitatively. In regard to the size of the networks (as an indicator of quantity), which can be measured by the total number of propositions and the number of different propositions, Table 1 shows the following results: While the students in the exploration group mentioned fewer propositions and fewer different propositions in the posttest compared to the pretest, the jigsaw group showed the opposite result. The number of propositions and the number of different propositions increased in this group. The analysis of variance shows that both groups of students differed significantly regarding the changes in the number of propositions named from the pretest to the posttest (see the value p for the interaction of the factors group * time in Table 1). According to this result, it seemed likely that the

Table 1: Size of networks.

	exploration group			jigsaw group		
	pretest	posttest	change	pretest	posttest	change
number of propositions	945	858	−9.2%	866	977	+12.8%
number of different propositions	546	485	−11.2%	452	485	+7.3%
average number of propositions per student	45	40.9	−9.1%	37.6	42.5	+13%
standard deviation of the number of propositions	12.4	12.6		11.9	12.3	

Analysis of variance[19]

Source[20]	SS	df	MS	F	p	d_{int}[21]
group	180.00	1	180.00	0.78	0.38	
time	2.562	1	2.562	0.04	0.58	
group * time	441.517	1	441.517	6.15	0.02	−0.7381

Legend: SS = sum of squares; df = degrees of freedom; MS = means of squares.

knowledge structure of the jigsaw group became more differentiated, while this was not true for the exploration group. This assumption had to be proven by qualitative analyses. Two possible methods of analyzing the quality of the networks are introduced in the following. The first method refers to mode networks, the second one to partial networks.

Mode networks   Mode networks give deeper insight into the quality of the depicted knowledge structures on the level of the whole group. Mode networks consist of

[19] The effects were tested by an analysis of variance. The analysis of variance was conducted using BMDP 2V (repeated measures design).

[20] The factor group consists of the groups "experimental group" and "jigsaw group". The factor time consists of the groups "pretest" and "posttest".

[21] d is a measure for estimating the size or the practical meaning of an effect. The value of d subjects the differences between the experimental groups to a norm based on the standard deviations of the experimental groups (http://www.phil.uni-sb.de/ ~ jakobs/seminar/vpl/bedeutung/bedeutung.htm). In case of pretest-posttest designs, corrected effect sizes that take the pretest differences between the experimental groups into consideration should be calculated. The corrected effect size is determined by: $d_{int(=interaction)} = d_{posttest} - d_{pretest}$. The pooled standard deviation from both experimental groups was used as standard deviation. (http://www.phil.uni-sb.de/ ~ jakobs/seminar/vpl/bedeutung/eskorr.htm).

propositions which are named by many students.[22] The pretest mode networks of both experimental groups were to a considerable degree (more than 20 propositions) in accordance with each other, but also contained individual elements (see Figure 2). Both networks consisted predominantly of flows of goods. These flows were magazine production and delivery, and delivery of paper and other material. Flows of information, which referred to ordering and invoicing magazines, paper, and material, ranked second. Flows of finances played a subordinate role. The flows which were only part of one mode network accentuated different parts of the same topic. In summary, mode networks mirrored basic parts of the processing of an order, which mainly corresponded to everyday economic knowledge. Based on its prior knowledge, the jigsaw group was able to integrate some specific details (e.g. order acknowledgement or purchase notice) into the network.

The posttest mode networks of both experimental groups (see Figure 3) were equivalent to the same degree as the pretest mode networks (17 propositions) of both groups. Most of the propositions in the posttest were named in the pretest, and mainly had to do with the ordering and production of magazines. In contrast to the pretest, both mode networks in the posttest contained flows of information which are important at the preliminary stage of taking an order, e.g. examination of customer reliability, or transportation via forwarding agent. Some pretest propositions were no longer part of the posttest mode networks, e.g. elements of the delivery process and payment of paper or material.

Apart from this shared knowledge, the mode networks of both groups contained propositions of their own, some of which were already contained in the pretest networks. In the exploration group, the new propositions were related to an alternative way of ordering magazines and to the production control department, which coordinates the whole production process. The jigsaw group then examined additional flows of goods and the payment for the products and the raw materials. The improvement in both mode networks in the posttest occurred because the students left out some propositions, e.g. parts of the processes for purchasing and paying for material or for recruiting workforce. These procedures were not important for the task assigned to the students. The results indicate that both experimental groups were able to differentiate and correct prior knowledge. In this context, the exploration group was better able to disregard irrelevant or incorrect relationships and thus to improve the knowledge networks.

Partial networks   In addition to information gained by the mode networks, detailed analyses of all the propositions named in the areas of flows of goods, finances and information can give further hints about the quality of the students' knowledge development. As a result, it can also provide information about the potential and the

---

[22] The number of propositions of the mode networks should equal the average number of propositions identified by the students (in this case about 40) (see Table 1). If the propositions are listed according to the frequency with which they are named, the result is that the fortieth proposition was named by five students in one group. If the 40 propositions named most often are multiplied by the number of times named (at least 5) and if the results are then put in relationship to the total number of propositions, the mode networks show between 30% and 37% of the total propositions named. Other studies concerned with network representations of knowledge reach a comparable standard.

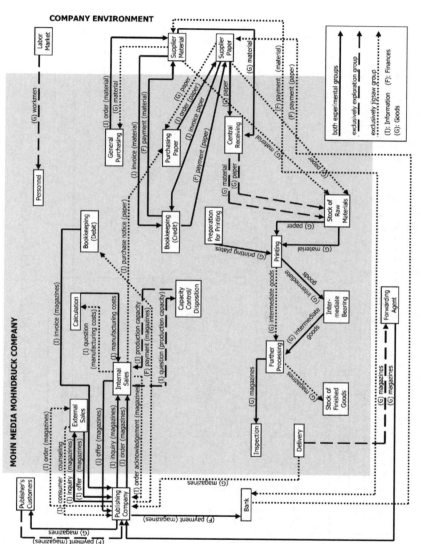

Figure 2: Mode networks — pretest[23].

[23] Note: The diagram shows both the mode networks of both the exploration group and the jigsaw group. The mode networks of the exploration group are shown by the solid and the dashed lines. The mode networks of the jigsaw group are shown by the solid and the dotted lines. Thus the solid lines are a component of the mode networks of both groups.

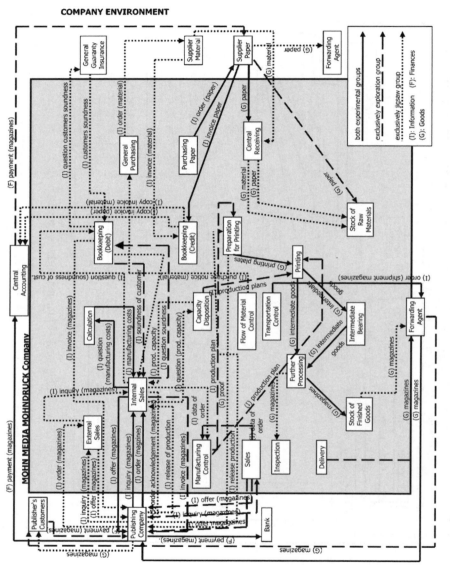

Figure 3: Mode networks — posttest[24].

Table 2: Quality of the development of knowledge regarding flows of goods.

flows of goods	quality of reconstruction	exploration group pretest %	exploration group posttest %	jigsaw group pretest %	jigsaw group posttest %	Anova[25] results
printing plate to magazine	correct	38.1	66.7	43.5	43.5	$p = 0.087$
	incorrect	57.1	33.3	56.5	56.5	
	no response	4.8	0	0	0	$d_{int} = 0.668$
paper	correct	57.1	80.9	39.1	47.8	$p = 0.488$
	incorrect	33.3	19.1	47.8	47.8	
	no response	9.5	0	13	4.3	$d_{int} = 0.426$
layout	correct	0	14.3	0	26.1	$p = 0.380$
	incorrect	0	9.5	4.3	13	
	no response	100	76.2	95.7	60.9	$d_{int} = 0.065$
proof	correct	0	4.8	0	60.9	$p = 0.000$
	incorrect	0	0	13	13	
	no response	100	95.2	87	26.1	$d_{int} = -1.243$

Legend: Anova: Analysis of Variance.

weaknesses of the arrangements as well as of the need to systematize classroom instruction.

Within the framework of order processing, different flows of goods can be distinguished, such as the main stream (printing plate to magazines) and the flow of paper (see Table 2). The main stream consists of the following components: the preparation department sends printing plates to the printing department, the printing department delivers intermediate goods to further processing, the further processing department sends magazines to the delivery department or to the finished goods warehouse. Finally, a forwarding agent transports the magazines to the customers. Another flow of goods is the procurement of raw materials, such as paper. The supplier entrusts a forwarding agent with the task of transporting paper to the customer. The paper is delivered directly to central receiving and from there either directly to the printing department or to the stock of raw materials. The layout for the magazine is usually done by the publishing company and then sent to the liaison in the sales department of the company, who sends it to the preparation department. The preparation department prepares a proof, or sample, that is representative of the finished product.

---

[25] The analysis of variance was conducted with BMDP 2V (repeated measures design). Only the effects of interaction — belonging to one of the experimental groups (factor: group) and to one of the points in time (factor: time) — are relevant to this study and are given here. The data were coded so that incorrect reconstructions were given the value of 1 and correct reconstructions were given the value of 2. Missing reconstructions were given the value of 0. Mean values were calculated.

The proof is usually sent to the customer, who can then either request changes or authorize printing.

In order to undertake a qualitative evaluation of sequences of propositions for flows of goods (or the flows of information or finances), the students' solutions were compared with a reference model developed in the preparation phase of the exploration (see Chapter 3.1). The students' solutions were counted as correct if they corresponded exactly to the reference solution or represented a reasonable alternative to it (see Chapter 5). In other cases the students' solutions were considered incorrect. In each case the evaluation refers to complete flows, that is, to a sequence of several propositions. This kind of evaluation corresponded better to the goal of teaching knowledge of interrelationships in school than the evaluation of individual propositions.

The analysis of the flows of goods showed, first, that in the exploration group the number of students who depicted the main flow and the paper flow correctly increased from the pretest to the posttest. At the same time, the number of students who depicted the respective flows incorrectly decreased. The jigsaw group had different results: the number of students who reconstructed the main flow and the paper flow correctly and the number of students who reconstructed the respective flows incorrectly stagnated in the posttest. Regarding layout and proof, different results were evident: although the percentage of the students who reconstructed the flows correctly increased slightly in the exploration group, the number of errors increased as well, and the majority of the students had offered no propositions on the subject. On the other hand, in the jigsaw group both layout and proof were considered by a greater number of the students, and the percentage of students able to reconstruct both flows correctly increased. This was especially true for the proofs, whereas there was an increase in the percentage of students who made errors in reconstructing the flow of goods for the layout. According to the results of the analysis of variance, the increase in learning of the jigsaw group concerning the proofs was significantly better than that of the exploration group (see the value p for the interaction of the factors time * group in Table 2). The reason for the comparatively poor results in the exploration group (especially as regards the proof) could lie in the fact that there was no interview partner from the firm in the preparation department (the department mainly responsible for this topic) available. Possibly, the interview partners from other departments did not emphasize the importance of layouts and proofs. This assumption was confirmed by a consensus validation of the networks.

Just as the flows of goods, the flows of information and finances can be differentiated, as shown in the left columns of the respective tables (see Tables 3 and 4). These flows, too, consist of sequences of several propositions.

On the whole, the exploration group showed an improved ability to handle flows of information. In almost every topic the percentage of students who reconstructed the flows correctly increased, and the percentage of students who reconstructed the flows incorrectly decreased. The jigsaw group, on the other hand, had problems with a number of topics. The percentage of students who reconstructed the flows correctly decreased in the areas of determining production costs and checking the paper inventory. Likewise, the percentage of students who reconstructed the flows incorrectly increased in the areas of ordering supplies of paper, examination of customer reliability and checking for free capacities. In addition, the analysis of variance shows clearly that the increase in

Table 3: Quality of development of knowledge regarding flows of information.

flows of information	quality of reconstruction	exploration group pretest %	exploration group posttest %	jigsaw group pretest %	jigsaw group posttest %	Anova[26] results
magazines ordering	correct	52.4	76.2	60.9	82.6	$p=0.725$
	incorrect	47.6	23.8	39.1	17.4	$d_{int}=0.091$
	no response	0	0	0	0	
paper ordering	correct	61.9	85.7	82.6	82.6	$p=0.162$
	incorrect	19	9.5	8.7	13	$d_{int}=0.557$
	no response	19	4.8	8.7	4.3	
examining customer soundness	correct	4.8	57.1	0	43.5	$p=0.282$
	incorrect	28.6	23.8	0	39.1	$d_{int}=-0.778$
	no response	66.6	19	100	17.4	
calculating production costs	correct	19	38.1	47.8	30.4	$p=0.118$
	incorrect	42.9	19	30.4	21.7	$d_{int}=0.709$
	no response	38.1	42.8	21.7	47.8	
checking free capacities	correct	19	33.3	13	26.1	$p=0.492$
	incorrect	19	9.5	21.7	26.1	$d_{int}=-0.267$
	no response	61.9	57.1	65.2	47.8	
strategy	correct	9.5	0	4.3	0	$p=0.262$
	incorrect	14.3	4.8	0	0	$d_{int}=-0.109$
	no response	76.2	95.2	95.6	100	
checking stock of paper	correct	23.8	42.9	30.4	17.4	$p=0.022$
	incorrect	33.3	23.8	56.5	39.1	$d_{int}=0.932$
	no response	42.9	33.3	13	43.5	

Legend: Anova: Analysis of Variance.

knowledge in the exploration group regarding checking the paper inventory was significantly better than that of the jigsaw group (see the value $p=0.022$ for the interaction of the factors time * group in Table 3).

There are many reasons for the difficulties experienced by the jigsaw group. Regarding the ordering of paper some students were of the (incorrect) opinion that the general purchasing department, rather than the paper purchasing department, was responsible for ordering the paper. The processes of examining the customer's soundness were depicted incompletely. That is to say, Mohn Media Mohndruck inquires about the customer's soundness but receives no answer to the inquiry.

Fewer students took production costs into consideration. Regarding checking for free capacities and checking the paper inventory, the students had difficulties identifying the

---

[26] (For explanations see footnotes 21 and 25).

Table 4: Quality of the development of knowledge regarding flows of finances.

flows of information	quality of reconstruction	exploration group pretest %	exploration group posttest %	jigsaw group pretest %	jigsaw group posttest %
payment for	correct	28.6	33.3	21.7	39.1
magazines	incorrect	57.1	57.1	78.3	56.5
	no response	14.3	9.5	0	4.3
payment for paper	correct	42.9	33.3	30.4	26.1
	incorrect	19	47.6	30.4	43.5
	no response	38.1	19	39.1	30.4
payment for	correct	9.5	14.3	0	4.3
shipment of	incorrect	9.5	14.3	0	39.1
magazines	no response	81	71.4	100	56.5

departments involved. For example, they assumed that the controlling or printing departments, rather than the capacity control department, determined free capacities. They thought that the calculation department or the company management rather than the materials handling department was responsible for paper inventory and disposition. Both groups had problems regarding strategy (for example, whether accepting an order would be profitable or not). The percentage of students who reconstructed the flows correctly decreased. On the whole, very few students offered propositions on this topic.

The greatest problems appeared in regard to the flows of finances (see Table 4). Although both groups showed positive changes in the quality of knowledge (for example regarding payment for magazines), these were not consistent. The problem can be identified very clearly in the payment of paper. It seemed to be difficult for both groups to understand the payment process and the function of central accounting. Apparently the fact that although an enterprise keeps its own books, its accounts and those of other profit centers are kept by a central business trust financial accounting department, rather than by the firm itself, contradicts their day-to-day business understanding or their prior knowledge. No systematic effects could be shown by analysis of variance.

On the basis of the data available so far, it can be assumed that exploration and jigsaw have different strengths and weaknesses. Neither arrangement is advantageous in all areas (as is shown clearly in the example of the flows of goods). The exploration arrangement does better regarding the flows of information.

A detailed analysis of the incorrect flows showed that the mistakes tend to fall into three categories: (1) Some flows were depicted with gaps (for example, the depiction of the main flow of goods lacked a link between the warehouse for finished goods and the forwarding agent); (2) Important functions and central departments or connections were not shown (for example the customer receives goods but does not pay for them); and (3)

Departments were given the wrong functions (for example the students confused the tasks of the printing and further processing departments or purchasing and warehouse or transport control and forwarding agent). Although all categories of mistakes occurred at the same rate in the exploration group, the jigsaw group made more mistakes in the third category.

Motivation

The data gathered were structured with the help of a factor analysis[27] of the motivation items. At the same time, an effort was made to determine the extent to which the structure of the data gathered is consistent with the variants of learning motivation described in the literature. A factor analysis often allows several acceptable solutions. The most important consideration for the decision on the number of factors was to maintain continuity with previous research. Thus, as far as could be justified on the basis of the eigenvalues of the factors and goals for this study, the number and names of the known variants of learning motivation were used. This approach was implemented to a large extent, but not completely. A factor analysis of the respective items showed that the following five factors adequately represented the data: (1) intrinsic motivation/interest; (2) flow; (3) identified motivation; (4) introjected motivation; and (5) amotivation/external motivation.[28] In contrast to the results in the literature, both of the negative variants of learning motivation, amotivation and external motivation, could be assigned to one factor. The same was true for both of the positive variants, intrinsic motivation and interest. In addition, the factor flow-experience was found.[29]

As stated above (see Chapter 4.3) the factors amotivation/external motivation and introjected motivation indicate more extrinsic or externally determined motivation, whereas the factors motivation, flow and intrinsic motivation/interest indicate more self-directed learning and subject matter, which were judged as increasingly important and challenging.

An analysis of variance[30] of the respective factor scores showed that the groups differed significantly with regard to intrinsic motivation/interest and introjected motivation (see Table 5).

Thus, the students of the exploration group judged content to be an incentive for learning and generally important. Furthermore, these students wanted to delve deeper into the subject matter beyond the current learning situation. One can assume that the

---

[27] The extraction method is a principle-component analysis (pca). The rotation is varimax with Kaiser normalisation. SPSS 8.0 for Windows was used.

[28] The factors have the following eigenvalues: intrinsic motivation/interest (4.774), amotivation/external motivation (1.563), identified motivation (1.137), introjected motivaton (0.945), flow (0.895), and they explain 76.9% of the variance.

[29] The following items may clarify the factors: intrinsisc motivation/interest ("I became acquainted with contents/topics that I want to learn more about"), amotivation/external motivation ("During the exploration/in class I didn't care about anything"), identified motivation ("I wanted to understand the contents"), introjected motivation ("I tried to do everything in the way that was expected of me"), flow ("The time seemed to fly by").

[30] A one-way analysis of variance was conducted by using SPSS 8.0 for Windows.

Table 5: Analysis of variance summary table for the variants of learning motivation.

	source of variation	SS	df	MS	F	p	est. ω^2
intrinsic motivation/ interest	between groups	10.661	1	10.661	14.736	0.000	0.271[31]
	within groups	25.339	35	0.724			
	totals	36	36				
Flow	between groups	1.563	1	1.563	1.589	0.216	0.016
	within groups	34.437	35	0.984			
	totals	36	36				
identified motivation	between groups	2.175	1	2.175	2.251	0.143	0.033
	within groups	33.825	35	0.966			
	totals	36	36				
introjected motivation	between groups	4.769	1	4.769	5.345	0.027	0.105
	within groups	31.231	35	0.892			
	totals	36	36				
amotivation/ external motivation	between groups	0.0084	1	0.008	0.008	0.928	0
	within groups	35.992	35	1.028			
	totals	36	36				

[31] ω^2 estimates the size of an effect associated with a treatment. The value of the estimated ω^2 is the percentage of the variance in the dependent variable which is to be accounted for by the independent variable.

Table 6: Students' evaluation of the arrangement –positive aspect.

arrangements — positive aspect	exploration group %	jigsaw group %
1. Good teamwork	47.8	52.9
2. Knowledge acquisition/ understanding complex interdependencies	38.1	0
3. Practice participation	33.3	0
4. Good interview atmosphere	10.0	0
5. Good classroom atmosphere	0	23.5
6. Self-directed learning	14.3	17.6

jigsaw group did not learn in a self-directed manner and did not judge the content to be a learning incentive to the same degree as the exploration group. The results show that the exploration setting suits self-directed learning better than the jigsaw arrangement.

Students' Evaluation of the Arrangements

In addition to the development of knowledge and motivation, some aspects of the students' evaluation are described in the following: The aspects which pleased the students of both groups were "good teamwork" and "self-directed learning". Good teamwork was particularly stressed as positive. In addition, 38% of the students in the exploration group students assessed the possibility to "acquire knowledge and understand complex relationships" as positive, 33% the "practice participation", and 19% the "good interview atmosphere". Neither of the latter two categories was mentioned by the jigsaw group spontaneously. But 23% of the jigsaw group students assessed the "good classroom atmosphere" as a positive aspect of the arrangement (see Table 6).

Negative aspects of the learning situation (which are not shown in the figure) were the difficulty of making appointments with the interview partners (29% of the students) from the perspective of the exploration group. Students of the jigsaw group complained about the frequency of depicting networks (18% of the students).

Summary and Conclusions

General Tendencies

Based on these results, one can assume that both arrangements enable students to reconstruct the most important processes of Mohn Media Mohndruck and to reflect on and modify initial assumptions. Thus, both arrangements contribute to the development of students' action competence. This is indicated by the qualitative improvement of mode networks (for example regarding the function of the production control department or order processing). The exploration seems to have a slight advantage in ability to correct misconceptions and to disregard unimportant information.

In addition, the detailed evaluation of the partial networks of the flows of goods, finances and information showed that the exploration setting had advantages in comparison with the jigsaw setting. This is especially true of the flows of information and partially true of the flows of goods. The percentage of students reconstructing these flows correctly in the posttest increased and the percentage of students reconstructing the flows incorrectly decreased in many areas. Thus, it can be assumed that the employees interviewed were able to communicate order processing procedures within the enterprise completely and effectively. The students in the jigsaw group were able to improve the quality of their knowledge, but not as completely as the exploration group. In addition, mistakes made by members of the jigsaw group often resulted from their inability to understand how individual departments function (for example transport control, materials handling, controlling etc.). This suggests difficulties in integrating new contents into existing knowledge. From a purely quantitative point of view, the number of propositions made by the jigsaw group in the posttest increased as compared with the pretest, while the number in the exploration group decreased; however this did not indicate a qualitative improvement in elaboration of knowledge in the jigsaw group. Further advantages of the exploration setting can be found in motivation, especially interest as one of the variants of learning motivation. Research studies show that interested learning causes extensive elaboration, deeper processing and better understanding of knowledge (Schiefele 1994). This could be true for the exploration group.

In addition, students in the exploration group highlighted the arrangement's potential to help them acquire knowledge and understand complex interdependencies. Finally, some teachers stated that the exploration group was better able to activate and apply knowledge gained in the process of learning new topics than the jigsaw group. Nevertheless, the exploration setting did not prove advantageous in every case or superior to the jigsaw setting. Problems were evident regarding the layout and proof, strategic considerations and ways of payment.

Potential and Limits of Authentic Social Settings and Classroom Settings

In order to explain these results, the specific characteristics and value of boundary-crossing, (i. e. practice, and at the same time the experience of the authentic social and collaborative environment of the enterprise) must be understood. The main aspect seems to be that the exploration group profited by experiencing workplace reality and by hands-on learning situations. Though the students were active only the very periphery of the enterprise in observing production and interviewing experts, even this peripheral participation provided insights into order processing activities. It is probably that the interaction with the company experts played a central role in this process. This interaction facilitated the transfer of expertise in a culture of expert practice which is specific to the activity system enterprise (defined by objects, subjects, mediating artifacts, rules, communities and divisions of labor). Apparently the employees conveyed their expertise in such a way that the contents to be learned acquired practical meaning and were "filled with life". This probably made it easier for students to gain abstract knowledge (such as the flows of information, which are more abstract than the flows of goods). It seems that written materials cannot do this in the same way. In addition, by interacting with experts, students learn to communicate ideas and to clarify their questions about departments and processes. In doing so, they are given direct feedback on their statements and questions. In this way leaving the isolation of the classroom offers additional possibilities for learning and experience (Barron *et al.* 1998: 285). This assumption is supported by the fact that the students in the exploration group singled out practice participation as a positive element within the framework of the total evaluation.

The limitations of the exploration setting could be seen when employees mentioned topics or areas that lie partially *outside of their day-to-day experience* and thus were not considered to the same extent or were more difficult to "fill with life". These topics can sometimes be taught in a better way by using written materials (as in the example of the use of layouts and proofs in the jigsaw group). Both teaching-learning arrangements met their limits when *abstract concepts were to be taught* that lie outside the experiences of the students' everyday lives, as was the case with strategic concerns and flows of finances. In these instances other media, such as simulation games that support the formation of experiences in a vivid way, should be used. Another problem of both arrangements lay in tapping into knowledge from *everyday life or existing economic knowledge*. This could also be seen in the example of the flows of finances. For the students it was hard to imagine that — unlike independent enterprises or private individuals — concerns do not keep their own accounts. The posttest showed that this knowledge was comparatively resistant to change. Here, too, follow-up work in the classroom is necessary and the use of other media to support the students' experiences should be considered.

In conclusion, it is evident that the exploration had advantages because it situated knowledge in real-world contexts, and because it enabled participation in a culture of expert practice. Thus, boundary-crossing in a combination of reification and participation (like boundary encounters) seems to be more conducive to knowledge acquisition and motivation than working with written materials in the school context (or boundary-crossing by working with boundary objects). Furthermore, if the exploration group is better able to link workplace experiences and knowledge learned in schools (as the teachers claimed), the exploration is more effective in activating the potential for brokering knowledge between schools and workplaces in the remainder of the apprenticeship.

Nevertheless, one prerequisite for a successful exploration setting seems to be that student participation be legitimate, on the one hand (as it is guaranteed in the dual system of vocational education). On the other hand, it seems necessary to coordinate their participation with their prior knowledge; otherwise, access to the cultural systems of meanings, as conveyed by the experts, will be impeded, and boundary-crossing will be adversely affected. This assumption is supported by the fact that the students in the exploration group stressed the importance of understandable explanations.

Independent of the results explained above, the company trainers judged the exploration to be an effective tool for understanding the complexity of the company both for themselves and for the students. They now use the description of the company processes and the charts in their own departments in order to train apprentices, trainees and other newcomers. Meanwhile, a comparable exploration has been developed and successfully carried out with apprentices in a technical field.

Acknowledgments

Special thanks to Terttu Tuomi-Gröhn, Fritz Klauser, Sten R. Ludvigsen, Pirjo Lambert, Diane C. Brandt and Roger Fox for their helpful comments on this article.

References

Achtenhagen, F., Nijhof, W., & Raffe, D. (1995). *Feasibility study: Research scope for vocational education in the framework of COST social sciences.* COST Technical Committee, Social Sciences, Vol. 3. Published by the European Commission: Directorate-General XIII, Science, Research and Development. Brussels, Luxembourg: ECSC-EC-EAEC.

Achtenhagen, F., Tramm, T., Preiß, P., Seemann-Weymar, H., John, E. G., & Schunck, A. (1992). *Lernhandeln in komplexen Situationen.* [Learning in complex situations]. Wiesbaden: Gabler.

Aebli, H. (1980). *Denken: Das Ordnen des Tuns, Band 1: Kognitive Aspekte der Handlungstheorie.* [Thinking as ordering of action. Vol. I: Cognitive aspects of action theory]. Stuttgart: Klett-Cotta.

Aebli, H. (1981). *Denken: das Orden des Tuns. Band 2: Denkprozesse.* [Thinking as ordering of action. Vol. II: Thinking processes]. Stuttgart: Klett-Cotta.

Aebli, H. (1989). *Zwölf Grundformen des Lehrens. Eine allgemeine Didaktik auf psychologischer Grundlage.* [12 types of teaching. General didactics on a psychological basis]. (4. Aufl.). Stuttgart: Klett-Cotta.

Aronson, E., Blaney, N., Stephan, C., Sikes, J., & Snapp, M. (1978). *The jigsaw classroom.* Beverly Hills, CA: Sage.

Axelrod, R. (Ed.). (1976). *Structure of decision.* Princeton, NJ: Princeton University Press.

Barron, B. J. S., Schwartz, D. L., Vye, N. J., Moore, A., Petrosino, A., Zech, L., & Bransford, J. D. (1998). Doing with understanding: lessons from research on problem- and project-based learning. *The Journal of the Learning Sciences, 7,* 271–311.

Becker, D., Oldenbürger, H.-A., & Piehl, J. (1987). Motivation und Emotion. [Motivation and emotion]. In: G. Lüer (Ed.), *Allgemeine experimentelle Psychologie* (pp. 431–470). Stuttgart: Fischer.

Brown, J. S., Collins, A., & Duguid, P. (1989). Situated cognition and the culture of learning. *Educational Researcher, 18,* 32–41.

Clarke, J. (1994). Pieces of the puzzle: the jigsaw method. In: S. Sharan (Ed.), *Handbook of cooperative learning methods* (pp. 34–50). Westport, CT: Greenwood.

Collins, A. M., & Quillian, M. R. (1969). Retrieval time from semantic memory. *Journal of Verbal Learning and Verbal Behavior, 8,* 240–247.

Deci, E. L., & Ryan, R. M. (1993). Die Selbstbestimmungstheorie der Motivation und ihre Bedeutung für die Pädagogik. [Theory of self-determination in the context of motivation and its significance for pedagogics]. *Zeitschrift für Pädagogik, 39*, 223–238.

Der Bundesminister für Wirtschaft (1978). *Verordnung über die Berufsausbildung zum Industriekaufmann.* [Training ordinance for industrial clerks]. Bonn.

Der Kultusminister des Landes Nordrhein-Westfalen. (1997). *Richtlinien und Lehrpläne für den Bildungsgang Industriekauffrau/Industriekaufmann.* [Guidelines and curricula for the apprenticeship of industrial clerks].

Deutscher Industrie- und Handelstag (1999). *Leitlinien Ausbildungsreform. Wege zu einer modernen Beruflichkeit.* [Guidelines for reforming apprenticeships. Ways to a modern professionalism]. (2. Aufl.). Bonn.

Dörner, D. (1976). *Problemlösen als Informationsverarbeitung.* [Problem solving as processing of information]. Stuttgart: Kohlhammer.

Engeström, Y. (1987). *Learning by expanding. An activity-theoretical approach to developmental research.* Helsinki: Orienta-Konsultit Oy.

Engeström, Y. (1990). *Learning, working and imagining. Twelve studies in activity theory.* Helsinki: Orienta-Konsultit Oy.

Engeström, Y. (1999a). Activity theory and individual and social transformation. In: Y. Engeström, R. Miettinen, & R-L. Punamäki (Eds), *Perspectives on activity theory* (pp. 19–38). New York: Cambridge.

Engeström, Y. (1999b). Innovative learning in work teams: Analyzing cycles of knowledge creation in practice. In: Y. Engeström, R. Miettinen, & R-L. Punamäki (Eds), *Perspectives on activity theory* (pp. 377–404). New York: Cambridge.

Engeström, Y., Engeström, R., & Kärkkäinen, M. (1995). Polycontextuality and boundary crossing in expert cognition: Learning and problem solving in complex work activities. *Learning and Instruction, 5*, 319–336.

Engeström, Y., & Miettinen, R. (1999). Introduction. In: Y. Engeström, R. Miettinen, & R-L. Punamäki (Eds), *Perspectives on activity theory* (pp. 1–16). New York: Cambridge.

Feller, G. (1995). *Duale Ausbildung: Image und Realität. Eine Bestandsaufnahme aus Lernersicht.* [Apprenticeships in the dual system of vocational education: image and reality. An inventory from the learners' perspective]. Bielefeld: Bertelsmann.

Frey, K. (1990). *Die Projektmethode.* [Projects as instructional method]. (3. Aufl.). Weinheim: Beltz.

Frey, K., & Frey-Eiling, A. (1993). *Allgemeine Didaktik.* [General didactics]. (6. Aufl.). Zürich: vdf.

Galperin, P. J., & Talysina, N. F. (1972). *Die Bildung erster geometrischer Begriffe auf der Grundlage organisierter Handlungen.* [Development of primary geometrical concepts based on organized actions]. Berlin: Volk und Wissen.

Gerstenmaier, J., & Mandl, H. (1995). Wissenserwerb unter konstruktivistischer Perspektive. [Knowledge acquisition from a constructivistic perspective]. *Zeitschrift für Pädagogik, 41*, 867–888.

Hacker, W. (1978). *Allgemeine Arbeits- und Ingenieurpsychologie. Psychische Struktur und Regulation von Arbeitstätigkeiten.* [General psychology of work and engineering. Psychological structure and regulation of working activities]. (2. Aufl.). Bern: Huber.

Hacker, W., & Skell, W. (1993). *Lernen in der Arbeit.* [Learning while working]. Berlin und Bonn: Bundesinstitut für Berufsbildung.

Hurrelmann, K. (1983). Das Modell des produktiv-realitätsverarbeitenden Subjekts in der Sozialisationsforschung. [The socialization research model of subjects who digest reality productively]. *Zeitschrift für Sozialisationsforschung und Erziehungssoziologie, 3*, 91–103.

Janis, I. L. (1982). Counteracting the adverse effects of concurrence-seeking in policy-planning groups: theory and research perspectives. In: H. Brandstätter, J. H. Davis, & G. Stocker-Kreichgauer (Eds), *Group decision making* (pp. 477–501). London: Academic Press.

Jonassen, D. H., Beissner, K., & Yacci, M. (1993). *Structural knowledge. Techniques for representing, conveying and acquiring structural knowledge*. Hillsdale, NJ: Erlbaum.

Keck, A. (1995). *Zum Lernpotential kaufmännischer Arbeitssituationen — Theoretische Überlegungen und empirische Befunde zu Lernprozessen von angehenden Industriekaufleuten an kaufmännischen Arbeitsplätzen*. [Learning potential of workplaces — theoretical considerations and empirical data about industrial-clerk-apprentices' learning processes in workplaces]. Göttingen. Seminar für Wirtschaftspädagogik. Berichte: Band 23.

Klauser, F. (1998). *Identitätsdynamik von Wirtschaftslehrerinnen und Wirtschaftslehrern in den neuen Bundesländern*. [Dynamics of business teachers' identities in the new German states]. Frankfurt: Lang.

Krumm, V. (1973). *Wirtschaftslehreunterricht*. [Business education instruction]. Stuttgart: Klett.

Lave, J., & Wenger, E. (1991). *Situated learning. Legitimate peripheral participation*. New York: Cambridge.

Leontjew, A. N. (1979). *Tätigkeit, Bewußtsein, Persönlichkeit*. [Activity, mind, personality]. Berlin: Volk und Wissen.

Lompscher, J. (1979). Theoretische und methodologische Probleme der psychologischen Tätigkeitsanalyse. [Theoretical and methodological problems of a psychological analysis of activities]. *Probleme und Ergebnisse der Psychologie, 68* (7), 19.

Miller, G. A., Galanter, E., & Pribram, K. H. (1973). *Strategien des Handelns*. [Action strategies]. Stuttgart: Klett.

Norman, D. A., & Rumelhart, D. E. (1978). *Strukturen des Wissens. Wege der Kognitionsforschung*. [Explorations in Cognition]. Stuttgart: Klett-Cotta.

Noß, M. (2000). *Selbstgesteuertes Lernen am Arbeitsplatz*. [Self-directed learning in the workplace]. Wiesbaden: Deutscher Universitäts Verlag.

Opwis, K., & Lüer, G. (1996). Modelle der Repräsentation von Wissen. [Models of knowledge representation]. In: D. Albert, & K.-H. Stapf (Eds), *Enzyklopädie der Psychologie. Themenbereich C: Theorie und Forschung. Serie II: Kognition. Band 4: Gedächtnis* (pp. 337–431). Göttingen: Hogrefe.

Preiß, P. (1999): *Didaktik des wirtschaftsinstrumentellen Rechnungswesens*. [Teaching accounting]. München: Oldenbourg.

Prenzel, M., Drechsel, B., Kliewe, A., Kramer, K., & Röber, N. (1998). *Materialien zum DFG-Projekt "Selbstbestimmt motiviertes und interessiertes Lernen in der kaufmännischen Erstausbildung: Eine Interventionsstudie"*. [Material for the German Science Foundation project: "Self-determined motivated and interested learning in initial vocational education"]. Kiel.

Prenzel, M., Krapp, A., & Schiefele, U. (1986). Grundzüge einer pädagogischen Interessentheorie. [Main outlines of a pedagogical theory of interest]. *Zeitschrift für Pädagogik, 32*, 163–173.

Prenzel, M., Kristen, A., Dengler, P., Ettle, R., & Beer, T. (1996). Selbstbestimmt motiviertes und interessiertes Lernen in der kaufmännischen Erstausbildung. [Self-directed and interested learning in initial vocational education]. *Zeitschrift für Berufs- und Wirtschaftspädagogik, 13*, 108–127.

Pätzold, G., & Walden, G. (Eds) (1995). *Lernorte im dualen System der Berufsbildung*. [Learning venues in the dual system of vocational education]. Bielefeld: Bertelsmann.

Pätzold, G., & Walden, G. (Eds) (1999). *Lernortkooperation — Stand und Perspektiven*. [Cooperation of learning venues — state and perspectives]. Bielefeld: Bertelsmann.

Rebmann, K. (1994). *Komplexität von Lehrbüchern für den Wirtschaftslehreunterricht.* [Complexity of business administration textbooks]. Göttingen: unitext.

Reetz, L. (1984). *Wirtschaftsdidaktik.* [Didactics of business education]. Bad Heilbrunn/Obb.: Klinkhardt.

Reetz, L., & Witt, R. (1974). *Berufsausbildung in der Kritik: Curriculumanalyse Wirtschafts- lehre.* [Criticism of apprenticeships: analysis of business education curricula]. Hamburg: Hoffmann und Campe.

Reigeluth, C. M. (1999): The elaboration theory: guidance for scope and sequence decisions. In: C. M. Reigeluth (Ed.), *Instructional design theories and models* (Vol. II, pp. 425–453). Mahwah, NJ: Erlbaum.

Reigeluth, C. M., & Stein, F. S. (1983). The elaboration theory of instruction. In: C. M. Reigeluth (Ed.), *Instructional design theories and models* (Vol. I, pp. 335–381), Hillsdale, NJ: Erlbaum.

Reinmann-Rothmeier, G., & Mandl, H. (1994). Wissensvermittlung: Ansätze zur Förderung des Wissenserwerbs. [Possibilities of fostering knowledge acquisistion]. In: F. Klix, & H. Spada (Eds), *Wissenspsychologie, C II G Enzyklopädie der Psychologie* (pp. 457–500). Göttingen: Hogrefe.

Rubinstein, S. L. (1977). *Grundlagen der Allgemeinen Psychologie.* [Foundations of general psychology]. Berlin: Volk und Wissen.

Schank, R., & Cleary, C. (1995). *Engines for education.* Hillsdale, NJ: Erlbaum.

Scheele, B., & Groeben, N. (1984). *Die Heidelberger Struktur-Lege-Technik (SLT). Eine Dialog- Konsens-Methode zur Rekonstruktion Subjektiver Theorien mittlerer Reichweite.* [Reconstructing naive (subjective) theories with the help of the Heidelberg structure-depiction technique]. Weinheim: Beltz.

Schiefele, U. (1994). *Motivation und Lernen mit Texten.* [Motivation and learning by using texts]. München: Universität der Bundeswehr.

Sekretariat der Ständigen Konferenz der Kultusminister der Länder in der Bundesrepublik Deutschland. (1995). *Rahmenlehrplan für den Ausbildungsberuf Industriekaufmann/Indus- triekauffrau.* [Skeleton curriculum for vocational training of industrial clerks].

Sekretariat der Ständigen Konferenz der Kultusminister der Länder in der Bundesrepublik Deutschland. (1998). *Überlegungen der Kultusministerkonferenz zur Weiterentwicklung der Berufsbildung.* [Considerations of the Conference of Educational Ministers concerning developments of vocational education].

Sekretariat der Ständigen Konferenz der Kultusminister der Länder in der Bundesrepublik Deutschland. (1999). *Handreichungen für die Erarbeitung von Rahmenlehrplänen der Kultusministerkonferenz (KMK) für den berufsbezogenen Unterricht in der Berufsschule und ihre Abstimmung mit den Ausbildungsordnungen des Bundes für anerkannte Ausbildungsbe- rufe.* [Guidelines for the development of a skeleton curriculum for vocational instruction in vocational schools and their coordination with the federal training ordinances for acknowl- edged occupations].

Shavelson, R. J., & Ruiz-Primo, M. A. (1999). Leistungsbewertung im naturwissenschaftlichen Unterricht. [Evaluation in Natural Science Instruction]. *Unterrichtswissenschaft, 27,* 102–127.

Star, S. L. (1989). The structure of ill-structured solutions: boundary objects and heterogenous distributed problem solving. In: L. Gasser, & M. N. Huhns (Eds), *Distributed artificial intelligence* (Vol. II). San Mateo: Morgan Kaufman Publishers.

Star, S. L., & Griesemer, J. R. (1989). Institutional ecology, 'translations' and boundary objects: amateurs and professionals in Berkeley's museum of vertebrate zoology 1907–39. *Social Studies of Science, 19,* 387–420.

Suchman, L. (1994). Working relations of technology production and use. *Computer Supported Cooperative Work, 2,* 21–39.

Söltenfuß, G. (1983). *Grundlagen handlungsorientierten Lernens. Dargestellt an einer didaktischen Konzeption im Simulationsbüro.* [Foundations of action oriented learning. Didactic conception of a simulated office]. Bad Heilbrunn/Obb.: Klinkhardt.

Tergan, S.-O. (1986). *Modelle der Wissensrepräsentation als Grundlage qualitativer Diagnostik.* [Models of knowledge representation as basis for qualitative diagnostics]. Opladen: Westdeutscher Verlag.

Tramm, T. (1992). *Konzeption und theoretische Grundlagen einer evaluativ-konstruktiven Curriculumstrategie — Entwurf eines Forschungsprogramms unter der Perspektive des Lernhandelns.* [Curriculum development — conception and theoretical foundations]. Göttingen. Seminar für Wirtschaftspädagogik. Berichte: Band 17.

Tramm, T., & Rebmann, K. (1997). Handlungsorientiertes Lernen in und an Modellen. In: G. Lübke & B. Riesebieter (Eds). *Zur Theorie und Praxis des SIMBA-Einsatzes in der kaufmännischen Aus- und Weiterbildung.* [SIMBA in initial and further vocational education — theory and practice] (pp. 1–38). Markhausen.

Ulrich, H. (1968). *Die Unternehmung als produktives soziales System.* [Enterprises as productive social systems]. Bern: Haupt.

Ulrich, H. (1984). *Management.* Bern: Haupt.

Ulrich, H. (1985). *Plädoyer für ganzheitliches Denken.* [Plea for holistic thinking]. Aulavorträge, Heft 32. St. Gallen: Hochschule St. Gallen für Wirtschafts- und Sozialwissenschaften.

Volpert, W. (1979). Der Zusammenhang von Arbeit und Persönlichkeit aus handlungs-psychologischer Sicht. [Connections between work and personality from an action psychological perspective]. In: P. Groskurth (Ed.), *Arbeit und Persönlichkeit: berufliche Sozialisation in der arbeitsteiligen Gesellschaft* (pp. 21–46). Reinbek bei Hamburg: Rowohlt.

Volpert, W. (1980). Psychologische Handlungstheorie — Anmerkungen zu Stand und Perspektive. [Psychological action-control theory — remarks concerning current state and perspective]. In: W. Volpert (Ed.), *Beiträge zur psychologischen Handlungsregulationstheorie* (pp. 13–27). Bern: Huber.

Von Cranach, M., Kalbermatten, U., Indermühle, K., & Gugler, B. (1980). *Zielgerichtetes Handeln.* [Goal-oriented action]. Bern: Huber.

Wenger, E. (1998). *Communities of practice. Learning, meaning, and identity.* New York: Cambridge University Press.

White, R. & Gunstone, R. (1999). Alternativen zur Erfassung von Verstehensprozessen. [Alternatives in the Assessment of Understanding]. *Unterrichtswissenschaft, 27*, 128–134.

Wygotski, L. S. (1964). *Denken und Sprechen.* [Thinking and speaking]. Berlin: Akademie-Verlag.

Chapter 6

Developing Competence During Practice Periods: The Learner's Perspective

Johan van der Sanden and Christa Teurlings

Referring to Cormier and Hagman's well-known publication on transfer (Cormier & Hagman 1987), Mayer & Wittrock (1996) have stated that transfer occurs "when a person's prior experience and knowledge affect learning or problem solving in a new situation". They go on to say that ". . . transfer refers to the effect of knowledge that was learned in a previous situation (task A) on learning or performance in a new situation (task B)" (p. 48). In these descriptions the 'new situation' can either be one in which there is a task to be performed or a problem to be solved, or one in which new learning is supposed to take place. In many other approaches to transfer, however, the focus only is on an individual's performance in a 'new situation' after she or he has been trained in another learning situation. As a negative example in the field of work and organizational psychology, we point to Broad & Newstrom (1992). These authors, as well as many others, have called attention to the problem that when employees are trained ". . . most of the knowledge and skills gained in training (well over 80% by some estimates) is not fully applied by those employees on the job" (p. ix). In the same vein Baldwin & Ford (1988) have claimed that as a rule only 10% of expenditures on training in organizations lead to on-the-job application.

What stands out in these approaches is the separation between learning and applying what is learned in a new situation. In our view especially theories and approaches that separate learning and applying are amenable to the 'portable knowledge' critique, as forwarded by theories of situated learning (see Chapter 2). It is difficult indeed to imagine somebody performing a new task in a new situation, without learning taking place. One could say that when no new learning is required, the 'new' situation activates relevant prior knowledge or triggers an automated previously learned response. Under such circumstances the situation is not a new one, or perhaps more importantly, is not perceived by the actor as a new situation. In that case it is doubtful whether one should speak of transfer; some might prefer the qualification very 'near' transfer.

In the research projects we are involved in, we do not ask ourselves how to devise learning environments that optimize learning in 'situation A' such that applying what is learned in 'situation B' proceeds erroneously. It is more fruitful to focus on the process of competence development in 'new' work or work-like situations and the factors that influence it. Thus, we are interested in the type of learning that goes on when boundaries between situations are crossed. Though 'competence' is often interpreted as 'having sufficient skill' or 'being sufficiently qualified' (Eraut 1994), we prefer to take a broader perspective (see also Van der Sanden, Terwel & Vosniadou 2000), and want to call attention to the organized whole of knowledge, skills, attitudes, and learning abilities that is typical of competent behavior. We deliberately include learning ability as an important aspect of competence. It is viewed as a mixture of metacognitive knowledge and learning skills, a disposition to apply and improve one's learning skills in varied potential learning situations, an adequate individual learning theory and the willingness to test, elaborate, and refine this theory.

According to Van der Sanden *et al.* (op. cit.) students' individual learning theories serve as personal frameworks for learning and instruction with regard to a particular domain. It is assumed that instructional strategies and measures do not directly influence students' learning processes and learning results (cf. Van der Sanden 1997; Vermetten 1999; Wierstra & Beerends 1996), but that "... it is the students' perceptions of the learning environment that influence how a student learns, not necessarily the context itself" (Entwistle 1991: 202). It is supposed that the way students interpret a learning environment is influenced by their individual learning theories. Van der Sanden *et al.* (op. cit.) have suggested that individual learning theories are composed of conceptual as well as procedural elements, and may consist of a more or less integrated and internally consistent set of the following:

- ideas, beliefs, and convictions about the entities and issues that are dealt with in a certain domain and, consequently, what learning in the domain is about;
- general and domain-related epistemological beliefs;
- general and domain-related learning conceptions;
- presumptions about the distinctive features of competent behavior regarding the subject matter area, about the typical difficulties involved in thinking and problem solving and about one's subjective competence concerning the field;
- individual goals and goal orientations;
- preferences for particular learning situations and learning activities;
- preferences for particular instructional events and measures, and ideas about the role of experts, teachers and fellow students in acquiring competence.

Though research into the development, and the role of individual learning theories is scarce as yet, a number of studies have shed light on the role elements of such theories play in school learning.

Ng & Bereiter (1992), for instance, performed a qualitative study on the influence of goal orientations on learning activities and learning results with regard to a BASIC programming course. On the basis of thinking-aloud protocols three different goal-orientations were found among adult subjects who voluntarily took the course: so-called task-completion, instructional, and personal knowledge-building goals. Subjects in the first group were striving for the completion of the tasks set by the teacher. Subjects in the second group were trying to reach the instructional goals specified by the teacher. Subjects in the third group were actively engaged in knowledge construction processes for which they set goals themselves.

Students who set themselves knowledge building goals were found to actively use their prior knowledge. They tried to reconsider and accommodate their preconceptions when they judged such cognitive activities appropriate. They generated additional questions, posed new problems, and eventually obtained the best learning results. Ng and Bereiter characterized the learning situation these subjects were involved in as a ". . . constructive interaction between prior knowledge and new information" and as ". . . a dialectical process in which prior knowledge not only influenced new learning, but new learning was used to reconstruct prior knowledge" (p. 258).

Subjects with instructional goals confined themselves to activities that were programmed by the teacher. Though they tried to use their prior knowledge in solving the assigned problems, they never appeared to reorganize or accomodate their personal knowledge base.

Students who set themselves task-completion goals turned out to work and exercise diligently and purposefully. Compared to the two other goal-orientation groups, they were found to spend the most learning time on the BASIC course. They also regularly wondered whether they were performing up to the standards set by the teacher. Prior knowledge, however, was only used to solve small problems and not to gain more insight into the BASIC programming language.

Differences between students with regard to the way they approach learning situations have also been studied from a learning style perspective. In the Netherlands, Vermunt's learning style theory (Vermunt 1998) is frequently referred to in this respect. Conventional learning style theories (e.g. Honey & Mumford 1982; Kolb 1984) usually pertain to individual differences in preferred learning activities. Vermunt, however, has broadened the concept and conceives of learning styles as general, relatively consistent, and characteristic combinations of learning conceptions, motivational orientations, preferred regulation activities, and preferred subject matter processing activities. In a number of studies performed in higher education it was found that students with constructive learning conceptions and intrinsic motivational orientations tend to use self regulation and 'deep' (Van Rossum & Schenk 1984) meaning-oriented learning activities, whereas students with reproductive learning conceptions mainly rely on external regulation and prefer shallow reproduction-oriented learning activities. Slaats, Lodewijks & Van der Sanden (1999) found similar results in the field of senior secondary vocational education.

An adapted version of Vermunt's Inventory of Learning Styles (Vermunt 1992) was used by Gordijn (1998) in a study on the effects of feedback, which was added to computerized modules on engineering and technology in junior secondary technical education. Gordijn compared simple (right-wrong) and elaborative types of feedback. The latter type was based on Merrill's Component Display Theory (Merrill 1983), which gives explicit prescriptions for the design of instruction (see also Dijkstra 1997; Reigeluth 1987). It was expected that this type of feedback would promote insightful learning and transfer for all students. However, compared to students who learned under simple feedback conditions, only the students with reproductive learning styles were found to improve their learning scores. Moreover, this effect only occurred with regard to reproduction type questions. It seems that these students did not to use the extra help and explanations offered by the complex feedback information for insightful learning, but for their preferred ways of reproduction-oriented learning. Essentially, again referring to Entwistle (1991), it is the students' perceptions of the learning environment that directly influence what they pay attention to and how they learn, independently of the instructional design-theory-based characteristics imposed.

Acknowledging the role of learning conceptions, epistemological beliefs and goal orientations in subject-matter oriented school learning (see also Slaats *et al.* 1999; Van der Sanden 1997; Van der Sanden *et al.* 2000), we were curious about the role these and other elements of individual learning theories play when students learn in competence-oriented practice periods. We set up a number of studies bearing on this theme; in the next section of this chapter the main findings of these qualitative and correlational studies are presented. As indicated above, we regard learning ability as an important constituent of competence. It is becoming increasingly important to design competence-oriented learning environments that foster learning ability and boundary crossing competencies. The question how to devise such learning environments is dealt within section 'Competence-Oriented Learning Environments'. An experimental study with regard to word processing competencies serves as an illustration. In the final section, individual and collective learning and transfer are treated in relation to each other (cf. Dixon 1994). We will describe some ongoing research projects in the field of teacher training that are inspired by recent theories on and approaches to collective and productive learning (Dixon 1994; Engeström 1987).

The Development of Competence During Practice Periods

In vocational education, practical training periods and internships are considered to play an important role in the development of competence. Yet little research has been done on the situated learning and transfer processes that take place during such practice periods. Typically students are put into an apprentice role, confronted with authentic tasks and problems and, as a rule, have direct and concrete experiences with employees, work-related events and phenomena. As a consequence, students' codified knowledge acquired in school settings is confronted with the more situated and episodic knowledge that results from workplace experiences (see also Guile & Young, this volume). Though practice periods can be partly prestructured, informal and 'everyday' learning from unplanned incidents is probably equally important (Center for Workforce Development 1998; Eraut 1994). Work experience places can be expected to differ with regard to the learning opportunities offered (Onstenk 1997). Besides that, students differ in the learning activities they apply. It is important in this respect to recognize, select and take advantage of opportunities offered, as well as create complementary learning opportunities under circumstances that may not always be beneficial to learning (cf. Onstenk 1997; Simons, Teurlings & Mulder 1998).

In this section we will review a number of empirical studies performed on work-related learning processes during practice periods in different vocational education settings (e.g.. health care education, technical education, social work education). Inspired by social-constructivist theories of learning (e.g. Byrnes 1996), we took the learners' perspective as a starting point. The emphasis is on learning activities and competence development during practice periods and the way these variables relate to, among other things, student learning conceptions, epistemological beliefs, and goal orientations as elements of individual learning theories. Student notions on the function and meaning of practice periods can be embedded in such theories and it seems reasonable to expect individual differences in this respect.

This section is divided into four parts. First, some descriptive studies with regard to learning activities during practice periods are presented. Second, relations between learning activities during practice periods, school periods and goal-orientations are examined. Third, some findings are presented from qualitative studies on competence development during practice periods, viewed from the learner's perspective. Fourth, the role individual learning theories play during practice periods is discussed.

Learning Activities During Practice Periods

In vocational education and corporate training practice periods, internships or on-the-job learning situations are frequently used to foster the development of work-related competence. Research into learning activities and processes of competence development during such work-related learning situations is still in its infancy; indeed, school-based learning has received a lot more attention from researchers.

In the studies we performed with regard to learning processes during practice periods, students' learning activities were central. It is assumed that the quantity and quality of these learning activities largely determine what, and how, much students learn from the many personal experiences encountered during those practice periods (Vermunt 1992). Our studies concerned learning and practice situations in different domains, i.e. nursery education (Fasol 1996; Van der Sanden, Fasol & Teurlings 1997), carpentry, bricklaying and metal working apprenticeship systems (In 't Groen 1996), higher commercial education (Rietbroek 1998), and higher social work education (Teurlings & Van der Sanden 1999).

In most of these studies, Slaats' approach to the study of students' learning activities in the school-based part of senior secondary vocational education was taken as a starting point. With her Inventory of Learning Styles (LSI-VE; Slaats 1997; Slaats *et al.* 1999) it is possible to measure the students' use of, among other things, 'integrative learning activities' and 'reproductive learning activities', as well as two categories of regulation activities, i.e. 'internal regulation' and 'external regulation activities'. As an example of the way learning during practice periods was studied in these field studies, we present some details of Fasol's study.

Fasol adapted Slaats' Inventory of Learning Styles to learning situations that were typical for practice periods in nursing education. She was interested in student differences with regard to learning activities applied during these practice periods (Fasol 1996; Van der Sanden *et al.* 1997). Two groups of student nurses participated in her study.

The first group of 42 students (taking part in the pilot study) had to complete a short questionnaire consisting of two questions. First, students were asked to describe situations in in-service training in which they had learned a lot, and second, they had to indicate what they had learned in those situations. In this study sixteen categories of typical instructive situations were gathered; these included 'confrontation with terminal care', 'observing expert nurses' and 'dealing with troublesome patients'. Ten of these categories were used to develop an adapted version of the Inventory of Learning Styles.

The second group of 146 students participated in the main study, and completed the original Inventory of Learning Styles to obtain information on learning activities during school-based learning periods as well as the adapted version to measure the use of learning activities during practice periods. For each of the ten situations, students had to indicate: (1) to what extent they found several 'candidate' learning activities desirable; (2) to what extent they found these learning activities applicable in the specified situation; and (3) to what extent they themselves would use the learning activities. In Fasol's study the differences between students' appreciation and intended use of learning activities during practice periods could be traced back to two factors. The first factor represented a tendency to prefer and apply self-directive, integrative, and reflective learning activities; the second factor pointed to a more externally oriented and reproductive learning orientation.

The same pattern emerged in the other studies mentioned above with students from other target groups as participants (In 't Groen 1996; Rietbroek 1998; Teurlings & Van der Sanden 1999). However, in these studies students were not asked to indicate what learning activities they would employ (as Fasol did), but to assess the extent to which they actually used a number of learning activities during practice periods.

Relations Between Learning Activities During Practice Periods, Learning Activities During School Periods, and Goal Orientations

In several studies we tried to find relations between preferred learning activities while learning at school and learning activities undertaken during practice periods. In 't Groen (1996) was interested in the learning activities of carpenters, bricklayers and metal workers who took courses under the Dutch apprenticeship scheme. He first interviewed a number of participants about their learning practices. Subsequently, he used the obtained information to construct two questionnaires: one referring to learning at school, the other one referring to learning during practice periods. He found strong relations between learning activities applied in school and those employed in practice situations. In the study discussed above Fasol (1996) came to the same conclusion. Though different types of knowledge are involved, students apparently do not differentiate between learning strategies for acquiring codified and situated knowledge (Guile & Young, this volume).

In other studies students' habitual way of studying at school was assessed by means of the Inventory of Learning Styles (ILS) developed by Vermunt (1992). Learning activities during practice periods were assessed by newly developed questionnaires

(Rietbroek 1998; Teurlings & Van der Sanden 1999). It was found that students who tend to integrate prior (codified) knowledge with new (situated) information and experiences during practice periods scored relatively high on the ILS scales measuring deep and concrete learning activities.

To examine relations between learning activities during practice periods and students' goal orientations, we developed a questionnaire to measure these orientations with regard to practice periods. The questionnaire was based on instruments developed by Nicholls (1989) and adapted by Duda & Nicholls (1992) and Vermetten, Lodewijks & Vermunt (in press; see also Vermetten 1999). Nicholls (1989) makes a distinction between task-orientation and ego-orientation. For task-oriented students learning has an intrinsic value; they apply learning activities with the primary aim of improving their competence. Ego-oriented students' learning activities, on the contrary, are mainly directed at establishing their superiority relative to others. So, instead of improving competence, their focus is on proving competence. Next to the categories 'task and ego-orientation', the questionnaire contained scales measuring an orientation towards the avoidance of tasks and feelings of superiority. We found that students who preferred deep learning activities (like reflecting, integrating and internal regulation) during practice periods were less ego-oriented, less task-avoiding, and less imbued with feelings of superiority. Students, however, with preferences for shallow and reproductive learning activities during practice periods turned out to be more ego-oriented.

Subjective Competence Development During Practice Periods

Recently, Eraut, Alderton, Cole & Senker (1998) published their report on 'development of knowledge and skills in employment'. In this report they present the findings of a research project that was part of 'The Learning Society' program of the Economic and Social Research Council in Great Britain. Their three main questions were: "(1) What is being learned at work?; (2) How is learning taking place?; (3) What other factors affect the amount and direction of learning in the workplace?" (Eraut *et al.* 1998: 3). Interestingly, they made no prior assumptions about the role of education and training in competence development. They collected information by means of double interviews (6–12 months apart) with 120 employees of work organizations in the engineering, business, and healthcare sectors.

We are presently engaged in a similar study on the development of competence of novice train guards, who are employed by the Dutch railway corporation. In these interview studies comparisons are made between off- and on-the-job learning, both being part of the introductory work period of novice train guards. We will return to this study later. First, we want to present some findings of an interview-based study on the competence development of higher social work students during school based as well as work experience place based learning periods.

Though we were interested in obtaining answers to the same type of questions as in the Eraut *et al.* (op. cit.) study, we took a different approach. Eight students whose performance during practice periods was evaluated positively and nine whose performance was evaluated negatively were asked to participate in our study. We held individual interviews with these 17 students, using the so-called 'story-line method' (Gergen 1988; Sannen 1997). Students were first asked to visualize their professional development by drawing lines in a diagram. Each student produced two graphs, one representing his or her development of competence as a social worker with regard to the study period as a whole, the other representing development of competence during a third or fourth-year practice period. With these story lines as a starting point, students were asked to explain the course of their professional development, and describe three of the most important factors, that in their view, played an important role. Subsequently, interview data were content-analyzed, using a phenomenographical approach (e.g. Marton & Säljö 1984). Because the students who were interviewed also participated in another part of the study, their learning style scores (pertaining to school-offered courses and measured by Vermunt's ILS (Vermunt, op. cit.)) were available to us as well.

Story-lines and interview data revealed considerable differences between students. Gergen's (1988) six types (ascending, descending, tragedy, comedy, romantic, and happily-ever-after) were apparent in the story-lines drawn by the apprentices. Moreover, two other types emerged, which were labeled 'growing' and 'not happily-ever-after after all'. Especially for students with negative evaluations, story-lines were found to be unstable (comedy, romantic, and not-happily-ever-after); students with positive evaluations as a rule gave evidence of increasing story-line types (ascending, happily-ever-after, and growing). These differences between positively and negatively evaluated students were especially conspicuous with regard to the story-lines representing the third-year practice period.

In explaining the course of competence development, about 40% of the factors held accountable by students referred to characteristics of the work experience place, about 25% to person variables, about 20% to characteristics of the school curriculum and teaching practices, and about 15% to personal relations. Person and work experience place variables often were reported to have had a negative influence, whereas school and teaching variables were judged more positively. Negatively evaluated students' development was largely attributed to work experience place and personal relation variables, and positively evaluated students' development predominantly to person variables.

The interviews further revealed that students differed with regard to their conceptions of the role of practice periods. Some students mainly see practice periods as opportunities for applying knowledge and skills acquired at school. For them it is important that they learn the 'right' things at school, because that makes them well-prepared for out-of-school activities. Other students accentuate the possibilities of further learning in authentic and context-rich work-related environments. In the railway guard study alluded to above we found the same type of differences with regard to the role of off- and on-the-job training situations (Voskes 1999). Most of the novice railway guards we interviewed were of the opinion that learning on-the-job (i.e. on the train) was by far more effective than learning off-the-job. This position is illustrated by the following statement of one of the participants: "During the course you are told by the trainer what to do on the train; being on-the-job, however, my coach asked me to quickly forget what was instructed".

Regarding the learning style data, we found that negatively evaluated students showed more characteristics of a reproduction-oriented learning style than positively evaluated students. Therefore we wonder whether differences in students' interpretation of the 'theoretical' school-based component can in some way account for the process of competence development during practice periods. Perhaps successful students view this school period as already having relevance for their personal development of professional identity. Practice periods constitute situations in which they can construct new knowledge and skills, rather than merely trying to apply previously acquired school knowledge. On the other hand, practice periods may confront unsuccessful students with their inability to apply not yet deeply rooted and personalized knowledge, which hinders the process of further task-oriented learning.

The Role of Individual Learning Theories in Learning During Practice Periods

In constructivist learning theories (e.g.. Driver, Asoko, Leach, Mortimer & Scott 1994; Dudley Herron 1996), learning is conceived of as the process of elaborating and restructuring prior knowledge (see also Boekaerts & Simons 1993). As Dixon (1994) has stated, a constructivist view of learning ". . . starts from the position that learning is the act of interpreting experience, that interpretation is unique to each individual and is both enabled and constrained by the individual's process of sense making" (Dixon 1994: 11). Constructivist theories of learning are usually contrasted with objectivist theories. In the latter, learning is seen as absorbing externally defined and stored knowledge, while teaching takes the form of handing down new pieces of knowledge by the teacher to increase the amount of knowledge in the learner's heads. Byrnes (1996) compares objectivist teachers to bricklayers involved in building a wall: they typically try to build a knowledge-wall inside the students heads by laying neatly organized bricks in the 'right spot'. Constructivist teachers, on the other hand, provide the bricks and help the students build their own wall (pp. 13–14).

Scientists develop theories with the aim of describing and explaining phenomena and to allow for predictions. It is, however, a human tendency to develop personal theories to create a frame of reference to describe and categorize things, people and phenomena, to explain and anticipate differences between events and to undertake purposeful action in a variety of situations (see Driver & Easley 1978; Van der Sanden, Terwel & Vosniadou, op. cit.). Such individual theories serve a conceptual-declarative function, but usually also involve procedural blueprints or action scripts. As examples we point to Kelly's cognitive theory of personality (Kelly 1955), in which individual naive personality theories are central, and the concept of individual action theories (Argyris & Schön 1978; Van der Krogt 1995) in the field of work-related organizational learning theory.

Our concept of individual learning theory is based on the position that scientific learning theories have their individual, naive and non-scientific counterparts. As is the case with scientific learning theories, these individual learning theories may be more or less internally consistent. Indeed, the studies on learning conceptions and goal orientations reviewed in this chapter, as well as other studies regarding these topics (see also Slaats *et al.* 1999; Van der Sanden *et al.* 2000) point to laymen variants of objectivistic as well as constructivistic learning theories. Conceptions about the role of practice periods seem to fit into these individual learning theories. Students with objectivistic individual learning theories may view practice situations as occasions for applying previously learned general, 'portable' and 'ready-made' knowledge. The separation between learning and applying, mentioned in the introductory section of this chapter, becomes apparent here. More constructivistic individual learning theories, on the other hand, may lead to an interpretation of practice situations as settings in which new knowledge, skills, and attitudes can be constructed or prior ones be reconstructed (Lodewijks, Schellings & Van der Sanden, submitted; Ng & Bereiter 1992; Teurlings & Van der Sanden 1999).

Competence-Oriented Learning Environments

In the previous section we reviewed a number of descriptive and/or correlational studies on students' learning processes and competence development during practice periods. As stated before, we hold learning ability to be an important constituent of competence. In agreement with this view we do not conceive of transfer as the ability to apply successfully what was learned in a training situation, but as the ability to learn constructively and to progressively recontextualize knowledge, skills, and attitudes (see also Van Oers 1998; Young & Guile, this volume). The question of how to design competence-oriented learning environments that foster learning ability and boundary crossing competencies is the core of this section.

We shall report here on an experimental study with regard to word processing competencies (for more information: see Teurlings, Van der Sanden, Simons & Lodewijks, submitted). To improve word processing competencies, we designed a learning environment focusing on the German Leittext method (Koch 1992; Koch & Selka 1991; Selka & Conrad 1987) and a number of cognitive apprenticeship based instructional strategies (see Collins, Brown & Newman 1989). The Leittext method, originally developed in German industry, aims at stimulating self-regulated learning and working. Because we were not satisfied with the learning-to-learn potential of the conventional Leittext approach, we added several instructional strategies and tools, based on the cognitive apprenticeship paradigm.

At the time of our study Word Perfect 5.1 was a commonly used word processing package in the Netherlands, and many training institutes offered courses that as a rule were designed according to traditional practice-and-drill principles. Lack-of-transfer from training to work situations was (and is) a frequently observed phenomenon. In our study we conceptualized transfer as the ability to learn constructively and independently in post-training situations. Following our views on transfer, we highlighted learning-to-learn word processing competencies in the cognitive apprenticeship-based learning environment that figured in the experimental condition of our study.

In our learning environment learners had to execute some authentic word processing tasks. To perform these tasks, they had to activate and recontextualize their newly acquired knowledge and skills. While working on the authentic tasks, learners had to communicate about the problem-solving process and the learning process with other learners and with the trainer, who was an expert in word processing. While executing the tasks, learners were required to follow the six phases of the so-called 'Leittext-method' The Leittext-cycle is depicted in Figure 1 and consists of the following six phases: informing (orienting), planning, deciding, executing, checking, and evaluating.

In the first phase, *'orienting'* or *'informing'*, learners were required to consult and gather information about the word processing task they had to perform. They were offered ways to learn how to execute certain skills by observing an expert (in real-life or on videotape). Learners were assisted by learning aids such as different types of questions (called 'Leitfragen' in German). These questions helped the learners analyze and build up an internal representation of the task. In the second phase, *'planning'*, learners planned what they were going to do and specified what standards had to be reached. During this planning phase they also selected the relevant materials and tools (for example the word processing functions) they were going to use. At the same time, they formulated the requirements the product (i.e. the letter) had to meet. Following the planning phase, learners discussed the plans and criteria they had developed with the trainer. On the basis of this discussion (the *'deciding'* phase) decisions had to be taken about how to proceed. During the fourth phase, *'executing'*, learners executed the task according to their plan. After finishing the task, learners first checked their own work

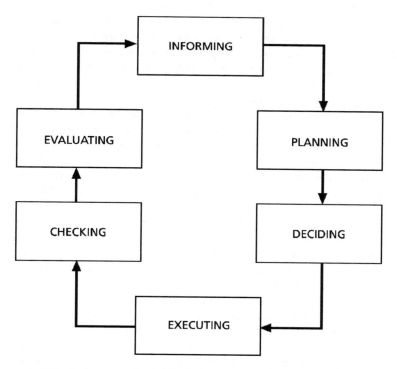

Figure 1: The Leittext method (Koch & Selka 1991; Selka & Conrad 1987).

(*'checking'*). After that, the trainer checked the learner's work. Finally, the learner and the trainer together *evaluated* how the task was done and what could be improved next time.

With these six Leittext-phases, some combination of coaching, scaffolding and fading, articulation, reflection, and exploration was provided for (see Teurlings *et al.*, submitted). Additionally, by presenting students with the six phases, the way experts go about performing (and learning to perform) tasks was made explicit. Therefore, the Leittext cycle can be regarded as a model of expert performance (including learning behavior). In addition to making the relevant thinking and learning activities explicit, we also demonstrated these activities (cf. Brown, Collins & Duguid 1989; Collins *et al.* 1989; Duffy & Jonassen 1991) by showing the learners a videotape on how to learn to use the word processor in producing texts. The tape showed an 'exemplary learner' who went through the six phases of the Leittext method while thinking aloud. We therefore made explicit *and* demonstrated the thinking *and* learning activities that we considered relevant for the domain of word processing (cf. Landa 1983).

Additionally, we considered the development of an adequate individual learning theory to be an essential part of word processing competence. In assisting the learners to construct (and elaborate) such an individual learning theory, we provided them with a concrete and application-oriented topical overview of the essential learning contents regarding the use of the word processor and their relations. This overview, called epitome (cf. Reigeluth 1987; Reigeluth & Stein 1983), was intended to help learners construct a frame of reference by which they could interpret new information and new experiences. It stressed relations with knowledge that learners had already required. However, the overview was also accompanied by a videotape figuring an 'exemplary novice'. In this way, the epitome was meant to be a concrete introductory illustration of both the essential learning contents *and* the learning and thinking activities described before (for example orienting, planning, checking).

Having completed the epitome, learners were confronted with a series of diverse tasks in which new learning contents were presented in an elaborative sequence. During the training, complexity was increased by adding more details to the previously presented overview of the learning contents. An elaborative sequence of the learning contents was thus created (cf. Reigeluth & Stein 1983). Moreover, learners were explicitly stimulated to apply integrative thinking and learning activities that were expected to lead to richer mental representations of the learning contents (to help them construct adequate individual learning theories). In elaborating the overview, and relating this representation to their own prior knowledge structures, learners were stimulated to form an integrative representation of Word Perfect related procedures, concepts, and principles, instead of more fragmented representations (cf. Teurlings & Simons 1992).

In doing so, learners confronted with the cognitive apprenticeship-based learning program were required both to perform word processing tasks by activating and recontextualizing their knowledge and skills, to learn new word processing skills, and to develop an adequate individual learning theory. In other words, we both emphasized the role of problem solving skills, autonomous learning skills and an adequate individual learning theory as essential parts of word processing competence (see also Van der Sanden, Terwel & Vosniadou 2000). Referring to Collins *et al.* (1989), this learning environment emphasized a mixture of domain knowledge, heuristic strategies, control strategies, and (especially) learning strategies and learning concepts (as parts of learning theories).

The experiment: main results and discussion   Forty-two volunteers were randomly divided into an experimental and a control group, which were found to be comparable with regard to age, level of education, typing speed, experience with computers, preferred learning and regulation activities, motivational orientations and learning conceptions (the latter variables measured by an adapted version of Vermunt's ILS; Vermunt 1992). The experimental group was trained according to the process-oriented cognitive apprenticeship-based learning environment described above. The control group was treated according to an expository and traditional training strategy, which mainly emphasized the practicing of skills. In this course, most potential learning activities (e.g.. setting criteria and making plans) were taken over by the trainer or the training program. Learning contents were first explained to the learners (*explaining*), after which certain skills were demonstrated (*showing*). In the third phase, the learners imitated the trainer (*imitating*), followed by some exercises (*practicing*), with the teacher evaluating their performance. Both courses were provided at Tilburg University and took up six meetings, totalling 32 hours each.

Both immediately after the course, and six weeks later, information was gathered with regard to several dependent variables. In this chapter we restrict ourselves to short-term and long-term learning-to-learn results, which were inferred from students' performance on new learning tasks (i.e. learning a new Word Perfect option), which they had to do on their own.

No differences between the two training groups were found on tasks requiring reproduction of acquired domain knowledge and skills $(F(1,39) = 2.44; p > 0.05)$. Learners from the experimental group, however, were more capable of independently learning new WordPerfect options. This effect was established both immediately after the course (Kruskal-Wallis Oneway analysis of variance: $H = 23.40; p < 0.00$), and six weeks later $(F(1,36) = 5.04; p < 0.05)$. For an illustration of these transfer (i.e. learning-to-learn) effects see Table 1.

Apparently the experimental learning environment was effective in fostering both the learning of more specific domain knowledge and skills, and the development of autonomous learning skills in the domain of word processing. We assume that the epitome and the elaborative way in which the learning tasks were sequenced, together

Table 1: Short- and long-term independent learning effects.

	Short-term learning effects	Long-term learning effects
Control training group	2.50	4.51
Experimental training group	10.00	7.77

with the explicit attention that was given to strategies for acquiring word processing skills, put students in a position to both develop adequate (i.e. constructive) Word Perfect related individual learning theories and effective learning skills. It can be concluded that the process-oriented cognitive apprenticeship-based learning environment enhanced students' word-processing competence, which enabled them to continue learning constructively and independently in new post-training situations.

Individual and Collective Learning

In the studies reviewed in the previous section, learning activities of students occupying work experience places offered by various work organizations were approached from an individual viewpoint. Students' learning activities and learning processes during practice periods were studied and related to psychological background variables, which were treated as elements of individual learning theories. As Dixon (1994) and many others do, we make a distinction between individual, group and organizational learning. According to Dixon (op. cit.) organizational learning is ". . . the intentional use of learning processes at the individual, group and system level to continuously transform the organization in a direction that is increasingly satisfying to its stakeholders" (p. 5).

When work organizations in the Netherlands create and offer work experience places to schools and students (within and outside the apprenticeship system), they do not do this because they want to learn as organizations from the students and schools involved. The typical situation is the other way around: they want to expose individual apprentices to existing individual and collective meaning structures, which can be tacit and explicit (Dixon, op. cit.). Far from being put into a change agent role, as is advocated in Engeström's views on expansive learning and developmental transfer (see Chapter 2), students are required to develop competencies the organization and its members already are assumed to possess.

Increasingly, however, work organizations find themselves confronted with rapid changes, which render a traditional apprenticeship system ineffective (compare Gott's lost-apprenticeship notion; see Wilson & Cole 1991). Partly as a consequence of this phenomenon, organizations are looking for partner organizations to jointly increase their capacities to anticipate and deal with all kinds of transformations. More and more vocational institutions and universities are asked to play such a partner role, and students are offered opportunities to participate in innovative projects to fulfill their practice period requirements. This creates new opportunities for individual as well as collective learning and competence development for all actors and organizations involved.

In the Netherlands, the school system at all levels is undergoing some major transformatory processes. Vocational institutions, for example, are required to develop and carry out curricula that emphasize broad instead of narrow competencies and to incorporate new ways of learning with the aid of information and communication technology. Learning to learn and autonomous learning are considered important key qualifications (Onstenk 1997). The quality movement requires schools to continuously improve existing practices and to find new answers to old and new problems, such as issues of internationalization and multiculturality. Schools are no longer treated as organizations that have to precisely put into effect what others (especially governmental bodies) have precisely spelled out for them. Their scope for policy-making has widened, which requires them to act as learning organizations (Simons *et al.* 1998). However, these processes are accompanied by an alarming shortage of teachers (especially in the field of science and technology). In the Netherlands there is a decreasing interest of young people to register for regular teacher training courses offered by teacher training institutes, which also creates major organizational and financial problems for these organizations.

To overcome these problems and to be better prepared for future developments, several national and regional approaches to school development and teacher training are being developed. As an example, we refer to new initiatives for recruiting and training teaching staff taken by Regional Vocational Training Centers together with institutes for teacher training. In cooperation with trade unions, a new qualification structure for teaching functions is being developed and implemented. Regional Vocational Centers and institutes for teaching training are jointly designing and implementing new combinations of in-company (i.e. school) training and part-time schooling.

These initiatives are a good fit for the new National Innovation Plan for Teacher Training Institutes, called 'Educational Partnership' (HBO-raad 1999), which was developed by the Higher Vocational Education Council. The main features of this innovation plan are as follows:

- school-based teacher education: teachers are prepared for continuous learning as members of learning school organizations;
- integration of learning, working and innovating: school development, personnel policy, teacher training and educational innovation are organized in relation to each other;
- enabling student teachers to take up responsibility for their own learning processes, focusing on clearly defined core competencies as desired by school organizations, supported by portfolio instruments and assessment procedures;
- educational partnership between teacher training institutes, schools and student teachers: joint responsibility for competence development;
- productive learning: learning by developing innovative products or solving authentic educational problems.

We are currently involved in a research project concerning the new dual vocational teacher training scheme described above. It gives us ways to study new forms of expansive learning and developmental transfer, as described in Chapter 2 of this book and in publications of the Helsinki Center for Activity Theory and Developmental Work Research (e.g.. Engeström 1987; Lambert 1996). In our view Engeström's approach is especially relevant for and suited to the implementation and study of innovative and collective forms of learning and work. With regard to the new dual vocational teacher training scheme, it can indeed be stated that representatives of different activity systems became involved ". . . in a collective activity . . .", taking ". . . the action of questioning the existing practice" (introductory chapter). Thus, expansive and collaborative learning cycles have been set up and it can be expected that they will evolve to find solutions for the common problems actors from the co-operating activity systems are confronted with.

In our new research project collective as well as individual learning processes will be considered. More specifically we are seeking answers to the following research questions:

- How did the participant organizations cooperate? What issues were addressed, in what ways, which problems were encountered and how were these solved? Special attention will be given to the way training institute teachers and vocational institution coaches cooperated.
- With regard to what issues did the participant organizations succeed in realizing an integration of learning, working and innovation and how was this integration brought about?
- What roles were ascribed to student teachers? How did they interpret these roles? What goals did they set for themselves?
- What learning activities were employed by student teachers? Did students differ with regard to these learning activities? To what extent and in what way did they integrate information and experiences gained during different learning tasks (e.g.. productive learning tasks) and learning episodes?
- How can processes of competence development of student teachers in dual learning situations be described and explained? How can competencies be assessed? What competencies did develop? What were the most important factors that influenced processes of competence development? How instructive was the work environment part of the dual training scheme?
- How does students' involvement in a collective learning endeavor influence their individual learning theories (including their conceptions of transfer)?
- What did the participants learn with regard to the way the common problems could or should be approached?

We think these are questions that deserve attention, because they point to the role individual as well as organizational variables play in both individual and collective learning and transfer processes. We deliberately want to pay attention to a) individual differences in the way members of different activity systems interpret the learning environment they are part of, and b) the quantity and quality of the learning activities they undertake in it. In this way we hope to contribute to the development of a sound knowledge base with regard to the processes that take place and the effects to which these processes lead when people are "... engaged in constructing their partially interdependent zones of proximal development" (see Tuomi-Gröhn & Engeström, this volume).

References

Argyris, C., & Schön, D. A. (1978). Organizational learning: A theory of action perspective. Reading, MA: Addison-Wesley.
Baldwin, T. T., & Ford, J. K. (1988). Transfer of training: a review and directions for future research. *Personnel Psychology, 41*, 63–105.

Boekaerts, M., & Simons, P. R. J. (1993). *Leren en instructie: Psychologie van de leerling en het leerproces.* [Learning and instruction: the psychology of the learner and the learning process]. Assen: Dekker & Van de Vegt.

Broad, M. L., & Newstrom, J. W. (1992). *Transfer of training.* Reading, MA: Addison-Wesley.

Brown, J. S., Collins, A., & Duguid, P. (1989). Situated cognition and the culture of learning. *Educational Researcher, 18* (1), 32–42.

Byrnes, J. P. (1996). *Cognitive development and learning in instructional contexts.* Boston: Allyn and Bacon.

Center for Workforce Development (1998). *The teaching firm. Where productive work and learning converge.* Newton, MA: Education Development Center, Inc.

Collins, A., Brown, J. S., & Newman, S. E. (1989). Cognitive apprenticeship: Teaching the crafts of reading, writing and mathematics. In: L. B. Resnick (Ed.), *Knowing, learning and instruction — Essays in honor of Robert Glaser* (pp. 453–494). Hillsdale, New Jersey: Erlbaum.

Cormier, S. M., & Hagman, J. D. (Eds) (1987). *Transfer of learning.* New York: Academic Press.

Dijkstra, S. (1997). Theoretical foundations of instructional design: introduction and overview. In: R. D.Tennyson, F. Schott, N. Seel, & S. Dijkstra (Eds), *Instructional design: International perspectives* (Vol. 1): *Theory, research, and models* (pp. 19–24). Mahwah, New Jersey: Lawrence Erlbaum.

Dixon, N. (1994). *The organizational learning cycle. How can we learn collectively?* London: McGraw-Hill Book Company.

Driver, R., Asoko, H., Leach, J., Mortimer, E., & Scott, P. (1994). Constructing scientific knowledge in the classroom. *Educational Researcher, 23,* 5–12.

Driver, R., & Easley, J. (1978). Pupils and paradigms: a review of literature related to concept development in adolescent science students. *Studies in Science Education, 5,* 61–84.

Duda, J. L., & Nicholls. J. G. (1992). Dimensions of achievement motivation in schoolwork and sport. *Journal of Educational Psychology, 84,* 290–299.

Dudley Herron, J. (1996). *The chemistry classroom. Formulas for successful teaching.* Washington, D.C.: American Chemical Society.

Duffy, T. M., & Jonassen, D. H. (1991). Constructivism: new implications for instructional technology? *Educational Technology, 5,* 7–12.

Engeström, Y. (1987). *Learning by expanding: An activity-theoretical approach to developmental research.* Helsinki: Orienta-Konsultit.

Entwistle, N. J. (1991). Approaches to learning and perceptions of the learning environment — introduction to the special issue. *Higher Education, 22* 201–204.

Eraut, M. (1994). *Developing professional knowledge and competence.* London: The Falmer Press.

Eraut, M., Alderton, J., Cole, G., & Senker, P. (1998). *Development of knowledge and skills in employment.* Final report of a research project funded by "The Learning Society" Programme of the Economic and Social Research Council. Brighton: University of Sussex.

Fasol, D. (1996). *Leren in stages. Voor A-verpleegkundigen en ziekenverzongenden.* [Learning during practice periods in nursery education.]. Unpublished MA dissertation]. Tilburg: Tilburg University.

Gergen, M. (1988). Narritive structures in social explanation. In: C. Antaki (Ed.). *Analysing every day explanation. A casebook of methods* (pp. 94–112). London: Sage.

Gordijn, J. (1998). *Computergestuurde feedback in modulen.* [Computer-controlled feedback in modular instruction]. Doctoral Dissertation. Enschede: University of Twente, The Netherlands.

HBO-Raad (1999). *Educatief Partnerschap. Innovatieplan Tweedegraads Lerarenopleidingen.* [Partners in education. Innovation plan for grade two teacher training]. Den Haag: HBO-Raad.

Honey, P., & Mumford, A. (1982). *The manual of learning styles.* Maidenhead: Honey Press.

In 't Groen, J. C. E. M. (1996). *Leren binnen het leerlingwezen. Onderzoek naar leeractiviteiten van timmerlui, metselaars en betonstaalvlechters.* [Learning in the apprenticeship system. Learning activities of carpenters, bricklayers and metal workers. Unpublished MA dissertation]. Tilburg: Tilburg University.

Kelly, G. A. (1955). *The psychology of personal constructs.* New York: Norton.

Koch, J. (1992). Diskussion: Ansichten, Einsichten und Missverständnisse in der Ausbildung mit Leittexten. [Views, conceptions and misconceptions on training with "Leittexte"]. *Bundesinstitut fuer Berufsbildungsforschung, 21,* 29–32.

Koch, J., & Selka, R. (1991). *Leittext — The Self-reliant way of learning. Information for seminar participants.* Berlin: Bundesinstitut für Berufsbildung.

Kolb, D. (1984). *Experiential learning.* Englewood Cliffs NJ: Prentice-Hall.

Lambert, P. (1996). Teacher education as a promoter of innovative learning in vocational institutions. *Nordisk Pedagogik, 16* (3), 155–166.

Landa, L. N. (1983). The algo-heuristic theory of instruction. In: C. M. Reigeluth (Ed.), *Instructional-design theories and models: An overview of their current status* (pp. 163–212). Hillsdale, N.J.: Erlbaum.

Lodewijks, J. G. L. C., Schellings, G., & Van der Sanden, J. M. M. (submitted). *Shades of epistemological beliefs.*

Marton, F., & Säljö, R. (1984). Approaches to learning. In: F. Marton, D. Hounsell, & N. Entwistle (Eds), *The experience of learning* (pp. 36–55). Edinburgh: Scottish Academic Press.

Mayer, R. E., & Wittrock, M. C. (1996). Problem-solving transfer. In: D. C. Berliner, & R. C. Calfee (Eds), *Handbook of educational psychology* (pp. 47–62). New York: Simon & Schuster MacMillan.

Merrill, M. D. (1983). Component display theory. In: C. M. Reigeluth (Ed.), *Instructional-design theories and models: An overview of their current status* (pp. 279–334). London: Erlbaum.

Ng, E., & Bereiter, C. (1992). Three levels of goal-orientation in learning. *The Journal of the Learning Sciences, 1,* 243–273.

Nicholls, J. G. (1989). *The competitive ethos and democratic education.* Cambridge, MA: Harvard University Press.

Onstenk, J. (1997). *Lerend leren werken. Brede vakbekwaamheid en de integratie van leren, werken en innoveren.* [Learning to learn at work. Broad professional skills and the interplay of learning, working and innovation]. Delft: Eburon.

Reigeluth, C. M. (1987). Lesson blueprints based on the Elaboration Theory of Instruction. In: C. M. Reigeluth (Ed.), *Instructional Theories in Action. Lessons Illustrating Selected Theories and Models* (pp. 245–288). Hillsdale, New Jersey: Lawrence Erlbaum.

Reigeluth, C. M., & Stein, F. S. (1983). The Elaboration Theory of Instruction. In: C. M. Reigeluth (Ed.), *Instructional design theories and models: An overview of their current status* (pp. 335–382). London: Erlbaum.

Rietbroek, J. C. M. (1998). *HEAO-studenten: leerstijlen, persoonlijkheidskenmerken en leeractiviteiten op stage.* [Higher commercial education students: learning styles, personality characteristics and learning activities during practice periods. Unpublished MA dissertation]. Tilburg: Tilburg University.

Sannen, H. (1997). De levensloop als verhaal. Jongeren en hun tijdsperspectief 1955–1995. [Course of life as a story. Young people's perspective of time: 1955–1995]. Tilburg: TUP.

Selka, R., & Conrad, P. (1987). *Leittexte — ein Weg zu selbständigem Lernen.* Berlin: BIBB.

Simons, P. R. J., Teurlings, C. C. J., & Mulder, M. (1998). *Het leren van docenten in veranderende schoolorganisaties*. [The learning of teachers in changing school organizations]. Nijmegen: The J. H. G. I. Giesbers Reports on Education, no. 6. Nijmegen: University of Nijmegen, Department of Educational Science.

Slaats, A. (1997). *Handleiding bij de Inventaris Leerstijlen voor het Middelbaar BeroepsOnderwijs (ILS-MBO)*. [Manual for the inventory of learning styles in vocational education]. Tilburg: Tilburg University/STAR-centre.

Slaats, A., Lodewijks, J. G. L. C., & Van der Sanden, J. M. M. (1999). Learning styles in secondary vocational education: disciplinary differences. *Learning and Instruction, 9*, 475–492.

Teurlings, C. C. J., & Simons, P. R. J. (1992). Learning to use a word processor: effects of the leittext method. *Journal of European Industrial Training, 16*, 29–38.

Teurlings, C. C. J., & Van der Sanden, J. M. M. (1999). *"Het vormt je in wat je eigenlijk wilt worden". Verslag van een studie naar het leren in stages gedurende de opleiding tot Sociaal Pedagogisch Hulpverlener van de Hogeschool Rotterdam en Omstreken*. [Report on a study of learning processes during practice periods in higher social work education]. Tilburg: Tilburg University.

Teurlings, C. C. J., Van der Sanden, J. M. M., Simons, P. R. J., & Lodewijks, J. G. L. C. (submitted). *Effects of a process-oriented learning environment based on cognitive apprenticeship: A study on learning to use a word processor.*

Van der Krogt, F. J. (1995). *Leren in netwerken: Veelzijdig organiseren van leernetwerken met het oog op humaniteit en arbeidsrelevantie*. [Learning in networks. Versatility in organizing learning networks with a view to humanity and work relevance]. Utrecht: Lemma.

Van der Sanden, J. M. M. (1997). *Duurzame ontwikkeling van leervermogen. Leren leren in het technische domein*. Intreerede. [Sustainable development of learning ability. Learning to learn in the technical domain. Inaugural Lecture]. Eindhoven: Technische Universiteit Eindhoven.

Van der Sanden, J. M. M. Fasol, D., & Teurlings, C. C. J. (1997). *Personality characteristics and learning activities during practice periods in nursing education*. Paper presented at the 7th EARLI Conference Athens, Greece, August 1997.

Van der Sanden, J. M. M., Terwel, J & Vosniadou, S. (2000). New learning in science and technology. In: P. R. J. Simons, J. L. van der Linden, & T. M. Duffy. (Eds), *New learning* (pp. 119–140). Dordrecht: Kluwer Academic Publishers.

Van Oers, B. (1998). From context to contextualizing. *Learning and Instruction, 8* (6), 473–488.

Van Rossum, E. J., & Schenk, S. M. (1984). The relationship between learning conception, study strategy and learning outcome. *British Journal of Educational Psychology, 54*, 73–83.

Vermetten, Y. (1999). *Consistency and variability of student learning in higher education*. Doctoral Thesis. Tilburg University.

Vermetten, Y., Lodewijks, J., & Vermunt, J. (in press). The role of personality traits and goal orientations in strategy use. To appear in: *Contemporary educational psychology.*

Vermunt, J. (1992). *Leerstijlen en sturen van leerprocessen in het hoger onderwijs. Naar procesgerichte instructie in zelfstandig denken*. [Learning styles and the regulation of learning processes in higher education. Towards process-oriented instruction in independent thinking]. Amsterdam: Swets & Zeitlinger.

Vermunt, J. D.(1998). The regulation of constructive learning processes. *British Journal of Educational Psychology, 68*, 149–171.

Voskes, M. (1999). *Je wordt het op de trein. Opvattingen van aspirant Hoofdconducteurs over competentieontwikkeling in hun functie*. [Novice railway guards's conceptions on job-related competence development. Unpublished MA Dissertation]. Afstudeerscriptie. Tilburg: Tilburg University.

Wierstra, R. F. A., & Beerends, E. P. M. (1996). Leeromgevingspercepties en leerstrategieën van eerstejaars studenten sociale wetenschappen. [Perceptions of the learning environment and learning strategies of first year social science students]. *Tijdschrift voor Onderwijsresearch, 21,* 306–322.

Wilson, B., & Cole, P. (1991). A review of cognitive teaching models. *Educational Technology of Research and Development, 39,* 47–64.

Chapter 7

Curriculum-embedded Mastery Learning as a Tool for Fostering Transfer

Frank Achtenhagen

Studying literature about transfer problems can be a frustrating task. Tuomi-Gröhn & Engeström (this volume) demonstrate this impressively by referring to many publications which can be classified according to different patterns of teaching and learning theories. They summarize and demarcate their approach of expansive learning and developmental transfer by focusing especially on three topics:

(1) Learning tasks are not considered as given. Problem solving and learning processes are typically not triggered by an instructor's tasks.
(2) The modeling of learning tasks has to explicitly include the possibility of future problem solving.
(3) Learning tasks should lead to practical consequences ("ascending to the concrete") in a twofold sense: as a transfer of new models into practice (the aspect of implementation), and as a transfer of local innovations and new forms of practice into other activity systems and organizations (proliferation). In both cases, the original models and new practices will also be transformed and negotiated as they are transferred.

It is important to consider these approaches carefully, but up to now there has been a lack of research and evaluation. The discussions are more or less run on a very abstract level, with a high degree of plausibility, but also with a large arsenal of catchwords — as Tuomi-Gröhn & Engeström clearly discuss. Their own approach tries to pave the way for more realistic procedures which can be evaluated empirically.

Nevertheless, a fascinating phenomenon can be observed: The whole discussion about transfer and its problems neglects the curricular dimension of the corresponding teaching and learning processes and does not sufficiently differentiate according to learning objectives as they are given — in an overarching shape — for initial vocational and occupational education and training or lifelong learning, etc. It also does not consider differences between formal and informal learning processes as well as those between knowledge production and knowledge adaptation as central learning goals. The arguments mainly focus on a single lesson, ignoring the fact that teaching and learning processes — especially in the fields of vocational education and training, but not only there — have to be constructed thoroughly and reflected in the curriculum. The literature on situated learning does not emphasize this topic. It favors a concept of (cognitive) apprenticeship which refers to medieval assumptions and, thus, does not systematically satisfy modern needs. It is a case-based approach which underestimates the needs of systematic teaching and learning. Achtenhagen (1988) showed — in reaction to Resnick (1987) — that the absence of systematization led the American enterprises to abandon their model of craft-oriented apprenticeship after the World's Exhibition. However, the German apprenticeship system which was at that time lacking, was revived by the introduction of the part-time *Berufsschule* as the place for theoretical and systematic teaching and learning.

It is — and this is the central thesis — necessary to discuss the curricular dimension of the transfer problem with regard to the interrelationship of casuistry and systematization. As most transfer approaches focus too much on cases (in a broad sense) and neglect the context in which the cases are embedded, they miss the point. Nearly all examples within the areas of "situated learning" and "cognitive apprenticeship", for example, ignore the goals and contents given in the specific contexts to be acquired as well as the problems of assimilating and accommodating them systematically. They more or less focus on "natural" developments leading to "expert" behavior and underestimate the importance of stringent qualification procedures, which are typically the guidelines for efficient and acceptable socialization processes. The distinction between a "learning curriculum" and a "teaching curriculum" and the focus on the "perspective of learners" is not sufficient (cf. Lave & Wenger 1996: 97) and the skeleton of the "cognitive apprenticeship" approach does not reflect deeper curricular considerations (cf. Collins, Brown & Newman 1989: 476 ff.).

These are not arguments against the necessity to interpret learning processes under a situational perspective. On the contrary: this approach was, and is, very helpful, especially with regard to a constructivist view on the effects of teaching and learning. But, on the other hand, it is necessary to focus on the fact that an overestimation of constructivist ideas blocks the view for the importance of teaching and curricula — which clearly have to be reformulated, especially with regard to ideas from the fields of situated cognition.

Our central thesis, therefore, is that all the different approaches for a solution of the transfer problem — up to that of expansive learning — need to be enriched by the development of curricular structures which support learning by reformulating the role of teachers, curricula, didactics, teaching and learning methods and media.

II

This idea seems to be paradoxical because at first glance there is an irreconcilable antagonism between the criticism of teacher-given tasks, an over-emphasis on past and present tasks, and the neglect of possible transfer effects.

In the following, we shall demonstrate how an evaluative-constructive curriculum approach known as *"Lernhandeln"* (learn-acting — a German coinage) might help to contribute to a solution of the transfer problem (cf. Achtenhagen, Tramm, Preiß, Seemann-Weymar, John & Schunck 1992; Reetz & Tramm 2000; Tramm 1992, 1996).

The concept of "learn-acting" was developed within a German research context but also in reference to Davydov, Leont'ev, Vigotsky, Lompscher and Volpert. It also is based on the work of Aebli, especially on his formation of concepts, and is situated in the German didactic and curricular tradition (in the German, but also the Scandinavian tradition *Didaktik* has a positive connotation — in contrast to the U.S.-American use of the term; cf. also Westbury, Hopmann & Riquarts 1999). In the fields of economic and business education, for which it was developed, favorable circumstances helped to form a strict definition of the approach: the traditional approaches of business theory were replaced by a systems-oriented approach (Hans Ulrich) and new ways of complex problem solving research (Dörner) supported the formulation of a systems-oriented strategy of *Handlungsorientierung* (action orientation) as a basis for the reformulation of teaching and learning strategies.

The concepts of *Handlungsorientierung* and *Lernhandeln* focus heavily on the curricular dimension of teaching and learning processes:

- Action orientation includes acting *and* thinking.
- It does not mean unreflected assimilation to specified tasks in school or at the workplace; critical thinking is basic.
- The individual shall be able to generate adequate actions in carrying out specified tasks. This includes an internal modeling of situations and the given system and the ability to change a situation step by step; the ability to master routine tasks, but also new tasks, by developing mental representations of modes of problem solving.
- Action orientation should improve the quality of learn-acting by providing content-related but also social-communicative experience and experiences with one's own behavior, including metacognitive activities.

With regard to these thoroughly operationalized topics, the following principles for teaching-learning environments, which are to help foster transfer, have been formulated for construction:

(a) The students must receive the opportunity to experience in school relatively complex facts and problems which can be related to "reality".
(b) The teaching should explicitly take into account prior and everyday knowledge and the interests of the students.
(c) Teaching should start with a complex goal and content structure which can serve in principle as an preceding organizer for all topics to be taught in the course.
(d) There must be a concentration on the intension and extension of terms and concepts. The decisive point for successful decontextualization is specified in this context. For example, the general concept of depreciation (the intension of that term) must also be used for the solution of more specific tasks, e.g. depreciation of machines, trucks etc. or for alternative procedures, e.g. linear or degressive depreciation — the extension of the term.

(e) The teaching-learning processes should foster a clear and distinct action and activity orientation. Knowledge should be developed through the solution of meaningful problems and by development of a deep understanding.
(f) In this action-oriented sense, illustrative clarity is more than pictorial demonstration. For the development of adequate mental models, learning objects are expected to be accessible and open to the experience of the students.
(g) The conflict between case-related and systematic procedures has to be balanced through the use of a systems and action-oriented perspective.
(h) The instruction should also foster a metacognitive perspective: through a "learning about the model" approach the conditions, necessities and restrictions of the environment should be emhasized and reflected on.
(i) Unstructured, ill-defined problems, which cannot easily be solved merely by additive 'team' work should be offered alongside of the ongoing instruction. In this way, the students can experience the importance of integrated collaborative work as well as the advantages and problems of distributed cognition.
(j) The complex teaching-learning environment should also provide tasks in the same manner in which would be carried out at the workplace — as direct preparation for the labor market, but also to aid students in understanding and performing similar or even new tasks at the workplace: this is known as the aspect of transferability and mobility.
(k) These overall criteria for didactic modeling take into account the fact that various dimensions of knowledge should be considered: namely declarative, procedural and strategic knowledge. Declarative knowledge is related to facts, concepts and networklike structures of facts and concepts which might give a first illustration of the systems character of an enterprise. Procedural knowledge is related to operations with facts, concepts and structures, e.g. to count purchase and production dates, or to relate them to each other to find optimal pathways. Strategic knowledge is mainly present in the form mental models. It helps to integrate declarative and procedural knowledge focusing on the intended main effects of acting and avoiding or being aware of unintended side-effects.

We developed a complex teaching-learning environment in accordance with these criteria: a virtual enterprise called "Arnold & Stolzenberg GmbH" which has a strong relation to the real enterprise "Arnold & Stolzenberg". It is a British firm close to Göttingen, has about 500 employees, produces industrial chains and serves one quarter of the world market (Siemon 1998).

We developed this virtual enterprise as a curriculum and training guide for the official apprenticeship for industrial clerks. For the first half year of the apprencticeship the curriculum formulates as introductory learning area: "the enterprise as a complex economic and social system". By using the virtual enterprise as an instructional vehicle (cf. also Seel & Winn 1997), who emphasize the importance of complex teaching-learning environments for an effective and efficient situated learning) its underlying business and production processes have to be explored and discussed under different aspects in over 60 lessons. This first learning area is supposed to foster declarative, procedural and strategic knowledge which can be used within the subsequent two and a half years of apprenticeship.

The educational goal was to support the learning processes of the apprentices in such a way that:

- they comprehend the subsequent teaching-learning processes in the Berufsschule better; and
- they become familiarized with categories by which they are able to identify similarities and differences with regard to the work processes in their individual firm — being different from those communicated by the virtual enterprise. This procedure provides the apprentices with the opportunity to get to the bottom of their work processes critically, but also to scrutinize the topics taught in the school.

One major problem is to consider: According to German law, each German who has completed at least nine years of compulsory school can commence an acknowledged apprenticeship — if a firm has agreed to accept him or her. Having been accepted, the apprentice has to work in the firm and at the same time he or she has to attend the *Berufsschule* one or two days per week, where special classes for apprentices with the same or related apprenticeships are run. Especially in the fields of business and commerce there are apprentices with very different ages and prior schooling (e.g. 9 years or 13 years with *Abitur*) in one classroom. This diminishes the learning chances of apprentices with lower academic schooling due to the fact that the teachers very often run their instruction according to the progress of the "upper" part of their classrooms. As a consequence, the apprentices with inferior school socialization have less chances to fully exploit the school instruction as well as to learn terms and concepts to understand the processes in their firms better. Therefore, the project runs a mastery learning approach, trying by the end of the 60 introductory lessons to bring all apprentices to a 90% mastery level as a basis for the concluding teaching and learning processes.

The mastery learning approach is supposed to serve the following goal and content structure (Figure 1).

Organizational and business information are presented and introduced by aerial views of the firm (Figure 2) and organigrams etc. This information was overtaken from the real enterprise.

We filmed within the real enterprise. The corresponding video clips provide informion about products, production, services etc. (Figures 3 and 4).

We also interviewed and filmed the employees and the managers; video clips explain their tasks and problems (Figure 5). This figure demonstrates that the text spoken by the interviewee is also presented in a written form.

We installed simulated computer terminals at the virtual enterprice. They provide information needed to treat specified tasks which can be solved by navigating through the virtual enterprise (Figure 6).

To structure the navigation through the virtual enterprise the apprentices have to solve "exploration tasks". The first of these tasks is to explore the earliest possible date for the delivery of a certain amount of industrial chains. The task is given by a video clip where an apprentice gets a call with the corresponding question (Figure 7).

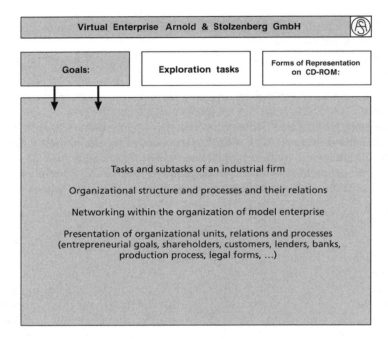

Figure 1: Goals and content of the virtual enterprise.

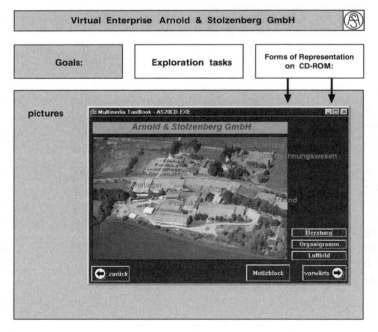

Figure 2: Aerial view of the real enterprise.

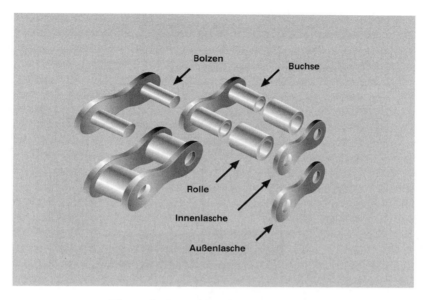

Figure 3: Parts of an industrial chain.

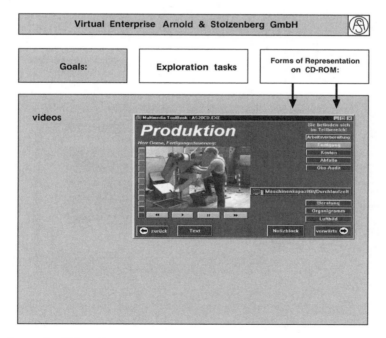

Figure 4: Videoclip about a production process in the real enterprise.

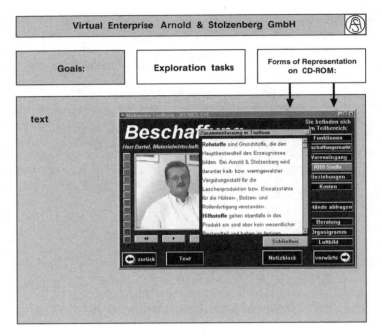

Figure 5: Videoclip (and additional text) about the purchase of raw material in the real enterprise.

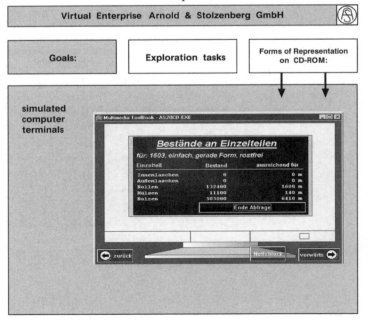

Figure 6: Simulated computer terminal of the virtual enterprise.

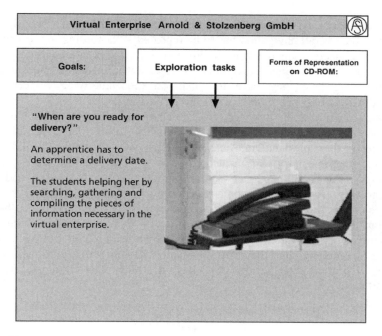

Figure 7: First exploration task: When are you ready for delivery?

Each apprentice in the classroom, then, has to navigate through the virtual enterprise to collect all necessary information. Via pictures, diagrams, videos, texts, and simulated computer terminals the apprentices get the pieces of information needed to answer the question. All navigation steps, their sequence and also the time of work with a special screen are recorded to get an insight into each learning process.

The apprentices additionally get the chance (via a notebook — "*Notizblock*") to record their sub-findings, which have to be combined for the final solution. In doing this, the students monitor their solution procedures.

All solutions are immediately assessed. If there are mistakes, the navigation through the enterprise has to be repeated.

After having worked out the answer — for this first task we configured one ideal-solution — the students see a video demonstrating how the answer is given to the client which closes the first exploration task.

As the students need different amounts of time to find the right solution for the first exploration task, a new task (in another format and mode of representation) is given to them immediately after they have finished the first exploration task successfully. This second task has to be solved in the same lesson. As the first classroom unit consists of three hours only, few students manage both tasks within class time. But all students have to come up with the right solution of the second task at the next classroom unit. This means they have to work at home or at their workplace in the firm (we received permission from their superiors). In this respect, additional learning time is administered outside the classroom.

In a second large exploration task (the client calls up and asks: "Why haven't you delivered?") the overall navigation has to be repeated — according to the Total Quality Management concept of the real firm. In this process, the apprentices are forced to solve the same task under modified conditions. The relevant information appears in another shape. In doing this, they have to focus on the underlying principles of the corresponding business processes.

Later a third exploration task is given. The apprentices have to solve the computer-driven tasks in their individual real training firm, thus, detecting all necessary information on their products and business processes — being totally different from those of the virtual enterprise (but also from those of the real enterprise "Arnold & Stolzenberg"). The results, together with an introduction into their firms and products, etc. have to be presented to the whole classroom in the presence of their trainers. The advantages of this procedure are manifold: the apprentices have to collect the relevant information in their training firm by reconstructing the given business processes, by interviewing clerks of different departments, and by translating the categories learned at "Arnold & Stolzenberg" into their "firm language". Coming back to the classroom they also have to present their results in a way in which their classmates are able to understand them.

III

In autumn 2000 our developments — as described under I and II — were confronted with the results and proposals of the "Committee on Developments in the Science of Learning", which was initiated by the American National Research Council (Bransford, Brown & Cocking 2000; Donovan, Bransford & Pellegrino 2000; Pellegrino 2003). Four major principles of "How People Learn" (Bransford *et al.* 2000: 23 ff.) with regard to designing and evaluating effective teaching-learning environments were formulated:

(1) Schools and classrooms must be learner centered.
(2) To provide a knowledge-centered classroom environment, attention must be given to what is taught (information, subject matter), why it is taught (understanding), and what competence or mastery looks like.
(3) Formative assessments — ongoing assessments designed to make students' thinking visible to both teachers and students — are essential. They permit the teacher to grasp the students' preconceptions, understand where the students are in the 'developmental corridor' from informal to formal thinking, and design instruction accordingly. In the assessment-centered classroom environment, formative assessments help both teachers and students monitor progress.
(4) Learning is influenced in fundamental ways by the context in which it takes place. A community-centered approach requires the development of norms for the classroom and school, as well as connections to the outside world, that support core learning values.

These central principles are also worked out in relation to the context of "learning and transfer" (Bransford, Brown & Cocking 2000: 51–78). The corresponding discussion also focuses on various approaches, presented systematically by Mayer & Wittrock (1996) or alternatively by Salomon & Perkins (1989). All of these considerations are influenced by aspects of constructivism and situated learning — with their mutual dependency. Consequently they lead to interactive environments, with the main goal of the promotion of (deep) understanding (cf. Cognition and Technology Group 1997; Greeno, Collins & Resnick 1996).

On the basis of the *Lernhandeln*-approach and the development in the fields of business administration and subject didactics of economic and commercial education, we constructed the virtual enterprise as a complex teaching-learning environment — using the described set of criteria. The virtual enterprise was then evaluated by a curricular implementation program of the State of Lower Saxony and a related research program (running a mastery learning approach) with a grant by the German Research Foundation (DFG: Ac 35/15-1). Transfer considerations had to be included as our field of development and research is the apprenticeship of industrial clerks (*Industriekaufmann*), who are trained and taught at the same time in enterprises and part-time vocational schools (*Berufsschule*). The transfer of experiences and knowledge gained in real enterprises to the school and of knowledge taught in school to the apprentices' individual firm is therefore a major topic. We collected data on these transfer processes more informally since the function of this study was primarily explorative; but now to we are trying to run an experimental field study in about 150 commercial schools in two German States which is designed to improve the transfer possibilities of this virtual enterprise.

One major purpose of this text is to relate our approach to the results of the overarching American project "How People Learn" — especially by comparing the lists of criteria. We see some similarities, especially with regard to the normative reference system, as we follow an approach which can be described as "enlightened, pragmatic and eclectic" (Achtenhagen 1984: 11).

In the following, we take the eleven criteria which were the basis for our development of the virtual enterprise "Arnold & Stolzenberg" and compare them to the criteria presented by the project "How People Learn". We believe that deep understanding (for us identical with strategic knowledge) and metacognition are the decisive variables — which is to be evaluated in our planned statewide study.

"How People learn" formulated 13 aspects concerning stilistisch the promotion of transfer:

(1) Amount and kind of initial learning.
(2) Opportunities to use knowledge to create products and benefits to others $\Rightarrow$ motivation.
(3) Time spent learning for understanding.
(4) Frequent feedback: students need to monitor their learning and actively evaluate their strategies and current level of understanding.
(5) Providing multiple contexts: to abstract the relevant features of concepts and to develop a more flexible representation of knowledge.
(6) Use of well-chosen contrasting cases.
(7) Abstract representations of problems.

(8) Common elements of tasks.
(9) Making thinking visible: chance to correct misconceptions.
(10) Cultural practices that support learners' prior knowledge (→ socialization; heterogeneity).
(11) Effective teaching: actively identifying the relevant knowledge and strengths that students bring to a learning situation.
(12) Transfer from school to everyday environments: rethinking school practices.
(13) Experts' abilities:
   (a) notice features and meaningful patterns of information;
   (b) content knowledge with deep understanding;
   (c) knowledge reflects applicability;
   (d) flexible retrieval of knowledge;
   (e) varying levels of flexibility in their approach to new situations.

Now, we are able to compare these aspects with our criteria of construction:

1. Amount and kind of initial learning	↔	(b), (c)

Aspect (1) of "How People Learn" corresponds to our criteria (b) and (c). We did our investigation on prior knowledge of the apprentices by administering the network tool COMASOTO (cf. Weber & Schumann 2000) or an essay on "How does an effective firm function?" We also asked for the students' computer skills by way of a questionnaire handling knowledge.

2. Opportunities to use knowledge to create products and benefits to others' motivation	↔	(a), (d), (i), (j)

The initial videoclip of the virtual enterprise shows Katrina having difficulties solving the first explorative task. The apprentices are asked to help her. Another example is the 3rd exploration task: the students have to present the knowledge that they have gained via real explorations in their real training firm to their classmates, but also to their teachers and trainers, who attend the classroom instruction for this purpose.

3. Time spent learning for understanding

This aspect is met by the mastery learning strategy using the virtual enterprise: 90% of the students are to reach 100% achievement by getting additional learning time if necessary.

4. Frequent feedback: students need to monitor their learning and actively evaluate their strategies and current level of understanding	↔	(g), (h)

The monitoring processes are mainly provided by the computer program: if an incorrect answer is entered the program suggests new (systematic) trials to help the apprentice find adequate information to answer the question correctly.

5. Providing multiple contexts: to abstract the relevant features of concepts and to develop a more flexible representation of knowledge	↔	(a), (c), (g), (i)

This aspect is met by our construction criteria for the virtual enterprise.

6. Use of well-chosen contrasting cases	↔	(c), (d), (f), (g), (i)

In addition to the virtual enterprise's three complex exploration tasks, alternative tasks are given. This additional material — e.g. newspaper reports on the real firm — is also provided by the CD-ROM.

7. Abstract representations of problems	↔	(c), (d), (e), (f), (g), (i)

Abstract representations are given e.g. by computer screens with information which is fixed but related to the solution of the exploration tasks.

8. Common elements of tasks	↔	(c), (d), (e), (g), (h), (j)

The virtual enterprise is based on business and production processes which are found on nearly all computer screens; these common elements are demonstrated especially by the shape of the three exploration tasks.

9. Making thinking visible: chance to correct misconceptions	↔	(b), (d), (e), (f), (g), (h), (i)

Coaching procedures are necessary in this process, especially for the apprentices with lower prior school socialization. Coaching was especially necessary for those students who had problems understanding the network structure of the business and production processes.

10. Cultural practices that support learners' prior knowledge	↔	(b), (d), (e), (f), (g), (h)

The individualized work with the computer reduces the influence of verbal-fluency processes which usually have an impact on the teachers' perception of students in the classroom.

11. Effective teaching: actively identifying the relevant knowledge and strengths that students bring to a learning situation	↔	(b), (c), (d), (e), (f), (g), (h), (i)

It is necessary to train the teachers to handle the virtual enterprise and the additional material effectively and efficiently; complex teaching-learning environments are not "self-runners" or "freestanding" resources, as many teachers naïvely believe.

12. Transfer from school to everyday environments: rethinking school practices	↔	(a), (b), (d), (e), (f), (g), (h), (j)

The necessary adaptation and change of categories gained by working with the virtual enterprise during the first two exploration tasks help to solve the third one in the real training firm. This helps to support the transfer of theoretical concepts to practical needs but also the reshaping of practical costums in the light of business theory. Fostering this questioning and reshaping (via dialogues and negotiation processes) could be seen as an innovative development (also in the sense of expansive learning and developmental transfer; cf. Tuomi-Gröhn & Engeström in this volume).

---

13. Expert's abilities:

    (a) notice futures and meaningful patterns of information

    (b) content knowledge with deep understanding

    (c) knowledge reflects applicability

    (d) flexible retrieval of knowledge

    (e) varying levels of flexibility in their approach to new situations

---

Here we provide different measures which shall be described briefly by their goals:

- We follow a holistic and systemic approach by which information is presented in the shape of meaningful patterns.
- We promote declarative, procedural and strategic knowledge which fosters the development of deep understanding. Again, we operationalize the concept of "deep understanding" by modes of strategic knowledge.
- Using the exploration tasks and the additional tasks we demonstrate different modes of applicability.
- We test the retrieval of information — especially with regard to strategic knowledge — on collecting dates six or eighteen months after the treatment.
- We provide different treatments for the solution of tasks by using a computer or information seeking in real firms.

To summarize, we can state that we used criteria and instructional methods within a given curricular frame which are very close to those of "How People Learn". We interpret these similarities as a sign that different researchers at different places (with different backgrounds) come to similar hypotheses about conditions which probably might be helpful for transfer. The following sketch demonstrates our idea of fostering transfer by developing strategic knowledge as the central mode of deep understanding. [CTLE: = Complex teaching-learning environment (the virtual enterprise)].

    The results of the tests show very high retention rates of strategic knowledge: about 85% on the average, which is very remarkable. We know that the reproduction of

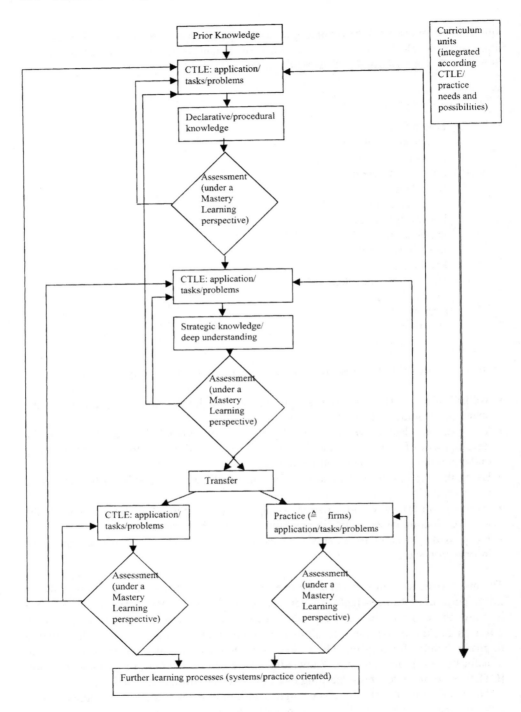

knowledge is not proof of transfer, but we interpret these results as hints that we are on the right track. We will therefore start the aforementioned state-wide field experiment in about 150 commercial schools.

References

Achtenhagen, F. (1984). *Didaktik des Wirtschaftslehreunterrichts* [Didactic of commercial teaching and learning]. Opladen: Leske + Budrich (UTB).

Achtenhagen, F. (1988). *Learning in School and Out — General vs. vocational education.* Paper presented at the AERA Annual Meeting, New Orleans.

Achtenhagen, F., Tramm, T., Preiß, P., Seemann-Weymar, H., John, E. G., & Schunck, A. (1992). *Lernhandeln in komplexen Situationen* [Learn-acting in complex situations]. Wiesbaden: Gabler.

Bransford, J. D., Brown, A. L., & Cocking, R. R. (Eds) (2000). *How people learn: Brain, mind, experience, and school.* Washington, D.C.: National Academy Press.

Cognition and Technology Group at Vanderbilt (1997). *The Jasper project: Lessons in curriculum, instruction, assessment, and professional development.* Mahwah, N.J., London: Erlbaum.

Collins, A., Brown, J. S., & Newman, S. E. (1989). Cognitive Apprenticeship: Teaching the Crafts of Reading, Writing, and Mathematics. In: L. B. Resnick (Ed.), *Knowing, learning, and instruction. Essays in honor of Robert Glaser* (pp. 453–494). Hillsdale, N.J., Hove, London: Erlbaum.

Donovan, M. S., Bransford, J. D., & Pellegrino, J. W. (Eds.) (2000). *How people learn: Bridging research and practice.* Washington, D.C.: National Academy Press.

Greeno, J. G., Collins, A. M., & Resnick, L. B. (1996). Cognition and learning. In: D. C. Berliner, & R. C. Calfee (Eds), *Handbook of educational psychology* (pp. 15–46). New York: Simon & Schuster; London: Macmillan; Englewood Cliffs: Prentice Hall.

Lave, J., & Wenger, E. (1996). *Situated learning. Legitimate peripheral participation.* Cambridge, New York, Melbourne: Cambridge University Press.

Mayer, R. E., & Witttrock, M. C. (1996). Problemsolving transfer. In: D. C. Berliner, & R. C. Calfee (Eds), *Handbook of educational psychology* (pp. 47–62). New York: Simon & Schuster; London: Macmillan; Englewood Cliffs: Prentice Hall.

Pellegrino, J. W. (2003). Connecting learning theory and instruction: Principles, practices, and possibilities. In: F. Achtenhagen, & E. G. John (Eds), *Milestones in vocational and occupational education and training* (Vol. I, pp. 17–42). Bielefeld: Bertelsmann.

Reetz, L., & Tramm, T. (2000). Lebenslanges Lernen aus der Sicht einer berufspädagogisch und wirtschaftspädagogisch akzentuierten Curriculumforschung [Lifelong learning under the aspects of vocational-educationally oriented curriculum research]. In: F. Achtenhagen, & W. Lempert (Eds), *Lebenslanges Lernen* [Lifelong Learning] (Vol. V, pp. 69–120). Opladen: Leske + Budrich.

Resnick, L. B. (1987). Learning in school and out. *Educational Researcher, 16* (9), 13–20.

Salomon, G., & Perkins, D. N. (1989). Rocky roads to transfer: Rethinking mechanisms of a neglected phenomenon. *Educational Psychologist, 24,* 113–142.

Seel, N. M., & Winn, W. D. (1997). Research on media and learning. Distributed cognition and semiotics. In: R. D. Tennyson, F. Schott, N. M. Seel, & S. Dijkstra (Eds), *Instructional design: International perspectives* (Vol. I, pp. 293–326). Mahwah, N.J.: Erlbaum.

Siemon, J. (1998). Virtuelles Unternehmen Arnold & Stolzenberg GmbH. *Wirtschaft und Erziehung, 50,* 6–7.

Tramm, T. (1992). *Konzeption und theoretische Grundlagen einer evaluativ-konstruktiven Curriculumstrategie* [Theoretical foundations of an evaluative-constructive curriculum strategy]. Berichte des Seminars für Wirtschaftspädagogik an der Georg-August-Universität, Band 17. Göttingen.

Tramm, T. (1996). *Lernprozesse in der Übungsfirma* [Learning processes in a practice firm]. Habilitation thesis. Göttingen: Georg-August-University.

Weber, S., & Schumann, M. (2000). Concept mapping software tool (COMASOTO) — Zur Diagnose strukturellen Wissens [Diagnosis of structural knowledge]. In: H. Mandl, & F. Fischer (Hrsg.). *Wissen sichtbar machen* [Visualizing knowledge] (pp. 158–179). Göttingen: Hogrefe.

Westbury, I., Hopmann, S., & Riquarts, H. (Eds). *Teaching as a reflective practice — The German Didaktik tradition*. Mahwah, N.J.: Erlbaum.

Chapter 8

Boundary-crossing in the Context of Intercultural Learning[1]

Susanne Weber

Context

The worldwide interrelationship of economy and industry, increasing globalization, and the enlarged European Market are promoting new management concepts and strategies at the worksite, such as integrated networks, mergers and acquisitions, cross-cultural knowledge management, and the like. In private life, people are traveling more to foreign countries, buying more and more foreign products and services, making friendships with people from other countries and cultures, etc. Both in private and in working life, more people than ever before are, as a result, interacting with foreigners and taking part in a global exchange of ideas and knowledge.

These developments encourage intercultural encounters, and these have to be managed and tailored to meet the specific requirements of the situations in which they occur, and they have, of course, to be harnessed to meet the challenges of work, learning and private life. Within such "boundary-crossing" situations (Engeström, Engeström & Kärkkäinen 1995), our familiar structures of acting, thinking, motivation, emotion, identities and interpersonal interactions are confronted with new and unfamiliar structures. Our "normal" actions, judgments and patterns of interpretation very often fail

---

[1] Intercultural learning and intercultural interaction in this article focus on an interpersonal interactive context within intercultural encounters. In comparison, international interactions refer to encounters on the national level (see the framework of Asante & Gudykunst 1989, pp. 9–10 for structuring different research areas in this context). A distinction also has to be made between intercultural and multicultural interactions, which mainly focus on interethnic or interracial issues and are — depending on the authors and their national background – mostly bound to particular political programs (e.g. Auernheimer 1995, pp. 194–210; Banks 1995). This does not however mean that assumptions made within this framework might not be fruitful or applicable to for these or other fields of research.

in these circumstances, leading to interruptions in the communication process, uncertainty, vulnerability, loss of autonomy, misunderstanding and loss of face, all of which ultimately lead to the breakdown of important projects (Holzmüller 1997: 792; Ting-Toomey 1999). Moreover, people do not tap or fully utilize the synergetic potential implied in the intercultural encounter situations they experience (Adler 1991: 95–119; Bolten 1995; Holzmüller 1997: 795).

In economic and business education (as indeed in other contexts too) it is necessary to foster the ability to cope with such complex and dynamic intercultural encounters — "boundary-crossing" situations — by furthering "intercultural competence" (e.g. Weber 1997).

Traditional Intercultural Training Programs, Their Underlying Learning Theory and Implied Transfer Concept

There is already a plethora of suggestions, especially in the field of business training, as to how to develop intercultural awareness, and intercultural competence. These courses are based on different learning theories and transfer concepts, depending on the contexts in which they are developed. The theoretical backgrounds range from recipes for reacting in the "right" way to certain stimuli in an intercultural encounter, see (A) behavioral approaches, through learning more complex patterns of "right" behavior, see (B) cognitive scheme approach, and learning different culture-related categories that influence human behavior, see (C) other cognitive approaches, to more constructivist and situated approaches which attempt to foster intercultural competence exclusively through participation within the new culture, see (D) constructivist and situated approach and without any teaching going on.

In the following, some of these training approaches are briefly introduced and their applications illustrated. Most notable among the many other approaches to teaching and learning intercultural competence not discussed here are the more attitude-oriented approaches, examples of which are the countless "study down" strategies which focus on determining individual variables suitable for predicting intercultural competence and performance in new intercultural situations. The corresponding data is collected primarily through questionnaires run on student sojourners and university populations; international research organization staff, diplomatic personnel, multinational corporation executives, quasi-diplomatic and military personnel, remain the exception. The analyses are mainly based on factor analytical methods, and review variables such as adjustment abilities and effectiveness, e.g. coping with stress, openness, empathy, tolerance, etc. (for example, Dinges & Baldwin 1996; Hammer 1989; Knapp 1995).

(A) Behavioral Approaches

The early literature is full of anecdotal, impressionistic reports on interculturally effective persons, biographies of successful businessmen and journey descriptions (see

Dinges & Baldwin 1996: 106). According to the theory of imitation (Miller & Dollard 1941 in Schunk 2000: 85), intercultural learners only have to imitate the "effective" behavioral patterns in similar situations in order to achieve the same "positive" effects. Furthermore, "study up" strategies are used for gathering experiences, critical incidents and specific occurrences from returning students and business people. Most of this information is used for creating lists of effective behavior or "culturegrams", as for example "How to Do Business in Sixty Countries. Kiss, Bow, or Shake Hands" (Morrison, Conaway & Borden 1994) or so-called "cultural assimilators" (Cushner & Brislin 1996; Müller & Thomas 1991).

Learning concepts based on this kind of approach reduce learning to the individual subject and rely on behavioral approaches. Accordingly, they draw on the behavioral transfer concept implied by the "theory of identical elements" (Thorndike 1913; Thorndike & Woodworth 1901). This stimulus-reaction theory assumes similar stimuli and reactions in learning and real situations (Gage & Berliner 1998; Osgood 1957). Culture, situations, persons and interactions are considered as static entities. They are also based on a one-way communication model. If a person displays a certain pattern of behavior in a certain situation, he or she will — according to the theory — be effective in the intercultural situation. This approach not only neglects the cognitive processes of learning, but also the goals and motives of the interacting individuals or groups, not to mention the complexity of multiple social and cultural backgrounds influencing situations and activities.

(B) Cognitive Scheme Approach

Cognitive cultural anthropologists believe that "culture" is an ideational system (Keesing 1974), and describe the common knowledge of a culture in terms of sets of culturally neutral cognitive schemes (Flechsig 1998; Tannen 1979; Wyer & Srull 1984). A central assumption in this approach is that facts, activities, behavior, value orientations and social interrelationships follow standardized patterns, e.g. how to eat in a restaurant, or how to open a conference.

The main difficulty with the implied transfer concept is to recognize similar patterns in new situations. This tends to be easier in school and familiar settings than in less familiar intercultural interactions. Furthermore, the approach encourages the adaptation and enactment of learned schemes in new situations, rather than the necessary questioning of standardized schemes in familiar situations.

(C) Other Cognitive Approaches

Besides these two influential approaches, a number of others rely on isolated issues (themes, cultures and situations) that arise in intercultural encounter situations (e.g. verbal and nonverbal communication styles, conflict management, intercultural adaptation, issues relating to opposite sex interactions within Japanese-North American relationships) (Asante & Gudykunst 1989; Ting-Toomey & Korzenny 1991). The well known model developed by Gudykunst & Kim (1992) *"communicating with strangers"* attempts to integrate many of these more or less isolated aspects. The authors assume that communicators within an intercultural interaction are delimited by a number of alternatives (conceptual filters) they choose from when encoding and decoding messages (Gudykunst & Kim 1992: 32). The filters are categorized into *cultural* (internalized cultural values, norms), *sociocultural* (belonging to a group, role taking, expectations), *psychocultural* (stereotypes, attitudes, prejudices, ethnocentric attitudes) and *environmental* (like climate, landscape) *factors*. Learning to structure the actual communication situation in accordance with these categories will reduce uncertainty and anxiety, thus contributing to effective intergroup communication and intercultural adjustment (Gudykunst, Guzley & Hammer 1996: 73). Although the model proposes that the structuring and the de- and encoding of messages be processed interactively (Gudykunst & Kim 1992: 32), it is, nevertheless, quite static. Its categories are more or less fixed, which means that it often fails to explain what is actually taking place in specific encounters between strangers, and how the limitations caused by the conceptual filters can be overcome by interactional efforts (Casmir & Asuncion-Lande 1988: 287;[2] Warthun 1997: 21).

A further critical issue relates to the deficient operationalization of these approaches for fruitful teaching and learning programs. Abstract categories such as "anxiety" are not broken down to practicable items, or fail to adequately encompass the context at hand. Techniques such as "meditation" or "yoga" are thus recommended for managing anxiety (Gudykunst *et al.* 1996: 75), without providing a stringent justification for these coping strategies. Learning goals to cover learners' special needs are generally not integrated into the corresponding curricula. The theoretical considerations are, therefore, normally only introduced at the beginning of the courses, followed by isolated general cultural methods such as Bafá Bafá, Barnga, cultural assimilators, role plays, simulations, exploration tasks dealing with different issues and content (cf. the matrix of intercultural trainings in Brislin 1989: 445).

Depending on instructional settings and activities, some of these intercultural trainings are based on a metacognitive transfer concept that emphasizes the acquisition and restructuring of knowledge (Bruner 1981; Gagné 1969). The structural character-istics of the learning situations are responsible for initiating cognitive processes and initiating meaningful understanding. Once experienced in a situation, these processes act as a strong support in the solution of similar or structurally equivalent problems (Tramm 1992: 94–95; according to Bergius 1964 and Messner 1978). Such learning processes are characterized by elaborating concept structures, integrating new elements into concept structures, processes of abstraction and generalization, reflection and systematization for making situations transparent and for acquiring purposeful orientation, etc. These activities are based on "learning *within* the model" and "learning *about* the model" (Tramm 1992: 208–216; for a detailed discussion and argumentation

---

[2] It should be noted that this criticism was directed at the 1st edition of the model (Gudykunst & Kim 1984), but the model was not changed in the 2nd edition, the criticism remains valid.

see the "learn-acting" concept described by Tramm 1992: 212–214[3]). In order to implement the concept, complex teaching and learning situations or arrangements in schools and at the worksite have to fulfill specific requirements. Achtenhagen *et al.* (1992), for instance, developed so-called "complex teaching-learning arrangements/ environments", mainly realized as complex case studies, business simulations or 'virtual enterprises' featuring carefully worked out curricula and applying pedagogical and instructional elements in a special systemic and interdependent manner suited to foster high levels of learning and development. In constructing such complex teaching-learning arrangements/environments they developed basic criteria (see Tramm 1992, 1996 and Achtenhagen *et al.* 1992 and Achtenhagen & John 1992).[4] The central issues are summarized as lists of criteria for constructing complex teaching-learning environments (cf. Achtenhagen this volume; comparable lists are formulated by the Cognition and Technology Group at Vanderbilt 1997, by De Corte 1995, 1996). Decisive criteria are:

- teaching-learning situations have to include complex facts and problems for developing solid declarative or procedural knowledge;
- teaching-learning processes should be organized in an action-oriented way to ensure space for learning activities of the learners;
- the acquisition of knowledge should be based on relevant problems;
- using the systems and learn-acting approach: the two elements: (1) practical, situative learn-acting; and (2) recourse to codified knowledge, theories and heuristics,

---

[3] This "learn-acting" concept is based on the (materialist) action psychology of Hacker (1978), Volpert (1979), Lompscher (1984) and Aebli (1980, 1981) (following proposals made by Leontjev (1975), Galperin (1967), and Vygotsky (1964), the developmental psychology of Piaget (1926), the pragmatic educational theory of Dewey (1964) and new constructivist approaches. The concept of 'learn-acting' implies the following aspects (Tramm 1992: 105; 1996):

- an adaptive-constructive interaction of the individual with his/her environment
- a socio-cultural embeddedness
- goal-orientation together with feedback and reflection phases
- relationship to specific learning objectives
- hierarchic-sequential organization (in the sense of a cyclic entity in accordance with the TOTE-entity of Miller, Galanter & Pibram (1973).

Even if the framework seems to consider an extended learning concept, the elaboration of the theoretical concept 'learn-acting' as well as the pedagogical realization focus primarily on the processes of knowledge and competence acquisition in terms of materialist action psychology. Immense efforts are made: (a) to analyze and promote high-standard 'learn-acting' with regard to the improvement of processes of cognitive orientation and acting procedures, especially concerning content, formal procedures, reflection and systematization; and (b) by recognizing the personal variables of a certain learning situation such as emotion, motivation, interest, ability, etc. (Tramm 1992, 1996). Nevertheless, aspects of social and cultural embeddednes and the interactions themselves remain mainly implicit. (For critical arguments against the "learn-acting" concept, see Faßheber 1999; for critical arguments against the materialist action psychology approach see Lempert 1998, pp. 33–35; Engeström 1999, pp. 21–22).

[4] The authors developed these criteria mainly in the field of economic and business administration for the purposes of teaching and learning economic and occupational competences (*ökonomische Handlungskompetenz*) to interact adequately, purposefully and responsibly in complex economic situations at work, school and in private life which goes far beyond teaching skills required at the workplace.

algorithms and techniques, should be brought into a sense-making balance (mainly through case-related and systematic procedures). This aspect is also discussed under the heading of "contextualization and de-contextualization";[5]

- metacognitive processes must be initiated and promoted by competent instruction; thus, conditions, necessities and restrictions of the teaching-learning environment become transparent for the learners and can, therefore, be discussed critically and reflectedly (as "learning *about* the model").

Although there are interactions between the learner and his/her environment, this learning- and transfer concept, and consequently the learning achievement, is mainly linked to the individual. Learning situations and, simultaneously, the concept of culture are still seen as static entities with regard to the social environment and the concrete interaction processes (Faßheber 1999; Lempert 1998: 48). As a consequence, the communication remains somehow ethnocentric or egocentric. It is assumed that the communicator somehow knows the elements of the influencing filters, and that she or he encodes "adequate" messages. Within this model, it is assumed that the alien communication partner is decoding messages in the same way. Misunderstanding merely occurs when individuals do not de- and encode the message in the "right". This implies an over-emphasis of the individuals' role and possibilities (Tuomi-Gröhn & Engeström, this volume).

(D) Constructivist and Situated Cognition Approach

Though 'learn-acting' and the corresponding metacognitive transfer concept described above includes some ideas of "situated cognition" and "constructivism", other authors argue that thinking and knowledge are completely bound to situations, for example the "situated cognition" approach of Clancey (1993) and Greeno (1992) (cf. Gerstenmaier & Mandl 1995). According to this variant of constructivist thinking, knowledge and learning occur purely through participation and without any teaching. Learning is seen as a natural by-product of productive activities, rather than the purely mental activity of an individual. It is assumed that the real situation delivers motivation and a richly supportive environment. "Only participating" would seen to be the main rationale of most exchange programs and intercultural contacts. Only about 20–30% of participants get the benefit of intercultural training or any kind of preparation (Bhagat & Prien 1996: 219; Klimecki & Probst 1992). Thus, learners have no choice other than to muddle through and somehow learn by chance in the natural environments they are exposed to.

A central assumption in this approach is that the interaction itself is investigated. The learning and transfer concept remains with the individual. Furthermore, leaving the learners alone with their learning processes in practical phases or abroad would seen to amount of a "survival of the fittest". Learners with highly developed skills (especially metacognitive skills) or keen intuition will manage the intercultural encounters, other

---

[5] A similar view — combining situated knowledge and generalization — is given by Guile and Young (this volume; Beach 1999 and Resnick 1989) to overcome the encapsulation of learning that occurs in both contexts.

learners will struggle more or less successfully against situational constraints and requirements. This leads very often to a decrease of commitment, to ethnocentric attitudes and behavior, and to giving up by leaving the intercultural encounter situation. A lot of literature on student exchange programs and managers abroad confirm these tendencies in reports on drop-out-rates, unsuccessful and prematurely interrupted projects, etc. (see Bhagat & Prien 1996: 217–218; Bolten 1995: 24; Kauffmann, Martin, Weaver & Weaver 1992).

Promoting Competent Intercultural Interaction by Using the "Mindful Identity Negotiation" Approach

The deficiencies of traditional intercultural training programs mentioned above can be substantially overcome by analyzing the intercultural encounter phenomena with the help of a systematic, situative, holistic and interactionist theoretical model such as the "mindful identity negotiation" approach proposed by Ting-Toomey (1999) (Weber 2000a, 2000b) (Figure 1).

Culture

Culture, here, is conceptualized as a social construct: as a perceived bound unit which upholds a set of shared traditions, beliefs, values, and ways of life (objective aspect) and

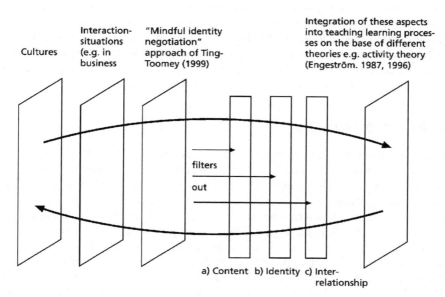

Figure 1: Simplified view of an intercultural encounter situation.

to which groups or individuals subscribe to varying degrees (subjective aspect) (Ting-Toomey 1999: 10). A culture in this sense can comprise an entire nation, but also religious communities, clubs, schools, universities, workplaces, departments, the youth or older generation, women, men, etc. A primary goal of intercultural learning in this approach is to overcome overgeneralizations such as "the Italians have good taste in designing products" or "the Germans are good in accounting". Comparing the objective aspect of culture to an iceberg with cultural artefacts (e.g. fashion, popular music) clearly recognizable on the surface, followed by increasingly less visible aspects such as norms, values and universal human basic needs (which are at the bottom of the iceberg, e.g. security, trust, inclusion, connection, stability), I conceptualize culture in a broader sense than it is done in most intercultural studies (Ting-Toomey 1999: 10).

Interaction Situation

The interaction within an intercultural encounter is seen as a dynamic process which is bound by the situation. Aspects which play an especially important role in providing orientation within the encounter are elements of behavior, goals or motivation of the participants, rules of behavior, different roles that people must play, physical setting and equipment, cognitive concepts, relevant social skills etc. (Ting-Toomey 1999: 20–21, referring to Burgoon, Buller & Woodall 1996: 193). The interaction situation is thus embedded in cultural and social contexts.

Speaking directly about difficulties one has with another person — without taking into consideration different cultural orientations — can lead to negative feedback or an interruption of the relationship. People with other cultural orientation and communication styles may perceive this kind of encounter management as threatening, and they may experience it as causing loss of face, if trust and harmony are essential for friendship within their culture frame. Treating people as foreigners, even if they have been living in the same culture for generations, for example by switching into "foreigner talk" in the presence of a 'foreign-looking' person, or by avoiding eye contact, is a further typical example of this kind of issue. Such behavior can easily be hurtful.

"Mindful Identity Negotiation"

The basic assumption of this approach is that everybody wants to be able to interact in intercultural encounters adequately, purposefully, competently and effectively.

On entering an intercultural encounter, individuals often notice that their patterns of behavior, value systems, beliefs, certain practices (e.g. in doing business), symbols and other artifacts either function differently or no longer work at all. They experience a loss of effectiveness in reaching their goals.Their counterparts would seem not to understand them. To solve the problem, the individuals or groups involved have to get into an object-orientated conflict situation such as the "mindful identity negotiation" process set out by Ting-Toomey (1999) (see Figure 2), or into an activity system which is mediated by cultural tools, rules, division of labor/joint practice etc. as described by Engeström (1987, 1996) (see Figure 3):

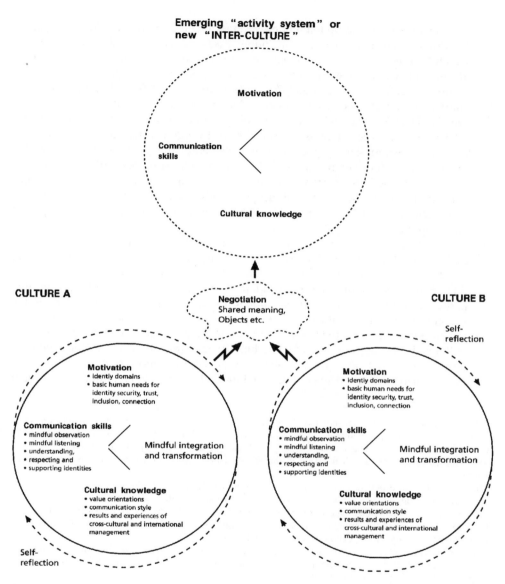

Figure 2: The "Mindful Identity Negotiation" — approach according to Ting-Toomey (1999).

Source: Reconstructed by Susanne Weber.

(a) The confrontation with different patterns of interpretation, practice and identities leads the individuals to a kind of self-reflection. They recognize that there are alternative ways of handling a phenomenon, and that the personally preferred alternative is only one option among several others. They realize that each person has different layers of identities, including a personal and a social identity,[6] each of which become relevant within a particular intercultural situation. At the same time, all individuals are seeking basic human needs for identity: security,[7] trust,[8] inclusion,[9] connection[10] and stability[11] (Ting-Toomey 1999: 42; Turner 1987; for similar theoretical structures and assumptions based on a social theory of motivation see also Deci & Ryan 1993), and they reflect, compare and question their own and other's practice. Very often, discussions in which both partners/groups try to evoke their own desired identity goals and motives and challenge or support the others' identities are not driven by harmony. Even where the participants of such a conflict situation or activity system would seem to agree on the surface, major contradictions are often seen at deeper levels. Nevertheless, an interculturally competent individual interacts in a way that allows all to feel understood, respected and supported.

(b) To get more insight into the alien patterns of interpretation and thinking, the individuals develop situationally adequate instruments for mindful observation, mindful listening, techniques to recognize the verbal and non-verbal cues in the interaction, identifying the roles adopted by the interaction partners in that particular situation, interview techniques for recovering the background of the persons, groups and/or situations, cultural aspects, social relationships, etc. Through this information, they are able to figure out the identity needs and attitudes of other individuals or groups (their cultural, ethnic, gender, role oriented identities and their degree of identification with the commonly shared orientations of their community), thereby also gaining a deeper understanding of their own. Interculturally competent

---

[6] *Personal identities* refer to an individual's self-conception that defines the individual in relation (or in comparison) to other individuals. *Social identities*, on the other hand, refer to an individual's conceptualization of the self that derives from membership in emotionally significant categories or groups (e.g. Ting-Toomey 1999: 27–28 referring to the social identity theory of Tajfel 1981; Brewer & Miller 1996).

[7] Individuals tend to experience identity *security* (refers to the degree of emotional safety concerning one's sense of both group-based membership and person-based identities in a particular cultural setting) in a culturally familiar environment and to experience identity *vulnerability* (refers to the degree of anxiety or ambivalence in regard to group-based and person-based identity issues) in a culturally unfamiliar environment [emotional level] (Ting-Toomey 1999: 40–41).

[8] Individuals tend to experience *trust* (a predictable or reliable interaction climate) when communicating with culturally similar others and to identity *distrust* when communicating with culturally dissimilar others [cognitive level] (Ting-Toomey 1999: 40–41).

[9] Individuals tend to feel *included* (refers to the degree of perceived nearness e.g. emotional, psychological, and spatial proximity) when their desired group membership identities are positively endorsed (e.g. in positive in-group contact situations) and to experience *differentiation* when their desired group membership identities are stigmatized (e.g. in hostile out-group contact situations) (Ting-Toomey 1999: 40–41).

[10] Individuals tend to desire interpersonal *connection* via meaningful close relationships (e.g. in close friendship support situation; "we" identity) and to experience identity *autonomy* when they desire relationship separations ("I"-identity) (Ting-Toomey 1999: 40–41).

[11] Individuals perceive identity *stability* (refers to a sense of identity continuation or consistency over time) in predictable cultural situations and to detect identity *change* or *chaos* in unpredictable cultural situations (Ting-Toomey 1999: 40–41).

individuals perform these analyses and modelling of the core contradictions mindfully (which means that they are tolerant of ambiguity, and open, flexible, respectful, adaptable, sensible and creative).

(c) Furthermore, with the help of their extended cultural knowledge (knowledge about cultural value orientations, verbal and non-verbal communication styles, development of relationships, group interactions, conflict management, adaptation processes, knowledge about international and intercultural business issues, etc.), they develop mindful intercultural skills (techniques for supporting identities, facework management, sitting arrangements, moderating multicultural group discussions, etc.) by integrating and transforming their knowledge to evolve expansive solutions.

(d) If this integration and transformation achieve the level of appropriateness and effectiveness and of satisfaction for each partner or group involved in the interaction — i.e. when all feel understood, respected and supported — they negotiate a commonly shared meaning and reach their goals. Through this negotiation process, the interacting individuals and/or groups develop a new culture of their own with shared meanings, values, norms and rules: a so-called "inter-culture" (Bolten 1995) or "boundary-object", a newly emerging "activity system" (Engeström 1999). On the basis of this, they go about their business and implement their solutions.

(e) This whole process really has to be gone through for each new encounter, but the procedure is usually automated for economic reasons. Actions are then run on the basis of their once negotiated results or shared meanings. This has to be checked from time to time in order to avoid misunderstanding and failure among the partners interacting within the activity system (Ting-Toomey 1999; Tuomi-Gröhn & Engeström, this volume). The outcome of an actvity system also has to be questioned, analyzed, discussed, modelled and re-negotiated when new individuals join the activity system, or when it is integrated into an existing or new activity system.

Three layers of meaning which are central to how people express themselves in communication processes are worth mentioning in this context (Ting-Toomey 1999: 19–20):

(1) Layer of Content Meaning

Even if a message is accurately decoded and the communicators come to a mutually shared content meaning on the factual (or digital) information level, a high potential for misunderstanding remains. Issues have to be addressed such as whether, for example, the content meaning has been presented in verifiable, factual terms ("Did you say that; did you not say that?"), or whether in a particular interaction situation it has been presented in an appropriate manner. Encounters often spend more time and effort debating and negotiating what has been said or not said than on identity meaning and relational meaning as described below.

(2) *Layer of Identity Meaning*

Each message includes some information about how one defines oneself and the counterpart in a particular situation. This information is more subtle than overt. Decoders typically infer (cultural, ethnic, gender, personal or interpersonal) identity meanings through the speaker's tone of voice, nonverbal nuances, different facial expressions, and selection of words, terms, idioms, which can express for example respect or rejection. To figure out such cues and salient identities is part of the identity meaning negotiation process.

(3) *Layer of Relational Meaning*

Relational meaning offers information about the state of the relationship between two communicators e.g. power distance meanings (equal–unequal), relational distance meanings (personal–impersonal). Relational meanings are inferred by nonverbal intonation, body movements, or gestures that accompany the verbal content level. For example, a teacher's "I want to talk to you about your grade in this class" will have a different meaning depending on how it is encoded and decoded — with a mildly requesting tone, a strongly demanding tone, or a sincerely caring tone. Relational meaning is closely linked to identity meaning issues. It is also often reflective of the expected power distance dimension in the relationship.

On the basis of these notions and assumptions "intercultural learning" and "intercultural competence" are conceptualized as "mindful identity negotiation". This concept integrates on the one hand individual knowledge internalized and possessed by an individual,[12] and on the other hand collective knowledge which is negotiated by members of a particular community or culture and distributed among them.

Integrating the "Mindful Identity Negotiation" Process into Teaching-Learning Processes

The "mindful identity negotiation" model describes the intercultural interaction situation and process from the perspective of communication (the smallest unit of identity negotiation).[13] Although Ting-Toomey summarizes the model's assumptions by

---

[12] With regard to the German connotation it refers to the anthropological competence concept of Roth (1966, 1971) and Reetz (1984, 1990), including aspects of content, self-reflection and social interaction as well as self-organized learning (Sembill 1992).

[13] The mindful identity negotiation perspective is an integrative theory that draws inspiration from four major scholarly disciplines: the work of social identity theory (Abrams & Hogg 1990; Brewer & Miller 1996), symbolic interaction (McCall & Simmons 1978; Stryker 1981, 1992), identity negotiation (Ting-Toomey 1988, 1989, 1993), and relational dialects (Baxter & Montgomery 1996). Integrating many of the empirical research studies conducted in these four academic areas, the theoretical ideas of the mindful identity negotiation approach are formed by psychological, sociological and social-psychological categories to describe and analyze the interaction situation in a holistic way. Furthermore, the "mindful identity negotiation" approach emphasizes on the one hand the relation between cultural value orientations and the *"self-concept"/identity*, and on the other hand the motives of *"identity security-vulnerability"* (Ting-Toomey 1999: 26).

formulating learning goals and giving recommendations for enhancing knowledge, motivation and skills which will encourage the development of "intercultural communication competence", there is a certain lack of solid learning and teaching theory. Very little is said about *how* or *in which way* one should learn this competence, or about how it is transfered to new intercultural encounters. From my review of the "mindful identity negotiation" model, I can see that this is not accomplished by merely acquiring particular knowledge. It does not suffice for the learner to know something about other cultural orientation systems, that one has different identities and that one should observe and listen mindfully, etc. What is needed is, rather, the integration and transformation of acquired cultural knowledge, personal motivation and mindful communication skills in order to initiate a process of self-reflection and identity negotiation. This can only be learnt sufficiently by using a mix of learning theory approaches, including real intercultural encounters in which mindful identity negotiation can be practiced and experienced, and where shared meaning can be developed.

According to the assumption made by Tuomi-Gröhn & Engeström (this volume), the different individuals and groups within an activity system *take and leave* the subject position as they produce specific goal-oriented actions. While holding the subjective position, the individuals can acquire: (a) cultural knowledge (value orientations, communication styles, conflict management etc.); (b) knowledge about the development and change of one's own and other's identities (different layers of identities); and (c) adequate mindful intercultural skills (instruments for mindful observation and mindful listening, facework management, etc.). Learning processes for acquiring and internalizing this kind of knowledge can be initiated through complex teaching-learning environments (role plays or simulations etc.) which should be based on different modern learning theories such as "learn-acting", self-organized learning, "anchored instruction", "situated learning", "cognitive apprenticeship", etc. Depending on the specific form and organization of such complex teaching-learning environments, the learners usually work in groups with other students and/or in real work contexts with field experts. During the interactions with members of the particular culture under review, socialization processes — in a narrower sense — occur. These mostly occur unconsciously, informally and as a by-product of other intended interactions. In order to draw benefit from them, the learning processes thus initiated (in which learners experience more or less reflectively the reciprocal culturation processes between the involved cultures or arising tensions and in which they probably change their identities) have to be partly explicated and integrated into the instructional processes and curricula.

Simultaneously, the learner may *take or leave the subject position* during these culturation processes. While successfully learning in discussion with the field experts, he or she learns to be open to novel or unfamiliar behavior, to think critically, to be tolerant about different value systems that influence others' self-conceptions, to be reflective about one's own reference system, to automatically take mental scripts of behavior explicit and conscious, to see unfamiliar behavior from a fresh point of view, to develop multiple visions and interpretations, as well as on overall mental flexibility, etc. When the learner takes the collective position during such practical phases, he or she engages in an activity system together with teachers, experts and/or tools. Within this activity system, he or she is much more deeply involved and unable to maintain the distance level (surface level) of a spectator. They have to negotiate common meaning and collaboratively develop common, innovative, creative and synergetic solutions for real situations or real intercultural encounters. They are no longer able to select the best choice from a number of available options, they have to create options. This might cause identity dissonances and identity changes, but can also give rise to personal growth. Being in such an activity system, all participants are seen as change agents for each other: participants of the familiar culture for the members of the alien culture, and the other way round. They become competent "boundary-crossers" (Tuomi-Gröhn & Engeström, this volume). This collective learning process, or mindful identity negotiation, could be stimulated by using the expansive learning — approach within an activity system in the sense of Engeström (1987, 1996) (see Figure 3).

Although they have different epistemologies, the two situated and interaction-oriented models of Ting-Toomey (1999) and Engeström (1987, 1996) display several comparable elements (e.g. both models focus on interaction as a unit of analysis, interpret the model as a creative conflict, include social interactions and recognize cultural embeddedness as well as rules of interaction and commonly shared meaning as outcomes, etc. (see Figures 2 and 3). Combining these two approaches would deliver significant benefit for an improved interpretation of the concept of "context". Context within the "mindful identity negotiation" approach is heavily based on assumptions of symbolic interaction. This implies that context is primarily interpreted by the individuals involved in the interaction situation. In the expansive learning-approach, context is seen as something determined by material practice and socioeconomical structures of the particular culture (Engeström 1993: 66, quoted in Kontinen 1999: 27; see also the discussion on the compatibility of these two approaches with Star (1996)). Both would seem to be relevant in order to interpret and understand the phenomena of intercultural interaction and intercultural learning.

Conclusion

To become a good and competent boundary-crosser within intercultural encounters, it is necessary to go beyond story-telling, cross-cultural descriptions and simple adaptation measures. The unit of analysis must include the interaction, or the negotiation process itself, embedded as it is in situational, cultural and historical contexts. The "mindful identity negotiation" approach proposed by Ting-Toomey (1999) seems to offer a fruitful route in unravelling some of the central aspects involved in any such negotiation (e.g. content, identities, relationships). In order to be able to competently develop a commonly shared meaning, or a new "inter-culture", the process of "mindful identity negotiation" should be based on and integrated into progressive teaching and learning theories and environments. Furthermore, individual and collective learning is essential. Therefore, a mixed learning framework combining ideas of the "learn-acting" approach, self-organized learning, anchored instruction, cognitive apprenticeship etc. with those of the expansive learning approach described by Engeström would seem to make sense.

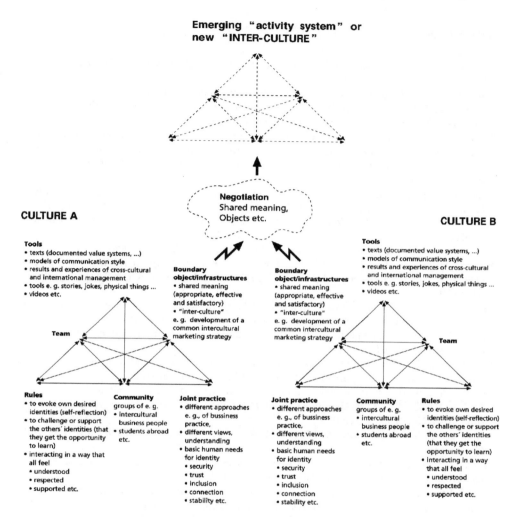

Figure 3: The activity system of Engeström (1987, 1992, 1996).

Source: Adapted by Susanne Weber.

Transferring a framework of this kind into action will require re-conceptualization of approaches and innovative, creative developments in the various disciplines. Such an approach should integrate accepted existing and new methods, instruments and practice into fruitful theoretical, curricular and methodically stringent learning frameworks, complex teaching-learning environments and projects or programs. Furthermore, these frameworks should be open to and flexible for further developments and innovations. Learning designs that meets these requirements are currently under construction.

References

Abrams, D., & Hogg, M. (Eds) (1990). *Social identity theory: Constructive and critical advances.* New York: Springer.

Achtenhagen, F. (2000). Reality, models and complex teaching-learning environments. In: J. M. Spector, & T. M. Anderson (Eds), *Integrated and holistic perspectives on learning, instruction and technology. Understanding complexity* (pp. 159–174). Dordrecht: Kluwer.

Achtenhagen, F., & John, E. G. (Eds) (1992). *Mehrdimensionale Lehr-Lern-Arrangements – Innovationen in der kaufmännischen Aus- und Weiterbildung* [Multidimensional Teaching-Learning Arrangements – Innovations within Commercial Education and Further Education]. Wiesbaden: Gabler.

Achtenhagen, F., Tramm, T., Preiß, P., Seemann-Weymar, H., John, E. G., & Schunck, A. (1992). *Lernhandeln in komplexen Situationen. Neue Konzepte der betriebswirtschaftlichen Ausbildung* [Learn-Acting in Complex Situations. New Concepts within Business Education]. Wiesbaden: Gabler.

Adler, N. (1991). *Organizational behavior* (2nd ed.). Belmont, CA.: Wadsworth.

Aebli, H. (1980). *Denken: Das Ordnen des Tuns, Bd. 1: Kognitive Aspekte der Handlungstheorie* [Thinking: The Arrangement of Actions, Vol. 1: Cognitive Aspects of Action Theory]. Stuttgart: Klett-Cotta.

Aebli, H. (1981). *Denken: Das Ordnen des Tuns, Bd. 2: Denkprozesse* [Thinking: The Arrangement of Actions, Vol. 2: Processes of Thinking]. Stuttgart: Klett-Cotta.

Asante, M. K., & Gudykunst, W. B. (1989). *Handbook of international and intercultural communication.* Newbury Park: Sage.

Auernheimer, G. (1995). *Einführung in die interkulturelle Erziehung* (2nd ed.) [Introduction into intercultural Education]. Darmstadt: Wissenschaftliche Buchgesellschaft.

Banks, J. A. (1995). Multicultural education: historical developments, dimensions, and practice. In: J. A. Banks, & C. A. McGee Banks (Eds), *Handbook of research on multicultural education* (pp. 3–24). New York: Macmillan.

Baxter, L. A., & Montgomery, B. M. (1996). *Relating: Dialogues and dialectics.* New York: Guilford Press.

Beach, K. (1999). Consequential transitions: a sociocultural expedition beyond transfer in education. *Review of Research in Education, 24,* 101–139.

Bhagat, R. S., & Prien, K. O. (1996). Cross-cultural training in organizational contexts. In: D. Landis, & R. S. Bhagat (Eds), *Handbook of Intercultural Training* (2nd ed., pp. 216–230). Thousand Oaks: Sage.

Bergius, R. (1964). Übungsübertragung und Problemlösen [Training Transfer and Problem Solving]. In: R. Bergius (Ed.), *Handbuch der Psychologie, Bd. 1.2, Lernen und Denken* [Handbook of Psychology, Vol. 1.2, Learning and Thinking] (pp. 248–325). Göttingen: Hogrefe.

Bolten, J. (1995). Grenzen der Internationalisierungsfähigkeit. Interkulturelles Handeln aus interaktionstheoretischer Perspektive [Boundaries of Internationalization. Intercultural Activities from an Interactive Theoretical Point of View]. In: J. Bolten (Ed.), *Cross-Culture – Interkulturelles Handeln in der Wirtschaft* [Cross-Culture – Intercultural Activities in Industry] (pp. 24–42). Sternenfels, Berlin: Wissenschaft & Praxis.

Brewer, M., & Miller, N. (1996). *Intergroup relations.* Pacific Grove, CA: Brooks/Cole.

Brislin, R. W. (1989). Intercultural communication training. In: M. K. Asante, & W. B. Gudykunst (Eds), *Handbook of international and intercultural communication* (pp. 441–457). Newbury Park: Sage.

Bruner, J. (1981). Der Akt der Entdeckung [The Act of Discovery]. In: H. Neber (Ed.), *Entdeckendes Lernen* [Discovery Learning] (pp. 15–29). Weinheim und Basel: Beltz.

Burgoon, J., Buller, D., & Woodall, W. G. (1996). *Nonverbal Communication: The Unspoken Dialoge* (2nd ed.). New York: McGraw-Hill.

Casmir, F., & Asuncion-Lande, N. (1988). Intercultural communication revisited: conceptualization, paradigm building and methodological approaches. In: J. Anderson (Ed.), *Communication Yearbook 12* (pp. 278–309). Beverly Hills: Sage.

Clancey, W. (1993). Situated action: a neuropsychological interpretation: response to Vera and Simon. *Cognitive Science, 17*, 87–116.

Cognition and Technology Group at Vanderbilt (1997). *The Jasper Project*. Mahwah, NJ: Erlbaum.

Cushner, K., & Brislin, R. W. (1996). *Intercultural Interactions. A Practical Guide* (2nd ed.). Thousand Oaks: Sage.

Deci, E. L., & Ryan, R. M. (1993). Die Selbstbestimmungstheorie der Motivation und ihre Bedeutung für die Pädagogik [The Self-Determination Theory of Motivation and its Importance for Education]. *Zeitschrift für Pädagogik, 39*, 223–238.

De Corte, E. (1995). Designing powerful teaching-learning environments. Conductive to the acquisition of cognitive skills. In: R. Olechowski, & G. Khan-Svik (Eds), *Experimental Research on Teaching and Learning* (pp. 67–82). Frankfurt/M.: Lang.

De Corte, E. (1996). New perspective of learning and teaching in higher education. In: A. Burgen (Ed.), *Goals and purposes of higher education in the 21st Century* (pp. 112–132). London: Kingsley.

Detterman, D. K. (1993). The case for the prosecution: transfer as an epiphenomenon. In: D. K. Detterman, & R. J. Sternberg (Eds), *Transfer on trail: Intelligence, cognition, and instruction* (pp. 1–24). Norwood, JJ: Ablex.

Dewey, J. (1964). *Demokratie und Erziehung* [Democracy and Education]. Braunschweig: Westermann.

Dinges, N. G., & Baldwin, K. D. (1996). Intercultural competence. In: D. Landis, & R. S. Bhagat (Eds), *Handbook of intercultural training* (2nd ed., pp. 106–123). Thousand Oaks: Sage.

Engeström, Y. (1987). *Learning by expanding: An activity – Theoretical approach to developmental research*. Helsinki: Orienta-Konsultit.

Engeström, Y. (1993). Developmental studies of work as a testbench of activity theory. In: S. Chaiklin, & J. Lave (Eds), *Understanding practice: Perspectives on activity and context* (pp. 64–103). Cambridge, U.K.: Cambridge University Press.

Engeström, Y. (1996). Developmental work research as educational research. Looking ten years back and into the zone of proximal development. *Nordisk Pedagogik, 16* (3), 131–143.

Engeström, Y. (1999). Activity theory and individual and social transformation. In: Y. Engeström, R. Miettinen, & R.-L. Punamäki (Eds), *Perspectives on activity theory* (pp. 19–38). Cambridge: Cambridge University Press.

Engeström, Y., Engeström, R., & Kärkkäinen, M. (1995). Polycontextuality and boundary crossing in expert cognition: learning and problem solving in complex work activities. *Learning and Instruction, 5*, 319–336.

Faßheber, P. (1999). Bestimmungsstücke wirtschaftspädagogischer Professionalität aus sozial-psychologischer Sicht [Deciding elements for Commercial Professionality from the view of Social Psychology]. In: T. Tramm, D. Sembill, F. Klauser, & E. G. John (Eds), *Professionalisierung kaufmännischer Berufsbildung. Beiträge zur Öffnung der Wirtschaftspädagogik für die Anforderungen des 21. Jahrhunderts. Festschrift zum 60. Geburtstag von Frank Achtenhagen* [Professionalizing Commercial Education. Contributions for opening up

Economic and Business Education to the challenges of the 21st century. Festschrift for Frank Achtenhagen's 60th Birthday] (pp. 370–383). Frankfurt/M.: Lang.

Flechsig, K.-H. (1998). *Kulturelle Schemata und interkulturelles Lernen* [Cultural schemata and intercultural Learning]. Unpublished working paper. Institute für Interkulturelle Didaktik der Georg-August-Universität Göttingen.

Gage, N. L., & Berliner, D. C. (1998). *Educational psychology* (6th ed.). Boston, New York: Houghton Mifflin.

Gagné, R. M. (1969). *Die Bedingungen des menschlichen Lernens* [Conditions of human learning]. Hannover: Schroedel.

Galperin, P. I. (1967). Die Entwicklung der Untersuchungen über die Bildung geistiger Operationen [Development of Research on the Formation of Mental Operations]. In: H. Hiebsch (Ed.), *Ergebnisse der sowjetischen Psychologie* [Results of Sowjet Psychology] (pp. 367–405). Berlin: Akademie.

Gerstenmaier, J., & Mandl, H. (1995). Wissenserwerb unter konstruktivistischer Perspektive [Acquiring knowledge under a constructivistic perspective]. *Zeitschrift für Pädagogik, 41,* 867–888.

Greeno, J. G. (1992). *The Situation in Cognitive Theory: Some Methodological Implications of Situativity.* Paper presented at the Meeting of the APS. San Diego 1992.

Greeno, J. G., Collins, A. M., & Resnick, L. B. (1996). Cognition and learning. In: D. C. Berliner, & R. C. Calfee (Eds). *Handbook of educational psychology* (pp. 15–46). New York: Simon & Schuster Macmillan.

Gruber, H., Law, L, Mandl, H., & Renkl, A. (1996). Situated learning and transfer. In: P. Reimann, & H. Spada (Eds), *Learning in Human and Machines: Towards an Interdisciplinary Learning Science* (pp. 168–188). Oxford: Pergamon.

Gudykunst, W. B., Guzley, R. M., & Hammer, M. R. (1996). Designing intercultural training. In: D. Landis, & R. S. Bhagat (Eds), *Handbook of intercultural training* (2nd ed., pp. 61–80). Thousand Oaks: Sage.

Gudykunst, W. B., & Kim, Y. Y. (1984). *Communicating with strangers.* New York: McGraw-Hill.

Gudykunst, W. B., & Kim, Y. Y. (1992). *Communicating with strangers* (2nd ed.). New York: McGraw-Hill.

Hacker, W. (1978). *Allgemeine Arbeits- und Ingenieurpsychologie* (2nd ed.) [General Psychology of Work and Engineering]. Bern, Stuttgart, Wien: Huber.

Hammer, M. R. (1989). Intercultural communication competence. In: M. K. Asante, & W. B. Gudykunst (Eds), *Handbook of international and intercultural communication* (pp. 247–260). Newbury Park: Sage.

Holzmüller, H. H. (1997). Bedeutung und Instrumente zur Handhabung der kulturellen Heterogenität im internationalen Unternehmensverbund [Importance and instruments for handling intercultural heterogeneity in international business alliances]. In: K. Macharzina, & M.-J. Oesterle (Eds). *Handbuch Internationales Management* [Handbook of International Management] (pp. 784–807).Wiesbaden: Gabler.

Kauffmann, N. L., Martin, J. N., & Weaver, H. D., with Weaver, J. (1992). *Students abroad, strangers at home: Education for a global society.* Yarmouth, Maine: Intercultural Press.

Klimecki, R. G., & Probst, G. (1992). *Interkulturelles Lernen* [Intercultural Learning]. Management Forschung und Praxis; Diskussionsbeitrag Nr. 4. Website [Management Research and Practice; Contribution for the Discussion, no.4. Web Site]: http://www.uni-konstanz.de/ZE/Bib/vv/verw/klimecki/klim04.htm vom 12.04.1999, 16:15h.

Knapp, K. (1995). Interkulturelle Kommunikationsfähigkeit als Qualifikationsmerkmal für die Wirtschaft [Intercultural communication ability as a qualification characteristic for Industry].

In J. Bolten (Ed.). *Cross-Culture – Interkulturelles Handeln in der Wirtschaft* [Cross-Culture – Intercultural Activities in Industry] (pp. 8–23). Sternenfels, Berlin: Wissenschaft & Praxis.

Kontinen, T. (1999). *The activity theoretical approach for studying NGOS in the process of development*. Working paper of the Institute of Development Studies, University of Helsinki.

Lempert, W. (1998). *Berufliche Sozialisation oder Was Berufe aus Menschen machen. Eine Einführung* [Occupational socialization or what occupations do to humans. An introduction]. Baltmannsweiler: Schneider.

Leontjev, A. N. (1975). *Probleme der Entwicklung des Psychischen* (5th ed.) [Developmental Problems of Psyche]. Berlin: Volk und Wissen.

Lompscher, J. (1984). Die Lerntätigkeit als dominierende Tätigkeit des jüngeren Schulkindes [Learning activities as dominant activities of young school children]. In: J. Lompscher u.a. (Eds), *Persönlichkeitsentwicklung in der Lerntätigkeit* [Personal development through learning activities] (pp. 23–52). Berlin: Volk und Wissen.

Mayer, R. E., & Wittrock, M. C. (1996). Problem-solving transfer. In: D. C. Berliner, & R. C. Calfee (Eds), *Handbook of educational psychology* (pp 47–62). New York: Simon & Schuster Macmillan.

McCall, G., & Simmons, J. (1978). *Identities and interaction*. New York: Free Press.

Messner, H. (1978). *Wissen und Anwenden. Zur Problematik des Transfers im Unterricht* [Knowledge and Performance. On the problematic of transfer in classrooms]. Stuttgart: Klett-Cotta.

Miller, G. A., Galanter, E., & Pibram, K. H. (1973). *Strategien des Handelns* [Strategies of actions]. Stuttgart: Klett.

Morrison, T., Conaway, W. A., & Borden, G. A. (1994). *How to do business in sixty countries. Kiss, bow, or shake hands*. Holbrook, MA: Adams Media Corporation.

Müller, A., & Thomas, A. (1991). *Interkulturelles Orientierungstraining für die U.S.A. Übungsmaterial zur Vorbereitung auf ein Studium in den Vereinigten Staaten* [Intercultural Orientation Training for the U.S.A. Prepatory Training Material for Studying in the United States]. Preparation No. 62, SSIP Bulletin. Saarbrücken, Fort Lauderdale: Breitenbach.

Osgood, C. E. (1957). A behavioristic analysis of perception and language as cognitive phenomena. *Contemporary approaches to cognition*. Cambridge, MA.: Harvard University Press.

Piaget, J. (1926). *The language and thought of the child*. New York: Harcourt, Brace.

Reetz, L. (1984). *Wirtschaftsdidaktik. Eine Einführung in Theorie und Praxis wirtschaftsberuflicher Curriculumentwicklung und Unterrichtsgestaltung* [Business Didactics. An Introduction into the Theory and Practice of Commercial Curriculum Development and Instruction]. Bad Heilbrunn/Obb.: Klinkhardt.

Reetz, L. (1990). Zur Bedeutung der Schlüsselqualifikationen in der Berufsausbildung [About the Importance of Key Qualifications in Vocational Eduction]. In: L. Reetz, & T. Reitmann (Eds), *Schlüsselqualifikationen. Dokumentation des Symposions in Hamburg "Schlüsselqualifikationen – Fachwissen in der Krise?"* [Key Qualifications. Documentation of the symposium in Hamburg "Key Qualifications – the crises of domain specific knowledge?"] (pp. 16–35). Hamburg: Feldhaus.

Resnick. L. B. (1989). Introduction. In: L. B. Resnick (Ed.), *Knowing, learning, and instruction. Essays in honor of Robert Glaser* (pp. 453–494). Hillsdale, N.J.: Erlbaum.

Roth, H. (1966). *Pädagogische Anthropologie. Band I: Bildsamkeit und Bestimmung* [Pedagogical Anthropology, Vol. I: Education and Destiny]. Hannover u.a.: Schroedel.

Roth, H. (1971). *Pädagogische Anthropologie. Band II: Entwicklung und Erziehung* [Pedagogical Anthropology, Vol. II: Development and Education]. Hannover u.a.: Schroedel.

Schunk, D. H. (2000). *Learning theories. An educational perspective* (3rd ed.). Upper Saddle River, NJ: Prentice-Hall.

Sembill, D. (1992). *Problemlösefähigkeit, Handlungskompetenz und Emotionale Befindlichkeit* [Problem solving ability, action competence and emotional being]. Göttingen: Hogrefe.

Star, S. L. (1996). Working together: Symbolic interactionism, activity theory, and information systems. In: Y. Engeström, & D. Middleton (Eds), *Cognition and communication at work* (pp. 296–318). Cambridge: Cambridge University Press.

Stryker, S. (1981). Symbolic interactionism. Themes and variations. In: M. Rosenberg, & R. H. Turner (Eds), *Social psychology: Sociological perspectives* (pp. 3–29). New York: Basic Books.

Stryker, S. (1992). Identity theory. In: E. F. Bogatta, & M. L. Bogatta (Eds), *Encyclopedia of sociology* (pp. 871–876). New York: Macmillan.

Tajfel, H. (1981). *Human groups and social categories.* Cambridge, U.K.: Cambridge University Press.

Tannen, D. (1979). What's in a frame? Surface evidence for underlying expectations. In: R. O. Freedle (Ed.), *New directions in discourse processing* (pp. 137–182). Norwood, N.J.: Ablex.

Thorndike, E. L. (1913). *Psychology of learning: Educational psychology* (Vol. 2). New York: Teachers College Press.

Thorndike, E. L., & Woodworth, R. S. (1901). The influence of improvement in one mental function upon the efficiency of other functions. *Psychological Review, 8*, 247–261, 384–395, 553–564.

Ting-Toomey, S. (1988). Intercultural conflict styles: a face-negotiation theory. In: Y. Y. Kim, & W. Gudykunst (Eds). *Theories in intercultural communication* (pp. 213–235). Newbury Park, CA: Sage.

Ting-Toomey, S. (1989). Identity and interpersonal bonding. In: M. Asante & W. Gudykunst (Eds), *Handbook of international and intercultural communication* (pp. 351–273). Newbury Park, CA: Sage.

Ting-Toomey, S. (1993). Communicative resourcefulness: An identity negotiation perspective. In: R. Wiseman & J. Koester (Eds), *Intercultural communication competence* (pp. 72–111). Newbury Park, CA: Sage.

Ting-Toomey, S. (1999). *Communicating across cultures.* New York, London: Guilford.

Ting-Toomey, S., & Korzenny, F. (1991). (Eds). *Language, communication, and culture: Current directions.* Newbury Park, CA.: Sage.

Tramm, P. T. (1992). *Konzeption und theoretische Grundlagen einer evaluativ-konstruktiven Curriculumstrategie – Entwurf eines Forschungsprogramms unter der Perspektive des Lernhandelns* [Conception and theoretical basis of an evaluative-constructive curriculum strategy – Design of a research program under the perspective of learn-acting]. Report of the Seminars für Wirtschaftspädagogik, der Georg-August-Universität, Volume 17. Göttingen.

Tramm, P. T. (1996). *Lernprozesse in der Übungsfirma. Rekonstruktion und Weiterentwicklung schulischer Übungsfirmenarbeit als Anwendungsfall einer evaluativ-konstruktiven und handlungsorientierten Curriculumstrategie* [Learning processes within a practice firm. Reconstruction and further development of a school-based practice firm as an example of a evaluative-constructive and action orientated curriculum strategy]. Habilitation thesis, Georg-August-Universität Göttingen. Unpublished manuscript.

Turner, J. C. (1987). *Rediscovering the social group: A self-categorization theory.* Oxford, U.K.: Blackwell.

Volpert, W. (1979). Der Zusammenhang von Arbeit und Persönlichkeit aus handlungspsychologischer Sicht [On the relationship between Work and Personality under a Action-Psychological View]. In: P. Groskurth (Ed.), *Arbeit und Persönlichkeit: Berufliche*

Sozialisation in der arbeitsteiligen Gesellschaft [Work and Personality: Occupational Sozialization in a Society based on the Division of Labor] (pp. 21–46). Reinbek: Rowohlt.

Vygotsky, L. (1964). *Denken und Sprechen* [Thought and Language]. Berlin: Akademie Verlag.

Warthun, N. (1997). *Interkulturelle Kommunikation in der Wirtschaf* [Intercultural Communication in Industry]. Bochum: Universitätsverlag.

Weber, S. (1997). Zur Notwendigkeit des interkulturellen Lernens in der Wirtschaftspädagogik [On the necessity of intercultural learning within Economic and Business Education]. *Zeitschrift für Berufs- und Wirtschaftspädagogik, 93*, 30–47.

Weber, S. (2000a). "Kiss, Bow, or Shake Hands" – Zur Entwicklung einer interkulturellen Handlungskompetenz in der kaufmännischen Aus- und Weiterbildung ["Kiss, Bow, or Shake Hands" – On the development of an intercultural competence within Commercial Education and Further Education]. *Zeitschrift für Berufs- und Wirtschaftspädagogik, 96*, 376–398.

Weber, S. (2000b). Zur Problematik der Vermittlung einer "interkulturellen Handlungskompetenz" [On the problematic of teaching an "intercultural competence"]. *Schweizerische Zeitschrift für kaufmännisches Bildungswesen, 94*, 79–101.

Wyer, P. S., & Srull, Th. K. (Eds). (1984). *Handbook of social cognition.* Hillsdale, N.J.: Lawrence Erlbaum.

Chapter 9

"Speaking from Experience" Boundary-crossing within a Pre-vocational Education Programme in Ireland

Gary Granville and Mary Reilly

Vocational education in Ireland has undergone significant re-orientation and restructuring over the past decade. A crucial development has been the systematic re-location of vocational education within the general domain of education as distinct from training. Within education, vocational education has been re-located for the most part, to the post-secondary education or Further Education phase, at approximately the age of 18 years. However, some significant policy initiatives have been introduced in the form of pre-vocational programmes within the second-level tier of education (Ireland 1995).

This chapter is concerned with one such national initiative at the upper secondary level of Irish education. The initiative in question is the work-related component of the Leaving Certificate Vocational Programme (LCVP) in Ireland. The LCVP aims to cross boundaries between school and work, between different school subjects and between different forms of teaching and learning.

The perspectives explored in this chapter are those of students and of teachers involved in the LCVP. The perspectives of these key participants are presented in their own words — "speaking from experience" — as far as possible, with special focus on the evidence emerging in relation to transfer of learning and to boundaries crossed. The chapter consists of five elements.

* First, the research study is located within a national policy and implementation context.
* Second, aspects of transfer and boundary-crossing within the LCVP are identified.
* Third, the views of students on their work experience and related learning are presented.
* Fourth, the views of teachers engaged in the programme are discussed in relation to the professional implications of their work-related experiences.
* Finally, some implications of the research for the zone of proximal development between school and work are addressed.

Between School and Work: New Perspectives on Transfer and Boundary-crossing
Copyright © 2003 by Elsevier Science Ltd.
All rights of reproduction in any form reserved.
ISBN: 0-08-044296-X

The Policy Context

A defining feature of Irish education, and indeed of Irish life, is the dominance of the Leaving Certificate programme at the end of the secondary cycle. Performance in the Leaving Certificate Examination is seen as the critical factor in future life prospects, in terms of education and employment. A major national review of the Leaving Certificate examination programme as a mechanism for selection for higher education has addressed the unique social significance of this public examination (Commission on the Points System 1999).

The Leaving Certificate programme carries all the hallmarks of the "classical humanist tradition" (OECD 1991: 69) which has been seen as characteristic of Irish education at primary and post-primary levels. The programme consists of some thirty-two subjects. Typically, full-time students aged 16 to 18 years choose six, seven or eight subjects, invariably including Irish, English and Mathematics (NCCA 1999). Student performance in six subjects is used as the basis for selection for further and higher education and for many forms of employment. Historically, the Leaving Certificate has been characterised by an academic orientation, reflected in an examination structure still dominated by the terminal, written external examination.

Recent education reforms in Ireland have sought to increase the participation and retention rates in upper secondary education. A national target of 90% completion of Leaving Certificate has been set (Ireland 1995: 50). Recognising the restricted curricular experience offered by the Leaving Certificate programme, the achievement of this national target was addressed by broadening that programme, specifically to introduce a vocational dimension to the curriculum. A new Leaving Certificate Applied programme was introduced, as a radical alternative to the traditional model (Gleeson & Granville 1996). At the same time, the Leaving Certificate Vocational Programme (LCVP) was introduced as an attempt to modify the traditional programme and to infuse it with a conscious vocational orientation.

The LCVP is a two-year programme in the upper secondary education cycle of Irish schools. It is designed to enhance the traditional academic Leaving Certificate programme through an increased emphasis on the vocational dimensions of teaching and learning across the curriculum. The LCVP is closely related to the established Leaving Certificate in terms of subjects offered. However, the LCVP requires the selection of two designated subjects in a vocational relationship to each other and the inclusion of a discrete set of Link Modules designed to link the other subjects to each other, to the world of work and to the overall learning experience of the students.

The curriculum structure of the LCVP can be described as follows:

- two designated vocational subjects;
- three vocational Link Modules (*Preparation for Work, Work Experience and Enterprise Education*;
- a modern European language;
- at least two other Leaving Certificate subjects.

The designated vocational subjects allow for the selection of two subjects from *specialist groupings* (e.g. engineering and technical drawing; home economics and art) or from *services grouping* (e.g. art and business, construction studies and business). The thrust of the LCVP is to develop links between these selected subjects and with the related world of work.

The Link Modules are the defining curriculum features of the LCVP. The modules take up a relatively small amount of time: two or three 40-minute periods per week are typical of school provision. Educationally, however, the Link Modules aim to have an impact far more pervasive than their strict timetable provision. The modules aim to *link* a number of teaching and learning experiences and to cross boundaries between school and work, between hitherto discrete subjects and between directed and autonomous learning.

The LCVP is a national initiative aimed at extending the range of learning within the educational experience of school students. "The LCVP prepares students for life after school — for further education, the world of work and the business of making a living" is the claim in support literature (LCVP 1998a) for the programme.

The programme aims to foster qualities and dispositions such as enterprise, initiative and creativity through autonomous learning, cross-curricular application of learning and activity-based learning. The LCVP initiative attempts to introduce new forms of teaching and learning, based on real life and on authentic work conditions, into the general educational experience of young people. As such it fosters a flexible approach to teaching and learning, the crossing of boundaries between school, work and the wider community, between school subjects and other forms of educational experience, and between traditional interpretations of vocational and general education.

A support service for schools operating the LCVP was established. The Support Service consists of a team of some five Development Officers led by a National Co-ordinator, all of whom are teachers on secondment from their schools for a period of three or more years. The function of the Support Service has been to provide in-career development for participating schools. This has taken the form of courses and ancillary materials for principals and for classroom teachers, with particular reference to school-work interactions and to innovative teaching and learning methodologies (Granville 2000).

Before the start of the school year 1998–1999, the Support Service described its work and immediate priorities in the following terms:

> The LCVP aims to change the existing culture within schools and to encourage the employment of new teaching methods, new relationships between teachers and students, new interdisciplinary relationships and cross-curricular co-operation between teachers (LCVP 1998b).

An Evaluation of the LCVP by the Inspectorate of the Department of Education and Science included a number of recommendations germane to the issues of boundary-crossing and transfer:

- the concept of an integrated curriculum and the promotion of a cross-curricular learning and teaching culture should be embraced by schools;
- teachers in the classroom should engage in active teaching and learning method-ologies;

- school cluster self-support networks should be fostered to facilitate the sharing of good practice in establishing effective interdisciplinary studies within specified subject groupings (Department of Education and Science 1998: 27).

The impact of the LCVP has already been considerable in Irish schools, as has been confirmed by the Inspectorate's evaluation of the programme. Some 462 schools are currently providing the programme to some 26,500 students and, through the support service, these schools have been exposed to the possibilities of a new approach to curriculum, emphasising certain generic skills as the basis for success in implementing and teaching the programme. These skills have been identified by the support service (LCVP 1998c) as the skills to:

- plan and implement an integrated approach to the programme;
- encourage and facilitate inter staff co-operation and team building;
- take part in group design and evaluation of the programme;
- design and use effective active-learning and experience-based learning approaches;
- develop new relationships through dialogue and negotiating with students about their programme;
- appreciate and emphasise the importance of the process of learning as well as content;
- employ resource-based learning and effectively use the wider community as a learning resource.

A particular feature of the LCVP that distinguishes it from other parallel curriculum initiatives, is its immediate engagement with the established Leaving Certificate examination programme. This programme is seen as the commanding height of Irish education, the "gold standard" by which all other courses and programmes are measured and through which access and progression to higher education and social advancement are mediated. The recognition by Higher Education institutes — Universities and Institutes of Technology — of student performance in the LCVP Link Modules for purposes of "points" calculation, was a significant validation of the programme (Commission on the Points System 1999: 158).

This proximity to the very centre of Irish education programming makes the LCVP experience particularly important and of immense potential significance. It makes the prospect of interdisciplinary and cross-curricular work in the programme all the more challenging. If such perspectives can be introduced into the Leaving Certificate programme the impact on teaching and learning in schools in general would be quite profound.

The tasks identified by the support service are the particular focus of this chapter, inasmuch as they refer to teachers' and students' experience of transfer and boundary-crossing. Specifically this paper is a study of the mid-term or long-term impact on students and teachers of the work-related components of the LCVP. The paper draws on research (Granville 2000) carried out with students who had completed or who were still following the programme, and with teachers engaged with the programme. The research reported on here took the form of structured interviews and survey work.

Transfer and Boundary-crossing within the LCVP

The LCVP is presented as a programme that prepares students for life after school, in further education and employment. Thus, literature from the Support Service (LCVP 1998c), directed at prospective students, states that:

> Skills learned through LCVP, such as planning, researching, writing reports and making presentations are a key to your success at third level. That's why an increasing number of third level institutions are recognising the LCVP.

and

> A modern worker needs to be well educated, a good communicator, multi-skilled and able to work in a team. Employers are enthusiastic about the LCVP because it encourages the skills and qualities which they value.

These statements are very much within the mainstream of current thinking on the role and definition of vocational education. Essentially, they are concerned with the development of skills of *transfer* and with the process of *boundary-crossing*.

Any rationale for schooling rests largely on the aspiration of the school to equip students with the ability to transfer their learning: to use what they have learned to solve problems in or to adapt easily to new situations. As an aim of schooling, it transcends traditional demarcations between general and vocational education. It is particularly applicable to vocational education, however, and is essential to the aims of the LCVP.

The dominant interpretation of transfer in education systems has been the cognitive conception, which stresses the degree to which behaviour will be repeated in new situations (Detterman & Sternberg 1992: 3). This cognitive conception has been described (Beach 1998) and criticised in the following terms:

- a very narrow band of what one learns in school and is used at work counts as *transfer*;
- the process of transfer as commonly experienced in schools, involves the *application of prior learning* rather than the construction of new learning: it recognises what goes on at school as *learning* as distinct from that which takes place at work, which is mere *application*.

In contrast to this restricted conception of transfer, the concept of *consequential transitions* has been proposed (Beach 1999). This concept recognises an extra dynamic in the process, one that must involve the exploration of new territory for which pre-learned response and solutions are unavailable. Consequential transitions involve the construction of new knowledge, identities and skills, or the transformation (rather than the application or use) of something that has been acquired elsewhere. A transition of this form, therefore, involves a notion of progress and is best understood as a developmental process. Such transitions may involve changes in identity, as well as changes in knowledge and skill. In other words, they are processes that involve the full person, not just learned attributes or techniques.

Table 1: Forms of transfer.

Form of transfer	Features	LCVP Examples
lateral transitions	between pre-existing social activities (*consecutive*)	transfer from school to working life
collateral transitions	between pre-existing social activities (*concurrent*)	transfers between school, community and home
encompassing transitions	within a single activity	impact of new technologies in classroom
mediational transitions	creation of a new activity	authentic and simulated experience of real work (incl. mini-enterprise)

An adapted typology of consequential transitions, as applied within the LCVP is set out in Table 1.

The LCVP — in particular the Link Modules component — is aimed at equipping students with skills of consequential transition as described above. Each of the forms of transfer can be identified within the LCVP, explicitly described in its promotional literature. Moreover, the programme of teacher support also aims at effecting consequential transitions within the professional self-identity of the teachers involved. The concept of boundary-crossing is introduced in a literal cross-curricular sense and in a more generalised sense of professional disposition and orientation.

The LCVP as a school programme can be seen to be committed implicitly to the development of the capacity in students to make consequential transitions. This commitment is manifested in the centrality of work experience and in the Link Modules' role in developing links, transfers of knowledge and skills, and active learning methodologies. In an equally valid way, the support programme for teachers involved in LCVP, the main focus of this research, is also concerned with the development of the capacity of teachers to engage in consequential transitions, developing a new identity as they engage with new forms of teaching.

The application of the insights and the findings of current research on the concept of transfer within vocational education are of significance to the LCVP in two respects. First, they provide a tool for the analysis of student outcomes of the programme, in a way that, for example, examination performance could not provide. Second, they offer a tool for analysis of the responses of teachers to the programme of support that is the primary focus for the present research.

It has been suggested (Young & Guile 1998) that an important aid to defining and focusing on the true meaning of transfer and transition in teaching and learning is to distinguish between *transferable skills* and *skills of transfer*. The concept of transferable skills is best understood as referring to certain pre-defined skills which can be learned and then transferred to other situations, if appropriate. This is a cognitive conception of transfer, as outlined by Beach (1999) — the application of prior knowledge.

The notion of *skills of transfer*, in contrast, refers to the capability of the learner to undertake activities in unfamiliar contexts, adapting prior knowledge or adopting new strategies and responses in the new situation. This is an exemplification of consequential transition, wherein the learner constructs new knowledge, with a reference point in the prior learning but perhaps no more than a mental set of attitudes rather than defined skills to apply.

Most of the LCVP literature tends to address the concept of transferable skills rather than skills of transfer. This does not, however, necessarily define the interpretation of the experience among the students of the programme. The perceptions of students, and especially of a group of former students, on their learning experiences within the LCVP were sought as part of the current research. The focus of this research was to ascertain the impact of the LCVP in respect of students' understanding of the teaching and learning processes involved and their subsequent application of this learning. The critical perspectives from which the student views are analysed are those of boundary-crossing and transfer.

Interviews were conducted with current and with former students of the LCVP and were analysed to ascertain the extent to which patterns of transfer are apparent in their perceptions of the programme. While the interviews relate to all four forms of transfer as set out in the typology described above, no attempt was made to explicate the concepts in the discussions with students.

The Student Research Study

The study described in this section of the chapter relates to two groups of students. The first group comprised graduates of the LCVP who completed the programme in either 1997 or 1998. Extended interviews were carried out, in person and by telephone (between 18 January and 7 March 1999) with sixteen such school-leavers, as well as with their school-based co-ordinators. The interviewees were currently either engaged in further or higher education or in employment. The interviews were designed to ascertain their consciousness of the modes of learning and content associated with the LCVP. More specifically, the interviews attempted to identify those areas of boundary-crossing where the students were seen to have benefited from and applied the forms of LCVP learning in their current occupations.

Structured interviews were carried out with students selected from class lists in two schools — one girls' secondary school in an urban area, one mixed-gender vocational school in a rural area. Schools were selected on the basis of identified good practice. Good practice was defined through consultation with the Support Service and with reference to the evaluation of the LCVP previously carried out by the Inspectorate of the Department of Education. This approach was adopted in a conscious attempt to address the added educational value derived through exposure to the LCVP as it was seen to be well implemented. Students were selected from the class lists on the basis of current employment or education status. Of the sixteen former LCVP students interviewed, eight were in higher education, two in further education (one nursing, one agricultural college), and six in employment (some studying part-time). The interviews were taped and subsequently analysed.

The second group comprised a current class of LCVP students in girls' secondary school in Dublin, along with other Leaving Certificate students in the same school, who were not taking the LCVP. These interviews and associated survey were designed to ascertain current students' views and understanding of the LCVP as implemented in school. In particular, these interviews are referred to in this chapter in so far as they indicate examples or perceptions of 'boundary-crossing' or skills of transfer. These interviews were video-recorded and the associated questionnaire survey was analysed (O'Neill 1999).

In relation to both groups of students, no attempt was made to take a representative sample of students nation-wide. The focus in the immediate context was on the generation of qualitative and illuminative data, by providing extended opportunity for the young people to express their views. The choice of schools was arbitrary, within the initial parameters of schools being identified as showing evidence of good practice. In other words, a bias was activated in favour of positive experiences: this was a conscious strategy, as the purpose of the exercise was to generate some evidence of what works in LCVP and from that evidence, to draw some informed inferences in relation to in-service implications. The selection of an urban and a rural school through which to identify LCVP "graduates" was the only gesture to representational parity.

The structure of the interviews was the same for each interviewee The comments culled from the interviews are grouped under three general heading:

• perceptions of the learning experiences of LCVP;
• current applications of LCVP learning;
• utility of LCVP in relation to overall Leaving Certificate performance.

Perceptions of the Learning Experience of LCVP

Comments from the former students were generally very favourable in relation to their LCVP experience. Most students referred to the LCVP in the sense of a separate subject among the suite of Leaving Certificate subjects, not as a programme in its own right.

This in itself is highly significant in terms of the boundaries to be crossed in the LCVP. One such boundary was that between subjects: the LCVP consciously attempts to link subject-based learning in interdisciplinary relationships. The work-related focus of the programmes is the cross-curricular theme within which this linkage is aimed to occur.

A few former students addressed their memory of the LCVP in terms of its being just another subject.

> It was my eighth subject, just something we did. We did most of the work
> in fifth year, like the project on our area (S.1).

Another said:

> LCVP was like Business, enterprise based. It wasn't easier or harder than other subjects, much the same really (S.2).

A more typical response, however, was recorded in another student's perception of the different experience that constituted the LCVP:

> We took charge! It was a fun subject, a hands-on subject. You'd have to find out for yourself. It was a nice break, it stimulates the brain again after the other subjects (S.3).

Some students took a particularly enthusiastic view of their LCVP experience, emphasising the freedom associated with the programme and repeatedly, the teamwork and associated responsibilities:

> It was good for coming out of your shell. If you didn't volunteer, it was your own fault. Team work was important: we'd have some disagreements but everyone had to take part or be told off by the group. In regular classes it'd be up to me to work or not. But in LCVP it was don't hold *me* back — because it was group work, it made others do it even if they didn't want to! (S.4)

The points raised by these students emphasise a change in learning environment from the standard school experience of didactic teaching to a more participative and experiential process in the LCVP. This process was substantially demanded through the work placement in various employment settings but was also maintained in the associated school-based but work-related sessions.

The inter-personal relationships and especially the emphasis on co-operative teamwork as compared with the dominant ethos of individualism and competitiveness associated with the established Leaving Certificate programme was noted in many comments. The motivational impact of this aspect was striking for some students: it also fostered a different form of peer-pressure, one more associated with positive achievement than the more frequently encountered negative forms.

> LCVP was good, you talked about different things. It was your own responsibility — we weren't treated like children. You had a lot more freedom (S.2).

> Needed to be able to be part of a team. We made our own decisions. There was a chance to do lots of things, we organised tasks then carried them out (S.5).

> You were more interested in what you were doing because you chose it yourself. You were let work on your own in class, and in groups (S.6).

One of the most frequently mentioned aspects of the LCVP that former students recalled was the relationship formed with their Link Modules teachers and with each other as students.

> We got to know the two LCVP teachers really well. We were treated as adults and we got on well with each other as well (S.7).

> There were about 16 of us in the class. The teacher guided you but you had do it yourself. It wasn't a pushy subject. You were responsible for learning (S.3).

The Leaving Certificate programme is a highly pressurised experience for most students. Typically a student will take six, seven or eight subjects for an external national examination, the results of which could be of life-effecting importance. The change of atmosphere encountered in LCVP learning, as part of such a high-stakes programme, is striking.

> You had more responsibility in class, it was easier to learn, you could ask anyone in the class if you had a difficulty, unlike in other classes where you might not know what was going on (S.8).

> There was a lot of learning going on in the classroom, people helping each other (S.9).

> LCVP was different to other subjects, like you learned through conversation and discussion with the group and the teacher (S.5).

The collaborative aspect to learning noted in these comments would be in stark contrast to the learning experiences in other aspects of the Leaving Certificate programme.

Current students tended to comment in similar terms on their LCVP experience. Their comments tended to emphasise two aspects of LCVP — the personal development dimension and the nature of the work involved.

> It's not just out of a book — it's first hand experience. LCVP has helped give me confidence, developed working on your own, not just the teacher saying it. It's up to you (P.1).

> It made me confident, out of my shell, not as nervous talking to people in authority (P.2).

> Really interesting, big advantage to it . . . learning, but fun at the same time (P.3).

Many current students referred to the amount of work involved in the LCVP, often expressing some surprise that it was so demanding. Other students, not taking the LCVP frequently express a view of the programme as something of a "doss" or a soft option — these references were picked up by some of the interviewees.

> It's a lot of work but it's very enjoyable. Don't realise it until you're doing it yourself (P.1).

> It's a lot of work — not a doss subject . . . have to take responsibility for work yourself (P.4).

> It doesn't take more time than it's worth. It isn't so much academic subjects — it's extra stuff (P.5).

> The bad side — having to have work done and the pressure. Too much work at the same time (P.6).

The current students tended to express a measure of sophisticated understanding of the importance of the newer forms of learning they were experiencing. The work-related aspects of the programme appealed to them and they were able to discuss in some depth the learning experience in terms of their own future career decisions. Their understanding of the concept of learning indicated a broadening of the traditional view of school learning.

One former student from a rural area now studying to be a nurse in the capital city, made an intriguing comment about the LCVP course she had completed two years previously:

> I worked in a local shop for work experience. LCVP was interesting, it was easier than other subjects . . . There was more research than learning in the LCVP (S.9).

While precise meanings and nuances cannot be inferred from verbatim comments taken from a long interview, that phrase — *there was more research than learning in the LCVP* — sums up in its slightly confused construction, the perceptions of many of the former students interviewed. They knew that there was something different in the LCVP but they couldn't quite articulate what it was.

It also provides an insight into the meaning of *learning* in the minds of many students. A tradition of didactic teaching and content-driven curricula has dominated Irish education. Situated learning in any environment other than that of the formal classroom has not been recognised, let alone validated, in national education programmes.

Current Applications of LCVP Learning

Questioned on current applications of learning, responses of former students tended to fall into the following categories — technical skills, study skills and personal/social skills. Most interviewees drew on their LCVP experience in two if not all three of these categories. (The quotations that follow are taken solely from former students, as the current students by definition were not in position to reflect on their completed experience.)

Constant features of the comments of former students in relation to the benefits of their work-related learning were the computer skills and the career-searching skills developed within the LCVP:

> Computer skills, filling out forms, mock interviews and project work, all those were good (S.5).

> Computer skills. The interviews were good and video was good. Work experience was very good. I think my boss thought it was great too — he said he learned a lot! . . . (S.11).

Work experience was almost universally welcomed by students as being both enjoyable and educative. The latter comment above reflected a comment frequently made by students (and also by employers, not reported on in this paper): the fact that employers cited their own beneficial learning was a strong endorsement of the boundary-crossing and consequential transitions referred to earlier.

Some students were particularly strong in crediting LCVP with positive inputs into their current study requirements.

> I got a good headstart in computer skills. LCVP helps self-confidence, study was up to you. LCVP is now a help in College, especially in communications class (S.12).

> We learned through experience. It was the best and easiest part of the Leaving Certificate. It was the "get up and go class"! There was a set time to do a task and you had to rely on yourself and your team effort. You had to interact with others. You learned decision-making skills and working in groups. And writing the portfolio took planning and time. The study skills I learned then are very applicable now in College (S.8).

> It was extra work but common sense work. There was individual work that you had to do for research and presentations. They were hard, alright. But that was very important for me now in College — assessments to be handed in on time. That all helped, it's not such a shock now. Doing those reports in LCVP was very important for College . . . (S.12).

> The projects were very beneficial because now there are projects to be done in college. Interview skills and application forms were useful as well (S.13).

Students also commented upon the application of work-based learning to subsequent work situations.

> LCVP was very useful when I was working in the pub, as well as selling not just petrol but also fishing tackle to, mostly, tourists. Tourism was covered in the LCVP and it was a great help in dealing with tourists. I could talk to them and could help them. I was self-confident as a result of the LCVP. Now that I'm in (*company name*) my computer skills are needed. I work on the factory floor and I have to get on with the others as well as putting descriptions of what I do into the computer (S.11).

The development of personal qualities figured in all the interviews. This was frequently seen in terms of relationships and of the development of self-confidence and motivation. Work experience was seen as a defining feature of the LCVP and was highly regard by nearly all the interviewees, on its own terms and as a motivator.

> Work experience was great. I was more interested in what I was doing (S.70).

> The work experience was the best part, and then the evaluation of the work experience afterwards. It helped you getting on with others, communicating with real people (S.14).

One student, summing up his views of the LCVP said:

> It was a nice break from traditional subjects. The teachers treated you differently, not as a child. You are responsible — you work if you want

to. The LCVP class is given a lot of leeway, we worked as a group. The work experience was very good ... The bad things were that some students weren't willing to do the work and this affected the rest of the class. Some of the class wasted time, they felt it was too much work (S.15).

Utility of LCVP in Relation to Overall Leaving Certificate Performance

The former students were asked a number of questions in relation to their attitude to the LCVP Link Modules, in terms of their assessment and certification arrangements. Generally, responses were favourable: a number of the students (four out of eight) had utilised the points dividend of the modules for successful entry to Institutes of Technology. A number of criticisms were made of the examination element of the Link Modules, in terms of the perceived lack of fit between the qualities of the LCVP and the structures of the exam:

The written exam should be more centred on the LCVP as it is or else change [the link modules] (S.2).

The main reason for doing the LCVP is for the points [for entry to college] (S.11).

It got me into College! It's not too hard to get full marks in it if you do it properly. Letters, reports, CV and so on — it's hard to lose marks! (S.16).

The comment of a student currently in school, but not taking the LCVP, reflects a commonly-held view of the programme:

I want to do engineering, law or medicine — all high points. I don't need the hassle of another exam that has lower points. I know that school shouldn't be about just getting points but the system at the moment is ensuring that it stays that way (P.8).

The recognition by the third level colleges of the LCVP Link Modules for the calculation of points for selection purposes has been greatly welcomed by most teacher and student participants. The belated recognition by the University sector was significant, but their reduced points dividend, as compared with the Institutes of Technology, is still seen as an indicator of relative status and thus of the target group of students for whom the LCVP is designed.

In general, all the former LCVP students interviewed gave either a moderate or a very strong endorsement of the LCVP experience, with the exception of one student who stated that she "hadn't really learned anything" (S.15). However, on closer questioning, her reservations tended to reflect her subsequent one-year Post Leaving Certificate secretarial course, after which she was rather scathing of the IT component of the LCVP. In other respects, her remarks were similar to those of the other interviewees, commenting that "the CV work was good, the group work was good, we helped each other . . ."

The evidence provided by the detailed interviews of former students gives a prima facie endorsement of the work of the programme in the achievement of the stated aims of the LCVP. This is especially true in terms of autonomous learning, boundary-crossing between school and work and between work-related learning and consequential transitions into higher education or employment.

When asked to recommend improvements in the LCVP, the most frequent item mentioned was the need for more *time* to carry out the LCVP work. While this is a positive endorsement of the work carried out in the Link Modules, it is also an implicit recognition of the relative failure of the cross-curricular dimension to impact on the consciousness of the students concerned. LCVP is viewed automatically among the students interviewed as the equivalent of another subject — different in quality from the other Leaving Certificate subjects but not impacting on those subjects. While the former students could articulate — in some cases very explicitly and convincingly — the tangible benefits of LCVP as transferred into their later experience of college or employment, not one student referred to any lateral transitions from the Link Modules into the parallel Leaving Certificate subjects.

The current students, while in many cases being extremely cogent in their analysis of work-related learning and of personal development features of the LCVP, made no reference to any tangible impact on other Leaving Certificate subjects. In other words, whatever links were being forged in the Link Modules, they were not with the other subjects.

The Teacher Research Study

In complementing the views of students, some comments of teachers on the professional impact of LCVP on them as teachers are presented here. This data was gathered as part of a wider survey of teacher responses to LCVP. A series of formal and informal meetings and interviews was held with participating principals, co-ordinators and teachers. A national survey also was carried out, in May 1999, of schools engaged in the LCVP.

Some 106 schools comprising slightly more than 23% of the total LCVP population were randomly selected for the survey, with an adjusted proportion of schools from each of the five phases of school enrolment on the programme. An initial response rate of slightly more than 54% was achieved, which was adequate for statistical purposes. However, a follow-up telephone call was activated with a further sample of schools (42), proportionally adjusted for each phase. This brought the rate of response up to a satisfactory 64.1%. The data in relation to school selection and response is set out in Table 2.

Some issues relevant to the teacher perceptions of boundary-crossing and transfer are summarised in this section of the chapter.

Table 2: Research Survey population.

Phase	No. of schools	Surveyed schools	% schools surveyed	School responses	% school responses	No. of teachers
1	68	18	26	11	61	12
2	58	18	31	13	72	17
3	144	29	21	17	59	21
4	140	30	21	21	70	30
5	43	11	25	6	54	9
Total	**453**	**106**	**23**	**68**	**64**	**89**

Professional Impact of LCVP Teaching

While the LCVP is a discrete programme, one of the aims of the support programme for teachers is to effect some deep changes in the overall school culture within which the programme is operating. In terms of boundary-crossing, this would involve teachers reassessing their professional practice in the light of the work-related teaching and learning components of the LCVP. The research study assessed the impact of their LCVP experience on teachers insofar as they transferred these to other aspects of their teaching.

Teachers were asked to assess the influence of the *transfer* impact of the LCVP on their teaching in three areas — traditional subjects taken as part of the LCVP, other senior cycle (non-LCVP) classes and junior cycle classes (12 to 15 year-old pupils). A four-point scale ranging from *very influential* to *not at all influential* was offered. The results are significant.

Strong positive reactions were registered regarding the influence of the in-service on their LCVP teaching (see Table 3). About 45% of teachers described the LCVP

Table 3: Extent to which teachers rated the LCVP transfer impact on other parts of the programme (internal transfer).

Extent of impact	%
Very influential	45
Quite influential	46
Not very influential	6
Not at all influential	3

Table 4: Extent to which teachers rated the LCVP transfer impact on other (non-LCVP) senior cycle courses.

Extent of impact	%
Very influential	7
Quite influential	35
Not very influential	44
Not at all influential	14

experience as being *very influential* and almost exactly the same proportion described it as *quite influential* in their LCVP teaching. This constitutes a remarkably positive response in relation to the impact of the LCVP initiative on teaching and learning styles in that programme: approximately 90% of responding teachers indicating positive impact of some kind.

In terms of impact on their wider professional role as teachers, the responses were not at the same high level. Asked about their teaching of other senior cycle classes (see Table 4), more than half the teachers indicated that the LCVP in-service provision had been *not very* (44%) or *not at all* (14%) influential.

While the participants in the LCVP programme of teacher support, by definition, was focused on LCVP teaching and learning, the orientation of the programme was consciously cross-curricular in many cases. It would have been reasonable to assume that a programme of support so positively received in its own terms might have significant over-spill into other parallel courses at senior cycle. This had not occurred to the extent that might have been expected.

However, while few teachers found the LCVP in-service programme very influential in teaching other senior cycle, some 42% in total of the teachers surveyed found the support programme to be influential to a greater or lesser degree. This in itself is a significant achievement and should not be minimised. In other words, the impact of LCVP in acquainting teachers with other ways of teaching and other forms of learning was reasonably effective in opening up new developments in their teaching generally.

In relation to junior cycle teaching, the pattern is more skewed towards the negative end of the scale (see Table 5). Some 38% of teachers said that their in-service provision was *not very* and 28% said it was *not at all* influential in their teaching at this level. These findings may be of some surprise in the context of such favourable views on the in-service provision itself. Some further impact on the wider culture of teaching might have been expected.

A related question was asked regarding the perception of individual teachers associated with the LCVP. The teachers in question, as co-ordinators and/or as Link Module teachers, were the most visible professional manifestation of the LCVP in their schools. Irish second level teachers have long been identified, by themselves, their peers, their students and others in terms of the subject(s) they teach. Teachers in this

Table 5: Extent to which teachers rated the LCVP transfer impact on junior cycle courses.

Extent of impact	%
Very influential	7
Quite influential	26
Not very influential	38
Not at all influential	28

survey were asked to consider to what extent, if any, their LCVP experience had affected their professional identity in the eyes of themselves, of their colleagues, of students in their school generally and of LCVP students specifically.

The responses indicate that the teachers themselves had taken on dimensions of a new professional identity. About one-third indicated that that they had taken on a new identity in their own eyes *to a great extent* while a further 40% indicated they had done so *to some extent*.

Respondents indicated that their LCVP students' identification of them as the LCVP teacher was even stronger: about 42% of the teachers believe that LCVP students would see them as the "LCVP" teacher (as distinct from their status as a traditional subject teacher) *to a great extent* and a further 38% *to some extent*. Teaching colleagues were beginning to develop an awareness of their new LCVP identity. About 50% of the respondents reckoned that their colleagues saw them as having taken on a new identity, to some or to a great extent. When considered alongside the nearly 75% of LCVP teachers who saw themselves taking on a new identity, there is evidence of something significant happening.

In the context of the traditional professional identity of teachers as associated with their subject, the data presented here may constitute the birth of a new category of professional within the Irish education system. In terms of boundary-crossing, the

Table 6: Extent to which teachers rated the LCVP experience in terms of changed professional identity.

Extent of impact	%
To a great extent	35
To some extent	41
To very little extent	14
Not at all	10

process at work with LCVP teachers involves forms of identity change such as Beach refers to: the LCVP, as a programme of professional activity, can be seen as a "boundary object" around which this sense of personal identity is evolving.

Implications for the Zone of Proximal Development between School and Work

An international OECD (1995) survey of public perceptions of education and schooling provides much evidence of the changing perspectives on the role and function of school programmes. The survey of adult citizens was carried out in a number of OECD countries. Three significant findings emerged from the survey:

- when asked to identify the most important qualities that schools should be seeking to foster, the most highly related qualities were *self-confidence and work-related/ employment skills*;
- respondents also indicated that the development of these and other similar qualities were more important than the teaching of school subjects;
- a significant majority believed that schools were well able to teach subjects but not adequately prepared to develop those very qualities seen as their most important mission.

These findings indicate an area of some concern for educational planners. In this international context, however, the LCVP experience in Ireland presents some positive indicators.

The LCVP has succeeded in crossing some of the more intractable boundaries associated with education systems worldwide. From the students' point of view, there is a priori evidence to suggest that the LCVP has facilitated them in effecting consequential transitions from the school to further education and, to a lesser extent, to employment. These transitions have been most visible in the lateral transitions, encompassing transitions and mediational transitions of Beach's (1999) typology. The boundaries between school learning and work-based learning have been successfully crossed in many cases through the LCVP modules.

The nature of the effect on students of LCVP work-related learning is ambiguous. While avowedly a vocational programme, the qualitative effects of the work-related learning, as exemplified in the Link Modules, relate as much to general educational objectives as much as to vocational training. Personal development in the areas of self-confidence and autonomous learning capacities were identified as outcomes at least as frequently and as significantly as vocational career focused outcomes or specific skills such as those related to information and communications technologies. To that extent, the relationship of workplace-learning to school-learning can be said to be "loosely-coupled" (Weick 1976). The specific vocational rationale for work-related learning may at times be the dominant feature of the student's experience of the workplace, but frequently the real learning facilitated by the work setting is in the realm of personal development and general education.

Within the school setting of LCVP, however, the boundaries between school subjects have remained uncrossed except in very rare circumstances. This is not very surprising: the strength of the academic tradition of separate subjects remains very high in Ireland as elsewhere. The students and the teachers interviewed in the present research displayed little success or indeed priority in respect of such cross-curricular boundary-crossing.

Perhaps most significantly, however, the experience both of students and of teachers indicates the appearance in the formal education sector of a new type of teaching and learning. Work-related and activity-based, it operates in the zone where school meets work. It is manifested in collaborative teaching and learning experiences, in changed student-teacher relationships and in situated learning of a kind hitherto unacknowledged in formal education programmes in Irish schools.

Paradoxically for an initiative in vocational education, perhaps the most significant indication of achievement in the LCVP is a broadening of the experience of general education among both students and teachers. Students, speaking from experience, identified significant aspects of boundary-crossing, in consequential transfer of learning as they moved on to further education or to employment. Teachers, speaking from experience, related limited but real boundary-crossing within their own professional practice, but most significantly in their professional identities.

References

Beach, K. (1998). *Transfer as consequential transition.* Paper presented at COST project workshop, Helsinki 12–13.10.1998.

Beach, K. (1999). Consequential transitions; a sociocultural expedition beyond transfer in education. *Review of Research in Education, 24,* 101–139.

Commission on the Points System. (1999). *Final report.* Dublin: Government Publications Office.

Department of Education and Science (1998). *LCVP: An evaluation by the inspectorate of the Department of Education.* Dublin: Government Publications Office.

Detterman, D. K., & Sternberg, R. J. (1992). *Transfer on trial.* NJ: Ablex.

Gleeson, J., & Granville, G. (1996). Curriculum reform, educational planning and national policy: the case of the Leaving Certificate Applied. *Irish Educational Studies, 15,* 113–132.

Granville, G. (2000). *In support of change: An evaluation of the LCVP in-career development programme.* Dublin: LCVP Office.

Ireland. (1995). *Charting our education future.* White Paper on Education. Dublin: Government Publications Office.

LCVP Office. (1998 a). *Information brochure.* Dublin: LCVP Support Service.

LCVP Office (1998 b). *An Enhanced Leaving Certificate.* Dublin: LCVP Support Service.

LCVP Office. (1998c). *Response to evaluation by inspectorate.* Unpublished paper, National Co-ordinator, Dublin.

NCCA. (1999). *From Junior to Leaving Certificate*: A longitudinal study of 1994 Junior Certificate candidates who took the Leaving Certificate examination in 1997. Dublin: National Council for Curriculum and Assessment.

OECD. (1991). *Reviews of national policies for education: Ireland.* Paris: OECD.

OECD. (1995). *Education at a glance.* Paris: OECD.

O'Neill, M. (1999). *A study of the comparative experiences of LCVP in selected schools.* Unpublished master's thesis, NUI Maynooth.

Weick, Karl. (1976). Educational organisations as loosely coupled systems. *Administrative Science Quarterly, 21*, 1.

Young, M., & Guile, D. (1998). *Notes on transfer and transitions in and between school and work.* Paper presented at COST project workshop, Helsinki 12–13.10.1998.

Chapter 10

Developmental Transfer as a Goal of Internship in Practical Nursing

Terttu Tuomi-Gröhn

Introduction

In Finland, health and social welfare services are confronting a serious challenge in the form of reduced budgetary allocations and calls for greater efficiency. This situation has arisen partly due to an overly complicated bureaucracy, partly due to rapid demographic changes, as the growing proportion of the elderly and chronically ill among the population has outstripped the ability of the state to increase services correspondingly. This has lead to structural changes in the working life and to the re-evaluation of working tasks. Education in the field of health and social welfare used to be based on narrow specialization. Nurses for hospitals, for the care of the mentally handicapped, for children's hospitals, daycare centers, etc., received training in different study programs which did not allow for mobility in working life. To solve this problem and to facilitate the flexibility and mobility of the work force, narrow specializations were merged into a broadly based program called "practical nursing". The new study program at the secondary school level system, prepares nurses for a range of careers spanning the entire social welfare sector. This reform also supports the ongoing merger of the health and social welfare sectors in municipal administration.

Nevertheless, these reforms have created a new set of problems. What content and forms of education can guarantee adequate expertise in such a broad field of practices? How should the structures and practices in the workplace be adapted to cope with the new situation: instead of training employees with specific technical and manual skills, students should now be prepared to acquire new skills and be better equipped to deal with people and social relations. Those who have the previous kind of education could upgrade their vertical expertise in their own narrow field as described in several novice-expert models (see, e.g. Dreyfus & Dreyfus 1986; Glaser & Chi 1988). However, the practical nurse should be able to work in a broad professional spectrum ranging from children to the elderly, from those in good health to those requiring intensive care. These situations require a different kind of expertise than previously. One needs courage to cross the boundaries of different work organizations, as well as to be able to quickly and efficiently seek knowledge from different sources, to be able to cooperate with different clients and experts, and to be willing to become involved in various processes of change. This kind of expertise can be called horizontal (Engeström, Engeström & Kärkkäinen 1995).

But what kind of education and training will produce horizontal expertise? Basically this is a question of transfer. Schools must equip students with the ability to transfer — to use what they have learned to solve new problems successfully or to learn quickly in new situations. Expansive learning (Engeström 1987), based on activity theory, gives one answer to this question. Activity theory redefines the unit of learning: learning of the collective activity system and learning of the individual are intertwined, and the individual's learning is comprehensible only if we understand what the learning of the activity system entails. Significant learning processes are achieved by collective activities. In this view (Engeström & Tuomi-Gröhn 1996), meaningful transfer takes place through interaction between collective activity systems. For example, the school and workplace may engage in collaborative interaction in which both learn something from each other. Solutions for novel problems are created by using the expertise of both activity systems. Transfer is not based on the transition of knowledge only, but on creating in collaboration new theoretical concepts and solutions to problems that lack ready-made answers. The collaborative way of creating knowledge and solving problems is transferred from one situation to another. This process is multidirectional and multifaceted, involving transitions from school to workplace and from workplace to school. On account of its dynamic nature, this transfer is called developmental transfer. The task of this article is to illustrate the concept of developmental transfer and to promote it in education.

The internship period, during which students work and practice in organizations, comprises a useful starting point for this kind of cooperation. This study focuses on the training of practical nurses at the Helsinki Institute of Social and Health Care. The education of practical nurses was extended a few years ago from 2.5 years to 3 years. Those students with only 2.5 years of training, were offered additional training amounting to 20 study weeks. This training includes an internship, which is the focus of this study.

During this internship the principles of the zone of proximal development (ZPD) were applied. Originally, this concept was created by L. S. Vygotsky (1978) for teaching children. The basic idea of the ZDP is that developing mental functions must be fostered and assessed through collaborative, not isolated or independent activities. Originally it referred to interaction between teacher and student. In the case of developmental transfer, the ZPD is expanded to encompass the collaboration of different activity systems: the school and workplace, not only the teacher and students.

The concept of the ZPD is based on the idea of enlightenment. According to this idea, there is valid knowledge towards which one should aim in teaching. The vertical tradition presents this kind of thinking. However, today, when the world is more complex than ever, it is hard to find absolutely true knowledge. Dilemmas are encountered, such as the relationship between technological development and sustaining the environment. It is difficult to find a single approach that is definitely better than the others. Or, when different cultures meet, different bodies of knowledge confront each other, and its is difficult to evaluate which is more qualified and valid. This is the case, for example, when Western and Chinese medicine meet. As mentioned in the beginning of this chapter, the work of practical nurses is expanding to cover a wide variety of clients, and it has become very difficult to settle exclusively on one approach. These factors favor the horizontal view of competencies. These considerations suggest that the concept of the zone of proximal development should be expanded to include both the horizontal and the vertical dimension of expertise.

In the following, the theoretical basis of internship in the training of practical nurses is discussed in more detail from the viewpoint of developmental transfer, horizontal expertise and the zone of proximal development. The evaluation criteria for the internship are based on these theoretical starting points. Finally, three case-study internships are described and analyzed in accordance with the criteria created.

Developmental Transfer

Classical notions of knowledge conceptualize transfer as an ability to apply school-learned knowledge in working life (for a discussion of views of transfer cf. Tuomi-Gröhn & Engeström, this volume). With regard to the demands for horizontal expertise, it is not possible to predict the problems practical nurses will encounter in these new work environments. Nor is it possible to provide them with a "learning kit" that would contain the answers to all the problems. The notion of portable knowledge is challenged by the theories of situated learning (e.g. Beach 1999; Lave 1988), which argue that knowledge is fundamentally situated one. One learns most effectively when learning is an incidental byproduct of genuine participation in meaningful activities, such as work. It follows that practice replaces knowledge as the crucial concept of learning and transfer. From the viewpoint of situated learning, the answer to the problem of meeting the challenges of the broad field of practical nursing is learning at work and learning from the more experienced experts. This novice-expert approach shares the vertical view of expertise that strives to turn novices into experts, and it therefore targets the characteristics of specialists as that which should be taught (Lave 1988; Lave & Wenger 1991). However, in a situation where workplaces are grappling with profound change, it is often the case that no one has answers or solutions to the problems encountered.

Expansive learning (Engeström 1987; Engeström & Tuomi-Gröhn 1996), based on activity theory, attempts to go beyond oppositions between the classical notions of learning and their situated challenges. From the viewpoint of activity theory, vertical and situated accounts of learning and transfer are inadequate to the extent that the unit of analysis is still depicted as an individual who is confined within a learner's relatively limited "domain of situations". An activity-theoretical view (Cole & Engeström 1993) defines the unit of analysis for cognition and learning as a collective activity system mediated by cultural artifacts (tools and signs) as well as rules, community, and division of labor.

In the activity-theoretical view (Engeström & Tuomi-Gröhn 1996), significant learning processes are achieved by collective activities. Activity theory approaches the issue of transfer developmentally. Since a student will enter a workplace which is inevitably caught in developmental turmoil, the best way to be useful and to learn is to become engaged in the change effort. Novices and outsiders can be valuable in change efforts because they see things from a fresh angle and have time to reflect on and take initiative in them.

Meaningful transfer of learning (Engeström & Tuomi-Gröhn 1996) takes place through interaction between collective activity systems. For example, the school and the workplace may engage in collaborative interaction in which both activity systems learn something from each other. Such transfer takes the form of negotiation and exchange between different cultures. What is transferred is not packages of knowledge and skills that remain intact; instead, the very process of such transfer involves active interpreting and reconstructing the skills and knowledge to be transferred. This expansion radically broadens the scope of learning. Thus, the teacher and students are used as agents of change in the organizations, such as elderly homes or daycare centers. The collective capabilities and resources of the schools are brought into these change efforts. Thus, the students and teachers act as mediators and boundary-crossers between educational institutions and workplaces (see also Wenger 1998).

The internship in practical nursing is a natural site for the new role of school as change agent. In development projects, collaborative teams of students, practitioners and teachers will have to develop knowledge and skills (cognitive tools) that meet the challenges of the projects. This is done by constructing and combining heterogeneous networks and "knots" of expertise (Engeström, Engeström & Vähäaho 1999). This is the essence of developmental transfer. An internship can create a zone where two activity systems, the school and the workplace, can jointly find and create mutually relevant boundary practices (Wenger 1998) or projects in which both derive benefit from collaboration.

Horizontal Expertise and Boundary-crossing

While the vertical dimension of expertise remains important, the horizontal dimension is rapidly becoming increasingly relevant for the understanding and acquisition of expertise. Engeström *et al.* (1995) have identified as two central features of the horizontal expertise polycontextuality and boundary-crossing. Reder (1993: 123) talks about polycontextuality at the level of tasks and work actions, emphasizing that the organization of work-group action evolves in such a way that multiple ongoing tasks can be smoothly interrupted, suspended and later resumed amidst a patchwork of other ongoing, yet intermittent tasks.

Engeström *et al.* (1995: 3–4) have enlarged the scope of polycontextuality to the level of larger collaborative activity systems. An activity system is a complex and relatively enduring "community of practice" that often takes the form of an institution. Polycontextuality at the level of activity systems means that experts are engaged not only in multiple simultaneous tasks within one and the same activity but are also increasingly involved in multiple communities of practice. Expertise in these conditions is not primarily manifested in higher or lower skills in performing a well-defined task. Problems are new, and there is little reason to expect that their solutions can be quickly turned into codified, repeatable procedures. These conditions give rise to horizontal expertise where practitioners must move across boundaries to seek and give help, and to find information and tools wherever these happen to be available. Leigh Star (1989) has introduced a useful tool to analyze the creation of new concepts and practices needed in the creation of horizontal expertise. This tool is the concept of a *boundary object*, which Star (1989: 46) defines as follows:

> Boundary objects are objects that are both plastic enough to adapt to local needs and constraints of the several parties employing them, yet robust enough to maintain a common identity across sites. Like the blackboard, a boundary object "sits in the middle" of a group of actors with divergent viewpoints.

Star and Griesemer (1989: 393) add:

> They (boundary objects) are weakly structured in common use, and become strongly structured in individual use. These objects may be abstract or concrete. They have different meanings in different social worlds but their structure is common enough to more than one world to make them recognizable, a means of translation. The creation and management of boundary objects is a key process in developing and maintaining coherence across intersecting social worlds.

A boundary object is a shared basis for cooperation between different partners. Wenger (1998) introduces the concept of the *boundary practice* by referring to the overlapping activities of the participating activity systems. A boundary object is a more precise, shared basis of cooperation (see, e.g. Lambert, this volume). Boundary objects can be concrete artifacts or shared mental models. For instance, a jointly developed form or a novel theoretical concept created cooperatively can comprise a boundary object that is important in facilitating boundary-crossing and cooperation between different partners. The salient characteristic of the boundary object is that it facilitates and promotes collaboration between partners.

Boundary-crossers are people who move from one activity system to another and work in two or more activity systems simultaneously, *sharing the boundary object and the work based on it* with some partners in the other activity system. In this study, the term boundary-crossing is used in this restricted meaning. Not all crossing between different activity systems is referred to here as boundary-crossing, but only those cases where a shared boundary object is created.

In an internship a team can generate a boundary practice that facilitates cooperation between the school and the workplace. With the advancement of cooperation, new problems emerge, requiring new tools and methods for their solution. Concrete or theoretical tools which facilitate joint development of ideas become boundary objects. Horizontal expertise is often developed through boundary objects by virtue of different perspectives that merge through dialogue and create more advanced knowledge and work practices. This is the collaborative learning process and the way boundary-crossing creates horizontal expertise.

The Zone of Proximal Development

Internship is studied here in the light of Vygotsky's (1987: 190–196) concept of the zone of proximal development (ZPD). The basic idea of the ZPD is that developing mental functions must be fostered and assessed through collaborative, not isolated or independent activities. What children can perform collaboratively or with assistance today, they can perform independently and competently tomorrow. The general logic of this method is that the subjects be given a task beyond their present capabilities, a task that could not be solved using the existing skills or tools. This method gives access to "hidden processes" and makes visible what becomes manifest only in the subject's interactions with the environment. The unit of analysis of learning is extended from the individual to the collective unit, including the interaction between the teacher and student. The following specifications clarify the characteristics of the ZDP and its difference from, for instance, conceptions based on pragmatism.

Engeström (1987: 174) defines the concept of ZPD on organizational level:

> It is the distance between the present everyday actions of the individual and the historically new form of the societal activity that can be collectively generated as a solution to the double bind potentially embedded in the everyday actions.

Double bind refers here to dilemmas, situations in which two available alternatives are equally unacceptable. Learning conceptions based on pragmatism do not take into account this contradictory nature of human action, emphasized in activity theory and expansive learning.

According to Moll (1990: 5–11) there are three aspects of Vygostky's theory that are essential for an understanding of his concept of the zone of proximal development and important for the clarification of the contributions of his approach to education. I shall call these aspects collaboration, everyday practice as a forum for mediation of theoretical concepts, and advanced activities. In the following, these aspects are presented in more detail.

(1) Collaboration
The essence of the ZPD is the qualitatively different perspective one gets by contrasting students' solo performance with their performance in collaborative activity. Learning is a social process where the teacher helps the student to exceed his or her present capabilities. The focus is not on transferring skills, as such, from those who know more to those who know less, but on the *collaborative use* of different kinds and different sources of knowledge. In such a teaching system, students develop "reflective

intervention" in the knowledge encountered: they can select knowledge as needed.[1] (Moll 1990: 11). In the case of developmental transfer, the collaborative team is expanded from a teacher and a student to a team of partners from two activity systems.

In traditional internship, the student works on tasks assigned to him or her under the guidance of a teacher or of a mentor from the workplace. The focus is on working alone and independently. In this new mode of internship, it is important to establish a collaborative team that jointly seeks after and creates knowledge and solves problems. Each collaborative team is intended to include student(s), a teacher, a mentor and other practitioners from the workplace. This is one of the very basic ideas of developmental transfer and horizontal expertise: it is important to learn to work in multiprofessional teams and to learn to seek solutions to problems which do not have ready-made answers.

According to this principle, one aim of the internship being studied here was to create a collaborative team to supervise the student during the internship. This team included a student, a mentor at the workplace, a teacher and in some cases other students and other practitioners.

(2) Relationships between theoretical concepts and everyday practices

Vygotsky (1987: 193, 219) emphasized that everyday and scientific concepts are interconnected and interdependent, and that their development is mutually influential.[2] One cannot exist without the other. Thus, scientific concepts[3] grow down into everyday practice, into the domain of personal experience, acquiring meaning and significance, and they facilitate the mastery of the more advanced aspects of the everyday concepts. This notion of interrelatedness between different types of concepts in learning, however, retains and reproduces the basic singular directionality of vertical movements. Horizontal expertise often requires sideways moves with step-by-step discussions and mediation between the scientific concept and experienced concept (Engeström 1999: 23–24).

This is the very basis for a functional cooperation between school and working life. It is often a problem that theoretical facts and concepts remain detached from everyday practice; they become a useless pool of knowledge. Likewise, many problems in work settings are solved on the basis of everyday experience, without drawing on already existing theoretical tools. The aim of the internship in this context is to help the student use theoretical knowledge in solving everyday problems. However, in a broader sense, the basic issue is to help the two participating activity systems utilize the internship to advance developmental transfer. The cooperation between the teacher and student and the practitioners will facilitate the activation of the most recent theoretical tools for

---

[1] This perspective is consistent with what Vygostky (1987) felt was the essential characteristics of instruction: the introduction of conscious awareness into many domains of activity; that is, acquiring control and mastery of psychological processes through the manipulation of tools of thinking.

[2] Vygotsky (1987) warns against atomistic reductionism in education. He rejects artificial divisions of abstractions and insists on what might be called a holistic approach; the unit of study must be psychological activity in all its complexity, not in isolation.

[3] Davydov (1988, 1990) discusses the difference between the terms scientific and theoretical. He prefers theoretical to scientific. This aspect is also taken up in the introductory chapter of this volume.

solving problems in the workplace, either in a vertical or a horizontal sense. At the same time, the school receives empirical feedback concerning the theoretical tools, their usefulness and their applicability.

(3) Advanced practices

Vygotsky's major focus on teaching and learning was not only on developmental processes as they normally occur, but especially on the effects of disruptions and interventions (Wertsch 1985: 18).[4] That is: a Vygoskian approach to education does not characterize teaching and learning as part of existent practices but as creating fundamentally new, advanced activities[5] for the student.

Applying this focus to education implies the need to study how current practices constrain or facilitate thinking, and the need to create new, more advanced, amplifying practices for students. The Vygotskian line of thinking is based on the idea that the teacher knows the advanced practices and that the task is to help students to learn them. The theoretical thinking behind the concept of expansive learning (Engeström 1987) and developmental transfer conceptualizes the zone of proximal development as a target unknown to everybody. The task of the collaborative work is to find and create new advanced practices. The very basic difference between the thinking based on traditional and expansive learning is that in the former the student either takes theoretical concepts learned at school and applies them in the workplace, or the student adapts to the existing working practices. According to the notion of expansive learning this is not enough: one should be able to create new knowledge and more advanced work practices. In our view, an internship aims to improve work practices genuinely by seeking more advanced practices of the workplace, school and student. By developing social networks that connect the team to outside resources, by mobilizing latent or dormant knowledge, and experiences of teachers and practitioners, new more advanced practices are created. The role of the school as an agent of change in this process is of crucial importance. The ethos of learning is to investigate and reconstruct, instead of adapting to existing practices.

Criteria for Internship Evaluation

An innovative internship for practical nurses is evaluated in this study through the use of the previously discussed aspects.

(a) What is the nature of the cooperation in the developmental project? Is there a collaborative team? Who are the participants? Are any boundary objects being created?

---

[4] A major theme in Vygotsky's approach is a reliance on a genetic or developmental analysis in keeping with his claim that psychological processes must be studied in transitions (Vygotsky 1978).
[5] According to the notion of expansive learning (Engeström 1987) advanced practices mean that the object of the activity system is perceived in a new way, and this affects the change in the motive, rules, tools and division of labor.

(b) How is theoretical knowledge used in implementing the developmental project? What kinds of everyday knowledge or everyday experiences are used in the project? What is the interrelationship between these two?
(c) What kind of networks and boundary-crossing has been created during the project?
(d) What are the benefits of participation in the developmental project to the different partners?
(e) What kinds of advanced collaborative practices have emerged? How sustainable are these changes?

Most of these criteria are based on the extension of the Vygotskian ZDP. Collaboration, interrelationship between scientific knowledge and everyday experiences, and advanced collaborative practices are all based on the Vygotskian ZDP. The advance vis-à-vis the Vygotskian conception is, however, that the collaboration in our case includes not only the student and teacher, but a collaborative team comprising members from two distinct activity systems. The interrelationship between theoretical knowledge and everyday experiences also brings horizontal transformations in addition to vertical ones. Moreover, the advanced practices are not something known by the teacher in advance, but are created together in the team.

Networks and boundary-crossing are based on the idea of horizontal expertise, which requires the ability to move across boundaries, to seek help and to find information and tools wherever they happen to be available, that is: to create and benefit from networks. Benefits for the different partners are used as criteria based on the concept of developmental transfer: cooperation between different activity systems must be useful for both partners. All these aspects are necessary prerequisites for developmental transfer to take place.

Research Target, Collection and Analysis of the Data

In 1998, the training of practical nurses in Finland was extended from 2.5 to 3 years. For practical nurses with a training period of 2.5 years, an additional training program (20 study weeks) has been arranged. The subject of this study, the additional program implemented in 1998 at the Helsinki Institute of Social and Health Care, applies the developmental principles described above. Students work e.g. on the hospital wards, elderly homes and daycare centers during the internship. The developmental project was organized in each of the collaborating workplaces. The teacher, student(s), and a local workplace mentor, established a team to support the student in implementing the local project.

During the internship period, the students, their teacher and the researcher, met at school once every three weeks to discuss and to work on improving their projects. During these school days, the students learned about other projects going on at other workplaces at the same time. At the end of the internship, each project was presented at the workplace in a joint meeting, called the "arena of learning" and attended by all those involved in the developmental project.

In 1998, nine different developmental projects were implemented by students in the additional training program. In this study, three projects with different kinds of results were selected as targets for this research.

Two of the projects studied here were conducted in geriatric settings and one in a childrens' daycare center. All three projects had a common theme, namely: activating the clients: developing recreational activities for the elderly and surveying possibilities for arranging physical exercise for the children. Two of these projects were carried out in spring 1998, and the third in autumn 1998.

The field researcher[6] who was originally a health care instructor, stayed with the three different workplaces studied here altogether for four months. She followed the ordinary activities of the workplaces and interviewed the workers, customers, teachers and students. The role of the school and teacher in the case of developmental transfer is the role of a agent of change. They are not passive participants in the collaboration. In this case, the field researcher also played an active role. For this reason, it was as if two teachers were working in these projects.

The data used here are based on the field researcher's field notes taken during her participatory observation, and on audio recordings of the student's mentoring-team meetings and the students' and teachers' meetings at school.

Description of Three Developmental Projects

The projects are first described in brief and then evaluated according to the stated criteria.

Project A: Geriatric ward "Silverhair"
(the names are fictional)

This psycho-geriatric ward consists of 24 beds and a personnel of altogether 10 nurses. During the study period, staff changed often because of numerous sick leaves. In addition, the nurse appointed to mentor the project-planning student had to take a long sick leave, and a young, newly recruited nurse took over that responsibility. The practical nursing student was a female, 29, who had specialized in nursing and care in her prior studies.

The basic idea of project A was inspired by the feedback received from the relatives of the residents. They had noticed that the elderly were lonely and complained about the absence of social contacts. However, the staff saw the situation differently. They pointed out that activities had been organized, but the residents did not want to participate them. The head nurse suggested that the aim of the project could be to increase the general satisfaction of the elderly. In addition, the student was assigned three personal residents whose recreation she should personally take care of. The aim was to follow up whether these efforts had any effect on the clients' need for medication. The project proceeded with seven themes. Although they were partly overlapping, they are discussed here

---

[6] The field researcher and the author of this report are two different persons.

separately, for the sake of clarity. Each theme describes a different way of trying to solve a problem or to promote the project. The excerpts serve to illuminate the basic idea of the theme, although due to the nature of the data, it was not possible to analyse all discussions systematically.

The Themes Dealt with in the Project

Theme 1: Activities planned on the basis of discussions with the personnel
The student began to plan the recreative activities by discussing the options with the nurses. However, they did not know their clients very well. The student organized quiz programs and singing sessions. Some of the residents took part in these activities. Later, dancing was organized and time for hobby crafts, but none of the residents participated. This initiative proved unfruitful. (Fieldnotes)

Theme 2: Residents' opinions are solicited in a joint meeting
The student noticed that the residents complained about the organized activities, and, as a result, the residents' opinion was solicited during a joint coffee session. However, during this session, nobody made any suggestions. (Fieldnotes)

Theme 3: The team meeting practice of the ward is reintroduced
The teacher recalled that the project should be a joint venture of the whole ward and not only the student's project. The consequence of this was that the joint team meetings of the whole ward were resumed again, after a long pause. These meetings were now to be held once every two weeks. The nurse responsible for the team meetings was on prolonged sick leave, and the chairman of the meetings changed from one meeting to another. At the same time, the head-nurse had the obligation to attend the meetings with the head nurses of the other wards. Due to this, the teacher had to assume more responsibility for the team meetings, thus, becoming a consultant. In the beginning, the staff did not perceive the purpose of the team meetings, and they suspected that the meetings were being held for the students' benefit only.

> Practical nurse: (as a chairman) Is it OK if we start discussing the residents' situation in these meetings, or what do you expect of these meeting, from the viewpoint of the school?
> Teacher: For our part, we are here for you, but you, of course, should use the team as you see fit.
> Nurse: Good, then we shall begin to discuss the residents and their needs.
> (The team meeting)

The team ends up discussing a subject important for the whole staff, that is, the situation of the residents of the ward.

In one team meeting, the student complained of being frustrated because she had understood that, first of all, the residents wanted more time with the nurses.

> Student: It is useless to present any of my own residents next time [the next team meeting]. Because all they need here is more time with the

> nurses. And for that — I cannot do anything about it. What am I doing here anyway?
> Researcher: You can use more time with the residents assigned to you, try to observe them and listen to their thoughts and then, here at the team meetings, we can jointly consider what we can do together to improve their contentment.
> Nurse: This made things more clear.
> Student (frustrated): But I have to do something [about it].

The team activities helped develop cooperation at the ward, but did not efficiently support the developmental project organized around the student.

Theme 4: Cooperation with people outside the ward
The student tried to contact an occupational therapist and a craft instructor in order to organize recreational activities, but these experts did not have time to help her. The cooperation attempt failed. (Fieldnotes)

Theme 5: A difficult male resident
The student decided to concentrate on a male resident who was named as her special resident. He turned out to be someone who the whole stafff had experienced as being a difficult person. He harassed the female staff members. The student tried to talk with him and also succeeded in that, but the resident was so demanding that the student got fed up with him.

> Student: I have tried all I can. In the beginning the discussions were OK, but then I felt that nothing is good enough for him, he only complains and asks for more. Last time he demanded that I should apply some ointment on his skin, but it looked perfectly healthy. I will give up the whole internship. (Students' meeting at the school)

Despite the threat to give up the whole internship, the student decided to proceed with the support of the teacher. The other students also gave decisive help in this situation. Finally, the student gave up on the male resident, who at the end of the research period, began to adapt somewhat better to the life of the ward. Yet, in this situation, the student felt that she had abandoned the old man.

Theme 6: Theoretical knowledge and training
Since things related to old peoples' sexuality were new to students, and this matter also seemed to trouble the other staff members, the teacher proposed to organize education on sexual matters with the help of an expert. Two afternoon training sessions were arranged on the theme: "Confronting sexuality in old people's care" These sessions were open to the whole elderly home, not only for the staff of this one ward. The feedback reflected controversy. On the one hand, the training was considered as important, but on the other hand, it was experienced as too distant from the everyday work on the ward

Nurse: Well, it was quite interesting, but it was only about one's own sexuality, then — I don't know how this is related to these old people here. (Team meeting)

In one team meeting the student said that the difficult male resident had talked with her about a study focusing on old people's care.

Student: He watches a lot of TV and he had heard yesterday about a study on old people's care. I would be glad to read it. Does anybody know about it?

Nurse: Yes, he really watches TV a lot, and especially news. He is quite aware of what is happening in the world.

The matter is passed over without further consideration of the chance of gaining new theoretical knowledge.

Theme 7: Dependent female residents

After giving up the male resident, the student concentrated on two female residents. She sat with them in the cantine, took them on walks out in the fresh air and took part in various other activities. However, jealousy developed between the residents about the student. She experienced the situation as very distressing, because one of the two had become so dependent on her.

Student: Shouldn't we circulate these personal residents in order not to make them dependent on the nurse? You cannot stand these things for a long time.

Nurse: Usually these long-term caring relationships are better, only in some exceptional cases it is better to change the personal nurse. (Team meeting)

In this case the situation remains unresolved.

In the following, project A is evaluated applying the criteria developed in Chapters 2 and 3. The results are analyzed from the viewpoints of the various participants. Thus, collaboration is marked either with + or – depending on who takes part in it.

The aim of the instruction based on the concept of zone of proximal development is to promote a fruitful relationship between the theoretical knowledge and everyday experiences. If this kind of relationship was observed, a T identifies those who provided the theoretical input, and E identifies those who brought in their everyday experiences as the complements of the theoretical concepts.

Creating networks refers either to seeking knowledge and help, or disseminating knowledge outside the collaborative team. This means interaction with persons outside the team or the ward, such as experts or organizations of experts. If successful, this kind of interaction may lead to boundary-crossing. However, not all contacts lead to successful results. Successful contacts, unsuccessful contacts, and the initiator of the contact are also explicated in the results.

The benefits are evaluated from the viewpoint of each partner either with + or – according to whether the partner did or did not benefit from the collaboration. It is well to remember that these evaluations are based on the field notes and recordings of the sessions at the ward and at school. Benefits are not evaluated here by the partners themselves, but, rather, on the basis of the new activities or the artefacts created in the project. This is a limitation, because there may be mental insights even in the cases where no new activities are reported. However, the data used here did not allow for these kind of findings.

Advanced collaborative activities mean that new kinds of activities are produced collaboratively. Due to the collaborative nature of activities, they are not evaluated from the viewpoints of the different participants. Instead, the aim is to evaluate the sustainability of the results to ensure their further development.

Table 1: Evaluation of the project according to the criteria created.

Criteria	Collaborative team	Theoretical knowledge integrated with everyday experiences	Networks and boundary crossing	Benefits
Student	(–)	(T)	–	–
Teacher/school	+	(T)	+	–
Practitioners/ward	+	(E)	–	+
Clients	(–)	(E)	–	–

Advanced collaborative activities: None

The signs: + = successful
(–) = was tried without success
– = not successful
T = theoretical contribution
E = contribution based on everyday experiences

Collaboration   In this project, there was no team which could devote itself to solve problems related to the developmental project collaboratively, in keeping with the notion of the ZPD. The student was left alone with her project. The effort to collaborate with the residents did not succeed. The team dealt mainly with the medical needs of the residents. The recreational activities and the means to enhance the residents' contentedness were discussed in the team meetings only from the viewpoints of the student's personal residents. The team that had been created on the ward was relatively well organized, but in terms of the project it had focused on the activities of the whole ward, instead of on the developmental project. The team served mainly the medical needs of the customers, not the aims of the project. Nevertheless, as the teacher worked as a consultant in the team, collaboration was not totally absent, and her contribution was of importance from the viewpoint of collaboration between the two activity systems as well.

The effort to establish relationships between the scientific concepts and everyday experiences also failed. Nevertheless, there were several good attempts. The teacher provided theoretical tools in her lectures, but it was not easy for the nurses to apply that knowledge in their everyday practice. There was a gap between kowledge of one's own sexuality and understanding the sexual needs of the elderly residents. In addition, the student tried to emphasize the need for theoretical knowledge, but the others in the team ignored this. Practical experiences were explored from both the residents' and personnel's perspective, but neither of these sources proved fruitful. The nurses knew neither the residents nor their needs, and an open joint meeting was not the forum to encourage the residents to reveal their own personal thoughts. The project was based solely on the training received by the student. She did not have any working experience with the elderly, nor had she received any specialized training in geriatric nursing.

Networks and boundary-crossing in project A can be described with the aid of the following diagram (Figure 1).

The diagram shows the collaborating partners in bold, and the direction of the point of the arrow indicates the person who started the collaboration. A bidirectional arrow in some diagrams represents mutual interaction, and an arrow with dotted shaft depicts a failed attempt to collaborate.

During this internship period, a network became established between the teacher and the personnel of the ward. The teacher is here a boundary-crosser who had a shared object with the personnel: the needs of the clients on the ward. The student with her own project remained outside this relationship. She tried to establish a network with the experts of the ward and the residents, but this attempt was not succesful either.

Benefits The cooperation between the school and the workplace was beneficial mainly from the viewpoint of the personnel of the ward. Their team meetings were reintroduced, and the teacher worked as a consultant in the team. However, the residents remained passive, and the student learned hardly anything else but how to cope with frustrating situations (her own comment at the school session).

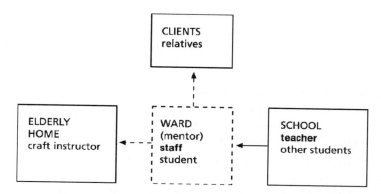

Figure 1: Networks and boundary-crossing in project A.

Advanced collaborative activities In this project, no advanced activities were created.

Project A failed for several reasons. It was inadequately focused, in many ways. First, one may ask whether the residents' basic feeling of loneliness was responded to adequately. The student gave several signals that the residents wanted more personal attention from the nurses, rather than recreational activities. This could be one of the reasons for the low participation by the residents in arranged events. On the other hand, the activities of the team were focused away from the purposes of the developmental project: the original object was the medical rehabilitation of the residents and not recreational activities. In this situation, the student did not receive support from the team as originally intended. Training based on a developmental project was new for the teacher as well as for the personnel of the ward. Therefore, the teacher directed the team to serve the needs of the ward when the personnel inquired about the purpose of the team and its aims.

In this project, the different partners derived only partial benefit: the ward benefited from the presence of the student and the teacher, but the benefits remained few. This was due to the different objects of the activity: the residents wanted more time with the nurses, but the student organized recreational activities. The staff tried to perform their everyday duties, and the teacher served as a consultant. Because the shared object was missing, there was no dialogue between the collaborators. Nevertheless, the project proved that collaboration between the two activity systems can be useful: the teacher's support was important for the ward activities. However, in this case no new, more developed practices evolved as a result of this support.

Project B: Geriatric ward "Golden age"

This ward is for those who suffer from dementia and depression. In 1998 at the time of the project, there were 21 residents and a staff of seven. There were only a few changes in the staff during the study period. The student responsible for this project was a 21-year old practical nurse, who had specialized in geriatric care in her previous studies.

The basic idea of the project arose from a study done with the relatives of the residents and on questions sounding out the residents' wishes. Both revealed that the elderly were lonely. Thus, the standpoint was similar to that of project A. Based on this, recreational activities were chosen as a developmental project. The project continued with the following themes, which were partly overlapping.

Theme 1: Surveying the wishes of the residents
As a result of the mentoring-team meeting, the student began to survey the wishes and needs of the residents. She interviewed all of them separately. A life-span questionnaire was used as an outline of the interview.

> Head nurse : We are now beginning to use this life-span questionnaire to ask the relatives about the residents' life cycle and its individual features. How about using this same questionnaire as the basis of the interview? (Mentoring situation at the workplace)

The result of the interview was that the residents wished for more outdoor activities, chatting and, especially, more time with and attention from the nurses.

Theme 2: A form for gathering information on the residents' life cycle and their interests

The student gathered, on a single form, all information available for each resident. This form was inserted in the care plan for all the new students and staff members to read.

> Teacher: One idea would be to gather a summary based on the interviews, and then present it in the ward meeting. This would help each of us to become more acquainted with the summary. (Mentoring situation at the workplace)

Later, the researcher proposed that this form could be added as an insert into the care plan. Following the interview, then, a summary of each personal profile was written to be used as a starting point for drawing the care plan. This had only seldom been done in the past.

Theme 3: Previous studies

In the meeting at the school and in discussions about the project, some previous studies were also mentioned. That material was given to the staff of the ward. It is not possible to judge from the documents of this research whether these had been used in practice on the ward. Nevertheless, the residents' interviews indicate that the idea of asking about the reasons for their dissatisfaction derived from the previous studies.

> Teacher: Do you think you should ask the residents also about their satisfaction with their present activities, the ward, or something like that . . .? (Students' meeting at school)

Theme 4: Training

A lecture on the recreational activities for the elderly was organized for the whole elderly home. The student and her mentor attended, too, however, the message of the lecture seemed to have no impact on the work of the ward.

The care plan was put into practice on the ward, and the researcher proposed that the teacher organize a training session about it for the whole staff. However, the head nurse dismissed the whole idea.

> Head nurse: I don't know . . . the teachers, . . . are easily too theoretical. There is not, necessarily, any help for us. The Roper model is used in many places, I guess it is OK for us without any training. (Mentoring session at the workplace)

Theme 5: Contacting persons outside the ward

There was a member of the work community whose job it was to take the residents out for a walk. She turned out to be so busy that she could not take on any more residents from this ward. Instead, the crafts instructor employed at the elderly home became interested, and the student began to cooperate with her. The crafts instructor was familiar with the recreational activities and the student knew the residents' wishes from their interviews. (Fieldnotes)

Theme 6: Organizing recreational activities
The student organized weekly meetings for the residents with the help of the crafts instructor. There were several themes, such as showing slides of the old buildings of Helsinki, reminiscence sessions based on these slides, completing old sayings and discussing the different meanings they carry, looking at the slides the nurse had taken in foreign countries, bingo and gymnastics. In addition to this, the student organized activity sessions which she led, alone, once a week. These activities became more popular during the study period, and residents from other wards joined the sessions. However, the student experienced that she was quite alone with her project, that the staff was not with her in the practical organization of things with the exception of the crafts instructor.

> Student: The staff tries to cooperate . . . those who happen to be there, but perhaps too easily, they always move away to some other tasks, for example, answering the phone and so on. (Students' meeting at school)

In the following, project B is evaluated, according to the criteria devised, from the viewpoints of the different partners.

Table 2: Evaluation of project B.

Criteria	Collaborative team	Theoretical concepts integrated with everyday experiences	Networks and boundary crossing	Benefits
Student	+	T	+	+
Teacher/school	–	(T)	–	–
Practioners/ward	+ –	T	–	– +
Clients	+	E	–	+
Elderly home	+	E	+	–

Advanced collaborative activities: None. Traditional activities only

The signs: + = successful
(–) = was tried without success
– = not successful
T = theoretical contribution
E = contribution based on everyday experiences

Collaboration   No teamwork was done during this internship period as it had been envisioned in the aims of training. In the beginning, the activities of the mentoring team at the ward were promising. The team guided the student to ask what the residents wanted. In the team meetings, the life span questionnaire was also devised as a tool to this end. However, the support from the team waned when the recreative activities were actually being implemented. Collaboration was carried out only between the student, the residents and the crafts instructor. It was an advantage to have determined the residents' wishes before planning the activities. The interview also motivated the elderly themselves to participate in the recreational activities. However, there was a problem: the crafts instructor was assigned to the elderly home and was not a member of the ward, and therefore, the new activities were not sustained after the student was gone. In addition, the input of the teacher and the school remained on a minor scale.

Relationship between scientific concepts and everyday experiences The life-span questionnaire proved to be a useful theoretical tool. The student conducted the interview of the residents on the basis of this questionnaire. The life course and interests of each resident were then summarized, and they remained as part of the care plan. The research results were also discussed during the meetings of the students and the teacher at school. Moreover, the teacher offered theoretical help to the personnel of the ward, but this help was rejected. In addition, the practical experiences of the collaborators were used. The life-span questionnaire helped by outlining the experiences of the residents and, in this case, the theoretical knowledge became fruitfully intertwined with everyday experiences. The craft instructor's previous experience in organizing recreational activities was also a beneficial everyday contribution from the viewpoint of the project.

Networks and boundary-crossing in this project can be summarized in the following diagram (Figure 2).

In project B, the network was created internally, inside the elderly home: between the student, residents and the crafts instructor. The school remained outside this network. The boundary-crossers were the student and the crafts instructor, who had a shared object: recreational activities as a basis of their collaboration. The teacher remained out of this collaboration and, therefore, it cannot be said that she was a boundary-crosser.

Benefits The residents wished for more personal attention and more time from the nurses, and this wish was fulfilled. First, the joint activities were planned according to

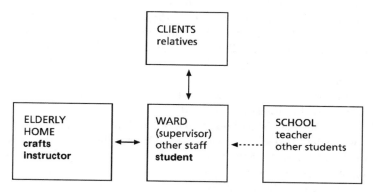

Figure 2: Networks and boundary-crossing in project B.

the needs of the residents; and second, while the student was engaged in organizing these joint activities, the staff members were left with more time for interaction with the residents personally assigned to them. As in project A, the elderly felt lonely, and the staff's response was the same: to organize recreational activities. However, the participation of the elderly was different: in project A, the elderly remained passive. The more active participation in project B may be due to the fact that the voices of the elderly were being heard. The activities were organized according to their wishes. This is an example of client-centerness, a principle emphasized in contemporary health care. However, the challenging question is how to do this in practice and how to develop suitable methods for sounding out the needs and wishes of the clients.

The other partners also derived benefits from the developmental project. The personnel of the ward were left with more time for other tasks, while the student organized and ran the activities. The life-span questionnaire remaind also as a tool for future use. The student learned to use methods of client-centered and recreational work. The teacher and the school derived the least benefit in this case.

Advanced collaborative activities   In this project, activities were created which were important and beneficial for the whole ward. However, these activities repeated the models used previously by the crafts instructor and were not new advanced activities in the sense of expansive learning and developmental transfer. In addition, the activities were not sustained as such. The staff had experienced the student as an efficient addition to the staff force, but after she left, the activities she directed were discontinued.

Several factors contributed to the success of this project. Theoretical knowledge was interwoven fruitfully with everyday experiences. It is noteworthy that the most important theoretical tool, the life span questionnaire, was based on a suggestion made by the staff of the ward. Theoretical knowledge does not necessarily come only from the school. It is also interesting that the boundaries of the ward were being crossed: the student was able to cooperate with an expert from the staff outside ward. In order to develop horizontal expertise, this kind of cooperation should be encouraged: knowledge should be sought from those who have it. A shared object of work was also developed among some of the partners: the residents, the student and the crafts instructor were intent on organizing new recreational activities. The other nurses of the ward had their everyday routines as the object of their work. These differences in the objects of work and the diminishing collaboration in the team led to a situation, in which the new activities could not be sustained. Regarding the successful results of those activities while they lasted, the collaboration with the residents can be regarded as having been of great importance.

It is also noteworthy that the theoretical knowledge offered by the teacher was rejected in project B. In project A, this kind of help was not rejected, but it could not be applied, either. This may be an implication of the difference of the two domains: the school may be too detached from the workplace. On the other hand, this may also be an indication of the importance of the training that strives to bring about developmental transfer. Collaboration makes it possible to develop shared boundary objects and boundary activities where theoretical knowledge can be better put forward to serve the practical purposes.

Regarding developmental transfer, this project was unable to bring sustainable benefits to either organization, the school or the ward; new sustainable and advanced activities were not developed. One might say that this kind of internship is close to the concept of the traditional internship: the student learns, and the work community gains work force benefits as long as the students' internship period lasts. In this project, not enough attention was paid to developing joint, collaborative teamwork. The teamwork started in a promising way, but as the team members did not participate in the implementation of the project and the sustainability of the activities, and thus the benefits for the various partners diminished accordingly.

Project C: Daycare Center "Toddlers"

This daycare center is fairly large, consisting altogether of five departments. The student worked with first grade children in the afternoons, after school. There were 13 children and one staff member in this department. The project assessed the possibilities for childrens' physical activities in the daycare center and in the vicinity. The aim of the student was to test, study and implement the different possibilities for various physical activities. The idea of the project came from a new kindergarten teacher working in the daycare center who was interested in this particular subject. She was also a mentor to the student. The student is a 23-year-old female practical nurse who was specialized in the care and education of children and adolescents.

Theme 1: Theoretical material
In order to start the project, the local mentor gave some theoretical material to the student dealing with the meaning of physical activities during different phases of life. In addition to this, the student consulted her old study notes on this subject. The mentor also gave her a table summarizing different areas of physical activities with a description of how, and when, an average child should accomplish in these areas. Other related materials were also sought from the library and the Internet. (Fieldnotes)

Theme 2: Team meetings at the daycare center
The head of the center, the mentor of the department, the students and the teacher conducted regular meetings to discuss the project and its progress. This team adopted an innovative approach to its task and to the use of new knowledge gained.

> Head of the center: Do you find the theme difficult?
> Student: Although I have not yet done much, I think this job is OK. Especially because I do not know much about physical activities yet.
> Head of the center: Yes, definitely.
> Teacher: Oh yes. And how much can one use the possibilities for physical activities, here, in this immediate environment? This could be one thing to study.
> Head of the center: And, then, working in small groups, trying out some new outdoor activities. Here, we have quite an excellent sports field right next to this house. Just take a few kids over there.

> Mentor: Or we can discuss the possibilities we have right here, for giving the feeling and experience of physical exercise. But do we have enough room . . . floor materials and equipment?

This team also appreciated the connection between motor development and the development of speech as a theoretically important insight.

> Student 1: Only yesterday we noticed that this child, who has some difficulties with his speech, cannot crawl either. We were wondering whether he had been able to crawl when he was a baby. I wonder if he has been moving about on his behind only.
>
> Mentor: I once asked the mother whether it was true that he did not crawl when he was a baby. Just recently someone has published research on this matter.
>
> Teacher: I haven't heard about that study, but NN is doing a licentiate thesis on such children. She is one of our teachers. If you are interested in this problem, please let me know how to reach you.
>
> Student 2: I want that information too. It was I who tried to locate the study.
>
> Teacher: OK, give me your phone number, I will call you [about the study]
>
> Head of the center: Well, what does the whole daycare center get out of this? Definitely we are getting information that helps us make observations. This is very important for all of us. This is the way these projects should bring us new information that can help us do our job. I just began to think about this child and his problems more thoroughly, you can really see the same thing in the group of the very youngest children. To help us make better observations, this is a really good project, indeed.
>
> *   *
>
> Head of the center: If we can develop our work through these projects and have enough interest in them, and if these new ideas add to our ways of doing the work — then we have come a long way.

Theme 3: Developing morning activities

Some problems arose in the middle of the physical activities project as one of the children was rejected by the group. The scope of the problem expanded, and the parents were also invited to the meetings. The problem focused on the activity area of the student, though the main reason for the difficulty was the activity of the whole department. The head of center worked on the problem, and the ground rules of the activities of the daycare center were reconsidered. This episode was rather strenuous and took a lot of the student's energy.

Theme 4: Interviewing children

A decision was made to interview the children to find out what they would be interested in. Nevertheless, the mentor and the student only ask the children what is fun in the daycare center.

Theme 5: Testing the physical abilities of the children

The mentor and the student tested together the childrens' physical abilities, such as throwing a ball and running.

> Teacher: What are the results?
> Student: For example, in the group test, surprisingly few were able to . . . And then, one very important thing: while walking, three kids held their arms straight to their side, the other hand almost rigid . . . two kids had something too, but I cannot tell what. And one kid: he was stepping on his whole foot, not only on the ball of the foot. (Meeting of the mentoring team)

The test proved to be revealing: over half of the children had remarkable problems in moving and in their physical abilities that would have consequences for their later development. The staff noticed that the children with motor problems also have problems in speech development.

Theme 6: Informing parents, and cooperating both with them and outside experts

The test results having become available, the head of the center decided to discuss the matter in a joint meeting with the staff of a mothers' counselling center.

> Teacher: I see this problem in a larger framework of how to help those children who have some problems. Through cooperation? Because the assistance should be coordinated, and no harm done to the kids.
> Student: I was thinking this morning, that these kids have just had their six-year check up. I was wondering about their speech: what happened in those check-ups?
> Head of the center: We cooperate with the mothers' counselling center. This new information is very important to me. Everything is not necessarily revealed in those check-ups, the situations are so tense and so on . . . You really don't see. But when you come to daycare, then these problems became visible.
> Mentor: I remember that motor development is connected to the development of speech, reading and mathematical skills later in life. Here we have this one kid, with excactly that kind of a problem. I mean, if you add physical activities, it may help him develop his reading and speech too. (Meeting of the mentoring team)

The matter was also discussed with the parents.

> Mentor: If you see that there is some kind of difficulty, and you have observed it in several situations, how should the parents be informed? How can the negative side effects be avoided?
> Student 2: I think we have not thought about this, anyway, though we have noticed these kinds of situations.
> Mentor: I think it is our duty to inform the parents. Some time ago, I was talking about one kid to his mother, and she rejected the whole matter.

> Head of the center: Yes, this is one thing that is very important and useful for us in this work community, these matters are part of our professional skills. However, they are difficult, but it is important to tell the parents. (Meeting of the mentoring team)
>
> *   *
>
> Head of the center: Yes, we shall have a meeting with the staff from the mothers' counselling center, they have put forward the same thing: parents should learn to focus on the right things. It must be a trend in small children's families these days: you just push the kids around in a cart and serve the kid, everything should be ready. You do not train these very basic skills. This is an important area, right here you should empower the parents. Parents can easily be doing harm to their kids by doing everything for them. We, as professionals, should really cooperate more with the parents, to wake them up, and to make them think. (Meeting at the work place)

Next year, the parents were able attend a series of meetings that discuss child development at different ages. These meetings were organized together with the Mannerheim League of Child Welfare, emphasizing the importance of physical exercise which was also included in the agenda of these meetings.

> Head of the center: This is a very interesting matter . . . Next year we shall start a series of meetings about child development at different ages. These meetings are planned to suit the parents: we shall discuss these developmental stages, how to observe how the child is using its feet, and we'll explain what is happening.

Theme 7: Training

It was noticed that the whole staff needed more training in this matter. The monitoring of motor development was neglected for other areas of education. The staff was not able to pay enough attention to this matter.

> Head of the center: In this other daycare center, the whole pedagogy is based on using the child's physical abilities as a tool . . . We can ask NN [an expert in motor development] to join us, she is experienced in these matters . . . It could be a very important stimulus for the whole daycare center to realize that these things develop hand in hand. (Meeting at the work place)

The teacher contacted her colleague who was specialized in studying the relationship between motor development and speech in children. This colleague was scheduled to give a lecture at the school for students and the same lecture was later delivered to the whole staff of the daycare center.

> Head of the center: . . . this is really something useful, for all of us. I mean, the results can be remarkable, we have a wonderful learning environment, and we have disscussed this when starting to improve our curriculum . . . Maybe we have been focusing less on it [physical

exercise], as other things have been more important. The balance between the different parts of the curriculum and the variety of activities are of the utmost importance in bringing up small children. (Meeting at the work place)

The speech therapist of the day care center was also consulted on this matter.

Theme 8: Information folder

The student worked out a manual like folder containing a summary of the central phases of the development of the physical abilities of a child, a test to measure it, guidelines to interpret the test, and several ideas of how to organize physical activities for small children.

> Teacher: What kind of literature do you have? I have got a really difficult book from NN.
> Mentor: The book is called 'Somersault'.
> Head of the center: Yes, we have that.
> Mentor: The book is awfully difficult, you have to read and think about it.
> Teacher: It is written for the professionals in the field of physical education.
> Head of the center: It could be part of our project, included in the materials. It could be important for us. We do not have it here in our library.
> Teacher: The University of Jyväskylä has a Faculty of Physical Education and a Faculty of Education, and they cooperate with one another.
> Student: Yes, I saw in the Internet some stuff regarding science and research.
> Teacher: In the near future, you are going to learn how to use the Internet for locating and retrieving information. Our teacher in computer skills will help you learn how to find information for the project.

At the top of the following page, project C is analyzed according to the criteria created.

Collaboration A team was nominated in the daycare center to work on the developmental project only. All partners participated in the teamwork. It is noteworthy that the head of the daycare center actively participated in the teamwork. The team created a common boundary object, namely the insight that children's motor development and speech are related. This insight is a boundary object based on a theoretical concept that includes a basis for dialogue between different practitioners: a speech therapist, a kindergarten teacher, the head of the center and an expert specialized in motor development of children. Each partner was able to contribute his or her own expertise to produce different kinds of practical applications: physical exercises, speech training, providing information to parents, and discussions with the representatives of other childcare institutes.

Table 3: Evaluation of project C.

Criteria	Collaborative team	Theoretical concepts integrated with everyday experiences	Networks and boundary crossing	Benefits
Student	+	T	+	+
Teacher/school	+	T	+	+ −
Practioners/ward	+	E	+	+
Clients	+	E	+	+
Daycare center		T	+	+
Organizations outside the daycare center			+	+

Advanced collaborative activies: Expanding activities

The signs: + = successful
          (–) = was tried without success
          – = not successful
          T = theoretical contribution
          E = contribution based on everyday experiences

Relationships between scientific concepts and everyday experiences   The expertise of different team members was used to define the common boundary object. The student searched for new theoretical knowledge from various sources: the Internet and previous studies. The teacher was in contact with an expert in the school to get a better theoretical understanding of the practical insights. The test of the physical abilities of the children proved to be especially useful. The test opened a new insight for the team members: children do have problems in their physical abilities. The practitioners contributed their everyday observations, and, in the team meetings, there was a horizontal movement, a fruitful dialogue between the everyday experiences and theoretical concepts leading to advancement of practices. In this project, theoretical concepts were interconnected with the everyday experiences in a successful way.

Networks and boundary-crossing   A diversified network was created around project C. This network is described in Figure 3.

The team working on the ward was in the center of the network. This team was based on the solid collaboration between the school and the daycare center. The expertise of the two activity systems was used: the motor expert at school and the speech therapist were consulted. The role of the head of the daycare center was especially important with regard to the creation of the network. She had many contacts with the organizations

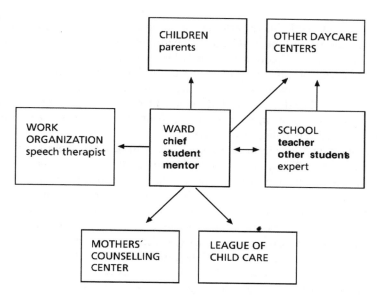

Figure 3: Summary of networks in project C.

outside her daycare center: with other local daycare centers, the mothers' counseling center, parents, and expert organizations such as the Mannerheim League of Child Welfare. She used these channels actively in order to expand the new insight for the benefit of the others. Parents were also included in the network. The teacher, student and the expert from the school were boundary-crossers in this project. They shared the same object with the practitioners in the daycare center: motor development of children.

Benefits The children clearly benefited from the project. Physical activities were organized for everyone, and those having the worst problems were sent for further treatment to experts. The whole work community derived many benefits: the practioners learned to observe children in a new way, and the educational aims were adjusted acoordingly. Regarding the concrete results, the information folder created by the student remained in the daycare center. Due to this folder the new knowledge did not disappear with the student. In addition, the students acquired a valuable tool for their future work: the ability to observe childrens' motor development. As in the other projects, the school derived the least benefit.

Advanced collaborative activities This project produced qualitatively developed, new activities. Later, the head of the daycare center reported that the idea of observing the motor development of the children expanded also to the other daycare centers in the area. Horizontal expansion occurred in the content of the project in the daycare center: when the next student came for her internship, she concentrated on the development of children's speech using theatre as a tool. While acting, the children practiced their speech and while cutting the paper dolls for the presentations they had to practice their motor skills.

This project fulfilled many criteria of promoting developmental transfer. A collaborating team was established, and each participant provided expertise to fulfill the purpose of the team. Theoretical knowledge was interconnected with everyday experiences in a fruitful way. The project was useful for all participants. It is noteworthy that the activities were expanded both spatially to other daycare centers and horizontally in regard to content. The development of the boundary object was of crucial importance for the success of the project, as it enabled a fruitful dialogue between the different partners and increased collaborative expertise.

Another important factor influencing the successful development of the project was the collaborative team. The troublesome incident with the morning group, as one of the children was rejected by the group, reduced the energy of the student. Without the support of the collaborative team and the firm hand of the head of the daycare center, the problem may have remained unsolved. In this case, the whole developmental project might have ceased. It is noteworthy that the object of the project changed from surveying the possibilities for physical activities into promoting the children's motor development and speech. As a product of the joint expertise of the team, the connection between motor development and the development of speech was recognized. This idea became so important that it replaced the previous idea. Without the support from the team, this important insight might not have been recognized at all, and the student might have proceeded with a minor project.

These three projects succeeded to a very different degree. Project A did not reach the aims set for this kind of internship. Project B was successful in a traditional way, and project C expanded to include the spatial expansion to the local environment and the horizontally with respect to the contents of the project. The boundary object was highly important for facilitating developmental transfer. In the project A, there was no shared object. In the very beginning of the project B, a promising shared object was envisioned by the student and the personnel of the ward. However, the activities later turned out to be implemented only by the student and a person outside the ward, and it was not possible to sustain the activities at the ward. In this project, no new theoretical ideas were applied. As a result, the activities were not advanced but remained traditional. Only project C was successful in establishing a genuine boundary object between all the collaborative members. A theoretically advanced idea was developed which led to expanded and advanced practices.

Conclusions

Previous studies have conceptualized transfer either as a transition of knowledge from one task to another, or from one situation to another; or as a transition of work practices from an expert to a novice. In this report, a different view of transfer is provided: an increase of collaboration between two systems of activity in order to develop new theoretical concepts and to apply them to solve everyday practical problems. The aim is to benefit all partners of collaboration and to give them tools for making sustainable changes in their own activity systems and for facing new challenges by using collaborative working models. How well was this aim achieved? What were the prerequisites for creating a new kind of work activity? We can say that the different projects gave varying results. The factors associated with successful results are discussed below.

It seems that the collaborative team is of the utmost importance. In those cases when the student was left alone or received help only from persons outside the ward, no sustainable results were achieved. The results indicate that collaboration is not self-evident. Is is not easy to establish a collaborative team, as the focus of the team must be on the developmental project and the teamwork must be continued throughout the project. In this study, a prerequisite for the genuine collaboration and new solutions seems to have been the finding of a shared boundary object. This was successful in one of the projects studied. It facilitated collaboration and merged the different perspectives of the two activity systems.

The dialogue between theoretical knowledge and everyday experiences seems also to enhance the development of new working practices. In this study, advanced practices were not created without theoretical insight. But how can a fruitful dialogue be created? In this data, there were two examples of how the relationship was *not* established: because the teacher's lecture did not meet the needs of the ward, her theoretical idea was rejected. This may reflect the problem of the traditional conception of transfer: knowledge as something that can be carried from school to the workplace, the teacher providing the right answers to the questions of the practitioners in a lecture situation. Reality did not work like this. The practitioners were not able to apply the knowledge in their everyday work. Studies on the developmental of transfer maintain that solutions to problems must be jointly devised in close connection with the everyday experiences. This is what happened in project C. At the beginning of this project, no one had an answer to the problem encountered. But because a collaborative team represented different perspectives, the right sources of knowledge were available. It is the very dialogue between the different perspectives and the networks related to them that made the novel solution possible.

An interesting horizontal dialogue occurred between the theoretical concepts and everyday experiences. The test of the children's physical abilities (theoretical knowledge) led to the observation that children with problems in their motor coordination had also problems with their speech. This observation, based on the everyday experience of practitioners, led to search for expert help. When the theoretical connection was understood, the practitioners decided to increase the amount of physical exercise, in other words, the theoretical concept became intertwined with everyday practice. But after this, there was an additional horizontal move based on the same insight at the daycare center: the speech of children was selected as a topic for a new project. The next student arranged and created, with the instrumentality of a children's theater, performances based on the popular novel (Pippi Longstocking). While acting, the children practiced their speech and while cutting the paper dolls for the presentations they had to practice their motor skills.

What can be said about the development of expertise in these projects? In project B, apprenticeship expertise was provided when more experienced colleagues taught the student to use client-centered methods to survey the clients' needs: the life-span questionnaire. Collaborative expertise was acquired when the crafts instructor crossed the boundary between the wards, and recreational activities were organized together with the student. The student alone could not have discovered the different types of recreation activities, and the crafts instructor alone would not have known the needs of the residents. In project C, apprenticeship expertise was transferred when the mentor taught the student the methods of testing the children's physical abilities. New creative expertise was gained in finding out why children with difficulties in motor coordination also have difficulties in the development of speech? No members of the team knew the answer to this question. This question moved the teacher, a boundary-crosser from another activity system, to contact an expert who could provide the theoretical explanation. These are examples of giving and receiving benefits and creating instances of different kinds of expertise in these projects.

One of the aims of the projects was that all partners should benefit from collaboration. How well was this aim was achieved? Workplaces seem to derive the most benefit in all the projects. They were on the receiving end of either the teachers' expertise, activities organized by the student, written material or a new theoretical insight with practical applications. Advantages to the workplace are understandable, as each developmental project was based on its needs. However, contrary to the notion of developmental transfer, the advantages are not necessarily sustainable. Sustainability has to do with a larger institutional context — how a project is "anchored" in the organization — supported by an understanding that it is an investment of time and energy and that it is an important initiative to improve the quality of services and the work environment. In the first case studied here (case A), this condition was not fulfilled. The ward was not aware of the nature of the new model of internship. In order for the results to be sustainable, the collaboration must also give birth to concrete results that are then institutionalized — put into daily use. This happened in cases B and C, but the results were not sustainable in project B because the collaborative team was missing. Sustainability is related to power and motivation, not only to learning — if these can be separated.

Advantages for the students were most evident in projects B and C. In these projects, the students received professional support from others, and they did not have to struggle alone. In project A, the student was left alone, except for the teacher's support during the time when she announced that she would quit her studies. This example illustrates the Vygotskian idea of the zone of proximal development: the collaborating student was able to exceed her present capabilities and achieve better results than when acting alone.

Were the students acting as change agents? Especially in project A, the student raised many critical questions in regard to the activities on the ward. For example, she found out in her survey that the elderly needed more personal time and attention from the nurses, not only recreational activities. However, her comments did not take root. Contrary to this, in the daycare center, the critical comments given by the student received serious consideration. It was her notion that although the children had been recently in the child advice center, the professionals there had not noticed the children's motor problems. This observation led to contacts with the mothers' counselling center. Thus, it is a matter of being receptive to the student's notions. There was potential for them to be change agents.

What about the clients? The projects were developed primarily to monitor and serve the needs of the clients. Therefore, they should be also the primary beneficiaries. Was this the case? They benefitted in two of the projects. In one (case B), recreative activities were organized for them, and in the other (case C), the clients' problems received serious attention and were treated in a professional manner. What might be the explanation for the different degree of success? In addition to the factors discussed above, there is one difference between projects A, on one hand, and B or C on the other. In the successful projects (B and C), clients were regarded as real partners in the project. In project B, the residents were interviewed, and in project C the children were tested for their individual problems. In project A, there was an intention to find out about the needs of the elderly, but it failed because the information was being gathered not in confidentiality, but in a joint meeting. This emphasizes that to activate clients as real subjects of collaboration is not necessarily an easy task.

Teachers seemed to gain relatively few benefits. However, in the interviews conducted later, they emphasized the importance of a long-term developmental project and a long internship period in regard to the requirements of their own professional development. Thus, they could better familiarize themselves with the contemporary work practices than when supervising a student during shorter periods of internship. The internship period lasted here for four months, whereas in the traditional internship it lasts only a few weeks. Recently, there has been discussion in Finland on the importance of vocational teachers' contacts with working life. A sabbatical has been created during which teachers can take part in the changing work life by working as ordinary practitioners. However, the successful application of the idea of developmental transfer brings even better advantages: teachers do not have to change their workplace, and they will become acquainted with not only the existing, but also advanced work practices and theoretical ideas.

However, changing the work practices at school seems to be difficult. In this study, the new kind of internship was regarded as an experiment. While this study was being finalized, it was not known yet whether the new practice will remain in the study program of the practical nurses or not. An alternative to a long internship in the same organization are short periods of internship with a selection of many different workplaces. The benefit of the long period is in providing a continuing authentic contact with the contemporary work practices and even more: their advanced forms. During a short internship there is no time availabe for establishing a collaborative team or creating networks to find new solutions, that is, for developing work practices. Consequently, there is no basis either for developmental transfer. The development of new practices during a shorter internship presupposes that the student stays in the same work place during several consecutive internship periods. As we see, developmental transfer is closely connected with the structures of training.

The creation and establishment of novel internship practices, based on the concept of developmental transfer, do not seem to be impossible today; nevertheless, their emergence into general applicability is not self-evident either. This report is part of a larger project, funded by the Finnish Research Academy, which aims to find different ways of conceptualizing and actualizing developmental transfer. This chapter explores this topic from the standpoint of the training of practical nurses. In their training, the structures of developmental transfer have been quite well developed. However, this is rather exceptional compared to many other training programs. The first phase in implementing the new conception of training is to create collaboration between the different partners. The creation of this collaboration is the focus of Leena Härkäpää. The aim is to describe and analyze the process whereby the collaborative way of working described here is transferred to the training of artesans. The theoretical concept describing this process is "trading", a term used by anthropologists that describes and analyses the discussions between school and work places to ensure the partners that this kind of new activity is beneficial to both of them. The aim of the study is to find out what is typical for successful trading processes and what kind of factors make trading difficult.

Developmental transfer is a new concept whose application presupposes the development of new kinds of tools. The study of Pirjo Lambert focuses on tasks given to students during and for the internship, and study by Riitta Konkola on mentoring discussions between the student, teacher and mentor which are held in the workplaces during the internship. Both the tasks and mentoring discussions are activities that are located at the boundary zone between the school and the workplace. This zone is a place where it is possible to integrate the different perspectives of the different activity systems and create a shared boundary object. The aim is to find out which prerequisites will enable the tasks and supervising discussions to produce boundary objects that are beneficial to all partners.

Traditionally, the school and work place have been working as parallel rather than collaborative systems. However, developmental transfer requires a new kind of relationship which can be called a "learning partnership". The aim of Kaija Hukka is to find out how school regulations or school authorities depress or promote the rise of this kind of learning partnership. These regulations are important to know in view of removing the obstacles to the new kind of collaboration.

The developmental transfer is a conceptualization that is still seeking its shape and applications. The experiments and experiences have been promising so far. However, it is also evident that the development of a new way of working is not easy. School systems are especially rigid, and in the future they must undergo some changes that will enable them to become beneficiaries of all that developmental transfer can offer.

References

Beach, K. (1999). Consequential transitions: a sociocultural expedition beyond transfer in education. *Review of Research in Education, 24*, 101–139.

Cole, M., & Engeström, Y. (1993). A cultural-historical approach to distributed cognition. In: G. Salomon (Ed.), *Distributed cognitions: Psychological and educational considerations*. Cambridge: Cambridge University Press.

Davydov, V. V. (1988). Problems of developmental teaching. Parts I-III. *Soviet Education, XXX*, 8–10. (Whole issues).

Davydov, V. V. (1990). *Types of generalization in instruction*. Reston: National Council of Teachers of Mathematics.

Dreyfus, H. L., & Dreyfus, S. E. (1986). *Mind over machine: The power of human intuition and expertise in the era of the computer.* Oxford: Basil Blackwell.

Engeström, Y. (1987). *Learning by expanding. An activity-theoretical approach to developmental research.* Helsinki: Orienta-Konsultit.

Engeström, Y. (1999). *Expansive learning at work: Toward an activity-theoretical reconceptualization.* Keynote presentation at the CLWR 7th Annual International Conference on Post-compulsory Education and Training.

Engeström, Y., Engeström, R., & Kärkkäinen, M. (1995). Polycontextuality and boundary crossing in expert cognition: Learning and problem solving in complex work activities. *Learning and Instruction, 5,* 319–330.

Engeström, Y., Engeström, R., & Vähäaho, T. (1999). When the center does not hold: The importance of knotworking. In: S. Chaiklin, M. Hedegaard, & U. J. Jensen (Eds), *Activity theory and social practice.* Aarhus: Aarhus University Press.

Engeström, Y., & Tuomi-Gröhn, T. (1996). *Complex learning environments, transfer and new forms of expertise in vocational training.* Research proposal within the framework of EU Cost Action 11: Flexibility, transferability, mobility as targets of vocational training.

Glaser, R., & Chi, M. T. H. (1988). Overview. In: M. T. H. Chi, R. Glaser, & M. J. Farr (Eds), *The nature of expertise.* Hillsdale, NJ: Lawrence Erlbaum.

Lave, J. (1988). *Cognition in practice: Mind, mathematics, and culture in everyday life.* Cambridge: Cambridge University Press.

Lave, J., & Wenger, E. (1991). *Situated learning. Legitimate peripheral participation.* New York: Cambridge University Press.

Moll, L. C. (1990). Introduction. In: L. C. Moll (Ed.), *Vygotsky and education. Instructional implications and applications of sociocultural psychology.* New York: Cambridge University Press.

Reder, S. (1993). Watching flowers grow: Polycontextuality and heterochronity at work. *The Quarterly Nesletter of the Laboratory of Human Cognition, 15,* 116–125.

Star, S. L. (1989). The structure of ill-structured solutions: Boundary objects and heterogenious distributed problem solving. In: L. Gasser, & M. N. Huhns (Eds), *Readings in distributed artificial intelligence* (Vol. 3). Menlo Park, CA: Morgan Kaufmann.

Star, S. L., & Griesemer, J. (1989). Institutional ecology, 'translations' and boundary objects: amateurs and professionals in Berkele's museum of veterbrate zoology. 1907–39. *Social Studies of Science, 9,* 387–420.

Vygotsky. L. S. (1978). *Mind in society. The development of higher psychological processes.* London: Harvard University Press.

Vygotsky. L. S. (1987). *Thought and language.* Cambridge: The MIT Press.

Wenger, E. (1998). *Communities of practice.* New York: Cambridge University Press.

Wertsch, J. (Ed.) (1985). *Culture, communication and cognition: Vygostkian perspective.* New York: Cambridge University Press.

Chapter 11

Promoting Developmental Transfer in Vocational Teacher Education

Pirjo Lambert

Introduction

A crucial element in teacher education in Finland is the so-called practice teaching component. It consists of student teachers listening to the lessons of competent teachers and then giving "proof lessons" of their own. Miettinen (1993) has shown that the basic structure of teacher education has remained the same for hundreds of years. The continuity of this institution can best be seen in the very mode of the proof lessons. The model has a long history that dates back to the nineteenth century. Student teachers had to give a proof lesson in front of a board of evaluators in order to obtain a teaching certificate. Little by little the proof lessons became an important part of teacher education programs, and their meaning changed as they were taken as indications of teaching ability.

In vocational teacher education, student teachers give their proof lessons in their own work places, usually in vocational training institutes where they work as teachers while completing teacher education. Figure 1 shows the model of a proof lesson where a student teacher is giving his or her lesson in front of the classroom while the teacher educator is following the lesson in a back seat.

Looking at this classical model from the perspective of transfer, an individual student teacher tries to transfer the pedagogical knowledge, for instance theories, models, principles and concepts, from the initial context of learning to the context of the classroom and to apply it successfully in analogous tasks. The teacher educator evaluates his or her success in doing this. The student teacher, teacher educator and the students, as a rule, do not engage together in a classroom discussion on the learning principles of the proceeding lesson. Even more, the lesson plan made by the student teacher easily prevents the student teacher from spontaneously changing the plan. Thus, the knowledge content remains the same, only the context of its use will change. The problem is that the status and meaning of knowledge is, however, different in different contexts.

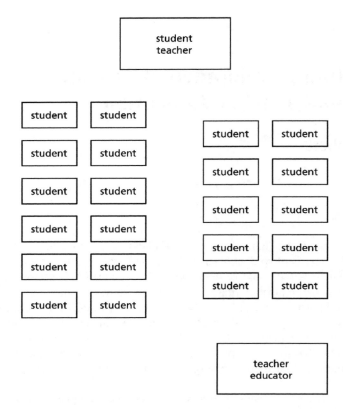

Figure 1: The model of a proof lesson in vocational teacher education.

At the same time, demands are being made for teachers to examine and develop their own work (e.g. Statute for Vocational Teacher Education 1996). In vocational teacher education, programs have been organized into large, multidisciplinary projects so as to improve the relevance of instruction for working life. Looking at this model from the perspective of transfer, the focus is on the context-boundness of knowledge and skills and on the need to reconstruct them afresh in each context. Learning is seen to occur most effectively not in a process of acquiring and storing knowledge and skills on the individual basis, but in a process of participating in the teaching work (see Lave 1988).

Y. Engeström & Miettinen (1999) see this problem in a temporal dimension. According to them (p. 12), the theory of situated learning depicts learning and development primarily as a one-way movement from the periphery, occupied by novices, to the center, inhabited by experienced masters of the given practice. What seems to be missing is the movement outward and in unexpected directions: questioning of authority, criticism, innovation, or initiation of change.

I perceive that teacher education is now developing in two directions: one being in the proof lessons, student teachers are practicing teaching; and the other direction, in the projects, they are trying to examine and develop their work as teachers. The problem is that the pedagogical interaction is restricted only to the classroom context, between the teacher and the students, and hence, the developmental work does not expand into school contexts, outside teacher education, but ends when the student teacher finishes the teacher education program.

Teachers' work is by nature communicative and interactive. However, new ideas, solutions and models will hardly improved, if we don't see also the developmental work as a communicative process and if we don't take these processes as objects for systematic research and development. As a result, it is becoming increasingly important to study the discussion and interaction at work. Y. Engeström (in press) points out: "Because the communicative and instrumental activities are related to each other in the development of work activities, it is unfruitful to examine the changes at work without taking seriously its communicative-interactive aspect".

The challenge is now to promote innovative learning in school contexts where the student teachers are working as teachers. The question is how to develop new instruments of transfer focusing neither on contents nor social process alone, but rather on the development of both. That is the idea behind *developmental transfer* (Y. Engeström 1998), which is based on the cultural-historical activity theory (Y. Engeström 1987; Leontjev 1978).

The view of distributed cognition (Cole & Y. Engeström 1993) redefines the unit of analysis of cognition and learning as a collective activity system mediated by cultural artifacts (tools and signs) as well as rules, community, and division of labor. In this view, significant learning processes are achieved by collective activities. Meaningful transfer of learning takes place through interaction between collective activity systems. Such transfer takes the form of negotiation and exchange between different cultures (Tuomi-Gröhn & Y. Engeström, this volume). The school and the workplace engage in collaborative interaction, in which both activity systems learn something from each other. Such a relationship presupposes that the two activity systems can jointly find and create mutually relevant "boundary objects" (Bowker & Star 1999; Star 1989; Star & Griesemer 1989), in which both benefit from collaboration.

In the following sections, I will first describe a new model of promoting transfer in vocational teacher education in health care and social welfare, called "the learning studio". I will then focus on one specific aspect of the complex process of knowledge creation and learning in the learning studio, examining, as concrete examples, how the boundary objects were developed as tools for constructing a shared object. I will use data from the discussions of the learning studios organized in two vocational training institutes. I will conclude by discussing the new challenges for promoting transfer in vocational teacher education.

The Learning Studio as an Instrument of Promoting Transfer

The Network of Promoting Transfer

Vocational teacher education in Finland is organized in polytechnics that provide the basic pedagogical education of vocational teachers, employed at polytechnics or vocational training institutes. The training consists of 40 study weeks. The design of the learning studio was part of a research and development project (Lambert 1995, 1996, 1999) carried out in the Helsinki Polytechnic, School of Vocational Teacher Education, in 1992–1995. The students participating in the teacher education program were working, at the same time, as teachers in behavioral, social, natural, medical, dental and nursing sciences in training institutes of health care and social welfare.

The project examined the teachers' work in the network of three activity systems: the aforementioned school of vocational teacher education, the training institutes of health care and social welfare, and the organizations delivering health care and social welfare services (Figure 2).

Activities are systems that have developed over long periods throughout history and typically taken the form of institutions and organizations (Cole & Y. Engeström 1993; Y. Engeström 1987). An activity system is seen as a collective and dynamic formation which has a complex mediated structure. The subject and the object, or the actor and the environment, are mediated by instruments, including symbols and representations of various kinds. The less visible social mediators of activity — rules, community, and division of labor — are depicted at the bottom of the model.

In Figure 2, the middle triangle, teachers' work in the activity systems of health care and social welfare training institutes represents the central work activity we were examining and developing. Teachers' work in this activity system was approached through teacher education (the triangle on the left), which denotes producing tools for promoting innovative learning in vocational institutions. The main object activity is the learning activity of the students who will work in health care and social welfare organizations (the triangle on the right).

The purpose of the experimental teacher education program was to develop work processes, and the curriculum was seen as a tool for changing these processes (see Lambert 1996, 1999). Thus, the curriculum was constructed in accordance with the phases of developmental work research (Y. Engesröm 1987, 1995). The focus was on

Figure 2: Network of activity systems relevant to teacher education in health care and social welfare.

learning the methods for developing work practices. The curriculum was basically a process of a collaborative formulation and testing of hypotheses and, simultaneously, a development plan for teaching work. The purpose of this process was to produce a cycle of expansive learning (Y. Engeström 1987, 1996). For which, teacher education implemented an *intervention* (Argyris 1970), which meant intentionally interfering with and affecting the prevailing conditions or processes in the working practices of the vocational institutions.

The health care and social welfare training institutes and service delivery organizations have a partially shared object: to supervise the learning of the students. Thus, it was now important for teacher education to develop new models of activity for examining the shared object, and for developing new instruments for collaboration between the central activity and the object activity.

The Learning Studio as a Scene for Boundary-crossing

The student teachers work in different kinds of projects of planning teaching and learning in training institutes. Many of the projects are connected to curriculum planning. Student teachers bring to these projects the instruments offered and produced in teacher education: theories, models, principles and concepts for developing teaching work. The projects of student teachers are often small and local experiments. However, most of the organizational innovations are often special and local, and one should examine them as dynamic processes, the productive potential of which depends on the quality of interaction between different viewpoints and areas of competence (Biemans 1992).

Student teachers produce research reports from their projects. Traditionally, such reports are handled in the seminars of teacher education, and they end up on the shelves of libraries, their impact being minimal or casual. In our teacher education program we began to develop new patterns of activity that disseminate the results of the projects through collective discussion, thus giving immediate feedback to the training community. Kvale (1989, 1996) discusses especially the communicative validity of knowledge that is tested in dialogue.

As a strategic intervention, special educational situations called "learning studios" were organized in the training institutes of health care and social welfare. These were based on the project of one local student teacher. The aim of the studios was to promote innovative learning in vocational institutions as an interaction process that crossed boundaries over the three activity systems (see Figure 3). Schön (1987) discusses a similar project aimed at creating bridges between vocational education, universities, and work practice. He presents a design studio as a common context in a project where the foundations of curricula were created.

Each student teacher designed and implemented the learning studio at the school they were working as teachers. This took place at the end of the teacher education program, when the student teacher had finished his or her own project at school.

The layout of an ideal type of learning studio is depicted in Figure 3. Different parties connected to the project, as well as parties whose problems were the initial motives of

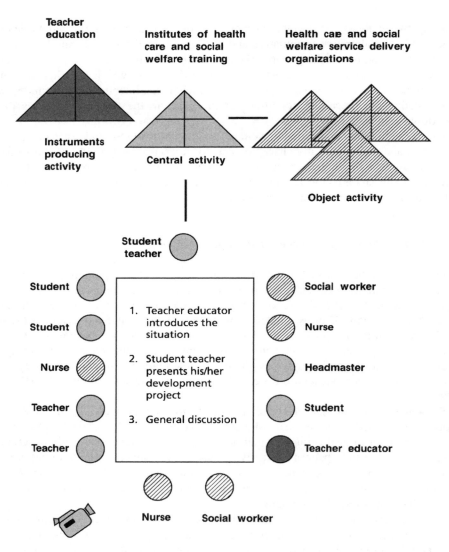

Figure 3: The learning studio as a scene for boundary-crossing.

the project, participated in the learning studio: teachers, students, the headmaster and the student teacher from the training institute, supervisors (e.g., nurses and social workers) from the workplace, and the teacher educator from the teacher education college. At first, the idea was to include also some patients or clients in the learning studio, but the task was not easy to organize, and the idea was left to mature. Figure 3 shows how the learning studio forms an interactive connection between the three activity systems.

The learning studio session consists of three parts. First, the teacher educator gives a short presentation of the framework and the principles of the teacher education program. Second, it is a student teacher's task to present his or her development project and its results as a basis for general discussion. The student teacher also leads the general discussion following the presentations. He or she directs the discussion to identify and solve common problems and to ensure critical feedback on models and tools produced. The teacher educator participates in the studio with a "collaborative voice". Her or his role is to facilitate the process of development.

The learning studio offers an opportunity to cross the boundaries between different professional areas. Y. Engeström, R. Engeström & Kärkkäinen (1995) point out that boundary-crossing is linked with the creation of new kinds of task combinations, collaborative connections and dialogical expertise that are breaking down boundaries between professions and disciplines.

Traditionally, collaborative interaction between the aforementioned activity systems had been minimal. Student teachers had been working in projects in training institutes, often together with their teacher colleagues and working life representatives. The teacher educator had visited the training institute only with the purpose of evaluating the proof lesson given by the student teacher. The teacher educator seldom collaborated with the students or the colleagues of the student teacher and never with the working life representatives. The curriculum planning had usually been teacher-centered; students and working life representatives had seldom participated in it. Also, the headmasters of the training institutes had been left outside from the pedagogical work done by teachers. None of these parties had ever before discussed at the same table, and this was the issue they all saw now as of crucial importance.

The following boundaries can be seen as especially important from the point of view of the development of the teaching work in the vocational institutions: (1) boundaries between experts and customers, that is: teachers and students; (2) boundaries between designers and users, that is: teachers and supervisors; (3) boundaries between hierarchical levels of organizations, that is: teachers and the leading staff; and (4) boundaries between the researcher and the people being examined, that is: the teacher educator and the different parties participating in the learning studio.

The learning studio can be seen as an instrument of *developmental transfer* (Y. Engeström 1998) in two ways. First, in the learning studio the participants are actively and collectively interpreting, modifying and reconstructing the knowledge and skills produced in the teacher education. Second, the interactive model of the learning studio itself can be modified to be transferred for use in different vocational training programs.

In the process of transfer the student teachers have an important role as change agents. The learning studio, as a place for boundary-crossing, offers a suitable forum to make this role concrete. The learning studio was, however, a new idea; there was not any ready made tool-package to offer the student teachers for managing the situation. But what kinds of potentials for change did the student teachers have when producing developmental transfer?

While working as a teacher in the training institutes, the student teacher is a member of the school community. At the same time, and in the same context he or she is also a student of teacher education. The student teachers have now an opportunity to bring with them the new instruments, offered or developed in teacher education, for instance, pedagogical theories, models, principles, concepts etc., to enrich the discussion of the learning studio. They have also been provided with tools for guiding a multiprofessional discussion. The student teachers have now the potential to act as *mediators* and *brokers* (Tuomi-Gröhn & Y. Engeström, this volume) between educational institutions and workplaces.

The idea of developmental transfer becomes more understandable if we examine the activity-theoretical concept of knowledge. Y. Engeström (1995) points out that knowledge manifests itself at two levels: at the level of internal and external knowledge and at the level of processes and structures. He describes knowledge as a movement between external materials and actions and internal, mental models and processes.

In the discussion of the learning studio, the participants express their internal models in external form with the help of pictures, signs, symbols and language. Language for its part, opens up possibilities to develop new internal models and external materials. The knowledge preserved in materials, signs and texts and mediated by language is transformed into practice only by going through the internal interpretations and models of those involved. Of interest here are the transitions where knowledge is changing its form of existence. How are, for instance, the participants in the learning studio sometimes supported by external materials or tools that are, in speech, internalized into thoughts and transformed into visions packed in a fixed form or into new models of activity? The concept of developmental transfer thus focuses on the continual movement of knowledge between people.

Boundary-crossing means jumping to unknown areas and presupposes the formulation of new mediating concepts (Y. Engeström, R. Engeström & Kärkkäinen 1995). The learning studios are videotaped, because they serve as a place for developing instruments for boundary-crossing. Both the teacher educator and the student teacher analyze the interaction in the learning studio with the help of videotaping.

However, the interaction in the learning studio can be understood only as an aspect of some specific historically developed activity. Communication only gives form to activity (Davydov 1999).

The Learning Studio in the Hierarchy of Activity

According to Y. Engeström (1999), cultural-historical activity theory offers a good framework for analyzing innovative learning at work, because: "it is deeply contextual and oriented to understanding historically specific local practices, their objects, mediating artifacts, and social organization. Second, activity theory is based on a dialectical theory of knowledge and thinking, focused on the creative potential of human cognition. Third, activity theory is a developmental theory that seeks to explain and influence the qualitative changes in human practices over time" (p. 377).

Leontjev (1978) describes activity at three hierarchical levels. In the uppermost level, *activity* is a historically developed social system that is oriented towards objects. The object of the activity is, at the same time, the aim and the motive of the activity.

The activity is realized through individual *actions*. Actions are relatively short-lived and have a temporally clear-cut beginning and end. The middle level of individual (or group) action is driven by a more or less conscious goal. Through the actions, the object of the activity is enacted and reconstructed in specific forms and contents. The object determines the horizon of possible actions (Y. Engeström 1995). The object of activity is not fixed and clear-cut, but constantly developing. The creative potential of activity is closely related to the "search actions" of object construction and reformulating (Y. Engeström 1999). Below the collective activity and individual actions, there is the level of automatic *operations*. These are dependent on the conditions and tools of the action at hand.

In this research, the interaction in the learning studios is approached in the network of the three activity systems: the school of vocational teacher education, the training institutes and the health care and social work organizations (Figure 4).

In this activity hierarchy, the learning studio forms a "cluster" of actions. The presentations of the teacher educator and the student teacher, as well as the general discussion, can all be seen as single actions that in the whole context of the learning studio are closely connected and form a cluster. The aim of the learning studio is to promote innovative learning in the training institutes as an interactive process that crosses boundaries between the three activity systems.

In order for an action to be meaningful, individuals must be able to see that it is related to the motive and meaning of the whole activity. The goals of the learning studio can be seen as a part of the network of the three activity systems. However, the action is seen only as an act of constituting the meaning (Cole & Y. Engeström 1993), because when actions are detached from activity, they arouse conscious meanings, goals and plans (Leontjev 1978). The collaboration of many people presupposes intersubjective communication, which relates to the object, instruments, division of labor etc. of the activity. The learning studio as a cluster of actions that carry out the activity provides the participants with an opportunity to reflect, to consider and evaluate one's own actions, words and thoughts on the basis of external, cultural rules.

In any activity specific concepts and means of expression characteristic to that activity always arise. At the level of operation highly automatized operations of speech, speech genres can be found (Bahtin 1986; R. Engeström 1995, 1999). These are the typical modes of utterances, the means of producing speech.

Analyzing Interaction in the Learning Studio

Y. Engeström (1996) approaches the development of activity theory and raises the challenge of developing conceptual tools in order to understand dialogue, multiple perspectives, and networks of interacting activity systems. Mihael Bahtin's (1986) theoretical work on the dialogical nature of human cognition and activity is seen here as an important basis. R. Engeström (1995, 1999) has pulled together Bahtin's ideas and Leontjev's concept of activity. Holland & Reeves (1994) approach the development of perspectives, Hutchins (1995) discusses distributed cognition, and Star (1989), as well

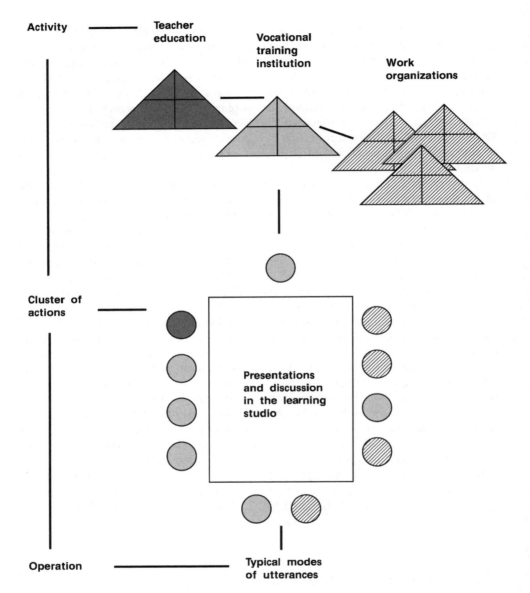

Figure 4: The learning studio in the hierarchy of activity.

as Y. Engeström, R. Engeström & Kärkkäinen (1995), have been developing the concept of boundary-crossing.

From the point of view of activity theory, examining work as a communicative and interactive process means taking into account the object-orientedness of interaction and the mediating artifacts (Y. Engeström 1999; Leontjev 1978). The discussion in the learning studio is seen as a part of the object-oriented activity, and the discussion also includes an object or objects. The object is a task or a problem that the participants in the discussion are dealing or working with and that is developing and changing. It is not self-evident that in this kind of boundary-crossing situation the participants can see the object as a shared task or problem. In this discussion, they are only searching for a common understanding of it and are constructing a shared object (Figure 5).

Object-oriented activity is mediated by cultural artifacts. These include tools and signs, both external implements and internal representations, such as mental models. With the help of these tools, people can obtain knowledge from the object of activity, interpret and evaluate the state of the object and modify the object so that a purposeful result can emerge. Star (1989) discusses *boundary objects* which are shared by more than one context, but which adapt themselves to special needs of different activity systems and in this way make it possible to reformulate a shared, boundary-crossing object. Star identified repositories, ideal types, terrains with coincident boundaries, and forms and labels as types of boundary objects. Basically, these are different types of shared representations of a problem or a domain. According to Y. Engeström et al. (1995), it could be useful to consider also shared mental models and concepts as boundary objects.

When analyzing the interaction in the learning studio, one should also take into account that, in interaction, the discussants are in relation both to the object and to each other. Therefore, it becomes important to analyze also the argumentation, and how the participants learn and create collectively new knowledge when constructing a new object, problem or task (Figure 5).

Argumentation means usually presenting and stating arguments. Billig *et al.* (1988) draws a distinction between individual and social argument. As one articulates a point of view, one can be said to be developing an argument. Equally, the word "argument" can also refer to a dispute between people, wherein opinions, or individual chains of reasoning, clash in the context of a social argument. Any individual argument is actually, or potentially, a part of a social argument.

The processes of knowledge creation are related to cognitive processes, such as memory and perception, thinking, reasoning, and problem solving. Cole and Y. Engeström (1993) and Hutchins (1995) discuss cognitive processes as socially shared or distributed. Then the unit of analysis of learning is seen as a collective activity system, where the subject and the object are mediated by cultural artifacts (tools and signs), rules, community and division of labor. Knowledge creation and learning are, thus, products of collective activity.

The research data in this project was collected in the Helsinki Polytechnic, School of Vocational Teacher Education. It consisted of 11 videotaped learning studios, interviews with various parties immediately after the learning studios, and telephone interviews with the student teachers two months later. The method used in the analysis of the interaction was one type of discursion analysis, called *voice analysis* (R. Engeström 1999), where the discussion at work is examined in such a way that the microlevel phenomena are connected to the whole structure and the contradictions of the activity system. In this research, interaction in the learning studio has been examined as taking

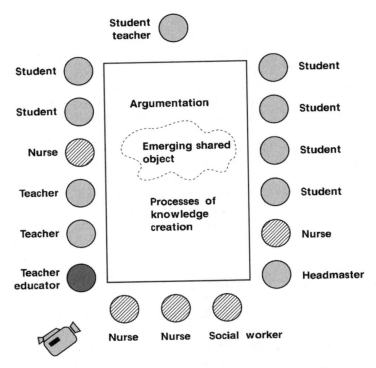

Figure 5: Interactive processes in the learning studio.

place in the network of the three above-mentioned activity systems (see Lambert 1999).

The two cases used in this article represent two different ways of developing and using boundary objects. In the first case, a type of a form was offered by the student teacher, and, in the second case, a type of a concept was developed during the discussion. Both cases are also examples *of* expansive boundary-crossings (see Tuomi-Gröhn & Y. Engeström, this volume). In the first case, I will focus on presenting how the object of the interaction expanded, covering a larger area in the activity system of the training institute. In the second case, I will concentrate on showing how the boundary object, emerged in the discussion, became the driving force for the new collaborative model of activity. Analyzing these cases I will try to find out:

- what kinds of forms the boundary objects acquired in the discussions;
- how the boundary objects were developed during the discussions; and
- what kind of meaning the boundary objects received in the boundary-crossing situations.

Boundary Objects as Tools of Object Construction

Case 1: Boundary Object Offered by a Student Teacher: A Form

In this particular learning studio, the participants were eight practical nursing students, four teachers, one student teacher and one teacher educator.

After an opening statement made by the teacher educator, the student teacher presented her research project and its findings. She had examined the practical nursing students' opinions about how the learning principles set forth in the curriculum had been put into practice. The object offered in the discussion by the student teacher was thus the relationship between the written and the actual curriculum:

Student teacher:

> My purpose is to compare the curriculum [as planned] at the school level
> . . . with the [actualized] curriculum at the student level; how a student
> sees the teaching and what kind of meaning he or she gives to it.

The results showed a conflict between the written and the actually implemented curriculum: the students could not see how the written principles were implemented in practice. The curriculum of the practical nursing education had been planned, as usual, by teachers only, and the students' task had been only to implement it.

To create the necessary conditions for boundary-crossing between the students and teachers, the student teacher had to translate the expressions of the students' demands and needs into the language of curriculum and, again, the concepts of the curriculum had to be connected to the reality of student learning. So, the student teacher offered *a form* (see Star & Greisemer 1989) that she had made as a boundary object in the discussion. Figure 6 shows that there is a paper in everyone's hand. As we can see, this instrument was *available* (Y. Engeström 1992) to everybody at the same time.

What did the form consist of? The student teacher had made an analysis of the curriculum context, and had also used a questionnaire to find out the students' opinions about how the principles had been put into to practice. She created the form on the basis of these analyses. The form included direct quotations pertaining to the learning principles written in the curriculum (for example individuality, cooperation, meaning of experiences, work research approach). There were direct quotations of the students' assessments on how these principles were implemented in practice. These were listed in sequence in the form.

The form here was a boundary object where the different kinds of representations of the same phenomena, namely teaching, had been put together. The form was simultaneously abstract, including the principles and concepts of the curriculum, and a very concrete description of the opinions the students had expressed. The form contained now, at the same time, the reality of both the teachers and the students. Its structure was, however, common enough to hold together the worlds of both.

In collective knowledge creation, the boundary object served most importantly as an instrument of *questioning and analyzing*. Y. Engeström (1999) discusses the role of questioning in expansive learning, when participants pose questions, criticize, or reject some aspects of the accepted practice and existing wisdom. Analysis involves mental,

Figure 6: Boundary object in the hands of the participants.

discursive, or practical transformation of the situation to find causes or explanatory principles (ibid.).

Students saw now before them a concrete text of the curriculum and direct quotations from their assessments. Questioning was started by one student, and immediately a debate ensued in which the students strongly criticized the written curriculum and the teachers kept defending it. The principles of the curriculum collided strongly with the teaching reality as expressed by the students. Figure 7 shows a practical nursing student showing the form while criticizing the text in the curriculum:

student:

> ... These kinds of separate, fragmentary, beautiful thoughts of growing as a human being and professional are scattered throughout this paper, but we [can] see in the classroom, that they aren't realized in practice at all. We can't find them at all where we are. Then you begin to think it is metaphysics, it isn't part of our reality. This is just what we call a paper theory!

Questions turned soon to analysis. The students and teachers began to discuss whether a view of a human being and learning was necessary in the curriculum at all. The teachers again defended the curriculum while the students criticized it:

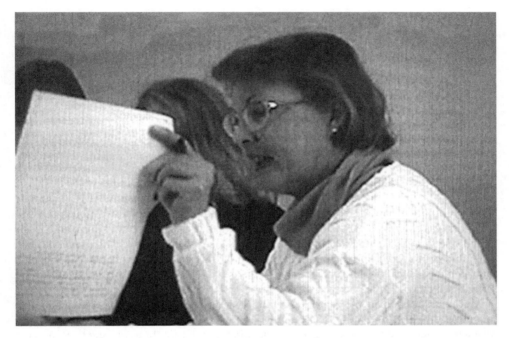

Figure 7: The practical nursing student using the form as an instrument of questioning.

student:

> I was wondering what the spirit is in this school. Is there some limited
> view of human beings which not all of us can agree on? Can this [school]
> system function in spite of that?

teacher:

> Or should the professional practical nurse . . . have some kind of common
> basis of values? In my opinion . . . there must be some common
> professional basis of values that is meant to be transferred to students by
> the instruction. That's why we have it in the curriculum.

Little by little, the teachers began to see the conflict between the written and the
implemented curriculum. The boundary object helped them to identify this conflict. The
following statement of one teacher resembled an appeal to the students to plan their own
curriculum:

teacher:

> . . . How do we handle these serious tasks in order to make them alive in
> teaching work in such a way that everyone could benefit from it? I feel
> this is very difficult. It can become just like this [curriculum]. (the teacher
> turns to the students)

Teachers and students began to discuss together how to develop the content of the curriculum. During this, one student began to reflect on the process as she saw it:

student:

> ... If this [curriculum] is being developed all the time, then why couldn't the students participate in it?

The participants then began now to discuss how the students could participate in the process of curriculum planning. A new shared object was emerging: *the process of curriculum planning*. The object was reformulated through a new shared perspective: *students can be partners in curriculum planning*. The object had been expanded from the written curriculum to the whole process of planning the curriculum.

The expansion of the object can be depicted with the help of the model of an activity system (Figure 8). In the beginning of the discussion, the teachers' relationship to the students was examined as mediated by an instrument, the written curriculum, and, at the end of the discussion, this relation was examined also as mediated by a division of labor, the process of curriculum planning. Expansion of the object means that the relationship between the subject and the object are now mediated by the relationship between several different elements in the activity system.

In the discussion in the learning studio, a new model of collaborative curriculum planning emerged and was subsequently implemented in practice. The students and teachers established a new team for planning the curriculum of practical nursing education together. Y. Engeström (1995) calls this kind of innovation a *trajectory innovation*, in which the whole production process is changed.

Interview with a student teacher:

> By Christmas, the planning team had met twice, starting immediately after the educational situation [the learning studio]. Students were very excited about their opportunity to contribute. They were highly motivated to participate. It didn't even matter that it would cause extra work for them.

Curriculum planning enjoys a central role in teachers' work. The question is about organizing the learning of the students, and this turns the process of curriculum planning

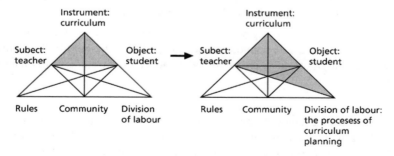

Figure 8: Expansion of the object in the learning studio.

into examining the object of the teaching work. Traditionally, curricula are planned by the teachers and given as ready made for the use of the students. The new solution was different from the prevailing practice in appointing the students as designers of their own learning, and the curriculum as an instrument for it.

As became clear during the discussions in this learning studio, the form as a boundary object:

- made it possible to cross over the boundary between students and teachers;
- served as an instrument of questioning and analyzing;
- raised "colliding" perspectives;
- made it possible to develop a shared object, and
- supported the emergence of a new model of activity.

Case 2: Boundary Object Developed in the Discussion: A Concept

Six teachers, four students, eight representatives of working life (supervisors), one student teacher and one teacher educator participated in the second learning studio. After an introduction by the teacher educator, the student teacher presented her research project and the results gained. The research dealt with vocational qualifications of practical nurses and the challenges of their education. The topic was of current interest because the education of practical nurses was at this moment a subject of dispute and people had divergent views of the goals and actual implementations of the education. The research data were collected using questionnaires distributed among students, teachers and supervisors and by participating in a meeting between the teachers and supervisors.

The student teacher presented the research results on a transparency. It was her intention to use the collected data as if an information *storage* (see Star & Griesemer 1989) in which the views of the different parties participating in the learning studio were drawn together. Star (1989) discusses modularity as a characteristic of boundary objects. The information storage was a boundary object through which the qualifications of practical nurses could be examined simultaneously from the points of view of the teachers, students, and supervisors. The property of an information storage, of "coming back to the knowledge" (Star 1989) did not, however, work successfully with the transparency. Thus, the information storage functioned only as a temporary boundary object. It was the first idea, or springboard (Y. Engeström 1987) to the formulation of a new boundary object, namely the *concept* of "the basic tasks" that was soon to be developed in the discussion. Next, I will describe, how this concept was developed little by little to become a boundary object.

The concept of "the basic tasks" was not new, as such. In the discussions on nursing and social welfare it often cropped up in a usual and customary manner. It was "given from above", therefore reflecting the national curriculum (Board of Education 1995):

> A practical nurse provides basic care and social welfare services at homes
> and in various communities.

When presenting the research results, the student teacher mentioned that teachers had found the examination of the practical nurses to show competence to work at the basic level in health care and social welfare. Participants started to approach the qualifications for practical nurses with the help of the concept of "the basic level tasks". They used it as a *where to* artifact (Y. Engeström 1992) when analyzing the future state or potential development of the qualifications of practical nurses:

teacher:

> I just heard the basic level tasks mentioned again. How are they specified?
> ... I wonder whether there is "an evil demon" here .... Where is the practical nurse good enough, what are her basic level tasks? Is it the work community itself that specifies what the basic level tasks are? On the other hand, this can lead to the old model of task-based division of labor that we have been trying to get rid of, at least in hospitals.

In the following discussion, the concept of "the basic tasks" was linked with the efforts to promote collaboration between the school and working life. A new model of curriculum planning began to emerge around this concept. The concept became the cornerstone of the new model of activity:

student teacher:

> Yes. It has come up here a few times already that it would be good to start searching for these basic level tasks and to create a team, as Lena suggested, to include different kinds of representatives of working life, as well as the current teachers and students of our school. Then we could start to think about education at the level of the curriculum.

teacher:

> How could we get a list of basic tasks to work in such a way that one person does not [only] take the bed pan and another one give the injections?

student teacher:

> How could we start planning now so that we really could define these [basic tasks]?

working life representative:

> I agree with you. I have just pointed out that we are discussing the basic level tasks, what they would be, because on the other hand, we are moving in the direction of crossing boundaries in these tasks. If the education turned back on itself again, then we would be back in that multiscale system.

Application of the concept of "the basic tasks" made it possible to relate the analysis to the context of both teachers and working life representatives. The supervisor discussed the problem from the point of view of a customer, and the student teacher from that of the curriculum. The concept was thus adapted to the demands of the central and the object activity:

working life representative:

> I don't understand how we could specify the basic care or basic tasks, because, as I see it, at least with us, the basic task is to help our customer and that's it.

teacher:

> As a matter of fact, it just occurred to me, when reading this national curriculum, that it is all here, that this is the basic task of practical nurse.

The concept, used as a boundary object, was referred to by many names in the discussion: "basic tasks", "basic level tasks", "the whole of the basic tasks" and "basic care". With the help of these modifications, the participants could discuss the different elements of the working process of practical nurses: the subject ("these basic level tasks . . . where is a practical nurse good enough?"), division of labor ("a kind of a whole of basic tasks that is is not like one person taking the bed pan container and the other giving the injections") and the object ("basic care or basic tasks . . . is helping our customer and that's it".).

At the end of the discussion, an idea of a new model of collaborative curriculum planning emerged. It consisted of a team, including the teachers, students and supervisors, and was put into practice immediately after the learning studio:

Interview with the student teacher:

> The students have placed there [on the curriculum planning committee] four persons. They have organized their efforts and feel that they can do more in the education of practical nurses. All the representatives of working life have also been invited. . . . This is the way this kind of a permanent [curriculum] team was established.

The concept of "the basic tasks" had a strong influence on the composition of the team. The process of creating the concept showed the difficulty of formulating a shared object when discussing what kinds of qualifications the education of practical nurses should provide. This led to demands of collaboration in order to develop the education of practical nurses. Most importantly, the boundaries between the teachers and supervisors in curriculum planning could now be crossed. The teachers began to see the curriculum as a means to examine the qualifications of practical nurses together with the students. One might say that the concept of "the basic tasks" and "the openness" of that concept were the motivating forces behind the discussion for developing the teaching.

Discussion

In this chapter, I have described how a new model of activity came into being for developing transfer in vocational teacher education. The model of the learning studio was an intervention that aimed to promote innovative learning in vocational institutions, where student teachers were working as teachers.

I have been approaching the transfer issue developmentally (Tuomi-Gröhn & Y. Engeström, this volume). The student teachers have received a new role as agents for change; they have been brought to act as mediators and boundary-crossers between teacher education, vocational institutions and work organizations. Expansive learning in teacher education is no longer seen simply as movement forward; it is also seen as horizontal movement (Y. Engeström 1996). In this research project this has meant that successful implementation of developmental transfer presupposes both crossing the boundaries that prevent learning and mutual cooperation, as well as developing new instruments for boundary-crossing. This can be made concrete in the following four design tasks of teacher education.

First, we have a challenge to develop *new boundary-crossing places* (Lambert, manuscript) where students can act as boundary-crossers and mediators between educational institutions and workplaces. Wenger (1998) discusses *boundary encounters* as single or discrete events that provide connections. These can take various forms, such as meetings, conversations, and visits. The learning studio is one example of this. It relates a communicative aspect to the developmental work done by student teachers in their own workplaces, at schools. The contents of their projects were transformed in the learning studios into new ideas and solutions that were implemented in new models of activity in the vocational institutions. When a boundary encounter is established, it can provide an ongoing forum for collective brokering. Wenger (ibid.) discusses these as *boundary practices*. The model of the learning studio was also further developed in the course of the teacher education. Its theoretical idea was also transferred and reshaped for the use of vocational training programs.

Educational institutions are knowledge-producing organizations. Knowledge is no longer created at the desk of a single teacher only, but more and more collectively and dialogically. For this reason we need new instruments to produce knowledge appropriate for boundary-crossing processes. Places designed for boundary-crossings carry the potential of producing these instruments. Second, boundary-crossings have to be taken as *a shared research and learning task* by both students and teachers. This means active recording and critical analysis of the events. The discussions in the learning studios were, therefore, videotaped in order to give an opportunity for both the student teachers and the teacher educator to analyze the interaction. Some student teachers also continued this intervention process in their own schools: together with their colleagues and students they analyzed the videotaped interaction using the tools offered in the teacher education.

For the students, it is often a new and a difficult task to operate in boundary-crossing situations. These are, however, important change agents. I see now as the third task, *supervising the students to act as boundary-crossers and mediators*. The findings of this research show that especially the boundary objects seem to be promising tools to facilitate boundary-crossings. These gave possibilities to formulate shared boundary-crossing objects and to find innovative solutions in development of teaching work.

The burden of the students grows easily too heavy, however. As we remember (see Figure 3), also the teacher educator gives a presentation in the beginning of the learning studio. She brings into the discussion the principles of the teacher education program, first and foremost the collaborative work research approach. She also endeavours to provoke the participants into debate, outlining the boundary-crossing function of the discussion and stressing it as an important place for collaborative learning and developing teaching work. Thus, the student teacher is not left alone in her or his work as a change agent. Finally, we shall have to see that the idea of expansive learning and developmental transfer translates into turning *teacher education into a collective change agent* (Tuomi-Gröhn & Y. Engeström, this volume), that works in partnerships with vocational training institutes and workplaces.

References

Argyris, C. (1970). *Intervention theory and method.* Reading: Addison-Wesley.

Bahtin, M. (1986). *Speech genres and other late essays.* Austin: University of Texas Press.

Biemans, W. (1992). *Managing innovation within networks.* London: Routledge.

Billig, M., Condor, S., Edwards, D., Gane, M., Middleton, D., & Radley, A. (1988). *Ideological dilemmas: A social psychology of everyday thinking.* London: Sage.

Bowker, C., & Star, S. (1999). *Sorting things out. Classification and its consequences.* Cambridge: The MIT Press.

Cole, M., & Engeström, Y. (1993). A cultural-historical approach to distributed cognition. In: G. Salomon (Ed.), *Distributed cognitions: Psychological and educational considerations.* Cambridge: Cambridge University Press.

Davydov, V. (1999). The content and unsolved problems of activity theory. In: Y. Engeström, R. Miettinen, & R-L. Punamäki (Eds), *Perspectives on activity theory.* Cambridge: Cambridge University Press.

Engeström, R. (1995). Voice as communicative action. *Mind, Culture, and Activity, 2* (3), 153–215.

Engeström, R. (1999). *Toiminnan Moniäänisyys. Tutkimus Lääkärinvastaanottojen Keskusteluista.* [Multivoicedness of activity]. Helsinki: Yliopistopaino.

Engeström, Y. (1987). *Learning by expanding: An activity-theoretical approach to developmental research.* Helsinki: Orienta-Konsultit Oy.

Engeström, Y. (1992). *Interactive expertise: Studies in distributed working intelligence.* University of Helsinki. Department of Education. Research bulletin 83.

Engeström, Y. (1995). *Kehittävä Työntutkimus. Perusteita, Tuloksia ja Haasteita.* [Developmental work research. Foundations, findings, and challenges]. Helsinki: Hallinnon kehittämiskeskus.

Engeström, Y. (1996). Developmental work research as educational research. Looking ten years back and into the zone of proximal development. *Nordisk Pedagogik, 16* (3), 131–143.

Engeström, Y. (1998). *Reconceptualizing transfer and remodeling internship.* Paper presented in seminar in Helsinki 12–13.10.1998. COST Action 11: European Cooperation in the field of scientific and technical research. Flexibility, transferability, and mobility as targets of vocational education and training.

Engeström, Y. (1999). Innovative learning in work teams: Analyzing cycles of knowledge creation in practice. In: Y. Engeström, R. Miettinen, & R-L. Punamäki (Eds), *Perspectives on activity theory.* Cambridge: Cambridge University Press.

Engeström, Y., Engeström, R., & Kärkkäinen, M. (1995). Polycontextuality and boundary crossing in expert cognition: Learning and problem solving in complex work activities. *Learning and Instruction, 5,* 319–336.

Engeström, Y., & Miettinen, R. (1999). Introduction. In: Y. Engeström, R. Miettinen, & R-L. Punamäki (Eds), *Perspectives on activity theory*. Cambridge: Cambridge University Press.

Holland, D., & Reeves, J. (1994). Activity theory and the view from somewhere: Team perspectives on the intellectual work of programming. *Mind, Culture and Activity, 1* (1–2), 8–24.

Hutchins, E. (1995). *Cognition in the wild*. Cambridge: The MIT Press.

Kvale, S. (1989). To validitate is to question. In: S. Kvale (Ed.), *Issues of validity in qualitative research*. Lund: Studentlitteratur.

Kvale, S. (1996). *Interviews. An introduction to qualitative research interviewing*. California: Sage.

Lambert, P. (1995). *Terveydenhuolto-oppilaitosten Opettajien Työn Kehittäminen. Kehittävän Työntutkimuksen Sovellus Ammatillisessa Opettajankoulutuksessa*. [Developing the work of teachers at health care institutes]. Helsingin yliopisto. Opettajankoulutuslaitos. Lisensiaa-tintutkimus. Helsinki: Educa- instituutti.

Lambert, P. (1996). Teacher education as a promoter of innovative learning in vocational institutes. *Nordisk Pedagogik, 16* (3), 155–166.

Lambert, P. (1999). *Rajaviiva Katoaa. Innovatiivista Oppimista Ammatillisen Opettajankoulu-tuksen, Oppilaitosten ja Työelämän Organisaatioiden Yhteistyönä*. [Boundaries fade away. Innovative learning through collaboration between vocational teacher education, training institutes and work organizations]. Helsingin ammattikorkeakoulun julkaisuja. Sarja A: Tutkimuksia 1.

Lambert, P. (manuscript). *Boundary-crossing place as a tool for developmental transfer between school and work*.

Lave, J. (1988). *Cognition in practice: Mind, mathematics, and culture in everyday life*. Cambridge: Cambridge University Press.

Leontjev, A. (1978). *Activity, consciousness, and personality*. Englewood Cliffs: Prentice-Hall.

Miettinen, R. (1993). *Oppitunnista oppimistoimintaan*. [From lesson to learning activity]. Tampere: Gaudeamus.

Schön, E. (1987). *Educating the reflective practitioner: Toward a new design for teaching and learning in the professions*. San Francisco: Jossey-Bass.

Star, S. (1989). The structure of ill-structured solutions: Boundary objects and heterogeneous distributed problem solving. In: L. Gasser, & M. N. Huhns (Eds), *Readings in distributed artificial intelligence* (Vol. 3). Menlo Park, CA: Morgan Kaufmann.

Star, S., & Griesemer, J. (1989). Institutional ecology, "translations" and boundary objects: Amateurs and professionals in Berkeley's museum of vertebrate zoology 1907–39. *Social Studies of Science, 9*, 387–420.

Statute for Vocational Teacher Education 455/1996. Ministry of Education. Helsinki.

Wenger, E. (1998). *Communities of practice. Learning, meaning, and identity*. Cambridge: Cambridge University Press.

Part III

Learning in Workplaces

Chapter 12

Learning in Working Life — From Theory to Practice

Petra Angervall and Per-Olof Thång

Introduction

Work-related learning in the engineering industry is more and more becoming a field of both scientific and market economic interest. This is true, especially of learning phenomena in relation to production and labor. In general, the growing interest in learning systems stems from various social developments, including changes taking place within organizations.

This chapter is concerned with different aspects of work-related learning as observed in connection with a specific Learning-Network-Program. The principal aim of this program is to try out methods and models for developing lifelong learning projects and continuing education within the engineering industry in the western part of Sweden. In addition, the program also aims to create opportunities for collaboration between small and medium-sized enterprises within the region. These aims are in turn related to more general strategies, such as developing an engineering industry that will emphasize lifelong learning. In this study, aspects of learning opportunities, terms and strategies within the Learning-Network-Program are analyzed, as well as employees' possibilities and wishes to collaborate in different learning projects. How knowledge gained in one context can be transferred into another, and finally, in what way work is affected by learning activities are also discussed. Our arguments and conclusions are based on empirical data and are to be seen as preliminary results within our ongoing study of activities within the Learning-Network-Program.

Education and training systems within industry are still characterized by a lack of flexibility, but are getting more and more attention as a result of technological and other changes.

> In the past few decades, education and training have acquired high status in the countries of Europe. In particular, in the wake of the structural change in the world of work, and in trade and industry, in the wake of internationalization and globalization, and in view of the increasing

Between School and Work: New Perspectives on Transfer and Boundary-crossing
© 2003 Published by Elsevier Science Ltd.
ISBN: 0-08-044296-X

penetration of "technology" into social and cultural life, the structures of and courses offered by training and further training are playing an increasingly important part (Sellin 1999).

After a introductory presentation of the western Swedish engineering industry and the Learning-Network-Program, we discuss the concepts of learning and transfer in the context of the program. Finally, selected parts of our results will be presented to clarify how the practices and processes of learning can be understood.

The Western Swedish Engineering Industry

There are a few criteria that are distinctive of the western Swedish engineering industry. First of all, the culture and traditions within the region's engineering industry are mainly influenced by five major corporations: Volvo Car Corporation, Volvo Bus Corporation, Volvo Truck Corporation, Swedish Ball Bearing Corporation (SKF AB) and Ericsson AB. These five concerns constitute the actual core of the engineering industry and its labor culture in the region. They have all developed into large, international and highly advanced companies, with well-established traditions.

Even so, these corporations have changed a great deal over the years. They were originally, to a large extent, conservative and hierarchical organizations. This was certainly the case with the Swedish Ball Bearing Corporation, which was founded in the beginning of this century and was initially a bureaucratic organization very much inspired by the ideas of Taylor and Fayol (Rubenowitz 1994). This means that the Swedish Ball Bearing Corporation was built upon the philosophy that instrumental effectiveness is the same as economic profit. The other corporations, namely Volvo and Ericsson, have been developed, at least in part, on the basis of a different outlook and are to this day looked upon as more technologically advanced and organized. The results of a recently published study (Davidsson & Svedin 1999) of the conditions for learning in working life in Sweden imply that residues of tayloristic organizational principles are still present in many companies. Other studies (Karlsson 1999), also suggest that not enough is known about the rhetoric underlying the assumption that tayloristic organizational principles have been abandoned.

> A lot of rhetoric and little real knowledge — that seems to me is the case in much of the current debate on working life. The rhetoric says that we are in the middle of a total change from the old to the new, a change that is for the good of all and in which the new in every respect is the opposite of the old (Karlsson 1999).

Despite their differences, these companies show many similarities with respect to union commitment, labor culture and politics.

A second criterion that is typical of the western Swedish engineering industry is the network of small and medium-sized engineering companies that are heavily dependent on the larger industries for economical survival. These companies are fighting a hard battle against a large number of competitors and economic changes in the market. Most of these companies are also way behind in both special skills and more general competence levels. This has mainly to do with lack of time, financing and knowledge of the importance of continuing education in working life (Larsson & Thång 1994).

The Learning-Network-Program

In November 1994, several private and municipal organizations and industrial companies in western Sweden formed a network based on social and economic interests as well as on a mutual interest in learning in working life. The underlying cause of this interest was an acknowledged problem among small and middle-sized enterprises as to how to respond to a growing need for special training, skills and lifelong learning. This network has the creation of a competitive industrial region as its goal. Above all, the program focuses on the workforce and their present and coming needs of continuing education within the engineering enterprises. The Swedish Security Fund, and EU's Structure Fund Target 4 are funding the program.

Over the years, the Learning-Network-Program has tried out a number of models and methods of continuing education within a large number of enterprises in the region. The program focuses on four main areas:

- developing methods and tools for competence analysis;
- designing training projects and offering guidance for continuing education;
- developing methods for training and education;
- developing organizational strategies for continuing education;
- creating opportunities for networking.

Two of the region's largest industries, Volvo Car Corporation and the Swedish Ball Bearing Corporation, have played important roles in the program. They have supported the network financially, developed various types of learning activities with the help of the Learning-Network-Program and acted as mentors for some of their own subsidiaries. Other parties involved in the Learning-Network-Program are the Secretariat for Private Commerce and Industry, the County Labor Board, The County Employment-Training Group, Gothenburg City Education, Göteborg University and Chalmers Technical University.

In all the companies involved, the actual education and training has taken place in learning centers. Here the participants have been given the opportunity to learn, most often by the use of a computer, and with the help of a trained teacher. In some cases the learning has been aimed at special technical skills or has focused on more general knowledge of computers, languages, economics etc. The teachers have either been recruited from industrial schools or adult education centers (municipal adult education or labor market training), or in some cases the staff has taken the role of teachers (supervisors).

The teachers have used different teaching methods, and the participants (employees) have been recruited for a variety of different reasons. In some cases the employees volunteered and in others they were selected as having an "educational need". In several learning centers, the teaching has been very traditional, but more progressive approaches like "distance-learning" have also been used. In these centers the participants started by attending a short introductory course in general computer knowledge. This gave them the opportunity to practice their knowledge and learning activities more freely later on in a distance-learning framework.

How to Understand the Concept of Learning?

Several recently published government reports have discussed the Swedish engineering industry in terms of development and competence strategies. Due to technical development and structural changes, terms and conditions in the engineering industry are rapidly changing. For the most part, the increasing demand concerns not only work-related competence and skills, but also social competence and ordinary formal schooling (SOU 1996). Group-based work is rapidly increasing and presupposes a highly communicative ability.

During the last decade the demand for qualifications has shifted from being process-dependent and process-oriented to more general and process-independent. Terms of employment have also changed during the decade to become more demanding. This trend reflects that the period when industrial work was rigidly divided into "executive and conceptual, intellectual and practical workers, intellectual and technical intelligence would appear to be over" (Sellin 1999).

It is the development towards increased demands in general and process- independent knowledge and skills (compared with process-*dependent* knowledge and skills), combined with a generally low level of education that is putting the focus on education and training in working life.

> To be able to cope with the working tasks of the future the worker has to be multi-skilled while at the same time having a deeper knowledge within a particular subject area/. . ./The claim on suitable knowledge of language, math, physics, and chemistry will augment/. . ./There is a number of relatively unquestionable and characteristic features in the industry of the future/. . ./The new industrial worker needs theoretical knowledge, understanding of the industrial process, group-based work, initiative and improvisation ability, flexibility and continued learning (Helgesson & Johansson 1994).

Higher-order thinking skills are becoming more important compared with the traditional vocational qualifications. New demands in working life are of great importance, such as the ability to:

- decide which foundation of facts and which lines and methods are needed to solve a problem;
- know which additional information is required as well as where and how it can be acquired;
- treat situations as uncertain when routes to goals are not given;
- carry out more complex tasks which place demands on planning, the organization of work and holistic thinking; and

- move outside of routine practices in order to encounter unexpected situations and capture opportunity on the run (The National Agency for Education 1994).

This is also the new qualification that the industrial worker is confronted with "ability to grasp the meaning of things, to comprehend and to make judgements, is the first factor in adopting economy and labor market change" (European Commission 1995). A higher degree of competence on the job could mean a higher grade of independent ability to solve upcoming problems. You could also say that the broader the knowledge and skills are, the greater the ability to compete successfully (Koike 1984).

Lyttkens (1994) is also certain of the benefits of a positive student attitude toward education. He argues that the stronger the individual's intention to acquire and improve competence, the greater the scope of action and the less risk of experiencing loss of meaning. Lyttkens also argues that the most important task in education and development of competence is to get people to retain a sense of the purpose of their own learning and competence development.

Individuals in our society depend on strategies and opportunities for learning and continuing education. Adults who lack motivation, learning strategies and insights risk being side-stepped in the competition for work (Tuijnman & Van der Kamp 1992). As the learning process is very difficult and complex to understand, a wider spectrum of research on adult education is necessary. This research should take aspects of transfer into consideration, i.e. responsibility, quality, methods and informal strategies of learning.

Ellström (1992) calls attention to the importance of analyzing interaction in daily life in order to understand the process of learning instead of just analyzing "school-based" learning. In this way learners are forced to re-think the development of knowledge and to understand the continuity of activity and learning from one changing situation to another. Most on-the-job learning is based on experiences, and the lack of analytical thinking and reflection has implications for the individual transfer process.

According to Ellström, Gustavsson & Svedin (1996), learning activities are to be looked upon as social processes. Employees are involved in a social and cultural network, which means that they are active participants in different social relationships at work. These relationships join employees together in culture, understanding, reflection and taking action, which in return affects each individual's development and learning. At work, learning is an ongoing process that most employees are unaware of, i.e. incidental learning. They try to solve day-to-day problems, seek information, solve conflicts and organize their work surroundings. Informal learning is often an unconscious process that could be organized as a form of self-directed learning (Borgström 1988). A third way of understanding learning is in formal settings, i.e. planned, conscious and structured education.

> Creative learning occurs when individuals or groups of individuals within an organization begin to reflect upon and transform established ideologies, routines, structures and practices (Ellström 1999).

Different conditions for learning have substantial implications for knowledge and skill transfer. One prerequisite for on-the-job training and skill formation is the presence of an environment that promotes education and learning, as well as aspects of motivation

(Thång & Wärvik 2000). According to Ellström *et al.* (1996) three main factors are crucial in the process of creating terms of individual development and learning: action, reflection and transfer. Every learning situation has to contain:

- means for action;
- time for reflection; and
- exchanging experiences (transfer).

We understand learning at work as a social and continuing process between individuals and cultures in an organization.

Results and Analyses

Below, we will make a few statements based on the results of our study of the Learning-Network-Program. The results originate from several studies completed in 1999. The empirical data is based on interviews, observations and the responses to a questionnaire.

To begin with, we present a short example of one of the learning centers in our study and describe its set-up and activities. A brief resume of the more general results follows thereafter.

Production-based Learning

In most of our studies, activities in so-called "learning centers", are the focus of attention. These learning centers are situated near the production facilities of small, medium-sized and large enterprises. Altogether we have studied eight learning centers, where 15 to 20 companies have been more or less involved. A learning center is to be understood as a physical room, where participants are offered different types of learning-activities. This room is established within the actual production area in order to stimulate learning and make the process of transfer as unproblematic as possible.

These learning centers are different in many respects, which should be taken into consideration when looking at the results. First of all, the learning centers are located in different areas within or near production, which means different degrees of disturbance and availability. They are more or less available in the form of traditional classrooms, containing desks, whiteboards, etc. Other differences can be noted in the pedagogical aspects of learning, and different methods are used such as distance-learning and learning activities with for example CD-Rom discs. Aspects of teaching and supervising within the learning centers are also important to consider.

Even so, there are many similarities. The participating groups are on the whole similar to each other, as well as the goals and aims. The following example illustrates the activities in one of the learning centers.

This particular learning center (Angervall 1999) was situated in a small production-based section of the Swedish Ball Bearing Corporation. The actual "room for learning" was in the dining room, normally used for breaks during the workday. The people in charge of the learning activity had put six computers, along with small desks and a whiteboard in the room. A delegate (project supervisor) from the Learning-Network-Program was responsible for the project, but the production manager and personnel officer were also involved. Curtains were used to separate the "learning activity" from people having their breaks during the day.

The learning activity started with an introductory course in computers (ECDL) designed to provide basic computer skills, including how to work with the Internet and distance-learning. Participants were able to attend this course during working hours (2 hours per day). The teacher came from the corporation's own industrial school.

After 13 hours of basic training, the participants went on to a distance-learning course in production techniques. This course progressed through several levels, and the participants were expected to work independently. All participants were to practice distance-learning during breaks when production was slow and/or before or after work. Four supervisors were selected from among the staff to offer guidance to the participants. The supervisors were generally known to have a good knowledge of computers and to have pedagogical skills.

Twelve participants were selected on the basis of three criteria: no (or very little) basic knowledge of computers, their need for continuing education and, the wish to participate. The production manager and personnel officer, who made the selection, assured the rest of the staff that there would be opportunities to participate later. This was to prevent the workforce from questioning the selection.

The results illustrate that managers and personnel officers in general are much more positively disposed towards continuing education than the participating workforce. Several participants felt that the corporation does not put in enough effort into promoting continuing education. Instead, the staff is often expected to initiate their own training in their spare time. When the management initiates continuing education projects they are often experienced as being irrelevant to the actual job. This has negative implications for participation and motivation. One participant exemplified this by commenting:

> I am not used to this kind of learning activity (referring to the distance-learning course). Instead I need to discuss tasks with somebody, face to face. If I don't understand something I need to discuss the problem . . . get an explanation. We were supposed to write to somebody and within 24h get a reply. This model is not easy for me to understand . . . To communicate with somebody you will never meet? (P1)

This quotation illustrates the great difficulty and danger in establishing learning centers without at the same time making any effort to integrate the activities and make the actual content meaningful.

Table 1 shows the relation between the participants' general experiences of training that concerns work assignments and their experiences of the distance-learning course described above.

The table clearly indicates the imbalance between what the participants found to be important in continuing education and the type of education they were offered. The participants were in a more general sense positive towards training that concerned their

Table 1: Participants experiences of continuing education.

	Positive	Uncertain	Negative	Total
Training that concerns work arrangements	10	–	2	12
Experiences of distance learning	3	4	5	12
Total	13	4	7	24

work assignments. At the same time they had a negative attitude towards the distance-learning course they participated in. One explanation might be the participants' difficulty in connecting the distance-learning course with ordinary work. As Beach (1999) points out, learning is an ongoing relation between changing individuals and changing social contexts. In that respect this specific learning activity was sealed off from ordinary work and the social context, which probably affected attitude and motivation.

Clearly the participants did not understand how the distance-learning course could give them the feedback and personal benefits they were looking for. Another explanation might be the participants' experience of how management dealt with the aims of continuing education. A distance-learning course puts a lot of responsibility on the workforce, and each participant is expected to work independently during his/her spare time. Instead the organization should take more responsibility, claim several participants and support a developing workforce. Finally, the table also brings to surface the important question of method versus content. Apparently, some of the participants have found distance learning difficult to understand, no matter what the course contains. This might imply the importance of putting content before method in continuing education.

General Results

We find that learning is a matter of participation and that it's success is determined entirely by how meaningful the learning activity is experienced to be in relation to the actual job (Angervall 1998, 1999). In light of this, we conclude that all participants are, in a general sense, very positively disposed towards learning activities. Continuing education is important and gives satisfaction at work. Even so, most of the participants differ in their understanding of the importance of learning, how learning affects their everyday life, learning ambitions and learning strategies. Two employees working for different companies made the following statements. The question they responded to concerned their goals for participating in a learning center:

My aim was to learn more about computers. I want to be able to use the computer on my own. I used to be afraid of computers. At least I am now prepared to have to learn more, if needed, at work. (P2)

... education is always something positive, for the individual and the company. Employees become more positive and alert, simply because they know more. You can go far with just "common-sense", but learning give you new perspectives, even if it is difficult to learn. (P3)

These quotations illustrate different aims of participating in learning activities. The first response indicates how one participant valued and was motivated by continuing education. He felt that the contents have to be connected to work in some way. The other response is not as sharply focused on the importance of content. Instead the employee discusses learning as a way of making work more interesting and worthwhile.

Other distinctive results show that most of the participants feel similarly about different learning opportunities at work in different companies. For example, out of a total of 92 responses from seven different learning centers in large, medium-sized and small companies, 86 (*) stated that their primary interests were in learning something that related to their present work. Table 2 illustrates this.

This table shows how the culture within the organization and production influences the labor force and creates norms for living, working and learning. The table also illustrates how the participants value different kinds of learning opportunities. Clearly

Table 2: Choice of learning.

Type of learning activity	Yes	No	Uncertain
Large companies (47)			
– General education	36	9	2
– General technical training	24	11	12
– Training that concerns work assignments	43*	2	2
Total	103	22	16
Medium-sized companies (8)			
– -General education	8	–	–
– General technical training	5	3	–
– Training that concerns work assignments	8*	–	–
Total	21	3	-
Small companies (37)			
– General education	25	3	5
– General technical training	16	11	6
– Training that concerns work assignments	35*	–	2
Total	76	14	13
Total	200	39	29

they find learning activities to be an important strategy for living and that effort will give them opportunities for economic rewards and career advancement. Another interpretation might be that participants not only prefer learning that is related to their work, but also learning activities that are *situated* at work.

It is quite surprising that as many as nine out of ten wanted more job-related education and training. There was no difference considering the size of the company. On the whole, larger industries offer better possibilities for education and training among the employees compared to small and medium-sized enterprises. As many as three out of four answered that they needed better general education, i.e. better knowledge of subject matter in mathematics, natural sciences, languages, etc. The results show no difference between large and small companies. When comparing different needs of education, our findings are all the more interesting, as few participants expressed the need for better technical education compared to general education. This is in accordance with earlier Swedish studies (Petersson & Thång 1996).

Apparently, choices of education tell us a lot about learning possibilities and transfer. One issue to consider here relates to the conditions of learning in a production-based system. One employee gave the following explanation for the difficulties encountered:

> . . . Possibly we were not given enough time to be able to sit down in the
> learning center and actually learn. When I finally found time to sit down
> by the computer, someone called and I had to start working again. (P4)

When are participants given the time and circumstances they need in order to learn? One employee stated that learning activities are only encouraged and provided when they concern actual improvements in production.

> . . . only when new machines are being introduced. Then we have to learn
> more and get better at using them. Then it becomes a real need and
> learning-activities are being put forward. Then we have to learn . . . (P5)

There are apparent difficulties in finding the time and space for learning in production-based engineering industries. Our study shows that this mainly has to do with ideologies of short-term strategies, which means production systems on a daily basis. Apparently, this system does not provide much room for *en situ* continuing education. This suggests that it might be worthwhile to discuss the benefits of long-term strategies, such as continuous learning processes, employee development, and continuing production development.

Swedish studies show (Statistic Sweden 1995, 1996) that many employees in small and medium-sized engineering enterprises are not benefiting either from competence development or from other forms of educational contributions. Members of labor unions have access to a PC at work or in their home to a lesser degree than groups with higher education on the Swedish labor market. The paradox is that blue-collar workers get more opportunities for adult education and training when they are unemployed. The level of education among employees within the engineering industry in Sweden is relatively low by Swedish standards.

Another interesting observation (Statistic Sweden 1995, 1996) is that opportunities for staff training and human resource development among white-collar workers and academics increased much more than among labor union members between 1987 and 1997. In 1998, 64% of the blue-collar workers did not participate in any form of staff training.

The great interest in education and training shown in Table 2 is worth further discussion. Swedish studies (Larsson, Alexandersson, Helmstad & Thång 1986) show that there is a direct relationship between level of education and attitude towards education. The shorter the education, the lower the motivation for both general and vocational education, as well as education and training at work. The lower the level of education, the greater the lack of motivation for adult education and the more unqualified working tasks and the less learning possibilities at work. This affects ability and flexibility in attempting to adapt to changes in working life changes and is called the theory of "the vicious circle".

> The short educated lack education. Therefore they acquire the jobs that do not demand craftsmanship. The jobs are therefore often in such a way that no knowledge can be won from them and no need for knowledge. When the short educated have a narrow and instrumental view of knowledge they do not feel the need for vocational education if the job does not demand it (Larsson *et al.* 1986).

Another important result is that most companies in our study prior to this have taken very little interest in learning and continuing education. According to supervisors and managers, the reason for this is that learning is either considered unimportant for production or that learning strategies are expensive and time-consuming. This means that the workforce has been expected to create its own learning strategies and opportunities in life, at or outside of work. Several of our interviewees, however, point out that their understanding of the industrial climate and competition is changing, which means that learning strategies could play a more important role in the future. In this respect, Glick's (1997) recommendation to challenge the traditional understanding of working tasks is important.

Final Discussion

Our results suggest that learning most often concerns the participants' strategies for living and not their strategies for life. This means that learning can be misunderstood as a theoretical conception that has no relevance for real life, at least if it's understood in the sense of "developing for life". It has become clear to us that the engineering industry has difficulties in getting themselves and their workforce involved in learning activities. Work-related learning (training) is looked upon as something very positive by the workforce as long as it is related to the actual work performed (Petersson & Thång 1996). Other learning activities are sometimes experienced as pointless, expensive and time-consuming, especially in small and medium-sized enterprises. We believe that to be able to practice the concept of continuing education, companies must first of all start to develop long-term strategies for work and life. However, there are important theoretical questions to bear in mind when developing such learning strategies. For example, how does one know when workers/staff grasp the meaning of things? In what way is that important? Several studies (Beach 1999) show that work contains unintentional processes of education and learning. In that sense, might formal learning activities, such as learning centers, even be unnecessary? Maybe it is necessary to ask who needs formal learning activities, or whether the learning centers in our studies might have served a different purpose than that which they were aiming at?

Finally, one important question for us to bear in mind for future discussions and analyses is why people choose not to participate in learning activities when they have the opportunity. One very clear example of this problem occurred within one of the biggest government-funded projects in continuing education in Sweden: the Adult Education Initiative (AEI). This project was designed to support unemployed people in Sweden financially to enable them to finish their upper secondary schooling (The National Agency for Education 1997). AEI started in 1997. The more humanistic goals of adult education from the seventies were replaced by a focus on economic growth and employment. Structural changes in working life, due to the rapid technological and organizational development, increased the need for a more highly-skilled labor force. The basic assumption is that access to a skilled labor force will result in better conditions for economic growth. However, according to recent statistics concerning participation in the AEI, men with a low educational background chose not to participate in contrast to women (approximately 75% are women and 25% are men).

Most of the participants in our study were men. Most of them were in general positively disposed towards learning activities, especially training that concerned work assignments. This confirms McGivney's findings for the U.K. (Excluded Men 1998). According to McGivney (1998) women in the U.K. take more advantage of educational opportunities than men. When men are offered any form of continuing education, they tend to choose education that only concerns work assignments. In general, this means that men are more interested in education that gives direct qualifications for work. One reason for this, according to McGivney (1998), is that boys receive lower grades in school than girls, which affects boys' experiences of education negatively later on in life. Another reason is a matter of gender. Men "with blue collars" do not get an education or participate in more general learning activities. That is a "female" activity.

The question why men are more difficult to motivate into participation in learning activities than women, cannot be answered here. Clearly, there is a problem when men with only basic education — and who in many cases are positive towards learning — refuse to participate when the opportunity arises. It may be that cultural aspects and tradition interfere, or they may be afraid of failing in an increasingly demanding society. Another explanation might be the difficulties of transferring knowledge gained in one context to another. It is to be hoped that future research will help us to understand this phenomenon and its implications.

References

Angervall, P. (1998). *Unlimited learning*. Department of Education, Göteborg University.
Angervall, P. (1999). *Production-based learning*. Department of Education, Göteborg University.

Beach, K. (1999). Consequentional transitions: A sociocultural expedition beyond transfer in education. *Review of Research in Education, 28.*

Borgström, L. (1988). *Adults seeking knowledge: A study of self-determined learning.* Stockholm: Brevskolan.

Davidsson, B., & Svedin, P-O. (1999). *Learning in production. A study within the engineering industry.* Linköping: Linköping studies in Education and Psychology. Department of Education and Psychology, Linköpings University.

Ellström, P-E. (1992). *Training, education and learning in working life.* Stockholm: Publica.

Ellström, P-E. (1999). *Integrating learning and work: Problems and prospects.* Göteborg: Paper presented at the EARLI-conference in Göteborg.

Ellström, P-E., Gustavsson, M., & Svedin, P-O. (1996). *Learning within a temporary organization.* Linköping: Linköping University.

Engeström, Y. (1996). Developmental work research as educational research. Looking ten years back and into the zone of proximal development. *Nordisk pedagogik, 16* (3), 131–143.

Engeström, Y. (1999). Activity theory and transformation. In: Y. Engeström, R. Miettinen, & R-L. Punamäki (Eds), *Perspectives on activity theory.* Cambridge: Cambridge University Press.

European Commission (1995). *Teaching and learning. Towards the learning society.* Whitebook.

Glick, J. (1997). Discourse and development. Notes from the field. In: L. B. Resnick, R. Säljö, C. Pontecorvo, & B. Burge (Eds), *Discourse, tools and reasoning. Essays on situated cognition* (pp. 243–264). Heidelberg: Springer.

Helgesson, B., & Johansson, J. (1994). Work of the Future. In: SOU 1994:101. *Raising our sights: Teacher training for education at work.* Stockholm: Ministry of Education and Science.

Karlsson, J. Ch. (1999). Flexible work organizations – An empirical test of a rhetoric. In: J. Holmer, J. Ch. Karlsson, & B. Thomasson (Eds), *Making working life work. On change, competence and participation.* Karlstad: Karlstad University studies.

Koike, K. (1984). Skill formation systems in the U.S. and Japan. In: M. Aoki (Ed.), *The economic analysis of the Japanese firm.* Amsterdam: North Holland.

Larsson, S., Alexandersson, C., Helmstad, G., & Thång, P-O. (1986). *Work experience and labor workers view of educational opportunities.* Göteborg: Acta Universitatis Gothoburgensis. Göteborg Studies in Educational Sciences.

Larsson, S., & Thång, P-O. (1994). Principles behind the generation of adult education in local arenas. In: P. O. Benn, & G. C. Fieldhouse (Eds), *Training and professional development in adult education.* Oxford: University of Oxford Press.

Lyttkens, L. (1994). *Competence and individualism.* Rapport nr 8, Agenda 2000, Ds 1994:18. Stockholm: Ministry of Education and Science.

McGivney, V. (1998). *Excluded men. Men who are missing from education and training.* Leicester: National Institute of Adult Continuing Education.

Petersson, B., & Thång, P-O. (1996). *Possibilities to learn.* Department of Education. Göteborg University 1996:01.

Sellin, B. (1999). *European trends in the development of occupations and qualifications.* CEDEFOP.

SOU. (1996:164). *Lifelong learning in the employment market – A step towards the knowledge society.* Stockholm: Ministry of Education and Science.

Statistic Sweden (1995). *Staff training.* Örebro: Statistical report.

Statistic Sweden (1996). *Staff training.* Örebro: Statistical report.

The National Agency for Education (1994). *The national evaluation of primary school.*

The National Agency for Education (1997:1646). *Adult secondary schooling and the adult education initiative – 1998*. Report no. 4.

Thång, P-O., & Wärvik, G-B. (2000). Interest and motivation to participate in adult education. A study within the adult education initiative. In: S. Tösse (Ed.), *Adult education research in the nordic countries. Reforms and policy*. Trondheim: Tapir Academic Press.

Tuijnman, A., & Van der Kamp, M. (1992). *Learning across the lifespan*. Oxford: Pergamon.

Rubenowitz, S. (1994). *Organizational psychology and leadership*. Göteborg: Akademi-förlaget.

Chapter 13

A Model for Analyzing Knowledge Content and Processes of Learning a Trade within Alternance Vocational Training

Annalisa Sannino, Alain Trognon and Lara Dessagne

Introduction

Although educational institutions provide students with training in specific skills and practices relevant to the worksite, vocational education and work are far from being harmoniously collaborative entities. One reason for this incongruity is the gap between educational logic and the reality of the industry, which mainly follows the logic of production. Professionals within a company perform practical actions applying to theoretical knowledge. The incongruity between vocational education and work leads one to consider how the conception of action relates to actual performance within a given context. Educational institutions can be efficient in terms of teaching and learning only if they allow students to acquire knowledge and skills directly applicable to their future professions and to the different working situations they will have to cope with.

In France, the search for a compromise between educational institutions and business practices has led to the concept of *alternance vocational training*:[1] a pedagogical system which implements on-the-job learning. This implementation allows convergence between the two parties. But what is it that an apprentice learns on the worksite? How do the processes of learning a trade unfold in alternance vocational training? Despite the increasing desirability of this type of training, specialized literature provides few methodological tools for exploring learning contents and processes that are concretely implied. Our objective here is to introduce a methodology in order to identify

---

[1] Alternance vocational training (in French "*la formation en alternance*") has been promoted by the French authorities and business representatives since the early 1970s. It is a junction between school and work. Its objective is to provide apprentices with sufficient general knowledge as well as professional training within a firm so that they can acquire autonomy during the learning process and be capable of evolving throughout their professional life.

knowledge and processes that emerge from on-the-job interactions involving master craftsman/apprentice pairs.

The Context

The analytical approach presented here was implemented in order to conduct a study mandated by the New Qualifications National Mission (MNNQ) on the processes of constructing knowledge and know-how within the framework of alternance vocational training (Sannino *et al.* 2001). Alternance vocational training targets a young, and varied population, from the ages of 16 to 25 and requires that the participants spend a quarter of their training time in a training center and the rest in a company. The total training period lasts two years. The main objective is for the apprentices to acquire knowledge and know-how relevant to the chosen profession. It allows the trainees to develop social skills and to face concrete work situations. It also allows them to discover the effects of hierarchy and tension in a working group, to identify with a group of workers, and to become acquainted with a type of work that can stimulate reflection about real professional paths. Furthermore, this type of training has been shown to be an excellent way to motivate young people that have lost faith in the school system after a series of failures.

The MNNQ established a partnership with four construction companies in the Lorraine region. The first firm specializes in indoor and outdoor insulation and painting and carpentry for both new and old buildings. The other firms specialize in insulation and façade treatment. The professional training domain examined here is specifically focused on insulating the outer walls of a structure. The trainees have to progressively master the changing techniques and materials. They must also learn how to complete the individual tasks that constitute the job target (coating of thermal insulating material, hydraulic projection, placing of thermal insulating materials and siding) as well as complementary activities (erecting of scaffolding, concrete treatment, preparation of supports, placing of finishing accessories).

These objectives were designed to be achieved within trainer-trainee dyads. This is a particular guided situation where mediated learning by experts happens on-the-job. During the course of their working activity the trainers are in charge of creating the favorable conditions for the apprentice to acquire the practical skills the job requires (Portelli 1992). The interactions between craftsman and apprentice pairs imply guidance. Therefore, as in any tutorial relationship, these interactions involve individual and social dimensions. Supporting phenomena intervene at several co-reference levels and in different manners. In general, at the beginning of the training, the task is primarily managed by the expert. Then the task transfers to a joint activity, and finally the apprentice can accomplish it independently (Winnykamen 1996).

The Data Collection and the Analytical Approach

The intention of this study is to explore knowledge and know-how as they occur naturally. Thus, we needed to create a device for collecting data that would introduce as little distortion into the interaction as possible. Tests, standardized inquiries or any kind of verbalizations initiated by the researcher would not have been appropriate. Verbalizations-during-activities, though widely used in work psychology, would have provided less abstract data than interviews, but would have produced unnatural interactions. Therefore, we decided to record unsolicited conversations between master craftsmen and trainees. This choice is also justified because on-the-job learning occurs mainly during conversations within expert/apprentice pairs.

We selected pairs that had recently begun working together because more familiar craftsman-apprentice dyads may not have engaged in as much verbal communication. They could have interacted according to an implicit mutual knowledge or could have communicated by means of an operative language (Falzon 1989). We collected the dialogue of five expert–novice pairs by using tape-recorders each participant wore during two days of the working week. This resulted in a total of 80 recorded hours. By combining the recordings of the master craftsman and the apprentice we reconstructed the dialogues in the transcriptions. All the interlocutors are male.

Once transcribed, the data needed to be analyzed in order to understand the knowledge involved in learning a trade in alternance vocational training, and in order to understand the conversational dynamics by which this learning emerges. The analytical approach we used is Interlocutionary Logic (Trognon 1999; Sannino 2002 ch. 3), a model based on the double socio-cognitive dimension of the interlocution. From a theoretical point of view, Interlocutionary Logic integrates ideas from the General Formal Semantics of the natural languages, introduced by Vanderveken (1990), and the Hierarchical and Functional Model of Analysis of Conversations conceived by Roulet and Moeshler (Roulet 1981; Roulet *et al.* 1985; Moeschler 1985, 1989).

In order to describe this approach, we need to start from the concept of speech acts, i.e. the acts we perform when we pronounce utterances. Speech acts are characterized by an illocutionary force — F — and a propositional content — p; the reciprocal organization of illocutionary force and propositional content is generally formalized as $F(p)$. The force is the pragmatic function performed in conversation by expressing an utterance. Five main types of actions can be performed through the enunciation of a speech act: representative, directive, commissive, expressive, and declarative. These actions have the following properties: illocutionary aim of F, degree of strength, mode of achievement, propositional content conditions, preparatory conditions and sincerity conditions. The propositional content is the representation on which a given force is applied.

Interlocutionary Logic theorizes about the relationship between the satisfaction and success of speech acts within interlocutions (Ghiglione & Trognon 1993; Grusenmeyer & Trognon 1996; Trognon & Brassac 1992). A speech act is satisfied if its propositional content is true in the context of the utterance expression, and because of this utterance. For example, a request is satisfied if the listener gives the answer in the context of the utterance and because of the initial act. A speech act is successful if the speaker manages to get the listener to understand which act they are performing.

A speech act can also be successful even if the proposition stated by the speaker is not implemented within the context of the speech act or if it does not result in the psychological state required by the act. This introduces the concept of the defectiveness of a speech act. A speech act is non-defective if it is successful and if the preparatory conditions (i.e. what is presupposed or assumed to be true by the speaker who performs the act) and the sincerity conditions (i.e. the speaker's psychological state) are satisfied in the stated context. However, a speech act can also be defective if one or several preparatory or sincerity conditions are not satisfied in the context. For example, a request for information will be defectively successful if the listener has no means to do what is required, though he perfectly understands what the speaker requests and wishes to give the required information.

Interlocutionary Logic distinguishes four organization levels of interlocutions: interventions, exchanges, structures and transactions. These levels are mutually inclusive. Interventions are complex speech acts (Ghiglione & Trognon 1993). Two or more interventions form an exchange. Interventions and exchanges compose structures. Structures and interventions compose transactions. The intervention is the only reoccurring component of conversations (Moeschler 1989; Roulet *et al.* 1985). A series of two or more interventions gives rise to an exchange, such as, for example, in a question-answer pair. Exchanges are the smallest units of interlocution, as asserted by several authors (Goffman 1967; Kerbrat-Orecchioni 1996), and are complete when the interlocutors satisfy the initial act.

More macroscopically, exchanges are organized in structures based on two types of linking: linear and hierarchical linking. In the former type, exchanges are sequential and belong to the same speech level. In the latter types, exchanges are bound by interdependent relations. Some structures present a typical organization carrying out a collective intention, such as debating, animating a group or making collective decisions. The most macroscopic components of interlocutions are transactions. They refer to the conventionally established language games (Wittgenstein 1968) such as psychotherapy or man-machine dialogues. On the basis of these four conversation levels, Inter-locutionary Logic explains the intuitive knowledge the interlocutors have of a particular language game (like the tutorial dialogue, for example) and the socio-cognitive effects the game induces (like the autonomy the apprentice reaches and the knowledge emerging from a tutorial dialogue). More concretely, this architecture that gradually emerges from the conversation can be represented in the following table.

Table 1: Table of interlocutionary analysis.

Transaction	Structures	Sequential	Conversational	
			Illocutionary	Cognitive

In order to understand how Interlocutionary Logic is applied, follow the analysis of the conversation excerpt below (C and A respectively symbolize the craftsman and the apprentice; the numbers indicate the succession of the contributions to the dialogue).

C1: << The roughcast shouldn't be tackled laterally >>.

A2: (pneumatic drill).

C3: << That's the way you do it, that's much better >>.

T1: << *Le crépi ne doit pas être attaqué latéralement* >>.

. . .

T3: << *Ah ben, ça va nettement mieux* >>.

The master craftsman intervenes because the apprentice is executing a clumsy maneuver with the pneumatic drill. Thus, the apprentice, as indicated by the noise of the tool, tries again and corrects the initial mistake. These social and cognitive movements are presented below in the table of interlocutionary analysis.

Table 2: Interlocutionary analysis for the excerpt 1.

Structures	Sequential	Conversational	
		Illocutionary	**Cognitive**
⌐I	C1	Directive (Request for correction)	(p) To tackle the roughcast laterally
E—I	A2	(Action)	
⌐I	C3	Expressive and positive evaluation of the action in progress	(p) To tackle the roughcast laterally

The analysis of the transcript always starts on the second column of the table. Notice that the components detailed in this column are both discursive (like C1 and C3) and non-discursive (like A2). Later we will see that these contributions are organically articulated.

Once located in the sequence column, the contributions are interpreted as illocutionary and cognitive phenomena. When we look at the illocutionary aspects of a speech act, we focus on their force, i.e. what it enacts in conversation. Thus, C1 is literally a representative because the craftsman asserts something. However, non-literally C1 is a directive, because the craftsman requires the correction of an improper maneuver by the apprentice. C3 is a complex speech act formed by an expressive and a representative that evaluate the action under way. The interlocutionary analyst identifies the force of speech acts considering them from both a prospective and retrospective point of view (Sannino & Trognon 2003; Trognon 2000). Although we cannot detail this procedure technically, an overview will be provided in order to give a general idea of its functioning. When the craftsman pronounces C1, the concrete illocutory function of this utterance is not yet completely determined. At this stage in the conversation, C1 could be simply the affirmation of a general norm. But when the craftsman pronounces C3, this interpretation is no longer valid. Saying "that's the way you do it, that's much better", the craftsman indicates that A2 has satisfied a request of correction (C1). In other words, Interlocutionary Logic identifies the illocutionary function of a speech act by looking at how it stabilizes within the conversation.

The cognitive aspects of each contribution in the excerpt are the propositional contents of the speech acts the interlocutors perform. The propositional contents of C1 and C3 correspond to the same representation [(p) To tackle the roughcast laterally]. The only difference is that C1 situates this representation in a possible world, whereas C3 situates it in a real world. This difference underlies the preparatory conditions of the expressive by the craftsman (i.e. the apprentice is able to maneuver the tool correctly), and the know-how which emerges from the exchange.

In order to complete the explanation of the analytic table from excerpt 1, look at the first column on the left. Here, the interlocutionary analysis formalizes how the illocutions mutually organize into a structure. In the excerpt, the interaction structure is a repairing exchange (Goffman 1967), accounting for the way in which the apprentice is using the pneumatic drill.

Although non-discursive contributions are not inherently part of the speech, they become part of it when non-discursive actions induce speech, and the interlocutors appropriate them to carry on the discourse. There is a vast literature on the relation between discursive and non-discursive events within a conversation. One of its authors is Herbert H. Clark (1996) who has shown how the sequential organization of a conversation informs "the concrete world around" the interlocutors. Thus, by listening to the conversations between the craftsman and the apprentice, we "see" how the work evolves on the site.

The structure we have just described is a recurring structure within tutor-trainee dialogues, even if it hides within more complex architectures sometimes, like the one in the excerpt below.

C1: ≪ You're deviating ≫.

A2: ≪ The drill is too heavy ≫.

C3: ≪ Did you go out last night? ≫.

A4: ≪ I didn't sleep much ≫.

C5: ≪ Ah it's better not to party when you have to remove the roughcast the next day ≫.

C1: ≪ *Tu dévies* ≫.

A2: ≪ *Il est trop lourd le marteau* ≫.

C3: ≪ *T'es sorti hier soir?* ≫.

A4: ≪ *J'ai pas beaucoup dormi* ≫.

C5: ≪ *Ah il vaut mieux ne pas faire la fête quand on doit décrépir le lendemain* ≫.

The apprentice is still struggling with the pneumatic drill which he must learn how to use properly. The trainee doesn't manage to remove the roughcast in the exact place where it is needed. The apprentice explains his clumsy maneuver by stating that "the drill is too heavy". This statement provides the craftsman with an opportunity to suggest a general principle of living if one wants to be optimally efficient on-the-job: "it's better not to party when you have to remove the roughcast the next day".

Table 3: Interlocutionary analysis for the excerpt 2[2].

Structures	Sequential	Illocutionary	Cognitive C	Cognitive A
	C1	Evaluation of the action under way Implicit directive	**deviation**	
	A2	Answer Explication– Justification of the action		**Too heavy weight**→ deviation of the drill
	C3	Request for confirmation of an implicit hypothesis	**party**→ fatigue→ deviation	
	A4	Answer		party→ ¬**sleep**→ fatigue→ deviation
	C5	Assertion of a principle Implicit directive	**work**→ ¬**party**	

The statement C1 is an implicit evaluation of the action under way. This evaluation implies the directive, "do not deviate". Instead of immediately correcting his maneuver, as in the previous excerpt, the apprentice answers by explaining and justifying his faulty action: "I deviate because the drill is too heavy". The subordinated question C3 functions as a request of confirmation of an implicit hypothesis about the apprentice's fatigue. Thus we obtain the following chain of representations not always explicit in the dialogue: "the drill is too heavy" → "I went out last night" → "I didn't sleep much" → (I am tired). The answer A4 validates this hypothesis, as well as the previous logic chain. C5 serves two functions concurrently: to assert a principle for the management of the apprentice's personal time in relation to work activity, and to implicitly suggest compliance with this principle. This intervention by the craftsman reverts to the argumentation the interlocutors have built together throughout the excerpt. The principle

[2] The terms and symbols in bold correspond to what is explicit in the dialogue.

for the management of personal time emerges as an explanation distributed between the interlocutors within the progression of the dialogue.

In order to complete the description of our analytical approach, an additional excerpt from our data will be analyzed. We will investigate how the interlocutionary properties presented above condense within a more extensive dialogue than the one analyzed previously. In this excerpt the apprentice also has difficulties correctly manipulating the pneumatic drill.

A1:   ≪ Like this ≫ .

C2:   ≪ Pull a little toward you (. . .) just like that. That's it (. . .). What is really important is not to try to get too deep in the wall. You see your roughcast, it is too thick. Don't try too much to slightly limit the bevel ≫ .

A3:   ≪ Yeah, yeah ≫ .

C4:   ≪ (. . .) The point is that you don't use the tool enough, right. As long as you don't use it with the shovel like that, look (pneumatic drill) you see the difference in the work and then in your time and effort. (. . .) Anyway the less you use the drill, the longer time it will take you to remove the roughcast. (. . .) It is already heavy enough like that, without killing yourself. I'll tell you, this is not a piece of cake, I know what it is, right. When it gets to be too much you can rest and then start again. No one is telling you not to stop right. We know you can't take it. Even we take a break. Let's try to use your work tool correctly, after all it is no fun right, that's true it is hard ≫ .

A5:   ≪ Yeah ≫ .

C6:   ≪ Yeah, it's one of the toughest jobs in the world, you kill yourself at first but after you get used to it, you do it real fast. But then it's not great because you get tired but working fast that's no good because whether you work fast or not fast it doesn't matter, the concrete is not gonna fall by itself. After that kid we'll use pressurized water to wash so that the concrete can cling to the bricks, then after that, as soon as we're done with it we must clean out the roof down there. It certainly won't get done all by itself. Sure it makes more work. Go on you still have the bottom part to do ≫ .

A1:   ≪ *Comme ça quoi* ≫ .

C2:   ≪ *Tire un peu sur toi (. . .) tout comme ça. Ca y est (. . .). C'qui faut surtout c'est pas essayer de rentrer en profondeur dans ton mur. Tu vois ton crépi il est trop épais. Pas trop essayer de limiter légèrement en biseau* ≫ .

A3:   ≪ *Ouais ouais* ≫ .

C4:   ≪ *(. . .) Ce qu'y a c'est que tu l'utilises pas trop ta machine, hein. Tant que tu l'utiliseras pas avec la palette comme ça, regarde (. . .) tu vois la différence de travail et puis de temps et puis de fatigue. (. . .) De toute façon moins tu t'en serviras comme y faut de la machine là, plus longtemps tu mettras à casser. (. . .) C'est déjà assez crevant comme ça, sans se casser. Moi je te le dis, c'est pas de la tarte, je sais ce que c'est, hein ouais. Quand t'en as marre et bin tu la reposes et puis tu r'prends tout de suite. On te demande pas de pas t'arrêter hein. On sait très bien que t'y arriveras pas. Même nous on s'arrête. Allez essaye d'te servir comme il faut de ton outil le travail, avant tout c'est chiant hein, c'est vrai que c'est crevant* ≫ .

A5:   ≪ *Ouais* ≫ .

C6:   ≪ *Ah, ouais c'est un plus dur métier du monde, là tu te crèves comme ça mais après t'y arrives vite fait mais ça ça tu te crèves, mais travailler vite. Alors là ça va c'est pas génial parce que ça tu travailles vite ou pas vite ça fait rien, le béton y va pas le béton y va pas tomber tout seul. Après là tchio on mettra un coup de carcher pour laver pour dépoussiérer pour tout ça là un coup de carcher pour laver pour que le béton puisse s'accrocher après les briques, puis après, dès qu'on a fini ça y faut nettoyer tout le toit tout en bas ah. C'est sûr ça va pas se faire tout seul. C'est sûr ça représente du boulot. Allez vas-y à toi t'as encore le bout du bas* ≫ .

A7:   (drill)

C8:   ≪ You've had it buddy, right? ≫ .

A9:   ≪ Hum ≫ (pneumatic drill).

C10:   ≪ You've had enough, you're gonna get down, see Rob and tell him I've told you to stop. It's no use, you're not getting anywhere, you're gonna do what I told you, you're gonna get down, you see Rob, you tell him I've told you to stop. You say you're not doing well, your hand hurts, it's no use continuing, you're not getting anywhere, that's the only thing left to do for today. You go and see if he knows what you can do because as for me, I can't take care of you anymore. I don't have time ≫ .

A7:   . . .

C8:   ≪ *T'es cuit mon pauvre ami, hein* ≫ .

A9:   . . .

C10:   ≪ *T'es cuit, tu vas descendre, tu vas aller voir le le Rob tu lui dis que c'est moi qui ai dit que tu t'arrêtes. C'est pas la peine, t'avances pas t'avances pas, pis ça tombe en ruine hein oh oh, bon tu vas faire ce que je t'ai dit tu vas descendre tu vas voir le Rob, tu lui dis que c'est moi qui t'as dit d'arrêter. Tu dis que ça va pas, t'as t'as mal à la main, c'est pas la peine que tu continues t'avances pas du tout, y'a pu qu'ça à faire pour ce soir. Tu vas le voir tu lui dis qu'y voit ce que tu peux faire parce que moi, j'pourrais pas m'occuper de toi. J'ai pas le temps* ≫ .*

The excerpt presents two phases within the dialogue. During the first phase (from A1 to C4) a faulty maneuver by the apprentice induces the master craftsman to explain the proper use of the pneumatic drill. During the second phase (from C4 to C10) the master craftsman ascertains if the apprentice's maneuver improves on the basis of his explanation; however the interlocutors are faced with another failure.

In C2 the expert asserts that in order to use the tool correctly one should slightly limit the bevel instead of forcing the tool too deeply into the wall. These explanations are also indirect requests addressed to the trainee, by the expert (i.e. do not try to get too deep in the wall, but slightly limit the bevel). C4 (≪ The point is that you don't use the tool enough . . . ≫) indirectly enunciates the non-satisfaction of these requests. A request is both an action we perform on our interlocutor and the representation of the satisfaction conditions. In other words, a request is satisfied if what the interlocutor does corresponds to the action represented within the locutor's request. Here the interlocutor is the trainee and in order to satisfy the craftsman's requests he must manipulate the pneumatic drill adhering with the actions represented by the requests (i.e. the way to get in the wall and to limit the bevel). Also, a request is successful if its preparatory conditions are satisfied, namely if the interlocutor is able to perform what is required.

Thus, more precisely, what C4 enunciates is the non-satisfaction of the preparatory condition of the request, i.e. the trainee's inability to perform what is required. This explains why the following discourse is about how to manage the task and the efforts it requires, which are the necessary conditions to satisfy the initial requests. The explanations about the proper use of the tool are built on both the discursive and non-discursive levels of the interaction. The craftsman takes the tool away from the apprentice and shows him how to handle the pneumatic drill (≪ . . . like that, look . . . ≫). At same time the craftsman comments on the actions he is performing. He enunciates a rule of the appropriate use of the tool, which is also a technical explanation of the apprentice's ineptitude in using the tool (≪ . . . as long as you don't use it with the shovel . . . ≫). He explains the advantages of the appropriate use of the pneumatic drill in terms of work quality, performance, and comfort (≪ . . . you see the difference in the work and then of your time and effort . . . ≫). The craftsman also states the consequences of an inappropriate use of the tool (≪. . . the less you use the drill, the longer time it will take you to remove the roughcast . . . ≫). Then the craftsman evokes a common method to manage the strenuous nature of the work (≪. . . Even we take a break . . . ≫). The requests implicitly formulated in T2 as explanations are expressed directly in a speech act in T4 (≪. . . Let's try to use your work tool correctly . . . ≫). Also, it is interesting to notice that the propositional content of this speech act, implicitly expresses the non-satisfaction of the initial requests (you are still not using your work tool correctly, i.e. you are still trying to get too deep in the wall and do not slightly limit the bevel).

In T6 the expert situates the activity under way within the entirety of activities connected with the task (≪. . . After that kid we'll use pressurized water to wash so that the concrete can cling to the bricks, then after that, as soon as we're done with it we must clean out the roof down there . . . ≫) and enunciates his philosophy of the trade in relation to this particular circumstance (≪. . . you kill yourself at first but after you get used to it, you do it real fast . . . ≫). The requests implicitly formulated in C2 in the form of explanations, and then expressed in a direct way in C4 are reformulated here within the utterance "Go on you still have the bottom part to do". Despite the demonstration and the explanations provided, the apprentice's second try (A7) is not more successful than the first one and induces the craftsman to express a negative judgment (≪ You've had enough . . . ≫). Like in C2, in C8 and C10 the craftsman's speech aim is to explain the trainee's faulty performance; the only difference is that the explanation focuses on the trainee's physical condition, and no longer on his use of the tool. As the apprentice persists in the incorrect manoeuvre (A8), the craftsman asks him to stop working (≪. . . you're gonna get down, see Rob and tell him I've told you to stop ≫). Thus the craftsman reformulates his evaluation on the basis of the result obtained (≪. . . you're not getting anywhere . . . ≫), and he suggests that the apprentice should tell the boss that he has to stop because of the pain (≪. . . you tell him I've told you to stop. You say you're not doing well, your hand hurts . . . ≫). This part of the sequence deals with the failure to correctly engage in a work activity, but this practical incompetence remains in the background of the tutor's speech. The craftsman's explanation focuses on the apprentice's pain, and consequently, does not make him face his ineptitude in the use of the tool directly.

Learning Contents Emerging from the Interactions

By putting together the propositions in the right column of the interlocutionary analysis tables and grouping them by their themes, we have obtained a set of categories which define the learning contents that emerge from the sum of interactions between the expert and the novice. These contents are not solely concerned with how to perform the work in the literal sense of operative modes of performing a task. As shown in table 4, the apprentice primarily learns how to perform these tasks within the broader perspective of the profession and not as a restricted set of actions. Most of the categories concern the relationship with the work in a broader sense: how to manage the work in terms of organization, space-time and ergonomics, how to manage personal time in relation to work activity, how to adapt to diverse situations, and the philosophy of the trade.

Table 4: Distribution of acquired knowledge emerging from the interactions.

1. Organization, space-time and ergonomics management of the work	58%
2. Operative modes to perform the tasks	20%
3. Philosophy of the trade	10%
4. Adaptation to different situations	9%
5. Management of personal time in relation to work activity	3%

χ^2 $\quad$ p > 0.01

1. Organization, space-time and ergonomics management of the work — 58%. This category regroups the contents which will allow the apprentice to acquire the necessary competencies to plan his work, to implement his planning within the deadlines, and to optimally manage the work within the psycho-physiological constraints of the tasks in relation to the tools and materials. The craftsman teaches the apprentice that his work does not only consist of accomplishing one or several principal tasks, but is also characterized by secondary tasks which need to be integrated in daily planning, such as verifying materials to be brought, cleaning and tidying-up the work site.

<< Is the stuff ready? No, we need a ruler and the bucket there and then we can go >>.

<< Don't leave the screwdriver there ok stuck in the poly ... because I know what will happen, it will stay in the cement for six months >>.

<< *Est-ce que le materiel est prêt? Non, il nous faut une règle et le sceau là-bas, puis en route* >>

<< *Le tournevis tu ne le laisses pas là hein planté dans le poly ... parce que j'en connais ils restent six mois dans le poly* >>

The interlocutions collected in this study are organized according to a constant temporal unit, the work day, which allows the craftsman to set concrete goals that the apprentice must reach by the end of the day. This short-term perspective is designed to help the trainee assess his capacity in terms of timing and quality; he can first recognize his limits and then evaluate his eventual progress from day to day.

<< That's good we will finish the colors tonight, and then we will move on to the top floor >>.

<< *C'est bon on aura fini ce soir les couleurs, ce soir on est en haut* >>.

The craftsman often takes the time to teach the apprentice the ergonomic contents of the task, in order for him to learn how to control his physical effort. These concerns are always expressed during the execution of a task, and can be presented directly or indirectly.

≪ Don't force it too much, don't strain yourself too much. ≫ , ≪ Be careful, is your finger ok? Yeah, yeah, you can put some ointment on it a little later ≫

≪ *Force pas trop, te casse pas trop* ≫ , ≪ *Fais attention, alors ton doigt ça va? Ouais, ouais, tu mettras de la pommade t'à l'heure* ≫

≪ It's a pain, it's true that it is exhausting, it's the hardest job in the world, you're going to struggle like that for a while but after that you'll get it pretty quickly ≫

≪ *C'est chiant, c'est vrai que c'est crevant, c'est le plus dur métier du monde, là tu te crèves comme ça mais après t'y arrives vite fait* ≫

Concerning the use of the work tools, the tutor teaches the apprentice how to manage his body in relation to the tool, by explaining how to use it, and more importantly by teaching him the right attitude to adopt while using it.

≪ When you're fed up you need to put it down and then pick it up right away; you need to stop when you're tired but not too long, you have to keep yourself ready to go ≫ .

≪ *Quand t'en as marre tu la reposes et puis tu reprends tout de suite; il faut s'arrêter quand on est fatigué mais pas trop longtemps, il faut rester chaud* ≫ .

2. Operative modes to perform the tasks — 20%.   This category refers to all the craftsman's instructions concerning the operative modes of performing the tasks: how to utilize a tool, how to use and manipulate the materials on the work site, and what procedures have to be followed during the work activity. These instructions can appear any time; during the completion of the work or after. There are two types of situations in which the craftsman gives instructions during the execution of the task; either he performs the task himself by showing the steps to follow, or the apprentice performs the task, guided step by step by the tutor's explanation.

≪ (. . .) There should only be paint on the end of the roller bristles and not inside the roller and there, you have too much already, you see going like this you turn up the bristles (. . .) ≫ ,

≪ (. . .) *Il faut qu'il y ait de la peinture seulement sur le bout des poils et pas au fond du rouleau et là, il y en a déjà trop, tu vois alors en faisant comme ceci tu relèves ton poil* (. . .) ≫ ,

≪ (. . .) The weight of the roller alone is enough to make grains, you don't need to press, you are only there to hold the roller, you got it (. . .) ≫ .

≪ (. . .) *Le propre poids du rouleau suffit à faire les grains, tu n'as pas à appuyer, toi tu es juste là pour tenir le rouleau, voilà* (. . .) ≫ .

When the instructions are provided following the completion of a task, they help correct a mistake or imperfection by the apprentice. When the apprentice maneuvers the tool incorrectly, the tutor continues the work by showing him how to proceed.

≪ Give me your roller, if you don't put the product on it you won't have the same grain. That is what I told you, you need to load it regularly and to work it and when we work, we make large movements because you'll never be able to load it afterwards with small movements, ok that's good, try it (. . .) ≫ .

≪ *Donne-moi ton rouleau, là si tu mets pas le produit dessus tu peux pas avoir les mêmes grains. C'est bien ce que je te dis, il faut le charger régulièrement et le travailler alors quand on travaille, on fait des grands mouvements parce que des petits mouvements tu tu n'arrives jamais à à charger par la suite, allez c'est bon, essaye* (. . .) ≫ .

However, the craftsman can also give instructions in response to a more or less explicit request by the apprentice, i.e. when he expresses doubt about how to proceed or he wishes to know something:

A: << Roger, why don't we put a piece of cloth on the base? >>

C: << (. . .) Because for one thing it isn't meant to have it and for the other, because this coating isn't smooth so you can't put cloth on it (. . .) >> .

A: << Roger, pourquoi on met pas de la toile sur le soubassement? >>

C: << (. . .) Parce que c'est pas prévu d'une part et d'autre part, cet enduit qui n'est pas lisse alors tu peux pas mettre de la toile (. . .) >> .

The craftsman can also provide instructions in an indirect manner, for example by conversing with a third person while the apprentice is present:

A worker talking to the tutor in the presence of the apprentice: << How do you put them there, how do you put on the little joints? Do you pin them on from behind or do you stick them directly into the tip >> .

C: << We put it like this, first we draw a level line 15mm long on the big carbide and then we cut, and put the aluminum profile >> .

<< Comment que tu les mets là, comment les petits joints? Tu mets une épingle derrière ou tu le piques directement sur les tétines >> .

C: << On le met, non on tire un trait de niveau déjà au dessus du gros carbure de 15 mm et puis on coupe, et puis on met le profil en alu >> .

3. Philosophy of the trade — 10%.
During his everyday practice the master craftsman has integrated a set of values into his work that are also transmitted to the apprentice during the training period. One of them is to perform aesthetically well-done work.

<< The grain needs to stop here, otherwise it will looks ugly because here you can see the marks of the brush or the roller that are under it and crosswise, we shouldn't see anything but the grain, ah it's good >> .

<< Le grain il doit s'arrêter là, et il doit s'arrêter ici, sinon ça fait moche parce que là on voit les coups de pinceau ou les coups de rouleau qu'il y a en dessous de travers, on doit rien voir que le grain, ah c'est bien >> .

The craftsman also teaches the apprentice the notion of teamwork, i.e. how the work must be coordinated by different individuals.

<< We'll go to the end in order to leave here, they should be able to huh go to at least here, ya' know! See? That way they won't be blocked. By the time they make the plates on this side, you know, we'll be back >> .

<< On va jusqu'au bout pour partir d'ici, il faut qu'eux ils puissent euh monter au moins jusque-là quoi ! Hein ? Comme ça ils seront pas bloqués. Le temps qu'ils fassent les plaques de ce côté-là tu sais, on sera revenu >> .

4. Adaptation to different situations — 9%.
The apprentice often encounters new situations that he is not always prepared to face. The craftsman's role is therefore to teach the apprentice how to overcome these difficulties by understanding them and adapting to them.

<< Every time you have more than five floors, you make a joint so that it dilates, it's required >> .

<< A chaque fois que tu as plus de cinq étages, tu fais un joint d'effractionnement pour que ça dilate c'est obligatoire >> .

5. *Management of personal time in relation to work activity — 3%.* The management of personal time in relation to work activity represents a very small part of the data, nevertheless, it makes up a very interesting aspect of the relationship between the craftsman and the apprentice. As a healthy life-style has necessarily positive effects on work efficiency, the tutor sometimes asks questions such as

≪ Did you have a good night ? ≫   ≪ *T'as passé une bonne nuit?* ≫

Learning Processes Emerging from the Interactions

By grouping the illocutionary forces in the analysis tables we have obtained a set of categories that define the learning processes that emerge from the sum of interactions between the craftsman and the apprentice. Although the trainee sometimes fails to perform what the expert requires, and remains dependent on his tutor, he shows he is learning in other ways: by asking questions, reformulating the craftsman's discourse, evaluating his own actions, finding creative solutions to extricate himself from problematic situations, contributing to the common work and tutoring another trainee. Table 5 represents the distribution in percentages of these different forms of learning in relation to the degree of autonomy they express.

Table 5: Distribution of the learning processes emerging from the interactions, and degrees of autonomy.

Degree 0:	Complete dependence on the craftsman's directives	8%
1st degree:	Questions	12%
2nd degree:	Reformulations of the craftsman's discourse	16%
3rd degree:	Apprentice's evaluations of his own actions	16%
4th degree:	Creative solutions	4%
5th degree:	Contribution to the common work under way	36%
6th degree:	Capacity to tutor another trainee	4%
7th degree:	Complete autonomy	4%

χ^2 $p > 0.05$

Degree 0: Complete dependence on the craftsman's directives — 8%. This category contains all situations in which the apprentice shows no initiative. He is completely dependent on the craftsman:

C: ≪ You are going to get a cut here, ok, do you agree with me? ≫

A: ≪ No, but uh, that's why I was waiting for you, I didn't know what to do! ≫

C: ≪ Pull here, your gonna have little chips leftover, right? ≫

C: ≪ *Tu vas avoir une coupe ici, ok, d'accord avec moi?* ≫

A: ≪ *Non, mais euh, c'est pour ça que j'attendais, et j'savais pas quoi faire!* ≫

C: ≪ *Tire par là, t'auras une p'tite chute là hein?* ≫

1st Degree: Questions — 12%.   The apprentice asks two types of questions: questions which require information but are not necessary for performing the task under way (excerpt 1), and questions meant to resolve a problematic situation (excerpt 2).

Excerpt 1:

C: ≪ There aren't any chargers, do you have one? ≫

A: ≪ Yeah, yeah, it's a nice one and the yellow button, what's it for? ≫

C: ≪ *Y'a pas de chargeur, t'en as un?* ≫
A: ≪ *Ouais, ouais, oh il est beau et le bouton jaune, y sert à quoi au fait?* ≫

Excerpt 2:

A: ≪ How do you do that, the edge of the window? ≫

C: ≪ Here, you go like this here and then you come here and you . . . ≫

A: ≪ *Comment tu fais là, le rebord de la fenêtre?* ≫

C: ≪ *Alors, ici tu fais comme ça là tu viens ici et tu . . .* ≫

2nd Degree: Reformulations of the craftsman's discourse — 16%.   The apprentice shows that he has appropriated the expert's explanations when he reformulates them in his own terms.

C: ≪ The large ceilings are for the dryers because there are dryers and uh as there aren't any shutters, the ceiling is larger here and there is a shutter here, the first row there is a shutter there is a regular ceiling ≫ .

A: ≪ The first row there is, there is a shutter always ≫ .

C: ≪ *Les plafonds de large c'est pour les séchoirs parce que il y a des séchoirs alors heu comme y a pas de volets, le plafond est plus large là y'a un volet là, la première rangée y'a un volet y'a un plafond normal* ≫ .

A: ≪ *La première rangée y'a, y'a un volet tout l'temps* ≫ .

3rd Degree: Apprentice's evaluations of his own actions — 16%.   When the apprentice evaluates an action that he has just performed, he demonstrates that he knows how it should be done. This is the case in the following example where in A2 the apprentice evaluates the relationship between the tutor's request (C1) and what he has done.

C1: ≪ Here, let's see. Try to make grains because, there's no reason why you wouldn't, go ahead Patrick and try to avoid hitting your roller against the support otherwise you will crush the bristles, go ahead make the grains. Don't stop there, stop lower down because otherwise we can see where you stopped, you can tell here, you see, there aren't grains, you have to try to go lower ≫ .

A2: ≪ It has to be redone ≫

C3: ≪ Uh, yes ≫ .

C1: ≪ *Tiens. Essaye voir un petit peu toi de faire des grains, parce qu'il y a pas de raison, allez ça va Patrick et puis évite de taper ton rouleau contre le le sous-appui, sinon tu écrases les poils allez fait des grains. T'arrêtes pas là, t'arrêtes plus bas parce que sinon on voit là où tu t'arrêtes ça se voit là regarde tu vois, y a pas de grains faut toujours aller plus bas* ≫ .

A2: ≪ *Faut le refaire* ≫ .

C3: ≪ *Ben oui* ≫ .

4th Degree: Creative solutions — 4%.   On several occasions, the apprentice makes up new solutions, which for him are equivalent to those that the tutor teaches.

C: ≪Did you use a file?≫

A: ≪No≫.

C: ≪Did you use a saw! You'll never get clean work done with that !≫

A: ≪To hell with it, I used a rail to do the groove!≫

C: ≪*T'as pris une rainureuse?*≫

A: ≪*Non*≫.

C: ≪*T'as pris une scie! T'auras jamais des trucs tout propre avec ça!*≫

A: ≪*Fais chier hein, moi j'ai pris un rail pour la faire la rainure!*≫

5th Degree: Contribution to the common work under way — 36%.   This category contains all situations in which the apprentice brings additional contents into the interlocution with the craftsman, and contributes to the common work under way.

C: ≪Did you prepare the stuff? Your tools?≫

A: ≪Yeah, uh we need fiberglass, we also need some fiberglass beforehand≫.

C: ≪*T'as préparé l'machin? Tes outils?*≫

A: ≪*Ouais, eh faudra y faut d'la laine, aussi faut mettre d'la laine de verre avan*≫.

6th Degree: Capacity to tutor another trainee — 4%.   When the apprentice is able to correctly direct the actions of another trainee who is performing a task, he demonstrates he has fully integrated the contents of the training.

A: ≪Don't do that here. Here, only underneath, we only need to do it underneath≫.

B: ≪Underneath here?≫

A: ≪Yeah.

B: ≪We don't need to do anything here?≫

A: ≪No, don't touch, there is nothing needed to be done on the gutter≫.

A: ≪*Fait pas là ici. Là, on le fait en dessous, y a qu'en dessous à faire*≫.

B: ≪*En dessous là?*≫

A : ≪*Ouais*≫.

B: ≪*Ya rien à faire ici?*≫

A: ≪*Non, non touche y a rien à faire là sur les chénaux*≫.

7th Degree: Complete autonomy — 4%.   The highest level a trainee can acquire in the trade corresponds to the point when he is able to autonomously perform the tasks; the tutor's interventions become support and are no longer direct instructions.

C: ≪Go ahead Bruno, you see, go ahead. Ok, that's good≫.

Noises

A: ≪Do you want the cutter?≫

C: ≪No thanks, that's ok≫.

C: ≪*Allez Bruno, tu vois, allez. Eh, ben c'est bon*≫.

. . .

A: ≪*Tu veux le cutter?*≫

C: ≪*Non, c'est bon merci*≫.

Conclusions

What kinds of interactions occur between a tutor and an apprentice in on-the-job training situations? What learning takes place and by what means? Are the instructions of official programs always followed? How does the interaction unfold when the novice encounters a problematic situation that he cannot overcome? How does an expert help an apprentice develop the necessary skills for the trade?

Knowledge and know-how are sometimes discursive by nature, as in the "language sessions" analyzed by Spigolon & Specogna (1996) or in conversational exchanges which play an important role in the acquisition of a first lexicon (Veneziano 1997;

Bernicot & Trognon 1997). Knowledge and know-how can also have a conceptual nature such as those found in conversations about physical or arithmetical notions (Gilly, Roux & Trognon 1999). Finally, knowledge and know-how can have a practical nature when, for example, a novice learns during the course of a conversation about how to use software (Trognon & Saint-Dizier 1999), or in dialogues within tutor-apprentice dyads as examined in the present work.

Whatever their nature, knowledge and know-how are not informational items simply transferred from the tutor to the apprentice, but distributed and situated dialogical phenomena. They are dialogical phenomena because the semiotic mediation used by individuals to communicate encapsulates and determines them (Trognon 1997). They are distributed phenomena because usually they cannot be described as the resulting sum of the resources brought together by the interlocutors, but instead as conjoined original constructions emerging from the interactive dynamics. They are situated phenomena to the extent that they depend not only upon available resources, but also and especially upon the "here and now" of the conversation under way.

Hence, in this chapter, we wanted to present a model for identifying and describing contents and processes emerging from a tutorial relationship on the work site. Analyses based on this model can provide support for new methods and practical solutions for facilitating the transfer between the educational system and the working environment. Interlocutionary analysis shows how the progressing conversation produces representations (propositional contents) and relations (illocutionary forces). In this regard, they can reveal the difficulties encountered by the interlocutors when they perform a task, but more specifically, they allow us to observe how, throughout conversation, these difficulties are faced on the basis of the resources available to the craftsman and the trainee. Thus, this methodology, in terms of data collection and analysis, can help to *empirically* visualize the tension between "official educational programs" (i.e. what should be taught and how), and "situated programs" (i.e. what individuals actually learn on-the-job and how).

References

Bernicot, J., & Trognon, A. (1997). Dimensions de la conversation [Dimensions of conversation]. In: J. Bernicot, J. Caron-Pargue, & A. Trognon (Eds), *Conversation, interaction et fonctionnement cognitif* [Conversation, interaction, and cognitive functions] (pp. 15–39). Nancy: Presses Universitaires de Nancy.

Clark, H. H. (1996). *Using language*. Cambridge: Cambridge University Press.

Falzon, P. (1989). *Ergonomie cognitive du dialogue* [Cognitive ergonomics of dialogue]. Grenoble: P.U.G.

Ghiglione, R., & Trognon, A. (1993). *Où va la pragmatique? De la pragmatique à la psychologie sociale* [Where did the pragmatics go? From pragmatics to social psychology]. Grenoble: Presses Universitaires de Grenoble.

Gilly, M., Roux, J. P., & Trognon, A. (1999). *Apprendre dans l'interaction* [Learning within interaction]. Nancy: Presses Universitaires de Nancy.

Goffman, E. (1967). *Interaction ritual. Essays on face-to-face behaviour*. Garden City, N.Y.: Anchor Books.

Grusenmeyer, C., & Trognon, A. (1996). Structures of natural reasoning within functional dialogues. *Pragmatics and cognition, 4* (2), 305–346.

Kerbrat-Orecchioni, C. (1996). *La conversation* [Conversation]. Paris: Seuil.

Moeschler, J. (1985). *Argumentation et conversation. Eléments pour une analyse pragmatique du discours* [Argumentation and conversation. Elements for pragmatic analysis of discourse]. Paris: Hatier.

Moeschler, J. (1989). *Modélisation du dialogue* [Modelling dialogue]. Paris: Hermès.

Portelli, P. (1992). Une pratique d'autoformation tutorée dans les actions Nouvelles Qualifications [An auto-training tutorial in New Qualifications]. *Education Permanente, 112*, 115–123.

Roulet, E. (1981). Echanges, interventions et actes de langage dans la structure de la conversation [Exchanges, interventions and speech acts within the structure of conversation]. *Etudes de linguistique appliquée, 44*, 7–39.

Roulet, E., Auchlin, A., Moeschler, J., Rubattel, C., & Schelling, M. (1987). *L'articulation du discours en français contemporain* [Discourse srticulation in the contemporary French language]. Berne: Peter Lang.

Sannino, A., Trognon, A., Dessagne, L., & Kostulski, K. (2001). Les connaissances émergeant d'une relation tuteur-apprenti sur le lieu de travail [Knowledge emerging from a relationship between tutors and apprentices at the work place]. *Bulletin de Psychologie, 54* (3), 453, 261–273.

Sannino, A. (2002). *L'élaboration des avis dans une assemblée consultative de l'Union européenne: un jeu de langage dans un collectif complexe et en évolution* [Developing opinions within a Consultative Assembly of the European Union: language games within an evolving complex collective]. Villeneuve D'Ascq: Presses Universitaires du Septentrion.

Sannino, A., & Trognon, A. (in press). Un'introduzione alla Logica Interlocutoria: Come studiare l'interlocuzione per accedere alle dinamiche generative del pensiero e dei rapporti sociali. [Introduction to Interlocutionary Logic: Studying interlocution in order to access the generative dynamics of thinking and social relationships]. *Ricerche di Psicologia*.

Spigolon, G., & Specogna, A. (1996). Aspects socio-cognitifs d'une interaction adulte-enfant à l'école maternelle [Social and cognitive aspects of adult-child interaction in nursery school]. *Interaction et Cognitions, 1* (2/3), 367–396.

Trognon, A. (1997). Psychologie de l'échange parlé [Psychology of spoken exchange]. In: D. Luzzati, J. C. Beacco, R. Mir-Samii, M. Murat, & M. Vivet (Eds), *Le dialogique* [Dialogue] (pp. 195–206). Peter Lang: Berne.

Trognon, A. (1999). Eléments de logique interlocutoire [Elements of Interlocutionary Logic]. In: M. Gilly, J. P. Roux, & A. Trognon (Eds), *Apprendre dans l'interaction* [Learning within interaction] (pp. 69–94). Nancy : Presses Universitaires de Nancy.

Trognon, A. (2000). Speech acts and the logic of mutual understanding. In: D. Vanderveken, & S. Kubo (Eds), *Essays in speech acts theory*. Amsterdam: John Benjamins.

Trognon, A., & Brassac, C. (1992). L'encha'nement conversationnel [Conversational linking]. *Cahiers de linguistique française, 13*, 76–107.

Trognon, A., & Saint-Dizier, V. (1999). L'organisation conversationnelle des malentendus: Le cas d'un dialogue tutoriel [The conversational organization of misunderstandings: The case of a tutorial dialogue]. *Journal of Pragmatics, 3*, 787–815.

Vanderveken, D. (1990). *Meaning and speech acts*. Cambridge: Cambridge University Press.

Veneziano, E. (1997). Echanges conversationnels et premières acquisitions langagières [Conversational exchanges and initial linguistic acquisitions]. Dans: J. Bernicot, J. Caron-Pargue, & A. Trognon (Eds), *Conversation, interaction et fonctionnement cognitif* [Conversation, interaction, and cognitive function] (pp. 91–124). Nancy: Presses Universitaires de Nancy.

Winnykamen, F. (1996). Imitation interprétative et interactions tutorielles [Interpretative imitation and tutorial interactions]. *Bulletin de psychologie, 1* (3), 427, 63–69.

Wittgenstein, L. (1968). *Philosophical investigations*. Oxford: Blackwell.

Chapter 14

Workplace Learning across Activity Systems: A Case Study of Sales Engineers

Sten R. Ludvigsen, Anton Havnes and Leif Chr. Lahn

Introduction

Several authors (Säljö 1999; Sternberg 1990) have pointed to the fundamental metaphoric usage of professional education as one of "logistics": Theoretical knowledge is transmitted to learners in one specific institutional context (usually a school), stored in their heads and transported to new contexts as students go from academic life into professional life. Here, the novice is expected to be capable of mobilizing the stored knowledge and applying it to a context that widely differs from the context of acquisition. The idea of transfer as a transportation of abstract knowledge and skills is not restricted to our perception of professional education. It has also attained a prominent position in the literature on continuous training and workplace learning (Blackler 1995).

Studies of technical work in the so-called post-industrial era (Sørensen 1998b) focus our attention on a process of "customerization" where the added value of products is found in shaping a new context of use. A recent example is the way telecommunication companies promote mobile telephones by combining technical solutions, design, life style, marketing innovations, etc. Thus technical products could be seen as socio-technical products, and consequently the basic skills of engineers and technicians have been extended to include social competence (Adler 1992). A case study of sales engineers can illustrate this development.

Traditionally the skills of salesmen were believed to be acquired in their interaction with customers. However, the rise of "service management" in the late 1970s meant a revision of this practice and supported the idea that such skills could be learned "in vitro". Service-oriented behavior could be promoted by role-playing and simulating communication with clients and customers. Although much of this training has been practice-based, the metaphor of individual storing and transformation of skills prevails. Østerlund (1997) describes how this idea of training is manifest in a corporate culture, where people are trained to sell technically advanced machines. Despite using the framework of "situated learning", he tends to explain the success of salespersons as the individual acquisition of social skills generated by their ability to cross contexts and communities of practice. He fails to see salespersons as a collective body, and their activities as mediated by cultural tools of different kinds. The successful salesperson is one that is able to "assume the position of the other", whereas the unsuccessful salesperson is one that remains an engineer and has an interest in the technical domain. In this paper we will question this dichotomy between social skills and technical skills and show how cultural tools like ventilators, sales forms, catalogs, and drawings bridge the gap between different areas of practice and support mutual understanding and learning between salespersons and customers.

Tuomi-Gröhn and Engeström reframe the problem of transfer (this volume). Rather than viewing transfer as an individual mental process, they see it in terms of relations between situations. The unit of analysis expands from the individual to contexts of interaction and communication. In this chapter we will follow up this attempt by analyzing the work of sales engineers and the context of their learning process.

The broader background for the analysis is a set of assumptions about the role of learning in the information society or the knowledge industry. As a metaphor the term "knowledge industry" directs our attention to the idea that knowledge is traded as a commodity. It is not only traded in the sense that knowledgeable people are employed; it is also traded more directly by means of buying and selling. In our analysis of the sales engineers' work we have identified the selling of ideas, concepts or knowledge as a new "product".

One characteristic of modern society is that knowledge is highly specialized. In the production of goods and services, agents often have to adjust to different contexts and communicate across various specialized fields of knowledge. Communicating with people from other domains (with their own specialized language) is crucial. In order to complete a job, we are often dependent on communication across domain boundaries. This means that the transfer of knowledge that takes place across contexts and domains is characterized by simultaneousness rather than by temporal development. Learning and transfer of knowledge are related to a continuity/discontinuity across situations as well as a continuity/discontinuity in time. Correspondingly, Engeström, Engeström & Kärkkäinen (1995) point to the horizontal and vertical dimensions of learning and expertise. Beach (1999) uses the concepts of collateral and lateral transition to describe these two dimensions of transfer. In this article the main focus is on the horizontal or collateral transfer of knowledge.

The Study

In our analysis we will focus on how sales engineers move in, and between, different activity systems — their home base (Norex) and their customers. The analysis is based on an empirical study of learning and work in Norex, an engineering company in Oslo, Norway. The focus is on the activities of sales engineers, that is, how they operate as salespersons within the company and in relation to customers. The intention of this chapter is to conceptualize the complexities of learning among engineers as a process that is rooted in social practices where agents move in and between activity systems (or communities of practice).[1]

We will analyze these horizontal movements by using a specific set of concepts that have recently been applied to the theoretical analyses of activities: activity systems, boundary-crossing, boundary objects and polycontextuality (Engeström *et al.* 1995; Fujimura 1992; Henderson 1991a; Star & Griesemer 1989).

In most complex work situations agents have to move between activity systems. Sometimes the agents are familiar with these various settings. The organizational routines are well defined and transparent to the agents. At other times, agents can be more or less strangers or "visitors" in the activity systems with which they have to interact through their work. The situation is not transparent. This form of opaque activity can occur within a large company where work is project-oriented or between different companies with different expertise. Work is characterized by polycontextuality. The notion of polycontextuality allows for an analysis of how experts are involved in multiple communities of practice (Engeström *et al.* 1995).

When experts are involved in multiple communities, they are involved in boundary-crossing activities. For example, Wenger (1998) describes how project leaders have to act as brokers between different units in an organization. The only way the work can be performed is by creating new ways of organizing interrelated work processes within the organization.

The terms polycontextuality and boundary-crossing mainly conceptualize how different systems, tasks and actions are related and how agents move between situations. The notion of a boundary object addresses how artifacts or objects can mediate interaction between agents from different communities of practice. The concept could be defined in this way:

> Boundary objects are objects which are both plastic enough to adapt to local needs and the constraints of several parties employing them, yet robust enough to maintain a common identity across sites. They are weakly structured in common use, and become strongly structured in individual site use (Star & Griesemer 1989: 393).

We will show how drawings serve as boundary objects in the activity of sales engineers. Different communities of practice may attribute different meanings to a particular boundary object. An architect and a carpenter may not read the drawing in exactly the same way, but they both attribute meaning to it. Boundary objects have some elements in common that makes sense across communities. In other words, boundary objects are co-objects to which members of different communities attribute common meaning.

We are dealing with a set of more or less loosely defined terms. However, our aim is primarily exploratory in the sense that these concepts are introduced as guidelines that give our empirical work a certain direction. We will test whether they can reframe our understanding of work-life learning in interesting ways. As a tentative move we will

---

[1] An alternative to the theoretical position we have chosen is the actor-network theory. It is beyond the purpose of this chapter to discuss actor-network theory in relation to the socio-cultural framework that we use. See Miettinen (1999) for a discussion of activity theory versus actor-network theory.

describe two cases of engineers who work across organizational boundaries and identify the potentials of an activity's theoretical framework in our conceptual analysis.

This case study of Norex is part of a larger project that involves learning in interdisciplinary settings; it will also include another engineering firm and two primary schools. The methodologies utilized were observations and interviews. In Norex we observed several sales meetings where the sales engineers discussed their work. We also accompanied one of the sales engineers to a meeting with a customer, a firm with engineering consultants. We interviewed the technical director to get an overview of the company as well as two sales engineers (Tim and David) in order to understand how they perceived their work. The interviews lasted for approximately ninety minutes.

The remaining part of this chapter is structured as follows. In the next section we will give a short description of the company and the environment in which it operates. Then, we will address a potential unit of analysis, that is, the context in which the sales engineers' practices could be understood. Finally, we will discuss some of the concepts that we have used in our attempt to understand learning and work processes in and between activity systems. In the conclusion we will discuss whether the different concepts used in this analysis capture different types of phenomena or perhaps represent different perspectives.[2]

Presentation of the Company and their Business Environment

Norex is one of the market leaders in Scandinavia of products for industrial heating and ventilation systems and is part of an international group of companies. The company is involved in research, development, production and import of their own products. In this section we will present a brief overview of the context in which Norex operates.

The heating, ventilation and sanitary business are part of the construction industry. As a result of the emphasis on indoor climate and work environments, the cost of heating and cooling has increasingly become an important part of construction. The ventilation sector has reached a level that demands a high degree of competence. The percentage of the cost that goes into this aspect of construction will, of course, vary according to the different types of buildings. Design has also become increasingly important in this business. Products are chosen not only because of functionality, but because of esthetics as well. The technical director of Norex argues that the ability to remain on the cutting edge of developments and follow these lines of development — within climate, economic heating and esthetics — is important in order to remain competitive.

---

[2] There is a long tradition in the social sciences of studying engineering as a profession, e.g. how engineering relates to other professions and management (Henderson 1991b; Meikins & Smith 1993; Sørensen 1998; Watson & Meikins 1991). Another topic of discussion about the work of engineers has been the distinction between mental versus manual work and craft versus profession (Whally & Barley 1997). The problems with these types of studies and distinctions about engineers are that they do not focus on the work activities of engineers. In addition, engineers' work has been studied as practice inside an organization. Whally & Barley (1997) argue that a more promising strategy focuses on the work activities. Our focus was the activity of engineers at a very concrete level, e.g. the interaction with potential customers.

Norex has a history that goes back to 1920. In the early years 20% of the production was specialized and 80% was serial; today the proportion is reversed. The process of changing this proportion has taken several years.

Norex produces and purchases a large number of products. The competition is keen and, according to the technical director of Norex, 90% of the products are similar to their competitors' products, both technically and functionally. Only 10% of their products are unique. In the interviews with the sales engineers and the technical director, they argued that the relationship with the customers is more important than the actual products. In this relationship a series of factors is important for the sales engineers. These factors include trust, reliability, knowledge about the products (including the limits of the products), their efforts in problem-solving for the customer; and social aspects of the relationship between the customer and the sales engineer. This means that factors other than the technical aspects of their products create/are responsible for their competitive advantage in the market (Porter 1998).

Norex divide their customers into four categories: (1) pipe and equipment wholesale dealers (9 firms covering the whole country); (2) ventilation contractors (approximately 50 firms with district offices); (3) plumbing contractors (approximately 800 firms); and (4) engineering consultants or technical consultants (approximately 100 firms, primarily small firms but some have over 50 employees).

For a company like Norex, it is crucial to develop and maintain good relationships with established and potential customers and to monitor the construction business. The timing of their customer relations is crucial in order to affect the different types of customers at the appropriate time. Timing, for example, could entail the engineering consultants' use of products manufactured by Norex in their specifications. In fact, it is illegal to use the name of the products, but engineering consultants use data from the products that Norex sells in the specifications for their own products.

Educational background and competence within the different categories of customers vary in relation to making judgments about ventilation products. Their competence, their roles in the market, and their interest in buying from Norex differ. For Norex there is a considerable difference between dealing with a large engineering consulting firm and a local tinsmith, both with respect to the way of communicating with customers and the size of a potential order. Engineering consultants tend to be the most interesting "customers", even though they do not buy products directly; they tend to buy indirectly by specifying criteria that Norex's products fulfill.

Unit of Analyses — The Problem of Complexity

In recent years a series of alternatives to standard cognitivist approaches to learning and cognition has evolved. These include situated action (Mantovani 1996; Suchman 1987), situated learning (Greeno 1998; Lave & Wenger 1991; Nielsen & Kvale 1999), distributed cognition (Hutchins 1995), cultural psychology (Cole 1996), mediated action (Wertsch 1991, 1998), and activity theory (Engeström 1987; Engeström & Miettinen 1999). In spite of different terminologies, research traditions, and methodological preferences, these approaches have important aspects in common. They share the assumption that learning and cognition have to be understood as actions and activities integrated or embedded in a complex social and cultural context. A multi-level analytical approach has been used to deal with the complexities in human practice. Learning and cognition are studied as an integral aspect of social, institutional, cultural and historical practices. In general, the individual is not regarded as an adequate unit of analysis, even though an investigation may start out by identifying and analyzing a specific individual's practices within the system. The analytical focus is widened and includes the person's practice in relation to activities of social units, communities of practice, and activity systems. Engeström (1995) expands the unit of analysis beyond the context of one given activity system. He argues that the proper unit of analysis includes at least two activity systems that interact. In these approaches the focus is on the situatedness of human action and the researcher's interest involves understanding how social order is constructed, how coordination is achieved, and how innovations in complex settings evolve (Button & Sharrock 1998; Engeström 1995).

Engeström & Miettinen (1999) argue that collective and historical aspects of the cultural context are integral to the actions taken by individual agents. An agent's interaction with the environment should be understood as a semiotic system where meaning is continuously negotiated.

> Individuals act in collective practices, communities, and institutions. Such collective practice is not reducible to sums of individual action; they require theoretical conceptualization in their own right. When individual action is the privileged unit of analysis, collective practice can only be added on as a more or less external envelope (ibid.: 11).

In this chapter we prefer the notion of "activity system" to describe our unit of analysis. The unit includes ". . . an object, subject, mediating artifacts (sign and tools), rules, community and division of labor" (ibid.: 9). Activity systems are dynamic systems where change and transformation are created by tensions, contradictions, breakdowns, etc., within the system itself or in relation to other systems. An important feature of activity theory is that the system is driven by a collective motive that expands beyond the level of individual intentions. Activity systems are not reducible to a sum of individual actions; they have ". . . cyclic rhythms and long historical half-lives" (Engeström *et al.* 1995). In other words, activity theory affords analyses of social phenomena on different levels: *activity* — at the level of social systems; *action* — at the level of the individual agent acting intentionally; and *operation* — at the level of the concrete operation, procedure or behavior. Learning in an activity system should be understood as tool-mediated activities in a collective enterprise interacting with other enterprises. This implies that the analysis of an activity system includes the interaction with at least one other activity system. Graphically an activity system is depicted in Figure 1.

In an activity system there are potential contradictions or tensions between all components of the systems and an analysis implies investigating such tensions. The work of the sales engineers is a result of a complex social situation. It is mediated by tools, restricted through a set of explicitly or implicitly expressed rules and is integral to a division of labor within a wider social community. All these factors interact in the

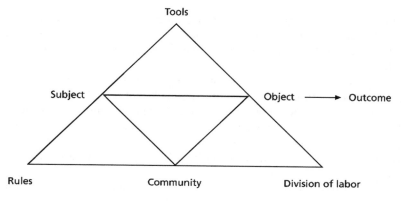

Figure 1: An activity system.

creation of the work practice and contradictions within the system impact on the work situation. When the unit of analysis expands to the interaction between different activity systems, the complexity increases. This chapter focuses on the relationships between different activity systems. The focus of this study was to demonstrate how the object of the activity of two activity systems overlapped during the process of selling. We were interested in studying tensions that occur when agents who represent different activity systems interact. We were particularly interested in how the objects of their activities overlap or differ. First, an overview of how the engineers at Norex work will be presented. Next, some critical episodes using these concepts will be analyzed. In the conclusion there will be a discussion of how the set of concepts that we have chosen serve as instruments for understanding the horizontal and social aspects of transfer.

Learning in and between Activity Systems

From a Newcomer to a Valued Participant

In the interview with the sales engineers, we asked them to elaborate on their experiences as neophytes in the company. Tim stated that he did not immediately get his own customer portfolio and sales budget. During the first four months, he was part of the team that answered phone calls from customers.[3] He took orders and was exposed to customer problems. Essentially he was simply responding to customers' requests. He also worked at the warehouse in order to become acquainted with the appearance of the different products as well as their construction and functionality. Tim and two of his colleagues also visited customers and estimated several bids in virtue. His comments concerning his more formal or explicit training at work included this remark: ". . . a two-minute session and then I had to try on my own". However, he also stated that an

---

[3] Both engineers described the same patterns. David was given his own budget after a year, but he was recruited directly from a technical college.

important part of his learning included working closely with a more experienced colleague. He emphasized that his colleagues shared their knowledge and experience. Each individual had their own budget, but the sales department's budget was the most important one.

When the sales engineers have there own budget they have to consider which factors are important when estimating and negotiating the "right price" with the customer. The sales engineers content that all bids are specific. Getting the right price is dependent on a number of factors which includes the type of customer, Norex's history with the customer, the type of products, the number of units sold, and the price they, as wholesalers, can get from their own industry. The sales engineers must work out a specific approach to most bids.

Some of the sales engineers have experience from other parts of the construction business. Tim stated that his experience as a building contractor was important for his present job. He was a customer of Norex in his previous job, and he had considerable knowledge about product functionality under different technical conditions. Several times during the interview he emphasized how important this was.

From the beginning, the newcomers at Norex are exposed to the main activity of sales engineers dealing with customers. They are socialized into a community where the motive of the activities is represented by questions related to customers. Even if the newcomer is physically located on the company's premises, the activities can be viewed as a form of boundary activity.

Sales Meetings — Monitoring the Market

One of the important settings within the company is the "sales-meeting". Every second week the sales engineers meet to discuss their achievements. Of the 30 employees located in Oslo, there are eight sales engineers and they all participate regularly in the sales meeting. All eight are involved in sales activities situated "inside" or "outside" the company.[4] Other employees are more indirectly connected to the sales work. These individuals are typically involved in administration, logistics, etc.

In one sales meeting there was a lengthy discussion concerned with determining the right timing for contacting different types of customers (see the description of different customers under point 2).

Among other things, they discussed how to use their networks and newspapers as well as a special "database" with information about activities in the construction business. One aspect of this discussion was related to the adequacy of their database and the computer system. Another aspect of being part of, and monitoring, the market involved the presentation of bids to the customers. One question related to whether or not the sales engineers should give detailed information about products. If they only sent bids with prices, the customer would not receive any product information. In this discussion they compared their own approach with that of one of their main competitors. Each sales engineer had to consider whether these specific customers wanted or needed product

---

[4] "Inside" in these settings means sales primarily by phone or written bid without visiting the customer.

information in addition to the price. They decided that they should follow up some instances where the customer had chosen another company's products, in an attempt to determine why they were not competitive. Beginning in the autumn they intended to meet for fifteen minutes once or twice a week to share information about new projects on the market. One area that particularly creates problems relates to monitoring in relation to new customers and the engineering consultants.

Working with Customers — Moving between Activity Systems

David was recruited directly from a technical college. In the following activity we accompanied him to a meeting with an engineering consultant firm. He expressed the concern that he needed some experience in the construction business because he felt that he did not have an adequate understanding of the processes involved in construction work. He knew that the engineering consultants were busy and his strategy was to get their attention by bringing several interesting products to the meetings. Let us look more closely at this situation by quoting directly from the observation data.

> The sales engineer (David) and I (the researcher) are going to visit a small firm with engineering consultants. The customer has said that they could not make an appointment with David because of lack of time, but he could just drop in when he had some time. When he shows up they will decide if they have time to talk with him. David has some products that he wants to show to the consultants. One of products is a new type of ventilator. The purpose of the visit, he tells me, is to get to know the consultants better. The visit is more related to building a relationship than actually selling. When we arrive, the chief consultant welcomes us. "We can talk for a few minutes", he says, "and then you have to show your 'stuff' to our assistant". They talked about Norex products in general for a few minutes, and the consultants asked questions about the different products that David had brought. The chief consultant said that this new ventilator was a very nice product. If he had seen it in the catalog, he would not have given it much attention, but now when he can see and feel it, he will consider it as a product that could potentially be used.
>
> The chief-consultant and one of the other senior consultants find the new ventilator so interesting that they ask the assistant to find some drawings from a project they were involved in. As the assistant brings the drawings, David and the consultants talk about the ventilator. After a while they start to discuss whether the ventilator could be used under the specific constraints in a specific room in the particular building they are involved in planning. They ask how many ventilators will be needed and how the ventilators could be installed (after a while the chief-consultant leaves, but the senior consultant stays). The consultant asks very detailed questions about the product. David answers as well as he can but finds it hard to deal with all the details. On one occasion David gives an obviously wrong answer and the senior consultant says (looking in my

direction as the observer): "Did you get that?" David should redo this 'calculation' as homework and call them with the result, he adds. They talk about both the technical functionality and esthetic dimensions of the ventilator while discussing whether it could be used in the building.

During the discussion David sometimes tries to suggest some 'clever' solutions to the problems that he and the consultant are discussing. The consultant 'corrects' him, saying: "We don't work in this way. We want both an adequate technical and esthetic solution". They continue to discuss different aspects connected to the project they are involved in.

The senior-consultant says that he has to do something else for a few minutes, but if we want, we could stay for lunch. We accept and David talks with the assistant about new products in the catalogs that he brought. During lunch David gets the opportunity to talk with the senior-consultant for at least twenty minutes.

This situation reveals at least four important aspects of the sales engineer's work. The first point relates to the difference between seeing products in a catalog versus actually seeing, touching and feeling them. In a way, the product serves as a tool for communicating about specifications or concepts. The second aspect is connected to David's behavior during the visit. He never brought up the subject of buying the products. He remained consistent with his purpose of simply making contact and introducing the company, the products and himself. The point was to build a relationship. The third aspect related to the type of solution this consultant preferred. When discussing the construction process, they tried to balance the demands of the technical problems with the esthetic dimensions. There was, in other words, a balance between the technical perspective and the esthetic perspective involved in negotiations with the engineering consultants. They were concerned with the micro and macro problems in an effort to construct both functional as well as visually pleasing buildings.

The fourth aspect is related to the use of knowledge in discussions. As a sales engineer, David must take part in discussions of the product's performance under different conditions, or to put it another way, David had to negotiate meaning for the products under different technical constraints. Only by being able to reason and argue at the same level as the consultants, while at the same time knowing when to be humble, will he be perceived as a person that they can trust. The balance between these aspects is rather complex. Generally speaking, the position of customers and their needs have been strengthened recently from management's perspective regarding quality and may be in contradiction with traditional ideas about technical quality being dominant in engineering culture (Sørensen 1998b).

Sales Activities as Boundary-crossing

The descriptions, episodes and opinions of the informants and the interpretations from the researchers provide glimpses into the activity of sales engineers at Norex and in particular how their practice is connected with various other activity systems. By viewing the activities and actions from an activity theory perspective, some features emerge from the data.

When the sales engineers have access to contexts where important business processes take place, different performance models become visible. We will argue that the method of learning the "trade of selling" for these sales engineers is accomplished by making different aspects of the company's activities visible. Most of these activities take the form of boundary-crossings and include taking the perspective of Norex, their own company, as well as that of the specific customer who is involved in another activity system. Since access could be considered the most important aspect in a learning environment, exposure to different activities where customer problems become visible seems like a powerful way of learning the skills needed for selling. Selling is a kind of boundary-crossing activity. This means that the sales engineer moves between activity systems and is challenged to make an operative picture of the different conditions and priorities that are "embedded" in various communities with whom he or she is working.

At the core of Norex's activity system is the delivery of a bid to the different types of customers. The bid, which is sent to the customer for further negotiation on the phone or in a meeting, should be considered as a kind of boundary object. This effectively means that the object can communicate meaning between different activity systems.

The sales engineers and the customers negotiate what the bid means to them. The sales engineer has to consider the prices that Norex will incur to cover their costs of making the product. There are various ground rules that he has to follow. Even though the customer is unique, the bid represents a standardized way of doing business in this company, a institutional practice. A bid is a form of boundary object which combines standardization and flexibility. It creates both common and different meanings depending on the position of the person who 'reads' the bid. Properly quoting bids is the most important part of work that newcomers have to learn.

It is important to understand that quoting bids is not limited to one activity system, but to the relationship between at least two activity systems. We can also include competing companies that are involved in the same — or rather a parallel — negotiating process. We will emphasize one aspect of the bid considered as a boundary object (Star & Griesemer 1989; Wenger 1998). A bid implies some form of standardization that gives both parties the opportunity to engage in a meaningful negotiation process. However, the bid as a boundary object is connected to several other types of objects; these are partly shared with the customer. Norex has several different catalogs where the products are presented and technical information is provided. One important aspect of information is the technical specification of the products. These specifications are part of a meaning-making process both for the customer and for the sales engineers. The specifications give meaning related to how the products can be used as part of the construction.

In the meeting with the customer yet another form of boundary object is identified. When visiting the consulting firm, David presented a new ventilator. The ventilator becomes a concrete point of reference for discussing similar and different products.

In the discussion about various possible solutions, the drawing becomes the boundary object. Drawings are visual representations to which different agents can attribute meaning. At the same time their format and the visual culture of engineering (Ferguson 1992) create a common ground for communication and problem-solving. In the discourse between the sales engineer and the consulting engineer, the boundary objects create a joint focus that helps to identify the demands of the consulting engineer in relation to the products David is able to offer. Henderson (1991a) refers to technical drawings as conscription devices that coordinate and realign local definitions and actions. By formulating the technical requirements of his product in a format that is supported by the visual consistency of technical drawings, David is able to produce a more persuasive argument. Boundary objects can be viewed as devices for abstract representation in the sense that everyone accepts the format as given. Any solution that is depicted in the drawing is given added weight in a discussion between practitioners or between sales engineers and customers. By labeling their products as well-designed "packages", this visual device may be an effective way of promoting sales. Drawings as boundary objects are a form of abstraction. Boundary objects could be different forms of abstraction such as "ideal types" (Henderson 1991a; Wenger 1998).

The two forms of activities mentioned thus far in the analyses have not been related to different types of customers. Figure 2 depicts the relation between Norex and the A customer.

Creating and maintaining this form of relationship is something that Norex and the sales engineers have accomplished with great success. As the figure depicts, there is a kind of dependency between the two systems. Norex has products that the customers need. The relation between the two systems is very clear. We have one system that needs to buy products, and one system that can provide a bid. The companies that constitute the typical A-customer are contractors, usually a small firm with expertise related more to the practical aspects of the construction than to the principles underlying how a product will work under different conditions. The sales engineers have at least three years of technical education from a college and can act as a consultant for the contractor. It is important to emphasize that the sales engineer acts in multiple roles in relation to the A-customers. They act as sales engineers, give technical advice, participate in concrete problem-solving, and provide service. Of course, their primary motive is to sell their products.

The relationship between Norex and the engineering consultants is quite different. Since it is of strategic importance for Norex to develop good relations with these firms, we will elaborate on this relationship. We will use the situation where David visited the engineering consultants as a staring point. The following model is the point of departure for understanding this relationship.

The main point in presenting these two models is to show the differences in sales activities when the secondary party is either an A-customer or engineering consultants. The sales engineers seem to need different types of competence as they function in the two different contexts. The Norex engineers' argue that their success in the future will depend upon their work in relation to engineering consultants. There is a set of important differences that constitute the different patterns. The products to be "sold" are very different. Solutions to a technical and esthetic problem do not have 'price' as a basic motive. Their main concern is related to knowledge about the creative use of the products under specific operating conditions.

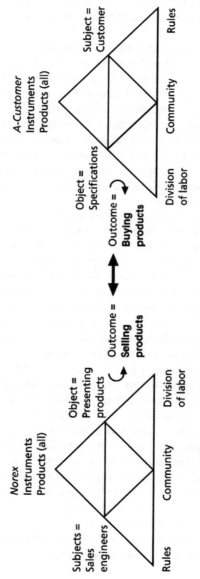

Figure 2: Norex and A-customers as connected activity systems.

In the negotiation with the A-customer, the driving motives are related to "price" and the products. The rules, community and division of labor are also different. When selling products to A-customers, cost and mutual trust are of key importance. The context of the activity is constituted by Norex, their A-customers, and competitors. The division of labor between Norex and their A-customers seems to have the character of a stable and fragile network.

When we look at the relationship between Norex and the engineering consultants, they are quite different. It is more problematic, as is symbolized with the broken arrow in Figure 3. Negotiation and collaboration are embedded in the activity of advanced problem-solving where a satisfactory solution has technical, esthetic and rhetoric dimensions. This relationship could be seen as an example of co-configuration work (Engeström *et al.* 1995) in the sense that the customization of products is a joint activity that involves both sales engineers and engineering consultants as customers. The context of activity is a discourse about the construction of a building involving a number of different agents. Some of these agents may be enlisted in ad hoc collaborative arrangements where the expertise of sale engineers may complement or compete with that of the engineering consultants.

The fact that Norex and the engineering consultants are part of the same business and engineering culture, the construction industry, means that they share a joint technical language and a professional interest in "good" problem-solving. Thus, boundary objects, like ventilators and technical drawings, are indexical of standards that are not articulated, but rely on a "tacit" collective understanding of how things are and what to do. At the level of specific problems, however, these boundary objects are often framed differently, and any collaborative outcome depends on the ability of physical or abstract objects to create a common focus and a partially shared understanding. This understanding involves an operative consensus that makes it possible to merge different interpretations and intentions into a joint action strategy.

A main characteristic of the work of sales engineers is that their position is situated between different activity systems within a larger community of constructional business. One of the key advantages of these agents is their ability to expand their system (increase the potential market and sell more products) and understand the position of the customers (solve local problems). These processes function very differently as we move from so-called mass-customization, where the customers get what they want, to co-configuration work. The latter is the case with engineering consultants. The sales engineers at Norex, who are responsible for this market, have to develop a symmetrical relationship with the customer. Their success is dependent on their ability to situate their initiatives and "listen" to the needs of other activity systems. This is the same for all types of customers, but it is a more straightforward task in the case of A-customers than in the case of engineering consultants. Polycontextuality may involve very different types of expertise depending on the dominant motives and the available resources that mediate these activities.

The most interesting aspect of boundary-crossing, when the differences between the pattern of activities in Figures 1 and 2 are considered, relates to the kind of knowledge that is in focus. The relationship with the A-customer basically follows the logic of regular selling and buying; price, trust, and knowledge about the product are the key

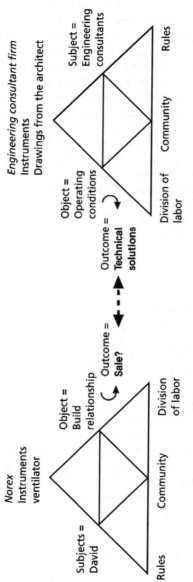

Figure 3: Norex and engineering consultants.

determinants. The discourse between the A-customer and the sales engineers is based on skills that the sales engineers have, as well as standardized devices such as catalogs and order formats.

The relationship between the sales engineers and the engineering consultants is quite different. Regular commercial interaction seems to be pushed into the background and replaced by a discourse that follows a less predictable path. Several definitions of problems, solutions, arguments and procedures are reordered and governed by physical objects and semiotic devices such as drawings and conceptual sketches. In this process, the Norex products meet the design problems of specific construction products and help to build an alliance with engineering consultants who will promote a "common" solution when ordering decisions are made. This type of argument may be supported by a "theoretical" explanation favoring one of several alternatives.

The willingness and the ability to use technical language in design work will, of course, vary among different individuals. However, the practical achievements are strongly contingent upon the artifacts used and the steps taken by collaborating agents. What seems to be an asymmetrical relationship between the sales engineers and engineering consultants may turn out to be a strategy on the part of sales engineers to involve clients in creating a joint product. The engineering consultants have the primary input in defining themes and focus.

Conclusion

In this chapter we have analyzed the expertise of sales engineers in terms of boundary-crossing activities. The Norex engineers learn the ropes of this trade by functioning inside and outside the company. They regulate the distance to the customer and give the novice a chance to adjust to the different customers. In the case of Norex, experience shows that the sales engineers are highly competent in interacting with the so-called A-customer.

Although the products that the sales engineers present to the A-customers work as boundary objects by integrating perspectives, preferences and actions, the number of moves and strategies are limited. The parties know the process they are involved in. Because price is the key determinant of this sales process, only trust or transactional costs (Ciborra 1996) can safeguard this type of liaison against the "hidden hand" of open market mechanisms. Thus, there is likely to be a minimal investment of privileged resources in these types of shaky customer segments. Thus, boundary-crossing in this context is a rather routinized practice that only rarely will expand into conceptual innovations.

In the case of Norex the collaborative strategy with consulting firms represents a new challenge. As described earlier, the key element here is not direct sales, but a kind of "co-configuration" with the engineering consultants. The aim of this venture is not to make them choose Norex products when designing new constructions in the first place. There is no actual selling of products and price is not necessarily the key determinant. However, from the perspective of Norex, the ultimate goal is obviously to sell their product.

The dual role of Norex's sales agents in a co-configuration strategy is quite evident. On the one hand they are loyal to their base organization and the imperative of sales output. On the other hand the sales engineers are recruited on a temporary basis for the project activities of construction design and planning. This loosely coupled structure of partly improvised activities tends to rely on a multitude of conscription devices that will guarantee progress and consistency, and it is of crucial importance to Norex that their products have allies in this process of elimination.

The sales engineers from Norex do not consider themselves as members of the project organization responsible for constructional design, but they try to make alliances with nodes in this network. If this relationship extends into a collaborative interaction where the clients are treated as "co-learners" and active partners in the development of Norex products, we may have an instance of horizontal construction of expertise (Beach 1999). However, this learning unit must constantly strive to find a way of negotiating the conflicting goals of the different activity systems involved. There is little evidence that those taking part in this type of "consumerization" are conscious of this co-configuration as a developmental arrangement. The motive for solving constructional problems may be relatively subordinated to that of selling "good" solutions or convincingly arguing for the Norex products. Thus, boundary-crossing in this case involves the use of conscription devices that make these products an integrated part of the overall design. Theoretical elaborations may promote marketing initiatives and generate new understanding.

In the introduction we referred to a study of technical salespersons conducted by Østerlund (1997). By pointing out the importance of boundary objects, such as drawings in supporting activities that could be called "co-constructive", we have tried to transcend the dichotomy between social competence and technical skills. However, in analysing his field observations, Østerlund highlights the difficulties of technicians and engineers when they have to "convert" to being salespersons. The latter group is not to be trusted, particularly when they pretend to be technical experts. By launching a collaborative strategy with consulting companies, Norex seems to place their engineers in a double-bind situation: they are salespersons, but they are not selling anything; they are just participating in a joint construction project. We do not know how these issues of mixed identities, suspicion and trust are handled by customers and engineers, but they are probably sorted out over a period of time. These observations and the study by Østerlund make seeing the context of transfer in working life as a "contested terrain" relevant (Burawoy 1981) where demarcations are drawn between professional domains and positions. In addition, these hybrid strategies create insecurity in social relations as they represent a category that is not clear cut. When contrasting these transitions — from engineers to salespersons and from sales engineers to co-engineers — with work-life "rites de passage" such as certifications, there are few cultural tools and ceremonies that regulate this kind of boundary-crossing. The objects are yet to be invented and institutionalized.

We have mainly used the term boundary object in relation to three different types of objects. One kind of boundary object is represented by the bids which Norex and their customers use to negotiate the sale. Another boundary object is represented by the ventilator. As a material object with certain distinct qualities, the ventilator bridges the gap created between the needs of salespersons to present their products and the requirements from the engineering consultants to see the technical and esthetic solutions. The third kind of boundary object is the drawings. They are introduced to the process by the consulting engineers. By definition, boundary objects create the ground for shared meaning among agents involved in different activities and situated in different communities of practice. As objects or artifacts, they are both material and conceptual (Cole 1996), and thus plastic enough to serve as reference for different agents in different situations. However, these objects have no fixed and predefined meaning and have to be contextualized and created in new situations. The artifacts we have discussed here could be seen as parts of a boundary infrastructure. This means that they serve multiple functions in different communities of practice (Bowker & Star 1999). In the engineering culture the artifacts are relatively stable points of reference as members move between different situations.

In this chapter we have shown how the perspective derived from activity theory enriches our understanding of learning and transfer processes as horizontal and collective phenomena. By observing how engineers move in, and between, different activity systems, we are able to conceptually locate them in larger social landscapes where operations, actions and activities are regulated by resources. These resources are both material and conceptual and trigger both the practical and theoretical skills of engineers when they create new practices by crossing boundaries. New practices reshape boundary objects, thus changing the relationships within and between activity systems.

In order to understand horizontal learning processes it is essential to look at the interactions between participants from different "communities" where co-design is made possible by the use of external resources. Still we need to know more about the dialectics between vertical and horizontal processes in the development of expertise. This can be accomplished by observing how engineers are both involved in individual trajectories and take part in the development of the system as a whole, that is, as a collective trajectory. In addition there are reasons to believe that these patterns will differ from one sector to another in working life. In some occupational cultures the textual aspects of physical objects are more prominent than in others.

A final methodological reflection in our study is worth mentioning. When defining an activity's theoretical approach to human-computer interaction, Nardi (1996: 95) has suggested some methodological guidelines: Boundary objects should be studied as they change over time, and the context of development should not be narrowed to episodic fragments. Broad patterns of an activity have to be observed. These principles are not easy to follow when studying workplace learning, but we take them as fruitful guidelines for our future fieldwork. In our presentation here we have not been able to describe processes of change over time which is essential if we want to explore learning.

Acknowledgments

This research is supported by the Norwegian Research Counsel within the research program entitled "Competence, Education and Value Creation".

We would like to thank our reviewers T. Tuomi-Gröhn and Y. Engeström, and B. Fürstenau, A. Sannino in the Cost Action A11 group for insightful comments on earlier drafts of this chapter. We would also like to thank participants in the Cost Action A11 group and Hilkka Ylisassi and Anu Peltola from the University of Helsinki for the discussions which have stimulated the work in this chapter.

References

Adler, P. (1992). *Technology and the future of work*. NY: Oxford University Press.

Blackler, F. (1995). Knowledge, knowledge work and organizations. *Organization Studies, 16* (6), 1021–1046.

Beach, K. (1999). Consequential transitions: A sociocultural expedition beyond transfer in education. *Review of Research in Education, 24*, 101–139.

Bowker, G. C., & Star, S. L. (1999). *Sorting things out*. Cambridge, MA: MIT Press.

Burawoy, M. (1981). Terrains of contest. *Socialist Review, 11* (4), 83–115.

Button, G., & Sharrock, W. (1998). The organizational accountability of technological work. *Social Studies of Science, 28* (1), 73–102. Cambridge: Cambridge University Press.

Ciborra, C. U. (1996). *Teams, markets and systems: Business innovation and information technology*. Cambridge: Cambridge University Press.

Cole, M. (1996). *Cultural psychology. A once and future discipline*. Cambridge, MA.: Harvard University Press.

Engeström, Y. (1987). *Learning by expanding*. Helsinki: Orienta-Konsultit.

Engeström, Y. (1995). Innovative organizational learning in medical and legal settings. In: L. W. Martin, K. Nelson, & E. Tobach (Eds), *Sociocultural psychology: Theory and practice of doing and knowing* (pp. 326–356). Cambridge: Cambridge University Press.

Engeström, Y., Engeström, R., & Kärkkäinen, M. (1995). Polycontextuality and boundary crossing in expert cognition: Learning and problem-solving in complex work activities. *Learning and Instruction, 5*, 319–336.

Engeström, Y., & Miettinen, R. (1999). Introduction. In: Y. Engeström, R. Miettinen, & R. L. Punamäki (Eds), *Perspectives on activity theory* (pp. 1–16). Cambridge: Cambridge University Press.

Ferguson, E. S. (1992). *Engineering and the mind's eye*. Cambridge, MA.: MIT Press.

Fujimura, J. H. (1992). Crafting science: Standardized packages, boundary objects, and "translation". In: A. Pickering (Eds), *Science as practice and culture* (pp. 168–211). Chicago: The University of Chicago Press.

Greeno, J. (1998). The Situativity of knowing, learning, and research. *American Psychologist, 53* (1), 5–26.

Henderson, K. (1991a). Flexible sketches and inflexible data bases: Visual communication, conscription devices, and boundary objects in design engineering. *Science, Technology, & Human Values, 4*, 448–473.

Henderson, K. (1991b). Social studies of technical work at the crossroad. *Science, Technology, & Human Values, 2*, 131–139.

Hutchins, E. (1995). *Cognition in the wild*. Cambridge, MA: The MIT Press.

Lave, J., & Wenger, E. (1991). *Situated learning: Legitimate peripheral participation*. New Jersey: Cambridge University Press.

Mantovani, G. (1996). *New communications environments. From everyday to virtual*. London: Taylor & Francis.

Meikins, P., & Smith, C. (1993). Organizing engineering work: A comparative analysis. *Work and Occupation, 20*, 123–146.

Miettinen, R. (1999). The riddle and things: activity theory and actor-network theory as approaches to studying innovations. *Mind, Culture and Activity, 6* (3), 170–193.

Nardi, B. A. (1996). Studying context: A comparison of activity theory, situated action models, and distributed cognition. In: B. A. Nardi (Ed.), *Context and consciousness* (pp. 69–102). Cambridge, MA.: The MIT Press.

Nielsen, K., & Kvale. S. (1997). Current issues of apprenticeship. *Nordisk Pedagogik* (Special Issue: Apprenticeship-Learning as Social Practice), *17* (3), 130–139.

Østerlund, C. (1997). Sales apprentices on the move. *Nordisk Pedagogik* (Special Issue: Apprenticeship-Learning as Social Practice), *17* (3), 169–177.

Porter, M. (1998). *Competitive advantage: Creating and sustaining superior performance.* New York: The Free Press.

Säljö, R. (1999). Learning as the use of tools. In: K. Littleton, & P. Light. (Eds), *Learning with computers. Analysing productive interaction* (pp. 144–161). London, Routledge.

Sørensen, K. H. (1998). *The spectre of participation: Technology and the work in the welfare state.* Oslo: Scandinavian University Press.

Star, S. L., & Grisemer, J. R. (1989). Institutional ecology, 'translations' and boundary objects. *Social Studies of Science, 19* (3), 387–420.

Sternberg, R. J. (1990). *Metaphors of mind: Conceptions of the nature of intelligence.* New York: Cambridge University Press.

Suchman, L. (1987). *Plans and situated actions. The problems of human-machine interaction.* Cambridge: Cambridge University Press.

Watson, J. M., & Meikins, P. (1991). What do engineers want? Work values, job rewards, and job satisfaction. *Science, Technology, & Human Values, 16* (2), 140–172.

Wenger, E. (1998). *Communities of practice. Learning, meaning, and identity.* Cambridge: Cambridge University Press.

Wertch, J. V. (1991). *Voices of the mind. A sociocultural approach to mediated action.* Cambridge, MA: Harvard University Press.

Wertsch, J. V. (1998). *Mind as action.* New York: Oxford University Press.

Whalley, P., & Barley, S. R. (1997). Technical work in the division of labor: Stalking the wily anomaly. In: S. R. Barley, & J. E. Orr (Eds), *Between craft and science. Technical work in U.S. settings* (pp. 23–52). Ithaca: Cornell University Press.

Chapter 15

Epilogue: From Transfer to Boundary-crossing

Roger Säljö

Introduction

The shared interests of the authors of the chapters in this volume concern how to conceptualize human learning, and in addition, how to orchestrate learning activities so as to somehow maximize the outcomes for learners. In addressing one, or both, of these issues, the authors find themselves in a research territory which is very much at the focus of public attention today. It is obvious that the changes in work practices in various sectors of the so-called knowledge or information society have raised the general awareness of the role of learning and knowledge in social change and in individual development. Powerful technologies, and the sophisticated types of knowledge and skills that are necessary for successful participation in many institutional settings, have contributed to putting the spotlight on issues of how to promote continuous development of human competencies. Learning experiences have to be potent. For research, this development implies that some classical issues of how to conceptualize learning and learning processes are back on center stage.

In their introductory chapter, the editors of this volume, Tuomi-Gröhn and Engeström, give a thorough historical account of how some key elements in the scholarly debate on learning over the past century have been understood. Central in this debate on learning and learning theory has been the phenomenon referred to as transfer. The basic issue in the context of transfer is to what extent skills acquired in relation to one type of problem or situation will carry over to a similar problem and/or setting. Typically this question has been asked in the context of schooling; how does knowledge acquired in school transfer to other situations and practices? The manner in which this question has been, and is being, asked signals a worry that there may in fact be less of such a transfer than has been assumed (cf. e.g. Bransford & Schwartz 1999; Detterman & Sternberg 1993). At least transfer does not seem to be follow automatically. This suspicion has been reinforced by the observations on the embeddedness of human reasoning in cultural practices demonstrated by sociocultural and situated approaches to

Between School and Work: New Perspectives on Transfer and Boundary-crossing
© 2003 Published by Elsevier Science Ltd.
ISBN: 0-08-044296-X

human action (cf., for instance, Beach, this volume; Greeno 1998; Lave 1988; Lave & Wenger 1991). The studies that perhaps most clearly brought this issue to public awareness were the ones on elementary mathematical reasoning among unschooled children operating as street-vendors reported by Carraher, Carraher & Schliemann (1985; cf. also Nunes, Schliemann & Carraher 1993). In these studies, children were found to be expert performers in the context of selling fruit for a living but far less skilled in handling 'identical' or isomorphic problems presented in writing and as school tasks.

But the observation of the problem of transfer between school and other activites is old, and the current debate is a revival of claims and arguments that have been made on many occasions. Dewey (1916/1966), for instance, argued almost a hundred years ago that "when schools depart from the educational conditions effective in the out-of-school environment, they necessarily substitute a bookish, a pseudo-intellectual spirit for a social spirit" (p. 38). And he continued by saying that when organizing schooling in this manner, learning "tends to preclude the social sense which comes from sharing in an activity of common concern and value" (p. 39). This observation is very close to the findings brought to the fore by scholars of today insisting on the situated nature of knowing and learning and on the central role played by communities of practice (Wenger 1998) in cultivating knowledge and promoting learning.

The analyses of how transfer has been handled by various traditions offered by the editors of this volume (and commented on in many of the other chapters) point to the current theoretical conflicts between dualist approaches (such as cognitivism), assuming that skills transfer from one situation to another, on the one hand, and what they refer to as the "situated challenges" represented by scholars such as Lave, Greeno and others, emphasizing the situated nature of learning, on the other. As an alternative to both these interpretations, Tuomi-Gröhn and Engeström suggest that the issue of transfer should be understood within an activity-theoretical frame in which the notions of expansive learning and developmental transfer are central. In such a framework, the "learning of the activity system and the learning of the individual are intertwined, and the individual's learning is understandable only if we understand the learning of the activity system" (Tuomi-Gröhn & Engeström, this volume). It is here that we find "collective developmental transfer" (ibid.), where individuals and collectives learn (cf. Tuomi-Gröhn, this volume).

I would like to contribute to the discussion of this volume by offering some additional reflections on the notion of transfer. Essentially my argument will be that this concept is highly metaphorical and elusive, and that it is time to move beyond issues of whether there is such a phenomenon as transfer or not. Transfer is a metaphor. The referent of this term does not remain constant across settings or theories. Attempts to prove or disprove that transfer takes place risk ending up in a play with words. But let me return to this

Transfer as a Theoretical Construct and a Metaphor

The concept of transfer is interesting in the sense that it has survived many, if not most, paradigm changes in research in the behavioral sciences (cf. Weber, this volume).

Already this observation should alert us to its vagueness. In early behaviorist approaches to the study of learning (i.e. conceived as the acquisition of behaviors), it is pointed out that "animals, like human beings, generalize". Thus, after "having learned to respond to a certain stimulus", they have "a tendency to transfer the response to other objects of the same class: such a generalization is called *transfer*" (Hebb 1969: 48, my translation, italics in original). Already Pavlov, in his pioneering work on the principles of classical conditioning a hundred years ago, claimed that "transfer is best considered to be the result of generalization (irradiation) whereby one stimulus serves to evoke the conditioned reflex learned to another" (Hilgard & Bower 1966: 70). In the behaviorist tradition, transfer is thus intimately connected to a notion of generalization of responses and behaviors. Also, generalization can be as much a problem as it is desirable; responses often generalize in dysfunctional manners. But the basic observation here is that as one S-R connection is acquired, there is a considerable likelihood that some other S-R connection(s) will be established as well. That is, learning cannot be contained, nor is it completely determined by the stimulus conditions.

In later, and more sophisticated, theoretical traditions inspired by behaviorism, transfer also plays a significant role. Gagné (1970) argues that "learning is managed and instituted for broader purposes than simply the modification of particular human performances. It is brought about in order to establish capabilities that will be of lasting and general usefulness to the individual" (p. 333). Gagné then goes on to distinguish between lateral transfer and vertical transfer, terms that appear also in this volume. The former "refers to a kind of generalizing that spreads over a broad set of situations at roughly the same 'level of complexity'" (p. 335), while the latter type of "transfer refers to the effects that learned capabilities at one level have on the learning of additional ones at higher levels" (ibid.). Vertical transfer thus implies that some learning is productive for the learning of more advanced or abstract skills or principles. Again, these claims can be said to illustrate that learning is not contained; it has implications for the ability to carry out similar tasks but it may also be instrumental for realizing that a specific task (such as learning to count apples) is an instance of a more abstract skill (counting in general). This notion of transfer thus follows from a theoretical perspective that allows for generalizations of two kinds, one having to do with moving 'sideways' and the other one with moving 'upwards'.

Similarly, in the verbal learning tradition, initiated by Ebbinghaus' (1885) research on memory and his invention of the non-sense syllable, transfer was always a hot topic. Over the decades, an endless number of experiments have been made to ascertain various kinds of transfer effects that occur when memorizing lists of words or syllables. For instance, some attempts have been made to study the influence of the similarity between the words or the syllables serving as stimuli on a new list of items to be memorized later. Would similarity increase the transfer and make it easier to learn the new list? Or would the opposite be the case? (for a summary of this kind of research, if anyone can stand to read it, see for instance Krech, Crutchfield & Livson 1969: 320ff).

For Gestalt psychology, represented by scholars such as Koffka (1935), Katona (1940/1967) and Wertheimer (1945/1968), the transfer issue is central, and Gagné's account is a step in the same direction. But, and this is interesting, the Gestalt interpretation of what transfer is all about is much more promising from a theoretical point of view than the previous ones, including the conception characteristic of cognitivism as described by Tuomi-Gröhn and Engeström. The reason for this is that in the Gestalt tradition transfer is discussed within an overall analysis of the nature of learning processes. In this tradition, 'learning' is not seen as a primitive concept but rather as referring to processes that may either be "mechanical memorization" (Katona 1940/1967: 242) of senseless associations, or "meaningful learning" of the principles underlying a certain problem or domain (cf. Wertheimer 1945/1968: 234). Katona's famous studies of the processes of Organizing and Memorizing (1940/1967) concern which "methods of teaching and learning result in the greatest measure of applicability? By what methods can the transfer effect be increased?" (p. 55). Katona reports a series of ingenious studies attempting to answer questions such as of "what significance is the number of the elements presented in the practice period? Must the elements be identical in the practiced tasks and in the test tasks, or must the principle be identical?" (p. 57). Without going into detail into these clever, but largely forgotten, studies, what Katona demonstrates, quite convincingly in my opinion (see Svensson 1976, for an extensive discussion), is that learning with understanding (i.e. identifying the principles underlying the solution of various problems) is superior in terms of transfer to memorizing solutions. The understanding of a principle (in contexts such as geometry, number series, card-trick experiments and so on) resulted in far better performance on similar problems and in a higher level of retention over time: "the knowledge acquired by understanding is retained for long periods of time without substantial deterioration" (p. 254). Katona even goes into a lengthy exercise of calculating "transfer coefficients" (269ff) to prove his point: learning of new material is easier for those who learned by means of understanding principles than for those who memorized the correct solutions.

What makes the discussion of transfer in the Gestalt tradition so interesting is that it is combined with an analysis of *what is learned*. That is, the transfer effect (a term not favored by most of the dominant representatives of this tradition) is strong in the case of "learning by understanding" since "reconstruction" rather than memorizing is the decisive character of the learning process (Katona 1940/1967: 254). In the case of memorizing, "knowledge can be reinforced only by repetition of the original situation and the original response" (p. 255). Transfer will be low since the gains in performance on other similar learning tasks are, at best, marginal.

Adding the comments I have made so far to the analyses provided by the editors and by some of the other authors in this volume, the highly metaphorical character of the concept of transfer should be evident. Scholars studying acquisition of behaviors, the learning of nonsense syllables, the understanding of scientific principles or card-games, various kinds of cognitive processes, or situated learning activities in factories and elsewhere, all use the term with different meanings, and they design their decisive research studies accordingly. Thus, the reasoning is circular within a paradigm or research tradition, and as a consequence attempts to compare findings and arguments across traditions come very close to being a play with words. Since, different theoretical perspectives have radically different units of analysis in the study of learning (behaviors, thought processes, memory traces, problem-solving strategies etc.), there is very little of common reference when using the concept of transfer.

A reasonable conclusion to this state of affairs is that "the concepts of learning and transfer cannot be distinguished", a point made by Smedslund (1953: 157) a long time ago (cf. also Beach, this volume). Thus, the problem of "predicting transfer is the problem of predicting what will be learned", and therefore, "the concept of transfer becomes unnecessary" (loc. cit.). At best this concept may serve as a general reminder of problems of seeing connections and parallels between situations and practices, but as a scientific term, transfer is, in Smedslund's terminology, a pseudoconcept. What we are interested in is learning, a detour via the concept of transfer adds little to our understanding. The many examples of successful boundary-crossing presented in the various chapters, in my opinion, are best conceived as learning experiences at collective and individual levels.

Learning Practices and Boundary-crossing in the Complex Society

The major contribution of the situated perspective on human action and learning is not the argument that human knowledge is relative to context and social practice. Rather, this claim follows from the much more decisive insight that human cognition and learning are social and communicative phenomena grounded in human activities pursued by means of interaction and physical action. In this manner, learning, memory, perception, and other cognitive phenomena, are possible to describe in conceptual frameworks that are commensurable with those of other research disciplines in the human sciences. Thus, cognition is neither seen as an abstract world of inner representations, nor is it construed in pseudobiological terms as the mere outflow of neurological and biochemical processes. Cognition is historically situated and produced through appropriation and mastery of meaning in communicative and other practices, to use Vygotskyan (1986) language. Mind — as studied in the behavioral and human sciences — is a social and historical phenomenon, and, consequently "education is neither a process of unfolding from within nor is it a training of faculties resident in the mind itself. It is rather the formation of mind . . ." (Dewey 1916/1966: 69), a view that comes very close to Vygotskyan and activity theoretical perspectives.

A significant consequence of this situated and sociocultural perspective is evident in the contributions to this volume; learning is studied as part of social practices. How learning events are structured, what affordances that are offered by various activities, and, in general, what learning means in society is accessible to study following such an approach. There is no such thing as a learning process *per se* that is identical across settings and that can be captured in a pure form. In addition, and as Lave (1993) has pointed out, learning may be taken for granted. People simply cannot avoid learning. The interesting issue is *what is learned* in various practices, and what kind of learning experiences that are potentially available if a practice is organized in a particular manner. Without attempting to do justice to the wealth of observations presented in the various chapters, I would like to draw attention to two major issues that are directly and indirectly addressed by the authors. One of these concerns the alleged gap between learning as it is orchestrated in formal institutions, on the one hand, and in other activity systems, on the other. The second point I want to make is to reinforce(!) the significance of studying learning as a problem of the relationship between collectives and individuals, and to attend to the dynamics at both levels. This is a problem that concerns the unit of analysis in research on human learning.

Learning in Formal Institutions and Outside

The situated (including sociocultural theory and activity theory) perspective has generated interesting critique of the traditions of learning characterizing formal institutions. Although this critique is by no means new, as I have already pointed out, empirical research illustrating the details of the characteristics of learning in such settings has provided interesting findings and theoretical insights substantiating this claim. The positive aspect of this insight is that researchers, including those contributing to this volume, have begun to scrutinize different activity systems to find out how learning is achieved within activities. However, as so often happens in research on education, this analytical perspective has also been turned into a normative ideology in which schools and other institutions of formal learning typically are portrayed as conservative, as too 'theoretical', and as more or less irrelevant for people's everyday activities or work skills. Even in some of the chapters in this volume, schools are described as divorced from 'real-world' contexts, a metaphor which I find very problematic, especially considering the fact that schooling is the activity system in society in which most people spend their day. In particular, apprenticeship learning has been hailed as the ideal learning situation where masters and their apprentices cooperate to achieve common ends. One of the most influential articles, in which this step of going from research to normative conclusions and ideology was taken, was the one by Brown, Collins & Duguid (1989), which is cited by some of the authors in this volume.

However, it is dangerous to jump to conclusions too quickly and attempt to convert research findings into normative claims about how education should be organized. This is the step that Jean Piaget sought to defend himself against most of his life by arguing that studying human development does not automatically imply that you can tell how to speed up intellectual growth or give advice on how schools should go about doing their business. Schooling is an institutional activity, and its mode of operation is grounded in many, partially conflicting, institutional constraints and normative assumptions. We can safely assume that through history, the position of being an apprentice, for instance within the authoritarian and rigid guild system, was a rather horrible context for a young person to be in. To be at the mercy of a master, who might have been a skilled worker but whose talents for teaching or whose interest in caring for young people may not have been very strong, was not always a rewarding experience. Also, and as Tuomi-Gröhn and Engeström point out, the conservatism that characterized many of the apprenticeship based crafts was considerable. The inability to cope with new technologies and changing work conditions were important elements causing this system to collapse in many countries some 150 years ago or so.

Any complex society, that is, a society with a high division of labour and advanced social and physical technologies, must have an activity system where learning opportunities are provided. Furthermore, to cover the range of potential present and future practices in which people are going to work and lead their life, this system must have some autonomy in how to organize its practices. Thus, not even in vocational education, which is the field that most authors analyze, can "the split between theory and practice" be "easily translated into a gap between school and work" (see Guile & Young, this volume). An uncritical acceptance of present work practices as providing ideals for learning, or arguing that such practices can be considered as 'reality' while education is not, is unwise. Again, one might seek advice from Dewey (1916/1966) who made a similar point a century ago. Thus, "industry at present time undergoes rapid and abrupt changes through the evolution of new inventions. New industries spring up, and old ones are revolutionized. Consequently an attempt to train for too specific a mode of efficiency defeats its own purpose. When the occupation changes its methods, such individuals are left behind" (p. 119). The assumption that present day work practices can serve as criteria for successful learning practices is grossly overrated.

In my opinion, the problem that the authors point to with educational practices is not that they are too 'theoretical' or that they do not prepare people for their later life and work. A major problem is that schooling has become abstract. The resort to abstract modes of teaching and learning, in which people are unable to use their daily experiences as support for what they do, has a long history in education. In part it is related to the manner in which learning is organized into separate disciplines that structure knowledge in ways unfamiliar to large groups. However, the recent information explosion has fuelled this development by making it much more difficult to localize and delimit the generative forms of knowledge. The traditional practices of schooling originate from a time when information was scarce and hard to come by, and when schools had more or less complete control over the information that people had access to. What people knew about foreign countries, the business of government or about nature was largely controlled by schools. Before the media explosion, the textbook in school conveyed information that most people had not encountered elsewhere. Today, schools have no control over the flow of information in society, and their main focus has to be reoriented towards helping people to operate in such a world and to discern what is relevant and reliable information/knowledge. This is a different, and to some extent much more complex, task than teaching some basic skills of reading and writing and testing whether pupils can regurgitate the information presented by the teacher or the textbook. And no other institution in society will deal systematically with this problem, education has to do it.

In my opinion, and this is probably in conflict with some of the authors of the chapters in this volume, schooling, including that in the area of vocational education, has unique responsibilities and cannot look to production or other activity systems to find out how learning should be organized. Cooperation with other activity systems, and the provision of rich opportunities for boundary-crossing, are to be encouraged (as is argued in the chapter by Granville & Reilly, this volume), but the criterion for what is generative learning is not necessarily to be found elsewhere. Learning is simply not the overarching motive or rationality of most other activity systems. Rather than repeating the rhetoric of schools not adequately preparing students for 'real-life' and work, the challenge for education, and educational research, is to organize learning experiences in such a manner that students appreciate being in a position of acting as learners. In the case of the study reported by Lambert (this volume), the purpose of practice teaching must not be reduced to performing a perfect lesson in front of a visiting expert teacher. Rather, this activity should be part of a process of learning about how to teach and develop school practices. To foster the "ability to learn constructively and to progressively recontextualise knowledge, skills and attitudes" (van der Sanden & Teurlings, this volume) is a very important ambition, and it is not identical with performing an action. Or, expressed differently, the successful educational activity makes people enjoy learning and see it as a worthwhile end in itself during some parts of their life. It should be experienced as providing values that cannot easily be found elsewhere. Thus, learning must not be construed as a bleak form of work, but as a valuable and rewarding activity in its own right. If vocational (or any other) education becomes merely instrumental and has as its sole ambition to copy activities in other activity systems, its role in society will rapidly diminish. It is in this context that the observation reported by Angervall & Thång (this volume) is so disturbing; people with a low education report being interested to learn, but they seem very sceptical towards institutionalized forms of schooling. This is most likely a very concrete outcome of present-day traditions, but it is a serious failure in a society aiming at promoting life-long education.

Learning in Collectives and Among Individuals

I have already pointed out that one of the most decisive contributions of a situated, activity theoretical and sociocultural perspective is that it takes learning out of its individualistic prison and studies it is as a social, historical and interactional phenomenon taking place in activities. This implies that what is studied are the exchanges that go on between and within individuals and collectives. Rather than taking the meaning of learning for granted, some of the studies reported illustrate how incredibly multifaceted and diverse learning is in a complex society. It would be naive to pretend that such intricate and practice specific phenomena could be fully captured under the heading of a simple process of learning. In the study by Ludvigsen, Havnes & Lahn (this volume), the intricacies of workplace learning among sales engineers as they learn a broad range of skills that have to do with how to position themselves in relation to different customers, how to move between the logic of their own organization and that of the potential customer, and how to design a bid as a boundary object between the negotiating partners, are demonstrated. These observations on how the sales engineers constantly move between social and technical skills and knowledge illustrate a kind of learning that people have to do in an activity system where they are put in a very specific position that can only partially be foreseen while attending an academic institution for basic training in economics or engineering. In a similar vein, the designing of a bid is of course a skill that can be taught in a general sense in another activity system (the university), but the precise manners in which one "combines standardizations and flexibility" to produce a bid that is sensitive to the various criteria that are relevant must be learned *in situ*. The performance of the individual builds on general skills, but knowing how to act in a situation of this kind with a diverse set of customers is a very complicated and contextual skill. Observations of this kind illustrate the division of labour that must exist between formal institutions (providing general, but still very complex, knowledge) and other activity systems where people are going to operate. The particular situation in which a sales engineer, to take just one example, is going to operate cannot be predicted in detail. Thus, the knowledge communicated in formal settings will have to be general, but still substantive. The use of this knowledge has to be negotiated in various practices through a learning process where one goes from the general to the specific, as argued by the editors.

Another interesting feature of the connection between collective and individual learning is to document exactly what is a productive learning experience in a practice. This is part of the story that Sannino, Trognon and Dessagne tell in their study of tutor-apprentice cooperation and communication when learning to use a pneumatic drill. Using recordings of authentic interaction, the authors illustrate how intimately intertwined discursive and manual activities are in the learning process. Thus, "transmission of knowledge" of how to handle "the tool is conducted in parallel on a manual level as well as a discursive level", and the "practical activities are formulated, assessed and explained as they unfold". The tutor formulates rules, corrects behaviors, provides comments, describes the activities to be performed, and gives the motives for various operations in close proximity to physical action. Thus, the instructional nature of the interaction is evident from the manner in which knowledge is made public and thematized in the dialogue. Furthermore, it is interesting that in quantitative terms, and even though we are dealing with a rather specific and limited learning task, the conversations only to a limited extent concern the technical aspects of how to operate the instrument. Instead, the interlocutors bring a broader set of relevancies into the picture, and they talk about management issues, autonomy, and other dimensions of their joint task. The specific actions thus trigger a much broader discussion than would be anticipated if we view the task of learning how to operate a drill as a very technical skill only.

The studies by Tuomi-Gröhn and Lambert also illustrate that learning is much more than a mere recycling of skills and knowledge that are already available (cf. also Fürstenau, this volume). A major idea in both of these pieces of action research is that one can learn about the practices that one is about to become socialized into by being involved in analysis and developmental work. The learner does not have to be completely on the receiving end. Instead of copying the knowledge and skills of expert members (nurses and teachers), learners contribute to scrutinizing daily practices and to modifying them as a means to developing knowledge. In these interactions and analytical encounters, the link between generalities and specifics can be publicly debated and analyzed. Involvement in argumentation of this kind is a rather different learning experience from a qualitative point of view.

Concluding Comments

Our collective assumptions of what learning is all about are still heavily coloured by the traditional metaphors of the exercise of mental faculties and the shaping of physical action as the prototypes of learning; to learn is to copy until perfection is reached. The corresponding metaphor of teaching is one of instruction functioning as a conduit in which information and knowledge, packaged in an easily digestible format, are poured into the minds of pupils. In both these metaphors, learning is essentially a passive and reproductive process; what people learn is a limited set of skills that can be defined as such and that should transfer to new situations. This mode of thinking, by the way, represents a classical academic mistake of mixing up the analyst's perspective on an event with that of the actor. Two situations that appear as similar to the scholar in terms of what kinds of knowledge and skills they require may not appear as similar in that respect for those involved. Today, these assumptions are challenged as too simple. To learn is to appropriate powerful intellectual and physical tools, and to realize how they can be put to productive use in a range of continuously changing practices. The more powerful the tools, the more of boundary-crossing has to be part of the learning process (cf. the concept of propagation of knowledge suggested by Beach, this volume). Learning opportunities arise when people are involved in activities. It is here that the gap between generalities and particulars can be closed. Learning takes place everywhere, but in a complex society schooling will continue to have unique functions; it is primarily here, time and resources can be set aside for systematically organized learning sequences that provide depth and overview. The challenge is to structure the activities in such a manner that people are willing to see learning as a worthwhile and interesting end in itself, and not as a watered down version of some 'real-world', where they would rather like to be. To balance the critique of schooling, it is important that researchers maintain a critical perspective on the nature of learning opportunities offered in other activity systems as well. Otherwise we will be too naïve and too ideological.

References

Bransford, J. D., & Schwartz, D. L. Rethinking transfer: A simple proposal with multiple implications. *Review of Research in Education, 24*, 62–92.

Brown, J. S., Collins, A., & Duguid, P. (1989). Situated cognition and the culture of learning. *Educational Researcher, 18* (1), 32–42.

Carraher, T. N., Carraher, D. W., & Schliemann, A. D. (1985). Mathematics in the streets and in schools. *British Journal of Developmental Psychology, 3*, 21–29.

Detterman, D. K., & Sternberg, R. J. (Eds) (1993). *Transfer on trial: Intelligence, cognition, and instruction.* Norwood, NJ: Ablex.

Dewey, J. (1966). *Democracy and education.* New York, NY: The Free Press.

Ebbinghaus, H. (1885). *Ueber das Gedächtnis.* [On memory]. Leipzig: Duncker.

Gagné, R. M. (1970). *The conditions of learning* (2nd ed.). London, England: Holt, Rinehart & Winston.

Greeno, J. (1998). The situativity of knowing, learning, and research. *American Psychologist, 53* (1), 5–26.

Hebb, D. O. (1969). *Psykologi på Biologisk Grund* [Psychology from a Biological Standpoint]. Lund: Gleerups.

Hilgard, E. R., & Bower, G. H. (1966). *Theories of learning* (3rd ed.). New York, NY: Appleton-Century-Crofts.

Katona, G. (1967). *Organizing and memorizing. Studies in the psychology of learning and teaching*. New York, NY: Hafner. (Original published in 1940).

Koffka, K. (1935). *Principles of Gestalt psychology*. New York, NY: Harcourt, Brace & World.

Krech, D., Crutchfield, R. S., & Livson, N. (1969). *Elements of psychology*. New York, NY: Knopf.

Lave, J. (1988). *Cognition in practice: Mind, mathematics and culture in everyday life.* Cambridge, MA: Cambridge University Press.

Lave, J. (1993). The practice of learning. In: S. Chaiklin, & J. Lave (Eds), *Understanding practice. Perspectives on activity and context* (pp. 3–32). Cambridge, MA: Cambridge University Press.

Lave, J., & Wenger, E. (1991). *Situated learning: Legitimate peripheral participation.* Cambridge, MA: Cambridge University Press.

Nunes, T. N., Schliemann, A. D., & Carraher, D. W. (1993). *Street mathematics and school mathematics.* Cambridge, England: Cambridge University Press.

Smedslund, J. (1953). The problem of "what is learned?" *Psychological review, 60* (3), 157–158.

Svensson, L. (1976). *Study skill and learning*. Göteborg: Acta Universitatis Gothoburgensis.

Vygotsky, L. S. (1986). *Thought and language*. [A. Kozulin, Trans.]. Cambridge, MA: MIT Press.

Wenger, E. (1998). *Communities of practice: Learning, meaning, and identity.* Cambridge, MA: Cambridge University Press.

Wertheimer, M. (1968). *Productive thinking*. London, England: Tavistock. (Original published in 1945).

Author Index

Subject Index